Balloon Madness

FOR MY PARENTS
WITH MY LOVE

A non esse, nec fuisse, non datur argumentum ad non posse
– Lunardi's motto

Just because something hasn't existed, or might not exist, doesn't mean it can't exist…

Balloon Madness

Flights of Imagination in Britain, 1783–1786

CLARE BRANT

THE BOYDELL PRESS

First published 2017

The Boydell Press, Woodbridge

ISBN 978 1 78327 253 2

The Boydell Press is an imprint of Boydell & Brewer Ltd
PO Box 9, Woodbridge, Suffolk IP12 3DF, UK
and of Boydell & Brewer Inc.
668 Mt Hope Avenue, Rochester, NY 14620–2731, USA
website: www.boydellandbrewer.com

A CIP catalogue record for this book is available
from the British Library

The publisher has no responsibility for the continued existence
or accuracy of URLs for external or third-party internet websites
referred to in this book, and does not guarantee that any content
on such websites is, or will remain, accurate or appropriate

This publication is printed on acid-free paper

Printed and bound in Great Britain by
TJ International Ltd, Padstow, Cornwall

MIX
Paper from
responsible sources
FSC
www.fsc.org   FSC® C013056

Contents

Illustrations

MAP

Acknowledgements

In writing the story of balloons in Britain in the 1780s, I have owed much to historians of flight. Though my book takes a different flight path, it often took bearings from the work of other scholars: Charles Gillespie, J. E. Hodgson and L. T. C. Rolt. I have also been grateful to collectors of balloon material, especially Sarah Sophia Banks and Major B. F. S. Baden-Powell, brother of the scoutmaster. As I sailed farther with balloons, books on them appeared in print by Richard Holmes, Paul Keen, Michael Lynn, Marie Thébaud-Sorger, Mark Davies and others, all of which made for inspiring, informative and lively aerial community.

I owe a big thank you to Julian Loose, who kept faith with the book for much of its aerial wanderings, as did Ewen Green. Thanks too to Kate Teltscher for saying the subject would make a good book, on the first outing of my balloon researches. Mari Shullaw at Boydell has provided wise words and encouragement to help with both landing and launching. Lyndsay Markham ensured the neatest stowage: I am grateful to her and the production team at Boydell.

I would like to thank all the librarians who gave me essential help, especially Mr Brian Riddle of the Royal Aeronautical Society Library, where I spent many happy hours, and Keith Moore at the Royal Society Library. I learnt much from them. Thanks too to librarians in Edinburgh, Liverpool, Bristol, York and Oxford. Colleagues at conferences, workshops and seminars have generously shared their work and responded to mine in ways that inform my thinking: I am grateful to all of them and to my students. Chris Ewers inspired me to think about speed, and Emma Newport about Chinese temples.

I am grateful to everyone who kindly sent me references, especially Ruth Richardson, Lesley Hall, Tim Webb, Lydia Syson and Vincent Quinn. Nicholas Rogers, whose books helped me think better about eighteenth-century history, shared adventures from the archives. Timothy Ashplant added vital and kind advice. For supportive contributions from King's, I am indebted to Max Saunders, Neil Vickers, Elizabeth Eger, Brian Hurwitz, Lara Feigel, Gordon McMullan and Rivkah Zim especially, and for creative friendship elsewhere, to Monica Soeting. I would also like to thank Regine Spätling and Christian Moser for inviting me to play.

For intellectual pleasures and much else I thank Charles Lock, whose learning knows no bounds nor his generosity in sharing it. Katherine Armstrong has been a sensitive and unfailing supporter. Helena Webb has shared her own inspiring flights of imagination. Thanks to my Carter family, especially Charles Denton, for their love and support. A special thank you to Richard Gordon for sanctuary and sustenance, and deep gratitude to my friends including Gordon Milne, Jo Denton, Sarah Spiller, Alex Thomson, Shirley Andrews, Andy and Gog Webb, Jacqui Mansfield and Jim Noble, Bridget Lubbock, Andy Kupfer, Josephine Wilmott, Katy and Hermione Waterfield, Vital Peeters and Jules Fletcher, Roger Perkins and Kay Sentance, Veronica and John-Dominic West-Harling, Henrietta Leyser, Matilda Leyser, Andy Letcher, Nicola Watson, Michael Dobson, David Gooding, Yun Lee Too, Nicholas Bunch, Peter and Kathleen Weiler and Jon Schneer. Special thanks to James Waterfield for mapping skills, digital rescues and indexing rigour. I wish Gooding could have lived to read the book she so loyally supported; her exceptionally acute visual sense would have informed more of my illustrations.

I owe a special debt to Sarah Murphy and Adrian Arbib for sending me aloft and for brilliant photographic salvage. Another flight, making a film for the BBC's *The One Show*, made me glad I pay a television licence.

Extreme circumstances blew me off course. When disaster struck, my family and close friends gave me love, help and hope. Love gives you courage: it is their love which has seen me through. I am especially grateful to my brother Chris, who read chapters at vital turns, and to Julia, Sarah and Katharine Brant for all the ways they cheered me on. My parents introduced me to aeroplanes at a young age. This book is dedicated to them with my love.

Abbreviations

BL   British Library
B-P   Baden-Powell Collection, National Aerospace Library
DNB   Oxford Dictionary of National Biography
WLA   Williamson's Liverpool Advertiser

'Imitation of the Foregoing Sonnet [by Guiseppe Parini]
    on an Air Balloon'

In empty space behold me hurl'd
The sport and wonder of the World;
Who eager gaze while I aspire
Expanded with aerial fire.

And since Man's selfish race demands
More empire than the seas or lands;
For him my courage mounts the skies,
Invoking Nature whilst I rise.

Mother of all! if thus refin'd,
My flights can benefit Mankind;
Let them by me new realms prepare,
And take possession of the air.

But if to ills alone I lead,
Quickly, oh quick let me recede;
Or blaze, a splendid exhibition,
A beacon for their mad ambition.

                                          Hester Lynch Piozzi

Map showing hotspots of balloon madness in Britain

Ascending

Beginnings

'It is really very pretty to see them go up; the thing is so new, so
subversive of our established habits, that the mind does not know
how to reconcile itself to the appearance.'
    Sir Charles Blagden to Sir Joseph Banks, 21 October 1783.[1]

ONE DAY AT THE end of December 1784, several thousand
people crowded into an inn yard in a town in the middle of
England. It was cold; sky and rooftops merged in winter gloom. The
shivering mass stood patiently. Many had travelled for miles, coming
in by coach, by horse, on foot from distant towns and outlying
villages. Some had spent the night half-frozen in stables, doorways,
any kind of rough shelters. Assembled with an excitement barely
dulled by cold, they waited. They waited for an hour, two hours,
three hours, four … even rumours moved slowly. Nonetheless, the
crowd did not thin; at its edges more latecomers arrived, all hopeful
for a sight of the balloon. There was a promise it would ascend that
day, with an aeronaut who would rise to the skies, a sight unlike
anything most of the crowd had ever seen before. Many of them did
not know quite what to expect. The demonstration was, the crowd
understood, a beginning – and there was much that could go wrong.
It was heroic to make the attempt. If it succeeded, the world of the
air was a step closer to being open to human endeavour. The sea had
once been uncharted; now the skies were on the brink of discoveries.
Who knew where those would lead? What would it mean if people
could travel like birds, as easy as eagles in the upper atmosphere?
Here in Birmingham they were about to see a flight of imagination
and new reality.

This crowd was enormous. Beyond the inn yard they swelled out
into the streets, where all the shops were shut up in expectation
of an event bigger than commerce. Some of those attending had
followed the progress of this new invention through newspapers,
pamphlets and the first of the new books discussing it. The less

literate depended on verbal accounts and glimpses of the balloon's advertising – handbills announcing that a Mr Harper would ascend in a balloon, showing a striped globe with an open appendage below, for carriage of the intrepid aeronaut. Those closest could see a swollen mass, tended by figures frantically attempting to get gas into it from pipes attached to casks; the half-inflated folds stayed stubbornly unfilled. One of those figures, Harper the would-be aeronaut, sent word to the local printer that he would stay up till midnight if necessary, a message whose omen of failure spread through the now restless crowd. Would the ascent happen after all?

A peal of bells signalled it would – but a last-minute fault created another delay. Now the crowd pressed forward, surging towards the balloon with violent intent. As a contemporary novelist noted: *'The curiosity of the public is no proof of their sagacity – Popular rage [is] more dreadful than the sting of the law.'*[2] Scaffolding around the balloon was demolished; fights broke out. A hail of sticks, stones, dead dogs and cats thickened the air and fell into the enclosure for spectators who had paid to see the balloon up close. Local constables stepped in, read the Riot Act and took scufflers into custody. One had a broken skull. A sort of order was imposed and the crowd dispersed.[3]

Damage to the balloon would take days to repair. Another ascent was promised. The balloon had been airworthy: it had been bought for £120 from James Sadler,[4] the first Briton to make a successful ascent, from Oxford on 4 October 1784. A week later, on 4 January 1785, all was ready again. The day was foggy and wet. Heavy rain fell. Nonetheless an even larger crowd assembled, said to be 150,000 strong, 'the most numerous Assemblage of People that was ever known', as one report put it admiringly.[5] Other sources, reporting a less swollen figure of sixty thousand, said people had travelled more than forty miles, and no carriage or horse could be hired for fifty miles around.[6] At eleven o'clock the bells rang to indicate the balloon was filling; it was filled by twelve, auspicious efficiency. 'The modest Adventurer took his Seat in a very increasing Rain, amidst the Gratulations of the admiring Spectators,' and two ladies loosened the cords. 'The whole apparatus rose with the greatest majesty, gratifying the most unbounded wishes by the sublimity of the spectacle.'[7] For six minutes the balloon rose in clear view and the aeronaut saluted the now exultant crowd below who fanned out to neighbouring fields to extend their view. For four minutes more the balloon ascended through the clouds before becoming invisible.

Above, Harper the aeronaut was having his moment in the sun. He took some measurements on his barometer, read his thermometer and monitored his compass, which varied with the air currents. Above the clouds he sailed through the air, observing the effects of altitude on his own body – a temporary deafness the only inconvenience – and eyeing with some unease the accumulation of water slowing down the balloon. Nonetheless, he stayed aloft for fifty minutes before making a steady descent. Through his speaking trumpet he hailed a person below to ask how far he was from Birmingham. 'About 40 miles, Master, but you are going the wrong way.'[8] Harper landed near Newcastle in Staffordshire, about fifty miles from the inn yard where he had started. It was the longest flight to date in Britain. A throng of people carried him back in triumph. Plaudits piled in:

> HARPER – to thee the palm belongs,
>   For struck with awe admiring throngs,
> Beheld the grand, the glorious sight;
>   No man besides can hist'ry say,
> Upon a dreary winter's day,
>   Ne'er dared to take so bold a flight.[9]

Encouraged by his success, Harper made a second attempt. This time the amount of ballast was miscalculated. The overloaded balloon rose awkwardly and swung into an adjacent house; a shaken Harper climbed out of the balloon to safety through an open window. The balloon was hauled down and a boy standing by got into it as ballast – then somehow the balloon rose. The involuntary aeronaut waved his hat to the spectators who cheered him enthusiastically, until enough gas escaped from the balloon for it to land by itself with the boy unharmed and a hero.[10]

Coming midway in the period of greatest excitement about balloons, Harper's aerial adventures were in many ways entirely typical of attempted ascents in Britain: epic and farce, sublime and riotous, taken seriously and sent up. The upshot was partly successful in taking a man aloft, a man able to make some observations with scientific instruments and able to describe some sensations of the novel experience of flight. It was partly unsuccessful, in that neither ascent nor descent was well controlled and there was no navigation. Accidental in its achievements, it demonstrated heroic determination, especially in braving the British weather. 'It was generally believed that the rage for air balloons had subsided as the winter advanced; but we find that the aerial Quixotes are not to be deterred by frost or snow, wind or hail.'[11] The same persistence was shown by those who came to watch. Like many crowds who came to see balloons, they can be described in opposed ways as polite spectators and an unruly mob, a polarity I explore later. Harper's adventure was also typical in that it produced a mixed literature: respectful notices in newspapers read around the country, congratulatory verses and satire that mocked the enterprise – perversely, not only for the ambition of its aspirations, but also for its limitation in achieving them. Satirists of course made a living from mocking anything, and unlike some other aeronauts Harper did not publish his own serious account to act as a corrective, though details of his temperature and height readings were passed to the press. Usually described as a barber, Harper had no obviously scientific credentials; that he – and the boy – could go up and down suggested anyone might. Nonetheless, his voyage was momentous, and it had a more than provincial reach. The first aeronaut attempting to cross the Irish Sea in a balloon studied accounts of it carefully.[12]

Harper's balloon ascent makes a convenient starting point, coming halfway through the curve of balloon madness in Britain, closely following events in France. The history of aerostation, or the art of sailing in air, began with the invention of the hot air balloon by the Montgolfier brothers in 1783 [Plate I]. On 5 June they successfully demonstrated in front of officials at Annonay a paper balloon raised by fire, which sailed for ten minutes or so to descend after a mile and a half. On 27 August, a balloon raised by inflammable air – hydrogen produced by running sulphuric acid over iron filings – was tested by M. Charles (a professor) and his collaborators, the brothers Robert. Ascending to three thousand feet from the Champ de Mars in front of a huge crowd, it fell fifteen miles away at Gonesse, to the consternation of locals. On 19 September at Versailles, in the presence of the king, queen and another huge crowd, the Montgolfiers sent up another fire balloon with a duck, cock and sheep in its basket – the first aerial travellers, who descended safely after a journey of two miles [Figure 1]. (The sheep was pensioned off in the royal menagerie.) On 21 November, the first human aerial travellers, Pilâtre de Rozier and the Marquis d'Arlandes, flew over Paris for twenty minutes in a fire balloon; on 1 December, the proponents of the *charlière*, Charles and the Roberts, flew for two hours in a hydrogen balloon, fitted with a valve, hoop and netting [Figure 2]; on a second-stage flight, M. Charles went on a further nine miles or so, witnessing a second sunset. The *montgolfière* was still in contention: on 19 January 1784, the Montgolfiers launched a giant fire balloon, 'Les Flesselles', carrying seven persons aloft over Lyons for fifteen minutes.

As these two versions of balloons developed, they set new records for height, distance and flight time. They also sparked debate about design. The *montgolfière* had the problem of how to enclose fire and make it more efficient; the *charlière* faced challenges in getting gas into the balloon and controlling it aloft. Both technologies required experimentation with different materials – paper, linen, silk, animal gut for the balloon; varnishes of different oils and gums; rigging and ballast. Cost was an issue: one report said the Montgolfiers could fill for a mere forty sous, whereas the inflammable air equivalent would

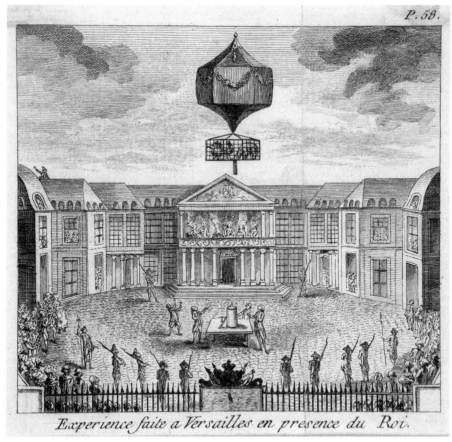

Experience faite a Versailles en presence du Roi.

The first aerial travellers: a duck, cock and sheep, launched by the   1
Montgolfiers on 19 September 1783. Engraving.

EXPERIENCE CELEBRE faite a Paris en presence de plus de 8 cent mille personnes dans le jardin des thuilleries le 1er Decembre 1783. a 1 heure 40 minute après midi. Cette machine montés par Mrs Charles et Robert descendit a 3 h. 3 quarts dans la prairie de Nesle a 9 lieues de Paris Mr Charles remonta seul dans la meme machine et redescendit a 1 lieue ⅞ du depart

2   The first human flight in an inflammable air balloon: Charles and the Roberts ascended from the Jardin des Tuileries on 1 December 1783. The little balloon was sent up first to test wind direction and speed. Engraving.

cost almost ten thousand francs (£400) – and take up to ten days.[13] Producing sufficient gas could be problematic, but Charles' design made ascent and descent relatively simple: one dropped ballast to rise and dropped gas to descend. 'Nothing more than minor refinements would be made to the gas balloon over the next two hundred years.'[14]

Accounts of these extraordinary developments – with facts, explanations, rumours and speculations – spread excitement from France around Europe and to America, and ignited balloon madness in Britain. But for all the attempts and ascents and aerial journeys that followed, balloons brushed up against an insuperable impediment to being vehicles of progress: they could not be steered well enough to make them dependable forms of transport. The balloon fell slowly from being a wonder of the age to an invention that could not quite deliver the new era that it promised. Interrupted by the French Revolution, re-adopted by Napoleon, balloons wobbled on as vehicles of adventure, glorious and ultimately short-lived, before settling into a nineteenth-century story of showmanship and spectacle, with occasional daring forays into territories of the unknown.

That potted history puts use value foremost. Balloons have, however, recently attracted attention from historians of eighteenth-century science, economy and culture. Richard Holmes places balloons in a masculinist story – even if it includes some women – of science penetrating nature's secrets:

> The notion of an infinite, mysterious Nature, waiting to be discovered or seduced into revealing all her secrets, was widely held. Scientific instruments played an increasingly important role in this process of revelation, allowing man not merely to extend his senses passively – using the telescope, the microscope and barometer – but to intervene actively, using the voltaic battery, the electrical generator, the scalpel or the air pump. Even the Montgolfier balloon could be seen as an instrument of discovery, or indeed of seduction.[15]

Well it could, and the excitement of discovery through the invention of instruments had powerful effects in the late eighteenth century. But balloons were described at the time in relation to ways of thinking more varied than our broad category of science. The experiments of aeronauts – both the experiment of getting airborne and the modest experiments conducted in balloons when aloft – were frequently related to 'philosophy', a word with capacious meanings including physics, but also embracing ethics.

To lock balloons into a history of science, even of imaginative science, means losing their history in imagination. To explain a little here of how this book contextualises balloons, I turn to Rita Felski's call to reconsider what makes a context. Literary scholars and historians who establish meanings wholly in relation to context, she argues, trap texts and phenomena in their own time: 'We are inculcated, in the name of history, into a remarkably static model of meaning, where texts are corralled amidst long-gone contexts and obsolete intertexts, incarcerated in the past, with no hope of parole.'[16] It is tempting to joke that establishing context is exactly what gives old texts their parole − parole in Saussure's sense in linguistics, where 'parole' means particular speech acts, which are then free to act again for a later readership. But Felski's point is that texts and objects act not just for us but on us: 'why not acknowledge that works of art can function as vehicles of knowing as well as objects to be known, why not make room for a multiplicity of media- tors?' She argues that a language of attachment should be valued as much as detachment. The significance of a text or object is not just what it reveals or conceals about the social conditions that surround it, 'but also a matter of what it elicits in the viewer or reader − what kinds of emotions it elicits, what kind of perceptual changes it trig- gers, what kind of affective bonds it calls into being.'[17] In their long period of existence, balloons − like novels − have engaged us with emotion, value and change. Whilst my approach values historical particularity, I propose a continuity in the way balloons imagine a kind of possibility for us − initially, the possibility of flight, but also of imagination. They come together in flights of imagination.

Felski accuses historians of another crime: 'our conventional modes of context take these multidirectional linkages and cast them into coffin-like containers called periods.'[18] While I propose a container-period for balloon madness in Britain, roughly the years 1783 to 1786, I hope it is not a coffin. It is simply the time when a craze for balloons spread all around Britain and then subsided. Though pockets of balloon madness persisted, public interest turned elsewhere. There were other collective enthusiasms before and after, but the rage for balloons had an intensity noted at the time as something new. My study of balloons explores their signifi- cance in Britain in a landscape of ideas which airscapes added to and changed. It is a necessarily selective analysis in that balloons sailed through numerous and extensive currents of thought even in their relatively short-lived heyday. My connective theme is how balloons came to reside in imagination, the beginnings of a history which is longer than this book can address, as my final chapter sketches out.[19]

My focus is on balloon madness in Britain, so I treat glancingly the rich story of aerostation as it unfolded across Europe. A full history of early balloons in France has been excellently told by Marie Thébaut-Sorger in *L'Aérostation au temps des Lumières*, and British ballooning has had fine narrative histories in J. E. Hodgson's *History of Aeronautics in Great Britain* and in L. T. C. Rolt's *The Balloonists: The History of the First Aeronauts*. Richard Holmes has told the aeronaut story over a longer period, or a bigger coffin, in *Falling Upwards: How We Took to the Air*. Michael R. Lynn has given late eighteenth-century balloons a context of historical science in *The Sublime Invention: Ballooning 1783–1820*, to which Mi Gyung Kim and others have added valuably.[20] Paul Keen has positioned balloons as a key part of the spinning nexus of literature and commerce in late eighteenth-century Britain in *Literature, Commerce, and the Spectacle of Modernity, 1750–1800*:

> In some ways, it was precisely this semiotic elasticity – the ease with which ballooning could mean so many different things to different people across a range of contexts – that made it so open to skepticism. Ballooning's endless adaptability on a symbolic level reinforced its power to evoke the fluidity of a commercial society generally; its very ubiquity amongst these sorts of satires (many of which played on the idea of ballooning as a "bubble") made it an easily recognized symbol for all manner of foolish or unstable or disreputable behaviour in a social order where the very concept of value had floated free from its epistemological foundations.[21]

This explanation helps define balloons in their comic, anarchic, unruly aspects. But they were also vehicles for values, and with ideological ballast. Sensible, stable and reputable behaviours were imaged through balloons too, and seriousness of purpose debated through them. The fun of balloons' flightiness should not completely overwrite their weightiness.

That mixed economy is present in Siobhan Carroll's study of Romantic atopias, or spaces that cannot be wholly converted into territorial possessions – the polar regions, the oceans, the atmosphere and subterranean regions – but she takes fantasy to be the instrument of greatest imaginative reach in this venture, and an instrument at odds with rationalism.[22] Certainly fantasy was active in balloon madness, yet between 1783 and 1786 fantasy around balloons had close relations with reason and examined possible extensions of British sovereignty with confidence and hope as well as anxiety. Sarah Tindal Kareem identifies equivocal feelings as a characteristic of eighteenth-century fictions which play with wonder: 'feelings that are at once destabilizing and exhilarating, and that foster a pleasure in the sensation of not knowing – of wondering – itself.' Kareem's idea of 'enchanted Enlightenment' argues for nuances and complexities which fit balloon madness nicely.[23]

The Birmingham crowd who stood for hours in miserable weather were in their way enchanted, anticipating an occasion memorable in their own lives and momentous for their descendants. Here was the future. It was bold, ambitious, daring; it also demanded faith. Success depended on planning, experiment, careful preparations and skill. Aeronauts needed luck too: fortune favoured the brave but rewarded them capriciously. In the air, a gust of wind or an eddy of air might catch the apparatus and dash it against buildings or trees. Those familiar with the principles might reasonably wonder whether freezing temperatures and the weight of rain would hamper ascent and dampen ardour. The spectators huddled expectantly were patient for a long time, as if they understood that possibilities like balloons were got aloft with difficulty. Why should anyone care? Some didn't. To them, ballooning was folly, a dubious invention that, like many in its day, became disappointing. But even cynics found attractions in flightiness, if only to vindicate their own cynicism:

> What is a *Balloon?* a thing lighter than air, composed of a flimsy, gaudy outside appearance, and within, containing nothing but *corrupted matter*; but by which it is buoyed up beyond its natural sphere. – This *bubble* ascends, while thus exalted in the air, *above the world*, is gazed at by mankind with admiration and astonishment, yet it is liable to be tossed about by the fluctuation of every wind that may blow, and to instantaneous explosion like the *fabric of a vision*. – In short, it is never free from peril a single moment, and when I reflect on these things, they afford me great matter for speculation. This bubble appears to be a true emblem, or picture of the corrupted manners of the present times.[24]

Yet for most people, balloons were the hopeful means by which the human race would fly. Louis-Sébastien Mercier, author of a utopian vision of the future in his popular fiction *L'An 2440*, published in 1771, reported the first ascent of humans in a balloon as a moment that changed the world:

> A memorable date. On this day, before the eyes of an enormous gathering two men rose in the air. So great was the crowd that the Tuileries Gardens were full as they could hold; there were men climbing over

the railings; the gates were forced. This swarm of people was in itself an incomparable sight, so varied was it, so vast and so changing. Two hundred thousand men, lifting their hands in wonder, admiring, glad, astonished; some in tears for fear the intrepid physicists should come to harm, some on their knees overcome with emotion, but all following the aeronauts in spirit, while these latter, unmoved, saluted, dipping their flags above our heads. What with the novelty, the dignity of the experiment, the unclouded sky, welcoming as it were the travellers to his own element, the attitude of the two men sailing into the blue, while below their fellow-citizens prayed and feared for their safety, and lastly the balloon itself, superb in the sunlight, whirling aloft like a planet or the chariot of some weather-god – it was a moment which can never be repeated, the most astounding achievement the science of physics has yet given to the world.[25]

After centuries of being imagined, the aerial age had arrived.

The story of balloons illustrates a paradox of Enlightenment: the act of breaking the bond with earth was a victory for reason over fear, superstition, religious orthodoxy and emotion, yet all of those forces accompanied balloons. Unreason's constant and complex dialogue with reason is arguably what defines Enlightenment reason. If Enlightenment optimism was widely promulgated through balloons, it was through passion as well as reason. Commenting on a report that the Grand Duke of Russia wanted to see a balloon made, one newspaper observed: 'For the credit of these times, it may justly be affirmed, that in no period of the history of the world have mankind ever discovered a greater ardour for knowledge, or so successfully pursued it in the paths of experiment, as at present.'[26]

For all their shock of the new, balloons had an impact on old ideas of monarchy, of war, of national boundaries. Their local appearances had global implications. They were also vehicles of a particularly Enlightenment questioning: what was useful to the world? How might balloons change the world, for better and worse? I make little if any distinction between Enlightenment and Romantic, in that I see it as part of Enlightenment thinking to be open to dreams – dreams about the future; dreams of exploration and discovery; dreams in which wonder and astonishment carried ambitions for individuals and for humanity. Those dreams could be described rationally, comically and poetically. Eighteenth-century reasoning was inseparable from humour: wit and satire defined folly as what can reasonably be mocked because it is unreasonable. Eighteenth-century people responded to the appearance of balloons on their mental horizons with confidence, uncertainty, anxiety, hope, comedy and contradiction. Like Harper's ascent, balloons were orderly and disorderly. They united polite and popular cultures in a common fervour of balloon madness.

Progress is often described as a march as if, like clock time, it happened smoothly and evenly. In reality, like time as it is experienced, progress is often a mad dash or a crawl and without a clear sense of direction. Besides, what is progress? What counted as progress was debated. In the eighteenth century, people talked of knowledge advancing; the hope it would do so benignly was also partnered by awareness that human nature made malevolent use of invention. In his study of the idea of progress in eighteenth-century Britain (a book whose cover illustration shows Lunardi's ascent), David Spadafora argues that the idea 'has many forms and is not monolithic'.[27] Although balloons clearly counted as innovation and advance, in 1784 it was not clear where that would lead: 'it is impossible to say how far the art of navigation may be improved, or with what advantages it may be attended'.[28]

With the benefit of hindsight, most versions of the story of flight include balloons among its beginnings. Aeronautical histories lead from those beginnings to a middle – the story of airships, fixed-wing aircraft, heavier-than-air flying machines and new heroes, like Sir George Cayley and the Wright brothers. Magnificent men were able to have flying machines, to which balloons then become precursors. If you take away that knowledge of subsequent aviation history, you return to a sense of beginnings where people could only guess middles and endings. Histories of ballooning describe developments with the logic of chronology. The story of ballooning isn't so linear. Like a balloon track, it circles and loops, it passes and pauses. The story is properly many stories into which balloons fit because they happened along, arriving in the middle, or the end, of other stories.

In tracing stories around balloons, we need to be aware of the preoccupations we bring, particularly how we tilt our mirrors to the past. The histories we make often have a motive of explanation: how things rise and fall, how things began, how one thing leads to another. But the past can be a strange place. We manage that strangeness with analytical frames: for balloons, a history of science, including 'wrong' science; a sense of spectacle; a theory of objects; the development of capitalism; a historical aesthetic of the sublime. All these include the particularity of eighteenth-century thinking. But they may also mask what is not translatable into our terms, the casts of mind that were practical in strange ways and produced dreams and debates in a landscape different from ours. Sailing through air was also a process of imaginative voyaging, undertaken in a world with horizons and maps that are not all graspable or reconstructable. The texture of imagination, like the silk of a balloon, is delicate.

Since the era of aerostation coincides with what many scholars identify as the emergence of Romanticism, one might see balloons as vehicles of imagination, passion and yearning for the skies. Balloons crashed into an existing typology of emotions: 'Who can describe the sensations of the spectators at a sight so majestic and sublime? Admiration and terror, joy and fear, succeeded each other so instantaneously, that they seemed to be but one and the same emotion.'[29] Certainly balloons attracted and generated emotions. Richard Holmes has imaginatively explored wonder as an emotion he relates to a new terror and beauty found in science in the late eighteenth century, for which balloons are a perilous vehicle. Romanticism is helpful as a way to explore how emotions have histories, but wonder was also structured in classical ways and related to real-world potencies of power. Balloons, said one commentator, 'give us the right of dominion, as it were, over other elements, and realise to us in some degree that fancied communication between earth and the celestial worlds, in which the enthusiasm of ancient poetry so much delighted.'[30] Literate people reached into a store of classical poetry to image balloons to themselves; they recalled passages from Virgil and Ovid, Milton and Homer, and they wrote their own poems in couplets and quatrains, jaunty stanzas that often mixed wonder and humour, scepticism and hope. Michael R. Lynn says of this mixture: 'Even as aeronauts conducted experiments, audience members swooned, gasped and generally emoted, belying the assertions of those who wanted to confine the new invention to the realm of science and reason. In this way, balloons epitomise the overlapping nature of the Enlightenment and Romanticism'.[31] But if the aeronauts were emoting too and the audience included reasoners, the relation between emotions and reason is one of synergy rather than opposition frogmarched into overlap, and not as simple as separate terms (coffins?) of Enlightenment and Romanticism. And one still has to account for how comedy managed emotions and structured reasoning. As Marie Thébaud-Sorger suggests, irony played an important role. The motor car was equally a fount of jokes, as if humour controlled the nervousness of recognition that here was a point from which transformations as yet unknown would emerge and change the world forever.

Balloons reveal the 1780s to be a hectic period, too easily over-shadowed by the immense events of 1789. To define the madness of balloons, Chapter 1 explains what sort of madness it was in theory and practice, and Chapter 2 explores an individual instance, a diarist who confided his obsession like a cartoon character with an empty thought bubble. With cast of mind established, Chapter 3 introduces a cast of people and places – by no means exhaustive – and examines a selection of aerial adventures to illuminate how balloon madness caught on around Britain. Its significance was determined as much by spectators as by aeronauts, so I devote Chapter 4 to exploring the behaviours of balloon crowds. Reason, science, technology and magic were especially crowded together at launches. Far from being respected as a savant, a failed aeronaut was likely to be compared to a pickpocket. Ideas of balloons as devices of fraud were reinforced by the activities of pickpockets in the crowds at launches. I establish the groundwork of this analogy to explain how pickpockets' activities resonated with the challenges of description and meaning around balloons.

In exploring how balloons took cultural ballast aloft, I suggest a light distinction between ideas of levity and of gravity. The madness of balloons was evident in fashion and satirical prints, and their seri-ousness was evident around concepts of monarchy and war. But the distinction is really for convenience. Chapter 5 shows how balloons joined the speedily evolving world of fashion, seemingly close to our own world of celebrities and consumerism. 'In this balloon age, custom, mode and fashion defend the most ridiculous and absurd proceedings.'[32] Balloon motifs, fabrics, colours, shapes, ornaments and accessories contributed new threads to the imaginative work of fashion. Speed, bounciness, voluminousness, lightness and aspi-ration were characteristics furthered by balloon symbolism. These aspects of modishness helped define a new modernity. Chapter 6 similarly places balloons in a topical milieu of politics to bring out meanings from fast-moving and partly-lost worlds. The politics of fashion flowed in and out of fashionable politics; balloons rode those currents. Material culture gave them tangible shape; visual culture gave them artistic forms. Very few representations survive of the material process of making balloons: one image in a composite sheet of a child copyist shows sempstresses sewing together the gores or sections of a balloon, probably Lunardi's second [Figure 3]. In comparison, the literature of balloons is immensely rich, if scat-tered.[33] Chapter 7 analyses literary flights of imagination and how

Lunardi's second balloon, which made successful flights on 13 May and 29 June 1785. Engraving published 18 April 1785 [*sic*], with vignettes showing stages in the production of the new balloon – its filling, ascending, zenith and descent. Fair text in copperplate: 'None can be Eminent without Application/ and Genius: To become an able Man in any/ Profession whatsoever, three things are necessary,/ which are, Nature, Study, and Practice./ By Diligence and Industry/ We come to Preferment./ O now, while Health and Vigour still remain,/ Toil, Toil, my Friends, to purchase honest Gain;/ Shun Idleness, shun Pleasure's tempting snare,/ Men of merit, find Friends every where./ Hilkiah Burgess, May 9th, 1785.' Hilkiah Burgess (1775–1868), here practising copperplate writing aged ten, was the son of an engraver. He grew up to become an engraver himself.

3

jokes helped manage uncertainty of meaning. In the swings between utopia and dystopia, comic epic proved popular, as its buoyant unpredictability matched that of balloons. Exploring how writers drew on old and new genres to place balloons in a long history of imagining air, I explain why they made special use of light verse and quixotic figures.

In all their manifestations, balloons acted as philosophical tools with which imagination toyed purposefully. The next part of the book, Gravity, shows how balloons contributed to the evolution of early modern into modern. Chapters 8 and 9 investigate how ideas about majesty and heroism acquired new features through balloons. Balloons also pressed new models of war, and an international order that had to absorb air as a space hitherto defined through classical and Renaissance terms.[34] Height and altitude are traditionally associated with social elevation, and so balloons entered the realm of exalted modelling. Gravity here plays on both the seriousness of the concepts discussed and the tug back to earth that came from ideological anxiety about intruding on divine territory. God and the King were sacred identities which Enlightenment writers negotiated carefully. Successful aeronauts were heroes. That they were also like celebrities is pleasing, but my focus is on establishing historical strangeness rather than similitudes, and in showing how the language around balloons drew on past and existing concepts to fit the new invention. Surrounded by prejudice and incredulity, Lunardi had 'gallantly soared above every barrier ... he astonished our senses, dispelled our doubts, confirmed our hopes, and established a truth in philosophy, which by perseverance may hereafter prove a blessing to mankind'.[35] Lunardi's publisher, who wrote this puff, was of course *parti pris*, but heroism was numinous and a ready sell. Ideas aloft had to adapt to new views from above, which Chapter 10 discusses through the aesthetics of the sublime and beautiful. The sublime fitted balloons in mixed ways; a ready passenger, it did not pilot aerial aesthetics. The prospect of aerial travel and dominion brought new pressure to bear on ideas of nation and their relations, which Chapter 11 investigates through the concept of aeronationalism, whose military applications in the possibility of aerial warfare disturbed deeply-held British identifications with the sea. Elevation in this context created the threat of war from above, the subject of Chapter 12. Nationalism warred with Enlightenment belief in humanity. Where nations advanced they gained power: how would this process be affected by balloons? A new sense of the world, of universal interests, contended with beleaguered patriotisms. Chapter 13 returns to earth with the parachute, whose reinvention in 1802 is a curious case of forgetting invention, and as a study in how much had changed around balloons – and how little. Becoming a customary appendage to balloons, parachutes were tested by pioneer animals – cats, dogs, sheep – in aerial voyages as early as 1785. Victorian balloonists took up or sent up less domesticated creatures – a remarkably calm tiger, a monkey, horses. Enlightenment flying animals were given a voice of sorts and visibility on stage and page, and they helped define that significance of being human which aerial voyages called into question and restaged in 1802.

Finally, Chapter 14 moves on to exploring a selection of imaginative appearances of balloons in twentieth and twenty-first century culture. It shows how balloons still inspire rational and comic attachments, and how their philosophical symbolism has meaning for us long after their technological or scientific uses have been superseded. Refining the Enlightenment's project of flights of reason, western culture turns to balloons for flights of imagination.

Madness and Balloons

1

'all the world is mad about balloons'

Caledonian Mercury, 18 August 1784

WHY DID PEOPLE talk of 'balloon madness'? What did they mean by it? The language around balloons after 1783 indicated their effect was startling. 'Balloon madness', a phrase widely used in the first two years of aerostation, has simple and deep meanings. Superficially, 'madness' refers to an abnormal, unstable cultural phenomenon, like the use of the word 'craze' in the twentieth century to describe mass enthusiasm for something. Close to 'craziness', the term 'craze' signals that a significant number of people is affected, and lightly pathologises their obsessiveness in terms of mental disorder. Madness and craziness involve disturbing ways of behaving. In the 1780s, this language of disturbance had resonances that came from deep-running ideas. 'Balloon madness' drew on at least four currents of thought that flowed together in intricate ways from medicine, politics, religion and fashion; each had a way of explaining how ideas caught on and spread. The force of the term 'balloon madness' in the 1780s came from a confluence that held an easy position in everyday language but was all the more powerful for being continuously fed by explanations also themselves evolving. 'Madness' seems obvious, and we still use it obviously to describe what we disagree with. What it meant in the 1780s also had a hinterland of ideas not all familiar to us now.

The pathology of madness had a large literature in the late eighteenth century. As Enlightenment medicine moved on from old models of imbalance of humours accounting for illness, it kept a sense of aggression as relevant. So do we: wounds can still be described as angry. A key term, 'rage', described how epidemics spread. In 1782 the sentimental novelist Henry Mackenzie wrote to the economist

Adam Smith hoping he had escaped 'the Influenza, which has raged in London and now begins to rage here'.[1] Disease raged through bodies: in 1784 a treatise on farriery discussed the staggers 'that rage so furious and fatal among Horses at this present Time'.[2] Heat was a treatment by analogy. Dogs were branded on the forehead as a preventative against rabies, otherwise known as *la rage*. Symptoms of rage in people had a readable set of symptoms: eyes rolling, neck outstretched, brow wrinkled into clouds, flared nostrils, strained muscles, heaving chest; actors and orators were advised to gnash teeth, stamp feet and clench their right fist to complete the posture.[3] The physical heat in anger and fever produced mental symptoms: when fever receded, 'it not unfrequently happens, that some degree of foolishness, or *mania* shall remain for a few weeks'.[4]

Here physiology and psychology slid together like the great statues by Caius Cibber installed above the gates of Bedlam in 1675, depicting Melancholy and Raving Madness. The history of how modern ideas of madness relate to early modern ones is slippery because some of the words they share have not quite the same meaning, but anger and madness shared a lexicon of possession. An Anglo-French dictionary translated *manie* first as madness, fury and rage, with a second sense of passion and fantasy.[5] Rage possessed people, as witchcraft did. Bodily madness was hospitable to creative delusion – Shakespeare had observed that wit was close allied to madness – hence mad was not necessarily bad. Where melancholy madness was thought to produce literary sensitivity,[6] angry madness was less likely to produce creative delusion. Since anger was traditionally one of the passions, it was likely to be on the wrong side of Enlightenment values where reason was to be promoted, even by those who argued for the virtue of passionate reason or passionate fury, which had been productive among classical gods. Madness, then, beyond the bounds of reason, had a boundary with reason that was not completely fixed.

Like medical language, religious language did not stigmatise all kinds of madness. Delusion might be visionary, as plenty of evangelicals in the late eighteenth century attested. One term widely in use to indicate disapproval of particular rhetorics of faith was 'enthusiasm'.[7] Like that happy-clappiness distasteful to some Anglicans now, enthusiasm described fervency – a word from the Latin for 'fever' – that was embarrassing in its lack of restraint. Enthusiasts were hot-headed. In 1780 Thomas Frewen, a medical specialist, glossed melancholy as a species of madness; he explained it could be produced by external objects such as doleful stories or affecting sights.[8] In the range of stimuli to the madness of religious melancholy, 'unnatural' and 'unusual' cover the lot ... and balloons were both.

Perhaps the commonest use of 'rage' was in politics. 'Rage of party' was an eighteenth-century cliché; in the 1780s it overlapped with fashion, as politics became intensely driven by personalities. A satirical poem of 1780 mocked such adulations: 'Now like the effects of opium – and wine – ... This venerated mania of the clime'.[9] Political rage had a vocabulary of height earlier than balloons, so it transferred easily from a fever-high metaphor. In a letter of 1780, Gustavus III, King of Sweden, wrote of how a rage of opposition to him had mounted to its highest point.[10] Important aspects of eighteenth-century politics were expressed through clothes, so politics joined with fashion to be ragingly fashionable. A generation before balloons, a French correspondent wrote of how the rage for culottes had passed him by;[11] in England, according to a satire of 1785, "Tis the rage in this great *raging* Nation/ Who wou'd *live* and not be in the *fashion?*'[12] Whether or not English borrowed the word 'rage' straight from the French, it certainly took up an association of fashionability from French, as it did again in the twentieth century when it adopted the word 'vogue'. (The expression 'all the rage' is jazz age.) English was also happy with its own word 'madness' to describe things wildly in fashion. The *Annual Register* of 1775 used both words in commenting on the 'present Rage for lotteries' in a comic letter from a country correspondent: 'I have been in town only a few days, but I have met with occurrences enough already to make me think half the inhabitants are out of their senses, especially those who are seized with the *lottery-madness*.'[13]

Madness, then, was a word easily attached to fashionable things, to delusions, disorder and irrational possession. Referring to both willed belief and wayward belief, it was a word stronger than folly, a concept which had some degree of agency attached – you could cure folly, possibly, by a dose of reason. Madness had contagion; it spread between individuals to affect groups; it fired imagination as strongly as sensation. Comparing mania and religious melancholy, Thomas Frewen positioned them as extremes: where religious melancholy sank the spirits, raving madness made them climb. Mania was violent, acute, unstoppable: 'arising from a perturbation of the imagination and judgment ... the dreaming of persons awake, wherein *ideas* are excited without order, or coherence, and the animal spirits are driven into irregular fluctuation'.[14] It seems almost uncanny that a language of madness should be so ready and waiting for ballooning, with its excitable ideas and fluctuations. The rage for balloons – the drive, one might say post-Freud – even provided suitable positives. Frewen suggested mania gave rise to strong imaginations – so the balloon-mad would imagine febrile possibilities, and 'that natural boldness which arises from *madness*'[15] would be gloriously evident among aeronauts, leaders of the balloon-mad.

Two stories from the 1780s show how madness was represented as something that medical science might treat, and as something that simply defied rational explanation. The first story features a seafarer who spent five and a half years in the Asylum for Maniacs in York. He was a desperate case who never spoke and spent all day curled up. Those who hand-fed him regarded him as an animal nearly converted into a vegetable. In the middle of May 1783, he suddenly uttered a greeting and politely thanked the servants for their care of him. A few days later he wrote a perfectly sane letter to his wife. He then returned to his family and took command of a ship in the Baltic trade, leaving one of the country's most eminent doctors astonished in his wake.[16] The second story began in February 1787 at a cotton factory in Hodder Bridge in Yorkshire, where a girl put a mouse into the bread of another girl who had a dread of mice and went into fits. Then so did others. By two days later a workforce of more than two hundred was unable to work, seized with the idea that plague was coming from a particular bag of cotton. Fits spread to another factory five miles away where more young women went into violent convulsions, convinced they too were being strangled by plague emanating from cotton sacks. A doctor was called. He applied electric shock therapy, ether, laudanum and hot blisters. The patients immediately improved. Their cure was completed by a cheerful glass and a day of dancing, after which everyone went back to work. Cases of mass hysteria are still mysterious; in this instance it was thought that although electrotherapy contributed something, the real cure was a big dose of laughter.[17]

A lunatic inexplicably recovered and a phobic reaction sparking psychosomatic symptoms demonstrate that madness was something reversible, contagious and baffling, which reason and comedy could palliate but neither could explain. As balloon madness spread across Britain, it drew in analysts and satirists in a case study of the reason and humour whose partnership characterised Enlightenment thought. Balloons were a vehicle for philosophical thought, moral and scientific ideas about progress, wild imaginings and amusement, and they were all these things at once. Neither reason nor satire could account for the airy turn thought took nor for the passing of that turn: balloon madness subsided, yet fits of it recurred. They still do. This book was begun when few scholars took up balloons as a potent subject; at the time of its completion, intellectual air space has become crowded. Is this not a mild recurrence of balloon madness?

The period in which balloon madness appeared, rose to dizzy heights and diminished is roughly 1783 to 1786, with 1784 to 1785 the height of balloon activity in Britain. It may seem microscopically learned to claim for a mere two years a whole book's worth of intellectual gravity, but what one sees under microscopes is often revelatory. Understanding the eighteenth century has been all the better for attention to the local and particular: it shows how ideas were lived. Balloon madness did not move evenly around the country, though there was a pattern by which some aeronauts went north from London or west to Bristol, following established theatrical tracks and lecture circuits to take in towns with enough prosperity and facilities to supply materials and audiences for viable ascents. But there were independent hotspots of balloon madness: James Tytler in Edinburgh and James Sadler in Oxford are instances.[18] Print culture's reach into remote places ensured a community of interest enhanced by networks of knowledge. Gentlemen in the country, like Tiberius Cavallo in his garden in Dorset, experimented with balloons they knew about from their London life. Newspapers and magazines printed reports, eyewitness accounts and correspondence that created as much as reflected balloon madness.

The height of balloon madness in Britain was evident in September 1784 in London: 'the cockneys seem *nocturnal* balloon mad. Balloons being advertised for sale at three shilling apiece, every idler purchases them and sends them up at night with a candle; so that in the evening you can see a balloon galaxy everywhere.'[19] The craze was individual and sociable: 'Even porter houses now collect company, by giving notice of their intention to launch a balloon at a certain hour, by which several of them are said to have made it well answer their purpose, so balloon-mad are the people in the metropolis.'[20] Fine weather brought out balloons night and day, real and phantom: 'The boys, and idlers that crowd the streets, run about crying, "An Air-Balloon! An Air-Balloon!" It sometimes happens that the report is true; but when it is not, which is oftenest the case, the disappointment of the gazing multitude is good fun to the boys, and sometimes to graver spectators.'[21] On the night before the Italian Vincenzo Lunardi made the first successful manned flight in Britain, ascending from the Artillery Grounds in Chelsea on 15 September 1784, London was convulsed with excitement. One correspondent wrote: 'It is impossible for me to write any-thing tonight but what relates to air balloons, for we can neither think, speak, nor dream, of anything else.'[22]

London's obsession mirrored the feverish excitement that had gripped Paris at the end of 1783. The Montgolfier brothers' first demonstration of a globe raised by hot air at Annonay on 4 June 1783 led swiftly to a demonstration of their new invention before royalty in Paris, but not before the Academy-sponsored rival balloon, filled with inflammable air or hydrogen, was also launched. A young woman wrote to her friend Sir Charles Blagden, Secretary of the Royal Academy in London:

My mama has already told you that a Globe full of inflammable air raised itself from *Champ de Mars* 27 August. It was 13 feet diameter; it rose quickly, and was soon out of sight, a cloud preventing us from seeing it, when the cloud was remov'd, it was a second time perceptible, but soon disappear'd: It travell'd three quarters of an hour, and fell at *Gonesse* (a village four leagues from Paris, towards N.N.E.) It was first perceived by two cart drivers, who took it for granted the Devil was coming to fetch them, in a form he had never before appear'd in: As soon as they recover'd from their Panick, they pelted him with stones; the air which came from the holes made by the stones added to their terror: they then were inclined to think it a *Sea-monster*: they allarm'd the village, which readily agreed to assist at the combat, and sallied forth valiantly armed with knives; they cut and mangled the poor globe most sadly. The Curate who headed the army, approach'd the Monster with religious confidence and after taking a Survey of the formidable animal, perceived a small oiled silk-bag containing a Letter offering a reward to the finder on condition he would send it safely to Paris. 'tis said its fall was occasion'd by its being fill'd too full of Air, which burst when arrived at a lighter Region of Air. Had it not been for the ill reception it met with at *Gonesse*, it might have been easily repair'd. M.M. *Faujas de St Fond*, *Robert* and *Charles* conducted the whole: The latter was the occasion of its falling so soon, by filling it too full of Gas. There was at Champ de Mars a ring formed around the Globe, to keep the crowd at a proper distance: M. Charles would not admit M. de Montgolfier within the circle, and the Public greatly disapproved of M. Charles behaviour. The same experiment at the expense of Academy will be repeated next week. – There were only three thousand spectators, (being subscribers) admitted into the Champ de Mars. I was of that number.[23]

Although Miss Delessert gives her narrative a comic turn and her detail of the balloon's landing is second-hand, she knows what she sends is hot news; she is proud of her ringside seat.

Two streams of thought fed balloon madness: serious attention and satire. Henry Smeathman, another friend of Blagden's who later designed his own balloon, was also in Paris and wrote a lengthy and enthusiastic account. Such elation filtered into print where it made converts and sceptics. The latter too were sending news from Paris, denouncing balloons as merely a new form of French frivolity. One wrote that Parisians

> seem not only in thorough good humour, but even transported, at the discovery of a volatile Air-Bladder! The enthusiasm of all ranks upon this occasion is beyond belief: It blinds them to the most glaring truths; produces levities the most ridiculous, and reasonings and expectations equally weak and extravagant.[24]

The same writer scoffed at the rewards said to be heaped upon Etienne Montgolfier: 'what is much more flattering and honourable to him among these people is, that almost every article in the composition of dress is now *à la mode de Montgolfier!*' The French, he concluded, were easily elated, and the balloon a mere novelty, 'an object of useless, expensive and dangerous curiosity'. Elation was an emotion at the heart of balloon mania, but elation was felt by serious minds. Another female correspondent of Blagden's told him, 'indeed the late Philosophical Discoveries are so wonderful, and curious, that I could almost imagine myself in a new World, I fear it presumption at my advanced age, to follow such elevated enquiries, yet so long as I breathe this air, (pure or impure) shall retain a thirst for information'. She concluded sagely, 'I cannot help remarking, that to one age is allotted the proposing of Queiries, to another the solving of them.'[25]

Some very serious minds in Britain scoffed at balloons. Joseph Banks, the President of the Royal Society, was one – although his sister Sarah Sophia assembled a fine collection of balloon-related materials and he did subscribe to Lunardi's balloon. Banks was lordly about what he saw as the prevalence of adventurism over scientific enquiry. He wrote to Blagden a week after Lunardi's historic ascent:

I shall probably hear from you on Saturday what the real effect of the success of Lunardi produced on the heads of the would-be philosophers whether the King gave him money & the Prince encouragement & in short whether we are in danger of having our turn of Balloon madness. I confess I feel interested to know how that is likely to be but hope for my countreymen [*sic*] that it will not rise to the absurd height we have seen in France it does not appear that Lunardi has made one real Observation to assist the Science of Metereology [*sic*] or indeed anything more than his Predecessors in the art of delivering themselves over to the Command of the Winds.[26]

Unmoved by balloon madness, Banks remained dismissive:

Many thanks for your letter which gave me exactly the Character of Mr Lunardi I expected to receive it is wonderful how many people have been tolerably at their ease in the air without making one observation worth a groat.

Mr Sheldon and Mr Blanchard have probably fallen out as I have not now heard a word of them from some time & I see by the papers an Oxford man [Sadler] has made a little trip already I fear the rage will prevail in its turn here as much as it has done among our volatile neighbours.[27]

Banks was at this time in the country, fishing, farming, eager for literary news. Blagden, however, was still intrigued by balloon news, which he scrutinised for technical advances:

The duc de Chartres was in the Air only 4 minutes his Companions had forgot to examine before they ascended whether the valve at the top of the machine was in order and when they were up found it was immoveable the duke and two of his companions were frighted beyond the power of assisting themselves one of the Roberts kept his presence of mind and disclosed much heavy ballast during the descent at last he threw over a long rope which a boy who happened to be under caught and directed the balloon by it from a deep pond which it would otherwise have fallen into he has a pension for life.

The Ballon [*sic*] of atmospheric air was inclosed (says my informer) in the other and floated in its gas reports are different whether or not it broke with a noise the Coup de Pic was given with a stick which made part of the wings.[28]

This account of amateurism and accident was distinctly less heroic than public versions, in which the duke more nobly drew a sword. Blagden, who himself let off little inflammable balloons, got information from French correspondents like the Abbé Berthollet; he also passed on pamphlets to Banks who for all his cynicism did enter into conversations about materials, mechanics and inflation processes, aiming to recover some scientific advantage from the mania around Lunardi. As he wrote to Benjamin Franklin, 'Practical Flying we must allow to our rivals Theoretical Flying we claim ourselves.'[29] His discomfiture was noted: 'the French nation has all the honour of the discovery and the Englishman is jealous', wrote one French author. 'The Royal Society of London (notwithstanding the respect I owe them) had not common sense on this occasion. – Jealousy, mere jealousy; – I am sorry for them.'[30]

In the course of 1784 and 1785, newspapers regularly announced that balloon madness was over and regularly retracted their pronouncements. The *Caledonian Mercury*, reprinting London items, declared in early August 1784, 'Balloons are now so common, that they are regarded as a mere bauble'.[31] At the end of November, 'Balloons are now growing stale ware, and soon will bring but a small price – Every person can now make one, and if he could afford the expense, could take an aerial journey when he pleased. The inventor only has any merit.'[32] Nonetheless, there was enough life in the craze to last the rest of the year. In December, a Scot declared cautiously, 'BALLOON Madness seems now to have drawn towards a conclusion. As we must always have something, however, to be in a *rage* about, it has very properly been succeeded by Cylindrical Lamps.'[33] Yet the newspaper to which he wrote hedged its bets: 'The rage for Balloons is not yet exhausted. ... There is an Italian Count preparing a Balloon, in the Strand, in which he is to ascend with a Lady.'[34] There was plenty ahead besides Count Zambeccari: Blanchard and Jeffries crossed the Channel the next month, on 7 January 1785, reviving excitement. In May 1785, the *Caledonian Mercury* declared that 'the rage for air balloons continues'. Three weeks later, it announced another death of balloon madness: 'The fatal accident by which two persons were lately killed, by an Air Balloon, has served very much to damp it.'[35] These two were French aeronauts, Pilâtre de Rozier and Pierre Romain, who were attempting to cross the English Channel in an experimental balloon that fatally combined hot air and hydrogen. Death struck out of the blue on a calm sunny day, 15 June. The violent and public death of popular young heroes did not end balloon madness, but it killed a significant element of aerostation, its romance.

In London, where novelties were discarded fastest, balloon madness was a fashion slow to wear out. The terrible crash was rationalised; the balloon that Romain and de Rozier had used was visibly dangerous from the start. Other aeronauts went on making safe ascents and descents. Around Britain, in towns like Norwich, Liverpool, Bristol and Oxford, large crowds continued to assemble to witness aerial journeys. British readers knew too of similar flights happening regularly in Europe and occasionally in America. In 1787 and 1788 airy fun was still being had with their imaginative possibilities, and not everyone gave up. The most dedicated aeronaut, Blanchard, continued to give displays including manoeuvres with an uncanny ability to direct his machine. 'BLANCHARD, notwithstanding the balloon madness is over, still preserves his credit with mankind,' opined one report, because Blanchard had brought balloons nearer to usefulness than his competitors.[36] But events in Europe were heading for revolutionary ferment, and the country that pioneered human flight was too occupied by political convulsions to continue to dream of possibilities that had so captivated the balloon-mad.

Paul Keen quotes Stephan Oettermann's suggestion that 'It may have been precisely [their] lack of efficiency that made the balloon such an appropriate symbol of human longings and hopes... Hot-air balloons and the gas-balloons that succeeded them soon after belong not so much to the history of aviation as to the still-to-be-written account of middle class dreams.'[37] One balloon dream manifested such longings and hopes. The dreamer, noting that dreams of flying are common, imagines himself joining balloon madness as a hero:

> I began to dream that I was in the midst of a crowd, where all shewed the most anxious eagerness to see a huge Balloon or Aerostatic globe, just ready to take its flight into the regions of Air; but in vain did they endeavour to find a man bold enough to expose himself on this fickle Element. I instantly felt a burning desire to mount the first – this desire ferments in my sleeping head – I see this chariot which attracts the eyes of all – I break thro' the crowd – I beg, I pray – my request is granted, and up I spring towards the celestial spaces.[38]

Beginning from 'a certainty that very soon Mortals should be seen flying aloft in air', this dream catches the excitement of that idea – a shared idea. My account takes up those dreams in relation to conscious ideas, communicated through writing and acted out in practice. The next chapter explores one such case: a balloon-mad MP whose diary tells us elliptically about how balloons sailed through imagination.

One Man's Balloon Madness

2

'the business of the biographer is often ... to lead the thoughts into domestick privacies'

Samuel Johnson, *The Rambler*, no. 60

IN FEBRUARY 1784 William Windham's head was full of balloons. An interesting thirty-four year old, Windham came from an old Norfolk family [Figure 4]. After extensive travels and a period in his local militia, he had begun a career in politics. In 1783 he had been appointed by the Fox-North coalition to the post of chief secretary to the Irish viceroy, Lord Northington. He served ably for a few months – he was a lifelong supporter of the cause of Catholic emancipation – before resigning on grounds of ill-health. In April 1784 he returned to politics as MP for Norwich, one of the few Foxite candidates to be re-elected. In February he was mostly in London, dividing his time between seeing people, going to the theatre – he was friends with Sarah Siddons – skating, which he did rather well, and scholarly pursuits. Always a man with a book in his pocket, Windham enjoyed mathematics and the classics. Having just started a diary, he confided to it, like many eighteenth-century people, a sense he was not getting enough done. On 7 February 1784 he wrote:'Did not rise till past nine; from that time till eleven, did little more than indulge in reveries about balloons.'[1] The day was not a vacuous one: he called on Sarah Siddons, then on Fox; he had intelligent company at dinner, in the persons of Edmund Burke, Samuel Horsley and Sir Joshua Reynolds, all members of the Literary Club, along with Samuel Johnson whom Windham fervently admired; and in the late evening, Mrs Siddons and Mrs Kemble paid him a visit. In the pattern of this sociable day, what did it mean to Windham to spend two hours in balloon reveries?

To understand what Windham represented in balloon madness in 1784, his diary gives us some help. Diarists use diaries differently and not everything that matters is written down. Windham used

4   Portrait of the Hon. William Windham by Sir Joshua Reynolds, 1787.
Oil on canvas, 29½ in. x 24½ in.

his to record his movements and confide some of his self-doubts. In
1790 he wrote to a friend that he was 'a little of two characters, and
good in neither: a politician among scholars and a scholar among
politicians'.[2] In 1784 his friends included both groups. He was
close to Edmund Burke and to another fine orator, clever Sir Philip
Francis, whom many have suspected of being the anonymous author
of the *Letters to Junius* which publicly needled George III. Samuel
Horsley was rising up the Anglican hierarchy thanks to his defence

of Trinitarianism against Joseph Priestley's smart case for Unitarianism. In 1784 Horsley was also leading opposition to Sir Joseph Banks in the Royal Society, where he furthered the cause of mathematics by publishing five volumes of Newton's works and papers. It was mathematics that made him and Windham friendly. Sir Joshua Reynolds' painting of Sarah Siddons as the Tragic Muse was exhibited at the Royal Academy in April 1784 to great acclaim, although Reynolds couldn't find a buyer willing to pay his sky-high price of a thousand guineas (the painting was eventually bought in 1790 by Charles-Alexandre de Calonne, Louis XVI's former finance minister, for seven hundred guineas).[3] The week before his first mention of balloon reveries, Windham had been to see another portrait of Siddons painted by George Romney the previous year. Given the craze for her acting and hence for portraits of her, Windham might have spent every day so employed.[4] So the sociable part of his day was passed in clever and talented company.

In his diary, Windham makes no comment on much of his activity; he simply records it. But he does write about what one might call cast of mind, the mental strengths and weaknesses as he saw them that came between him and achievement. This sort of moral accounting was influenced by Johnson's writings and conversation. It led Windham to ponder his own indecisiveness, his inability to decide how he should spend a day, even to the point of getting onto a horse and then not being sure where to ride to. He reviewed his sleep patterns, debating whether he should get up as soon as he woke up. He thought so, since it seemed to encourage positive activity – whereas Johnson, who also struggled with what he thought was indolence, thought the best part of the day was between waking and getting up, because you could lie in bed and think ahead to the day without anything having gone wrong.[5] Given that Windham often lamented inefficiency in himself, a balloon reverie might seem just another form of daydreaming in a man whose worldly career in politics was shot through with diffidence about his talents. But his scholarly abilities were very precise. In February he was translating Greek into Latin, an exercise he did intermittently thanks to perfectionism rather than laziness. Mathematics cheered him up; he loved to slip away to the country and hole up undisturbed with his books, writing abstruse treatises. This rich inner life co-existed with sociability: his friends thought him good company, an excellent conversationalist, an elegant, thoughtful and considerate gentleman. His reveries were not the empty sort.

At coffee-houses and club dinners, Windham heard balloon news. And he sought it out: on 13 February, after visiting Drury Lane, he went to see Dr Fordyce 'to consult about balloon'. George Fordyce lived in Essex Street, off the Strand, where he gave lectures on physics, chemistry and *materia medica*, or what we now know as pharmacology. Fordyce had been elected to the Literary Club in 1774; in 1776 he was elected to the Royal Society. A penchant for brandy, a very efficient memory and a capacity for hard work distinguished him among the eminent Scots physicians working in London. In 1784 he was attached to the Royal College of Physicians in a post held previously by the poet Mark Akenside. Since Fordyce was friendly with the balloonophile Sir Charles Blagden, he could have given Windham the latest news about balloons, and he could also have explained the science of aerostation, such as it was. Over the course of 1784 Windham visited Fordyce several times specifically to discuss balloons. Though parliamentary business occupied him more, he found time to do nothing. On 20 July he recorded: 'The greater part of the time till now, one o'clock, spent in foolish reveries about balloons.' In September he returned to London from Oxford; near Burke's house he got out of his phaeton and walked to meet his friends, who were also setting off to see Lunardi ascend. Overseeing the filling of Lunardi's hydrogen balloon was none other than Fordyce, who (according to one observer) did so 'with great coolness and success.'[6] All Windham notes in his diary for the momentous 15 September is 'Lunardi ascended'; he did not record the silence, shouts or cheers, nor the gasp when Lunardi dropped an oar [Figure 5] and an old woman who thought it was the aeronaut falling died of fright. But two days later he hunted up some lines from Oppian 'which apply very well on the present subject of balloons'. To Windham's well-stocked mind, a second-century Latin poem about fish and fishing, Oppian's *Halieuticks*, seemed just the thing:

> The pinion'd Flocks, that wing the lower Way,
> Or soar above the Clouds in purer Day,
> Are Slaves to Man, tho' central Earth denies
> Th'aerial Chace, and Freedom of the Skies.[7]

Balloons continued to divert Windham throughout the autumn. Like many others, he saw Blanchard's balloon (27 September) and Lunardi's balloon at the Pantheon. In November he was at work on a translation of Thuanus, berating himself for not giving more time to it: 'This morning, rose early, disposed to be diligent, but

for the EUROPEAN MAGAZINE

View of the Ascent of Mr LUNARDI'S *Celebrated air Balloon from the Artillery Ground Sept. 15 1784.*

Published as the Act directs by J.Sewell Oct.1. 1784.

The first official manned flight in Britain, by Lunardi on 15 September   5
1784. Hand-coloured engraving, published 1 October 1784, for *The*
European Magazine.

interrupted between ten and eleven by Lord Spencer: by him and consequent business, relative to balloons, together with a visit to Phipps, employed till past four o'clock.'[8] The next day, he began again with good intentions but was sidetracked into Euclid and reading Locke: 'Before this proceeded far Lord Spencer came in, and we soon after proceeded to the balloon, which, after several hours' waiting, we saw from the top of Lord Derby's house. A little before it went up we were joined by Burke.' So far Windham might not differ much from any interested spectator whose education led him to enquire into the workings of balloons. After seeing this ascent, Windham bunked off going to parliament and went to see another spectacle, a 'wager rowed for on the Thames'. One of his favourite amusements was watching boxing matches in which bare-knuckle bruisers squared up to each other and large bets were made.

On 24 December, Windham dined with Horsley, 'to whom I showed my idea about balloons'. His interest, then, was not simply spectatorial: he was getting involved with practicalities. In fact, Windham was in discussion with the Oxford aeronaut James Sadler about making an ascent with him and, even more adventurous, considering a plan to cross the Channel together. On Christmas Day 1784, his wavering settled on a decision: 'Sat meditating whether I should undertake with Sadler the enterprise of crossing the Channel; I had before determined against it, and now confirmed the determination.' In March 1785 he saw Zambeccari and Admiral Vernon ascend, and on 5 May he and Sadler took their turn. As the *Oxford Journal* reported:

> Thursday morning about nine o'clock, Mr. Sadler of this city, accompanied by the Hon Mr. Wyndham, formerly of this University, ascended from the gardens of Mr. Dodwell, at Moulsey-Heath, near Hampton-Court, in an air balloon, capable of accommodating four passengers, and which carried up more than 3 cwt. of ballast, besides mathematical instruments, &c. The balloon is said to have been filled in 25 minutes and ascended with uncommon velocity. Dr. Horsley, and many other Fellows of the Royal Society, were present, who were highly entertained as well as surprised at the various manoeuvres performed by these aeronauts, who were hovering about the spot for nearly an hour and a half before the balloon bore away.

> Mr. Sadler and his companion descended at the spot near where the Thames and Medway join; but owing to the aukwardness [*sic*] of the country people who assisted to secure the balloon, it got from them, and ascended into the atmosphere with great velocity; it went

in an E.S.E. direction, and was seen by a gentleman with a glass to
descend about three leagues beyond Nore.[9]

Windham was aware he ran a risk. He made his will and wrote a long
letter to George Cholmondeley, to be delivered only in the event of
his death. In it he settled various affairs between them, apologised
to his friend for keeping secret his plans to fly, and explained his
motive: 'From the moment of my hearing of Balloons, I felt, I believe
in common with every man of the smallest imagination, the wish
of adventuring in one; and as early as the beginning of the winter
before last, concerted with Dr. Fordyce that we should build one
and go up together.' He was anxious Cholmondeley should know
that circumstances – Fordyce's dilatoriness, Sadler's precipitateness
– had pushed him into making this flight at this time, and there
was no question of his having held off until Sadler had proved his
airworthiness. He would have liked to have been at the forefront: 'the
credit to one's resolution that would have attended such an adventure some time ago, I would not have been insensible to, though I
may safely say that that was but a part of my motive'.[10] Conversely,
to be thought he only desired to show courage was an argument
against going. This balancing act between foolishness and hardiness
shows how balloon flights were positioned uncertainly as the province of the foolhardy.

Windham's case also suggests that aesthetics and spectacle were
not important to everyone. Aloft, he conducted small experiments,
keeping memoranda of measurements of height, speed and direction.[11] What he wrote in his diary on 5 May shows he saw flight as
a transformative experience, an experience that equated attaining
height with psychological assurance:

> Went up in balloon. Much satisfied with myself; and, in consequence
> of that satisfaction, dissatisfied rather with my adventure. Could I
> have foreseen that danger or apprehension would have made so little
> impression on me, I would have insured [*sic*] that of which, as it was,
> we gave ourselves only a chance, and have deferred going till we had
> a wind favourable for crossing the Channel. I begin to suspect, in
> all cases, the effect by which fear is surmounted is more easily made
> than I have been apt to suppose. Certainly the experience I have had
> on this occasion will warrant a degree of confidence more than I
> have ever hitherto indulged. I would not wish a degree of confidence
> more than I enjoyed at every moment of the time.

Meanwhile Windham's closest friend was bursting to hear about the adventure. On 7 May, Edmund Burke wrote:

> When will you receive the congratulations of your Terrestial Friends on your return to Mortality? *O pater anne aliquis – iterumque ad tarda reverti corpora?* The rest does not hold exactly in the words. I really long to converse with you on this Voyage, as I think you are the first rational being that has taken flight.
>
> *Adieu, Star triumphant, and some Pity show*
> On us poor battlers militant below.[12]

Burke reaches for poetry as the most apt frame for his friend's success. He does not immediately ask, as we might, what did you see? Instead he suggests an understanding of how literal elevation might change humanity's sense of itself – as Windham had done by reaching for lines of poetry about the superiority of man. Let's look more closely at Burke's choices. His first quotation is from Virgil's *Aeneid* (Book VI, lines 719–21), translated by John Dryden in 1697 thus:

> O father, can it be, that souls sublime
> Return to visit our celestial clime?
> And that the generous mind, released by death
> Can covet lazy limbs and mortal breath?

Aeneas is asking Anchises about souls in the lake of Lethe. Burke cuts out the death reference and admits he is adapting – 'the rest does not hold exactly in the words', as no doubt Windham would know. His second quotation is from Jonathan Swift's mock-elegy, *On the Supposed Death of Partridge the Almanac Maker*, again slightly adapted. The original runs:

> Triumphant star! some pity show
> On cobblers militant below,
> Whom roguish boys, in stormy nights,
> Torment by pissing out their lights,
> Or through a chink convey their smoke
> Enclosed artificers to choke.

Together the two allusions, to Virgil's visitors from another world and to Swift's sublunary anarchy, position the aeronaut between epic and satire, metaphysics and astrology, grandeur and silliness. They serve a purpose of taking seriously and making light. They also show that people responded to ballooning by searching their cultural vocabulary for references to adapt to this new thing.

Enlightened minds reached for poetry. It could be classical or recent; either way, it was more relevant than a language of description. Or rather, it was the language of description: it translated an experience of elevation into existing terms. As the author of a key treatise on the sublime and beautiful published in 1757, Burke was well used to thinking visually. Neither was Windham indifferent to aesthetics. A few years later, touring Germany, he wrote in his diary that the view from a steeple in Strasbourg reminded him of a prospect seen from a low balloon.[13] That was the only reference in his diary after 1785 to anything balloon-related.

The high-flying world of poetry provided many people with frames of reference for balloons. That's not surprising if you take the view that new inventions co-exist with old ones, or that new inventions settle in to culture by means of forming a relationship with existing things. Studies of technological innovation in the nineteenth and twentieth centuries have memorably demonstrated how people give old meanings to new objects in a process of transference that accompanies assimilation. Carolyn Marvin shows how early users of the telephone shouted loudly into it, the more so if speaking long distance. That the telephone conveyed sound equally over unequal distances may have been intellectually understood by its users, but it took a while to get used to.[14] Balloons also altered behaviours slowly, and they altered some behaviours not at all. Marvin proposes that if you shift focus from a technological invention to its social context, what you have is still a drama, 'in which existing groups perpetually negotiate power, authority, representation, and knowledge with whatever resources are available. New media intrude on these negotiations by providing new platforms on which old groups confront one another.'[15] The novelty of balloons did not reduce the cultural capital of classical poetry as a way of thinking; indeed, the sharing of allusions to Virgil among the balloon-minded increased it.

William Windham provides a case study of how people, places and ideas intersect. We know some of what he thought from his diary, correspondence and manuscripts; we know some of what he did from the newspapers and life writings of others. He was present in London, Oxford and Norwich, all significant places for balloon activity; he made one aerial voyage himself and helped fund another aeronaut, James Sadler, who named his son Windham in gratitude; he aspired to crossing the Channel in a balloon. He saw his experience of flight as psychologically transformative – it changed his conceptions of self-confidence – and he is a possibly perfect example of balloon madness in that his head was full of balloon reveries and balloon designs for a short, intense period, after which he let them go. He could be generalised into a class, that of the educated balloon-mad, yet he is also particular, an individual who explored his own diffidence thoughtfully in a private space marked out from the very public world in which his distinctive talents were employed. He shows us how ideas are lived and he proves that imagination is a vital force in the history of balloons. Through his life in London and connections with Oxford, Windham also shows how ideas are shaped by where one is in the world. The next section explores how people in different places around Britain spread balloon madness round the country.

The Craze Spreads

People and Places 3

'the New application of Inflammable air to make flying balons has already invaded the whole Earth, and turned the head in every body. I am glad to hear that even the English do amuse them Selves about that play.'

Giovanni Valentino Mattia Fabroni to Sir Joseph Banks, 30 December 1783 (Royal Society Archives)

BALLOON NEWS SPREAD fast around Britain. Newspapers printed detailed accounts, local and international, so that readers in notionally provincial towns were often as well-informed as those in London. Some magazines too had national distribution, and private letters carried by an efficient postal system told of sightings and ascents. The balloon-mad read and talked avidly of aerostation in their area and worldwide. Benedict Anderson's classic work on the communication of ideas puts newspapers as a pillar of imagined communities, connecting people through common readership.[1] That model holds good for balloon news though with a question of tone. Eighteenth-century newspapers, like newspapers now, combined apparently dispassionate reporting with commentary or tone that angled the subject in positive or negative ways. Many newspapers published accounts sent by witnesses with explicit views; many also printed balloon materials – advertisements, poems, periodical-style pieces, some serious, some humorous – that both reflected and created a composite tone about balloons. Newspapers expressed pride, civic and national; they also poured scorn. Their volatile views on balloons embraced scepticism, enthusiasm and contempt; like crowds at balloon launches, their mood could suddenly turn hostile. So although they are an index of public opinion, they were not always in sympathy with the balloon madness of other actors, including their contributors and readers.

Enthusiasm for balloons created activity all round Britain. Some of it was independent of events in London, though metropolitan ascents were widely reported and made aeronauts known in provincial places. Lunardi, for instance, started in London and then toured north, taking in York, Liverpool, Edinburgh and Glasgow. But he did not bring balloon madness to a new audience: Edinburgh had had its own inventor, and York had aeronauts who came flushed from success in Norwich and Bristol. The wildfire spread of balloon madness had hotspots other than London. Liverpool in the north-west of England, York in the north-east, Norwich in the east and Bristol in the west were centres of trade that looked outward to the world. Liverpool and Bristol were transatlantic ports, globally important for slavery and sugar trade; Norwich was a port with strong links to the nearby Netherlands; York was the major staging post between London and Scotland.[2] By the 1780s, each had the civic amenities of cultural life – assembly rooms, playhouses, concert halls, societies and clubs. The prevailing south-westerly winds of England also gave them particular considerations for aeronauts: all were on or near enough to the coast for flights to run the risk of being swept out to sea. Strong winds could also buffet inland: all aeronauts had to contend with the vagaries of British weather. My selection of people and places in this chapter does not attempt either a geographically or chronologically comprehensive story, but one that explores significant and sometimes surprising locations of balloon madness around Britain.

SCOTLAND: ABERDEEN AND PATRICK COPLAND

One might think that Aberdeen, a town in the north of Scotland, would represent an outpost of aerostation. A balloon was let off here quite early, in the spring fever of ballooning. As the *Aberdeen Journal* reported on 4 March 1784:

> On Friday last an Air Balloon of 3½ feet diameter by 5 high was sent off from Castle-hill of this place; the wind was south, inclining a little to the east and pretty strong, which made it ascend, making with an angle of about 25 degrees from the horizon. It continued ascending as long as it remained visible from the hill, which was about two minutes and a half, when it disappeared behind a cloud. It is said to have been seen by a countryman a mile on this side of Ellon, about one o'clock, and at a great altitude in the air.

This short, sweet, attestable flight may not have been the first balloon in Scotland – John Scott, a chemist in Edinburgh, laid claim to that – but it was a serious one. The person who oversaw this launch was Professor Patrick Copland. Copland taught at Marischal College, founded in 1593. Officially he was Professor of Mathematics but he swapped jobs with his colleague, Robert Hamilton, Professor of Natural Philosophy, because in the practical classes Hamilton broke too much glass.[3] In 1780 Copland began a drive to raise funds for an observatory, an enterprise in which Edinburgh had tried and failed. Copland succeeded. He persuaded the town council, who donated twenty guineas, and nearly £400 was swiftly raised. On land the council had earmarked for a flagstaff, Copland set up a fine purpose-built observatory with an excellent set of instruments. He was well-connected – friends with Nevil Maskelyne, the Astronomer Royal – and infectiously enthusiastic. The great instrument-maker Jesse Ramsden laid aside more prestigious projects to work on instruments for him. Lord Bute donated two instruments said to be worth five hundred guineas.[4]

So although the Aberdeen Observatory was a geographical outpost, it was by no means remote from intellectual developments, even if some needed explaining. It was said that local people suspected Copland of controlling the weather, like Samuel Johnson's unhappy astronomer in *Rasselas*, and that Copland protected himself against possible attack on the street by carrying in his breeches a small vial of dangerous electrical matter which he could discharge against any assailant.[5] When his balloon fell after a flight of thirty-eight miles, country people thought it was a spirit or angel come to sound the Last Trump. Anyone who read newspapers was offered an alternative explanation: the balloon would have sailed on longer had the final stage of filling not distended pores in the silk, making gas leak out.[6] That detail of its angle to the horizon suggests Copland was following its progress with one of his fine instruments.

This is not, though, a story of high-faluting professor and superstitious peasants. Copland was an acclaimed teacher, keen to spread knowledge, and Aberdeen was a town where value was set on learning. In 1781 the governors of Robert Gordon's College, an establishment for educating poor boys, acquired the right to send four boys each year to join mathematical and natural philosophy classes at the university, in recognition of a gift of fifty guineas for astronomical instruments. And some who applied could teach the teachers a few things: 'A letter of 1787 recorded an instance of *"a common carpenter at Aberdeen"* who applied to attend the lowest mathematical class. On examination *"they found he had taught himself all they could teach him, and instead of receiving him as a student, they gave him a degreé*'.[7] Thanks to its observatory, Aberdeen was well equipped to follow aerostation as one of many exciting developments. Alas, this period was brief: in 1792, the Castlehill observatory was damaged during the construction of a barracks to protect against invasion; it was relocated, its energy ebbed away and its magnificent instruments disappeared.[8]

In the summer of 1784, Aberdeen was wet. The *Journal* reported Tytler's efforts in Edinburgh and Lunardi's ascent at London. By October, small balloons capable of staying aloft for fifteen minutes were on sale thanks to a local perfumier who promoted them alongside a fashionable stock of ostrich feathers. 'They provide as much pleasure and diversion as one of a hundred feet circumference', he claimed, and cost two or three shillings each.[9] In Elgin, slightly further north on Lossiemouth, it was reported that a mathematically-minded young man had sent up a balloon that fell down the chimney of a whisky-brewing landlord, injuring a woman.[10] The most northerly towns in Britain had joined in balloon madness.

SCOTLAND: EDINBURGH AND JAMES TYTLER

Balloons have a twist in their early history, as the Montgolfiers' original process of lift from hot air proved less attractive to imitators than inflammable air, or hydrogen. One exception was the Great Edinburgh Fire Balloon. This was designed early in 1784 by James Tytler in Edinburgh. Apprenticed to a surgeon, a student of chemistry, an inventor and an indefatigable writer of articles for a second edition of the *Encyclopaedia Britannica* which he expanded from three volumes to ten, he had a small printing press from which he issued abridged history and translations (of Virgil's *Eclogues* in 1781–82). None of this paid well and Tytler lived in poverty – in Robert Burns' description, 'a mortal man who trudges about Edinburgh as a common printer with leaky shoes and skylighted hat and knee breeches'.[11] Much of his writing was done on an upturned tub in the lodgings he and his family rented from a washerwoman.[12]

In such unglamorous surroundings Tytler built a stove, basket and balloon, to be paid for by subscription. Money came in slowly, too slowly, collected with the assistance of a golf caddy who ran a pub and resembled Lord North so much he was called by that name. Nonetheless, public interest was high and the press supportive: Tytler was 'our modern Daedalus', said one paper.[13] His balloon was large, cylindrical, forty feet in diameter and at least thirty in height; it had a rudder and wings. Another newspaper stated: 'Of its success no doubt is entertained in Scotland; and the curiosity of the people there to see a machine as large as a moderate sized house, ascending in the air with the Constructor along with it, is not more general than natural.'[14] Lack of funds hampered trials as much as technicalities, but finally Tytler managed to get the balloon free of the earth and float a short distance with him aboard. A larger exhibition was planned on 27 September 1784. The fire was lit and the well-filled balloon was hoisted halfway up its mast, to stay suspended for three quarters of an hour before the tethering rope broke and it sank slowly over the stove. It was hoisted again. Then the mast broke and the whole apparatus crashed. 'It must be obvious to every person present at the above exhibition, that a balloon raised by smoke, or rarefied air, such as Mr Tytler's is, cannot possibly ascend but when there is almost a dead calm, which cannot often be expected in this climate,' asserted one newspaper; inflammable air could defy the elements, 'but then it is attended with an expense infinitely beyond an Edinburgh subscription.'[15] Others were less kind. At the next public attempt on 11 October in Comely Gardens, 'the balloon, having rolled about a short time like an overgrown porpoise, at last rolled slowly and heavily to the height of about a hundred yards, but being without any director, it fell sideways on the ground, nearly on the spot from which it rose.'[16] Excitement turned to derision: 'It is scarcely to be conceived what a deal of time has been trifled away from first to last, by the various exhibitions of this bungling and mis-shapen *smoke-bag*.'[17] For a while Tytler persisted – he made the stove smaller and to lessen weight he abandoned his cork jacket and his beloved bagpipes, but in vain; the balloon was damaged in a further attempt, impounded, released, and so battered it had to be abandoned.

In defeat, Tytler was generous. When Lunardi's inflammable air-balloon eclipsed his efforts completely, he wrote a long heroic poem to celebrate his rival, glancing ruefully at his own failure. Lunardi printed it in his *Account of Five Aerial Voyages in Scotland*. In verse Tytler becomes a sort of balloon, filled with poetic fire and then sunk: 'Lost are my wishes, lost is all my care,/ And all my projects flutter in the air.'[18] His prose notes explained how he had been defeated by winds, public opinion and poor advice from friends who had insisted he make a smaller stove. To meet expectations, Tytler said he had filled his balloon dangerously full: 'this was the resolution of a *madman,* and which nothing but my desperate situation could excuse.'[19] He sounded a defiant note: the balloon was capable of performing all he had planned and more, but public opinion, like strong winds, blew against him.

> I was obliged to hear my name called out wherever I went, to bear the insults of every black-guard boy, to hear myself called Cheat, Rascal, Coward and Scoundrel by those who had neither courage, honesty, nor honour. I was proscribed in the newspapers, and pointed out by two of the Edinburgh News-mongers as a public enemy...[20]

Tytler observed how fickle public opinion construed his misfortunes as misconduct – and how there was no way of redress except by success, which eluded him. In the same summer months as he was struggling with obstacles, *montgolfières* in France were not doing much better. One in Bordeaux at the end of July rose a mere forty feet, and one in Paris in mid July that failed to rise was turned into a huge conflagration by an angry crowd.[21] Tytler's odd background gave him little protection; eventually he went to Ireland, then to America, where in 1804 he died falling into a claypit, drunk. It was a sad end for a persistent philosopher.

THE NORTH-EAST: YORK AND WELLER & DEEKER; NEWCASTLE AND VINCENZO LUNARDI

In 1784 York was a bustling cathedral city. Below its high walls and Gothic Minster, narrow and winding medieval streets known as the Shambles still housed artisans working in metal and leather. Mid-century prosperity led to extensive rebuilding; elegant town-houses were joined by an assembly room, a theatre and music rooms. York had solid and stylish Georgian character. It was home to Laurence Sterne, author of *Tristram Shandy* (published first in York in 1759), so it was perfectly familiar with comedy and sentiment; it was also familiar with political truculence through the anti-authority reform movement, led by Christopher Wyville, which in the 1760s pressed radical demands that continued to be vocal in the 1780s. A Freeholders' meeting in March 1784 typically urged members to 'repel the insolence of a few who seek to be lords over you and render you only the creatures of their will and pleasure.'[22] Such unwillingness to be kept down made Yorkshire folk interested in the freedom of the skies: the *York Chronicle* and *York Courant* were notably full of accounts of ascents elsewhere. Local signs of balloon enthusiasm included a new fast coach on a French model, built at Whitby early in 1784 and called the Air Balloon.[23] It appealed to Yorkshire thriftiness by enabling people to bypass a particularly expensive inn.

Balloons appeared in York almost simultaneously indoors and outdoors. In late February 1784 the Theatre Royal had a programme of plays all about magic and transformation. One of them was *Harlequin Philosopher*, in which a large balloon was visible on stage throughout and released at the end of the show. Meanwhile two local carvers, William and John Staveley, had built a ten-foot balloon: they sent it up in front of a crowd and extended their success to twenty minutes with another balloon a few days later. A gentleman from Lincolnshire wrote to tell the Staveleys their balloon had been found by a farmer's boy, who had pursued it as it bounded over hedge and ditch till it tangled in thorns with frightful hissing and cracking. The boy had tried to carry it off but a large bang made him sure the Devil was in it so he threw it down. The balloon was undamaged and kept some air for a day, looking like a petticoat.[24]

By early May the Staveleys had managed six successful launches. The north-east was firmly on the balloon map, with other launches at Hull, Halifax and Ripon. It was typical of how balloons first went up around Britain: artisan ingenuity capably built small unmanned balloons whose flights were eagerly watched and avidly reported. One such balloon, picked up a hundred miles away, was made by George Gibson, described as a carver and gilder and listed as a silk merchant in York's trade directory for 1784 – all trades that could be turned to balloon-making.[25] Such achievements seemed promising, though local experiments developed no further in 1784. Interest was fanned by lectures in York on electricity, which included a demonstration of the properties of inflammable air showing how much more suitable it was for balloons than hot air. In May 1785, an aeronaut from further afield blew in – James Sadler, on his second ascent from Manchester, landed at Pontefract in Yorkshire. Though Sadler was badly bruised on landing and keen to hurry back to Manchester, Yorkshire folk were hopeful of treating him: 'three or four dinners were provided at different places, where it was likely that he might alight.'[26] Balloon madness was fervently in evidence.

In August 1785 an advertisement appeared, announcing the imminent arrival of 'The Royal Balloon'. One of its two aeronauts was James Deeker, who had wowed the inhabitants of Norwich with a fine ascent in June, as he reminded readers by offering copies of his account for a shilling.[27] The place was to be Kettlewell's Orchard, just behind the Minster; the day depended on the weather but was cannily timed to coincide with race week, a big fixture in the York social calendar. The advertisement was genteelly worded – ladies and gentlemen who intended to favour the aerial experimenters with their company were invited to send their names beforehand, so accommodation could be prepared. Deeker's name appeared as Decker: more decorous, perhaps? Best tickets cost five shillings but there were also cheap rates for servants – 6d to see the balloon, on show at the Judge's Lodgings, a capacious house. Weller and Deeker invited applications from any liberal-minded lady or gentleman who wished to be a passenger.

Given that York gentry had been reading about balloon successes and disasters for months, this publicity was confident and intensely polite. Everything was to be convenient, agreeable, secure. Supposing the experiment to be a success, Weller and Deeker would move on to Hull; if it were not, subscribers were assured their money would be returned. Their term 'aerial experiment' gestured to science; their provision of a band to polite entertainment. Did this genteel talk allay doubts? The advertisement in the *York Chronicle* appeared alongside a lurid account of Lunardi's nearly-disastrous attempt in Liverpool, in which the aeronaut drew his sword on the crowd and a thousand screams of terror attended his messy take-off. The melodrama of that report must have coloured Weller and Deeker's bland politeness.

But the balloon sounded splendid. The Staveleys' last balloon was crimson and gold; Weller and Deeker's imaged far-flung worlds through fashionable China. It had a magnificent '*Triumphal Gondola* or *Car*, which supports an elegant Chinese Temple, decorated and ornamented in a Stile of unparalleled Elegance which has been allowed by many Thousands (who have already seen it) to be the most superb and complete Vehicle ever seen in this Kingdom'.[28] This magnificent Aerostatic Globe was to ascend from a green space near the Minster. All started well, if an hour late. In a quick two hours it was filled and, with Weller aboard, seemed to ascend with majestic grandeur. Then gusts of wind exacerbated by the lofty cathedral blew it against a wall, a tree and houses. Weller kept cool, throwing out sacks of sand, but the balloon overturned, wedging the elegant Chinese temple upside down against a chimney and detached from the globe which sailed on to deflate a few streets away. The audience was philosophical. Accidents of wind might happen to anyone. So people reappeared for a second attempt a few days later, this time sensibly sited on open ground near the race course. The globe, patched up, was three hours into filling when a terrible thing happened. The aeronauts ran out of oil of vitriol. No fresh supply could be found: 'the populace, which till now had waited with great patience, being, as is supposed, apprehensive of a disappointment, became outrageous, and broke in upon the balloon, which they liberated, after cutting away the car, &c.'[29] All those genteel ladies and gentlemen had become a less polite populace.

The subsequent row that broke out reveals much ambivalence about balloons. Perhaps commentators were influenced by a newspaper trail that featured bad news, as newspapers do, but which had also reported the success of James Sadler who at this time was managing to fly for up to two hours. The *York Chronicle* ran a long piece, headlined BALLOON, by a writer who described himself as 'neither a Balloonist not an Anti-Balloonist', but a man in whom human sympathy created feelings for other men, especially those injured or distressed. The recent attempts had created mental ferment in all ranks and some wild rumours; he would lay out the arguments impartially. Choice of a site near the Minster was obviously dangerous. 'Absurdity has even asserted, indeed that the man purposively dashed himself, first against the house, then the chimney, to prevent the Balloon's ascension; – in other words, that he deliberately put himself in *the most imminent and extreme danger of killing himself, from fear of killing himself.* – This requires no comment.'[30] Risking life to avoid suicide by balloon was mad reasoning. What was reasonable to examine was whether the aeronauts had imposed on the public. Were they cheats? That Weller and Deeker had squabbled about who should go up suggested both men were genuinely keen; Deeker had lost his public standing and a great deal of money.

> Their interest, their reputation, the security of their property, their personal safety; every consideration operated, that the public should not be disappointed. They had the greatest reason to expect success but have been *unsuccessful*; every future attempt of the kind has been defeated, and they are ruined.[31]

The key indicators here are about money. The author pointed out that York townspeople had voluntarily set up a subscription, and Weller had not left town as an impostor would. Like many of the era, this author believed that handling credit well made you creditable: Weller 'will make public the whole account, by the receipts and vouchers by which it will appear that he is both *honest and unfortunate*'. The value of equipment and balloon came to £140, a considerable loss.[32] More than that, it represented an investment in seriousness. In this case, the important context was not science but property.

The *Chronicle's* author deplored the way in which failed ascents unleashed anarchy, as he saw it:

> To sum up the whole of this plain and simple narrative, I submit it to the reflection of every sober person, What have these men done? How have they deserved to be pointed at as objects of the public odium? By what crime have they forfeited the protection of our laws? and what a disgrace to our Police, that in broad daylight, under the eyes of magistrates and persons invested with power to enforce public order, two innocent men should be abused; grossly insulted; robbed of their property; dragged about by a senseless rabble; and nearly escape undergoing the ignominious and horrid discipline of a pomp, which, to a person of any feeling, must be worse than death itself! Surely such scandalous violation of law, justice, decency, and humanity, calls loud for the attention of every thinking Englishman, and should be soon and effectually suppressed – when customs so shocking are tolerated or connived at, they speak our ferocity, and may well draw upon us, from a rival nation, the odious reproach of being *Les Sauvages de L'Europe* – the Savages of Europe.[33]

The possible crime of fraud on the part of the aeronauts was set against the irrefutable law-breaking of those who attacked them and their equipment. Balloons focused arguments about property: was it worse to take money by fraud or by destroying valuable property? The answer was important to the property-owning classes. Since property-owning was a qualification for enfranchisement, rioting around balloons threatened liberty. That patriotic idea was more potent to many readers than science.

What could Weller and Deeker say? Weller responded in the *Chronicle* with a pathetically polite apology: he lamented most sincerely all the misfortunes which had led to disappointment for the generous people of York and to a material loss to himself.[34] Deeker used the *Courant* to put out a more robust defence, pointing the finger at Weller for not having done his bit in supplying materials as he was supposed to. But Deeker also used the language of sensibility to give his exculpation more force. The discovery that the vitriol had run out 'was as a Thunder-Bolt to his very Soul ... The ablest Pen cannot convey the least Shadow of the Feelings of

Mr. D. at that fatal moment.'[35] Terms familiar from fiction indicated sensitivity to his fellow men in another version of the *Chronicle* writer's appeal to humanity. On 20 September, Deeker announced that his partnership with Weller was dissolved. What happened to the balloon meanwhile? 'Liberated by the mob of Knavesmire', it was taken up at sea around 7pm on 29 September by Captain Howe of *The Squirrel*, about fifteen leagues off Flamborough Head. 'When first seen it was at an immense height and appeared no larger than a bird, but gradually descending, it dropped into the sea about four miles to leeward of the vessel. The sailors were under the necessity of making an aperture in the Balloon to let out the gas.'[36] Balloon recovery returned to factual prose, though with latent irony – a balloon that aeronauts had failed to inflate had picked up enough volume to require manual perforation to secure it.

The York newspapers went on reporting balloon events from farther afield; ascents by Blanchard in the Netherlands and Poole in Cambridge were given heroic treatment. In December 1785, the heir to Duncombe Park came of age and three thousand people attended celebrations at Kirbymoorside. An ox was roasted in the marketplace and 'ale without measure' given to the people. Inns were filled with gentlemen making loyal toasts while church bells rang all day. After dark, the town was illuminated. Fireworks were set off and a grand ball got under way: 'At seven o'Clock a large Fire balloon was liberated from the Lund common, (with a Label to the Honour of C. Duncombe, Esq;) which had a most beautiful Aspect, took a North-East Direction, but the Night being foggy, was soon out of Sight'.[37] The balloon fitted neatly into a week of festivities around the Duncombe estate. There were hunts of hare, stag and fox, greyhound coursing, and charitable donations to any poor person lucky enough to meet with the Duncombe carriage as it travelled between jollities. With an emphasis on propriety, the balloon, fireworks, cannon and peals of bells laid claim to the air, while the pursuit of wild creatures secured the family's claim to the land. Balloons rejoined a conservative order of property.

At the end of August 1786, York had another visit from an aeronaut: Lunardi. The York public had followed his exploits around Britain in the previous year, his recent gallantries in Scotland and his rather mixed record. He arrived in town as Sarah Siddons was acting in *The Conscious Lovers*, and his announcement of his intentions was as respectful, confident and considerate as a desirably conscious lover. Daringly he chose the same spot as Weller and

Deeker – Kettlewell's Orchard near the Minster – where higher ground would be reserved for ladies and children. Tickets were three shillings to see the launch and one shilling to see the ascent. A balloon on a rope would guarantee some spectacle and minor experiment.

On 29 August the *Courant* reported:

> On Wednesday, at 40 Minutes after One o'Clock, the gallant Lunardi amply fulfilled his Engagement to the Public, by ascending with his Royal balloon from Kettlewell's Orchard, behind the Minster, amidst the Acclamations of several Thousand Spectators. His Ascension was truly sublime. The Balloon rose to a prodigious Height, so as to be distinctly seen in every Part of Town, and took a N.E. Direction. A very dark Cloud for some Minutes obscured the intrepid Aeronaut from the gazing Multitude, who had, however, soon the Pleasure of again observing his Progress at a great Distance, through the trackless Atmosphere. Mr. Lunardi's Dexterity in filling his Balloon, which was done in little more than 18 Minutes, and every Part of his Conduct throughout the Business, merited great Praise, and afforded the highest Satisfaction to every Beholder. – Mr. Lunardi descended an Hour after his Ascent in a Corn-Field, and observing People flocking from every Quarter towards him, by which he was apprehensive that the Corn would be injured, he therefore rose again and went out of Sight. At Three o'Clock he finally descended between two Hills, in a place called Greenock, in the Parish of Bishop-Wilton, about 18 Miles from hence. A few Shepherds came to his Assistance after he was perfectly anchored, and the number of his rustic Visitors increasing, he discharged the inflammable Air from the Balloon, and with their Assistance packed it up. Robert Denison, Esq; who had rode after him from his House at Kildwick Percy, arrived in Time to give proper Directions for conveying the Balloon safe to that Place; and having accommodated Mr. Lunardi with his Horse, took him home to Dinner, and afterwards most politely brought him in his own Chaise and Four to this City. Tho' it was Night when they entered the Town, the Anxiety of the people for Mr. Lunardi's Safety had been so great, and the Joy they felt on his Appearance such, that they took the Horses from the Carriage and drew him through the Streets to his Lodgings in Triumph. – Soon after, Mr. Lunardi dressed, and paid his Respects to the Ladies and Gentlemen at the Assembly-Rooms, where he was received with the warmest expressions of Welcome and Applause. Mr. Lunardi, when at a great Elevation from the Earth, experienced very inclement Weather; had Rain, Hail, and Snow; and was also in the Midst of electrical Clouds. The Neck of his Balloon was rather frozen, and himself quite benumbed with Cold when he descended.

Lunardi was unfailingly polite – explicitly appreciative of assistance, careful not to damage corn, assiduously grateful to his supporters, quick to pay his bills. Even his efficiency in filling was polite, in not keeping spectators waiting. He was a success with the crowd, urban gentry and rural labourers. Shepherds were rustic visitors, genteel pastoral. It is possible that Lunardi contributed to this account or approved it before publication. Its flattering light could not, however, overturn less polite facts: after York he went on to Newcastle, where his next attempt was a disaster. And there is a certain stasis in the *Courant* report; by 1786, balloon madness had settled into the merely pleasant unsettling of the sublime.

Lunardi had been invited to Newcastle by the mayor, with a thousand pounds and all expenses paid as inducement. But Lunardi's luck ran out. During the filling process, an uneven application of acid led to a sudden effervescence. The balloon bulged, with so terrible a noise and discharge of gas that the gentlemen holding the ropes on one side let go. Lunardi ran round to urge them to hang on, but too late – a young man, Ralph Heron, was caught up by a rope twisted round his arm, carried up several hundred feet where he let go, fell into a garden and was killed. His grieving elderly parents were inconsolable. So was his fiancée. They were to have been married the next day. Lunardi, appalled, made public professions of horror. Privately he wrote: 'I am so affected by the loss of this young man that my frame is entirely discomposed. I never suffered so much since I was born; I am inconsolable and I shall wear deep mourning for him.'[38] He was ill until December when he returned to London, to turn from balloons to designing an aquatic machine which came to a sticky end thanks to an uninvited crowd at Calais. Lunardi slunk back to Lucca, his home town, to resume attempts at balloon flights with no success and several violent disasters until 13 September 1789 at Naples.[39]

THE NORTH-WEST: LIVERPOOL AND CHESTER; THOMAS BALDWIN AND VINCENZO LUNARDI

In 1784 Liverpool was more of a working town than a smart city. A middle-sized seaport with a population of around thirty-five thousand, its streets were narrow and its public buildings unhandsome brick. Coach time to London was forty-three hours in 1776; in 1785 a flash new mail coach cut the journey time to thirty hours.[40] Its docks were busy with ships unloading cargoes of sugar, coffee, rum,

Baltic furs, amber and fish, especially from the Greenland fishery, important enough for sailors engaged in it to be protected against impressment. Its dirtiest business was slavery: in 1785 at least seventy-nine slaver ships passed through. These sea trades were serviced by timber yards, chandleries, taverns and brothels; it also had a ducking stool, still in use in 1779. But it was acquiring a more polite character: in 1772 came the Theatre Royal; the town corporation regularly feasted on turtle, and in 1784 it put on a festival featuring Handel's music. There were half a dozen inns, a few coffee-houses and three newspapers.[41] These took an interest in Ireland and America, Liverpool's nearest neighbours, and the principal newspaper, *Williamson's Liverpool Advertiser*, printed a great deal of balloon news from elsewhere in England and from the continent. Prevailing south-westerly winds made it likely that Irish aeronauts would come to land nearby: when Richard Crosbie made an ascent in late July 1785, it was said he was aiming for Holyhead.

The citizens of Liverpool, like those of York and other principal towns in England, had been offered a course of lectures by a Mr Walker, itinerant astronomer, in which the workings of the heavens were explained and demonstrated by a fine orrery which modelled the relative movements of heavenly bodies. In 1784 and 1785, Liverpool was also a place of inventiveness. It supplied portable soup, powders of beef, mutton, veal and chicken, said to be restorative for sickly slaves. It harboured news of diving bells, like that used to try to raise materials from an East Indiaman sunk off Dublin,[42] whose designer and his life-saving African partner made heroic efforts at salvage by moonlight. Interest was taken in developments likely to be of use to mariners, like a Flying Kite devised at Yarmouth, via which a message was sent by a storm-tossed crew to their captain onshore.[43] High value was put on use. One philanthropic local poet argued that Sunday schools were more use than balloons,[44] and though *Williamson's Liverpool Advertiser* was keen on balloons, it aired the problem of their utility in an editorial alongside an enthusiastic and detailed report of Lunardi's first ascent in London the previous day. It was a little tongue-in-cheek – 'Wonders! Wonders! Wonders!' was the tagline for Katterfelto, a shady figure associated with both science and magic. But then balloons seemed fabulous too:

> Our very kind neighbours the French having fomented a rebellion
> in, and compleated a revolution of our American colonies, and torn
> near one half of the British Empire from the other; are now very

obligingly condescending to make us amends, by amusing us with marvellous, incredible stories of air-balloons, trifles, baubles and children's playthings, like kites in the air; with galleries and accommodations carrying men and boys and beasts, like Noah's ark, up aloft in the air, two or three miles of perpendicular altitude from the surface of the earth, and flying like birds through those elevated regions, and descending safe in the fields, or in great cities, at their ease and at their own option, without the least inconvenience or difficulty. Wonders! – Wonders! – Wonders indeed! — But we must leave off wondering. We should not now wonder if the French should extend their plan next year, and send their aerial travellers to the Moon, from this dense atmosphere, through the pure ether to that attendant planet without any atmosphere at all, who would find no difficulty in making that ragged shore or surface without the assistance of any medium, element, or substance, but their own prolific brain, and dextrous steerage through all substantial and insubstantial spaces.[45]

A little behind Bristol in aerostation, Liverpool was equally interested. People in seafaring places were sympathetic to the art of sailing in air; their scepticism came from experience in the challenges of mastering an element. For all the complicated envy of the passage above, its author admires transferrable skills of navigation, steerage and discovery. The flight of men to the moon seemed a possibility, even though local achievements were several stages behind.

Chester got ahead with a splendid new Lamp Balloon, proudly described as the first of its kind launched in Britain. Nicknamed 'the Flying Room', it was raised by rarefied air (not inflammable), eleven feet high, with a tripartite structure and a fourteen-sided or double pyramid shape. Its inventor Thomas Baldwin was testing it out as a prototype for an ambitious version with wings and a tail, able to carry two persons aloft. Baldwin lived a little inland at Chester but his thinking chimed with marine imagination; his balloon would have sails and rigging and swim like a fish against the stream. His first model rose nearly a mile: 'the flying-room began to float in less than two minutes after the lamps were lighted'; in ten minutes it soared to a mile high, 'a Spectacle beautiful and sublime', visible from a great distance.[46] It landed gently and intact, until it was irreparably damaged by over-enthusiastic witnesses who returned the remains triumphantly to Chester.

Baldwin was experimenting with both fire and gas balloons. Since James Tytler in Edinburgh was seemingly on the verge of success with a fire balloon, *montgolfières* were still in contention.

The apparent advantage was that they might fuel a balloon for longer than inflammable air which could not be replenished without a descent to earth. On the downside, their flammability was risky. Baldwin had devised a way of arranging his cotton-wicked spirits of wine so the machine stayed upright and stable. In his second attempt, a gust of wind overset the apparatus. A previously welcome innovation was now criticised as extremely imprudent in the context of an all-too-flammable town. In August, Baldwin published proposals for a Grand Naval Air-Balloon with sails, oars and rudder, capable of carrying three or four people for up to twelve hours. His nationwide subscription aimed for a minimum of £700. Funds did not materialise.

Meanwhile, balloons in and around Liverpool took a comic turn. At the Theatre Royal *Harlequin Junior* was performed at the end of July, in which Harlequin crossed the Channel fantastically in a balloon – a gas balloon. Two other small balloons were let off by a Mr Heppenstall; he had bought them from Astley's in London. The first landed in a hayfield in Adlington having sailed forty-three miles in forty-one minutes. 'The fortunate finder, having recovered from his fright, and having blown it up with a pair of bellows, realised a good deal of cash by exacting all who durst view this tremendous phenomenon.'[47] He also claimed the finder's reward of two guineas – a sum halved for the second balloon, which was found near Chester by Ralph Drinkwater, a servant exercising a horse. He too charged spectators to view the remains in a barn.

> Not a little elated by the possession of so singular a prize, he remounted his Rosinante, placed the *Stranger* before him, and thus he (and his *Inflammable Captive*) entered the village with no small degree of triumph. It may easily be imagined that the curiosity of the inhabitants could not have been more easily gratified by the sight of the *Great Mogul*, had he entered the village, than by the appearance of this piece of *gummed Tiffany*, which they look up to with as much veneration as though it possessed something supernatural. – This *aerial Prisoner* is now securely lodged, in a suspended State, in a Barn, where it is likely to remain (in durance vile) till the Proprietor shall think proper to ransom it.[48]

An author who knew what a balloon was playfully made it quixotic, orientalist, comically transgressive.

In the summer of 1785, Liverpool citizens were weeping at Sarah Siddons performing tragedy and gaping at James Graham, exhibitor of an electrical bed whose convulsions re-excited desire and fertility.

Graham and his wife were also demonstrating the virtues of earth baths.[49] Buried all day up to their necks in a garden, viewable for a small fee, they were intent on proving Graham's claims that earth baths cured every ailment, restored vigour and increased potency, especially sexual potency. No doubt the earth moved for them. Quite why in an age of wigs and powdered hair Graham thought it desirable to reverse the greying of hair is a puzzle, except that this vegetarian inventor of sex therapy was ahead of his times and a master of publicity.[50]

Liverpool newspapers gave full coverage to Lunardi's exploits in London, so when he blew into town it seemed he would need little publicity. His first attempt attracted a crowd – not enough paying to see the filling process, whose slowness occasioned restiveness. It rained, with thunder in the distance. Lunardi persevered and finally got aloft to awed silence, then huzzas which he acknowledged by gracefully waving his hat. North-west winds suddenly veered south-east, looking as if he would be blown out to sea, but levelled out. Lunardi went north, in sight for fifty minutes, to land ten miles away near Symond's Wood. To stay aloft he had had to throw away half his fine uniform; minus hat, coat and waistcoat he returned shivering.

There was something unexpectedly low key about Lunardi in Liverpool. His spirits could hardly have been raised by the report of his first ascent appearing alongside an *Ode to Dead Aeronauts* in the *Advertiser*;[51] he was also financially drained. Crosbie was said to be coming in from Ireland in what would be a historic flight. It was a tight spot to be in. Lunardi took out an advertisement thanking the people of Liverpool for their approbation and promising to fulfil his engagement with a second ascent from the Fort, weather permitting. The delay meant word had time to spread, and people poured into Liverpool from the surrounding countryside. 'Expectation stood on tiptoe in every street.'[52] A south-east wind blew all day. It was too dangerous to ascend. People waited cheerfully. The next day it rained, which might at last bring a change in the wind. 'Everybody must wish the blustering Deity propitious'.[53] Lunardi grew visibly anxious. Thunder and hail were hopeless for aeronauts but ironically welcome to the assembling crowd: since 1780 rainfall had been on average less than half what it should have been, so the storms broke what was effectively a drought. Scant consolation for Lunardi.

All this swirled around in the rain. Lunardi had one card to play, which was to appeal to the ladies. Publicity materials had established an image of him as handsome, genteel, caressing his

6   Lunardi with his dog and cat basking in fame. Anonymous engraving with crowning verse: 'Behold the Portrait of the gallant Man, ye Fair,/ Who Soars above the World in his triumphant Carr,/ And calmly Sails upon the bosom of the Air.'

animal companions [Figure 6]. In Liverpool he set up separate
subscription arrangements for the sexes, an unusual arrangement
to generate sexual competition and make it visible. A letter from
'Philo' to the Ladies of Liverpool appealed none too subtly to the
ladies' generosity: 'can the gallant youth, who ventured his life
before your eyes, think you approve his conduct if you refuse to join
the subscriptions opened on his account; do not wait for a precedent;
let your only contest be who shall prove the most eager to set the
glorious example!'[54] Liberality of admiration was to be expressed
in hard cash. 'Philo' claimed, of course, to be a disinterested friend
of Lunardi; his style sounds fractionally less effusive than that of
Lunardi, who used the enforced interval to say he was enlarging
his balloon so as to take up a lady or gentleman, and to rush out an
account, priced at a shilling, of his previous excursion.[55]

To scotch rumours that he had no intention of ascending, Lunardi
went to the Fort and refused to leave. 'While the fierce blasts of the
north west wind howled dreadfully in his ears, he had the magnam-
inity to dress his countenance in smiles and gave a true picture of
exalted fortitude and resignation.'[56] He was certainly acting – but
would he act? Yes; the balloon was filled. In moving it to the centre
of the Fort, it wobbled so wildly in the wind that people rushed
forward to hold it down.

> In vain did he cry out "Let me go – For God's sake, let me go!" they
> still persisted to keep him down by holding the hoop to which the
> boat was fastened. The balloon was burst in two places, several of the
> cords loosened, and the netting almost torn to pieces; at this moment
> he seemed giving way to dispondency, and lying down, cast up his
> eyes and exclaimed "Oh Dio!" but, in a moment, as if started by a
> sudden recollection, he arose, drew his hanger and threatened to *cut
> every hand that should touch the hoop*.[57]

They let go; the balloon and Lunardi shot upwards, torn netting
and ropes streaming in the wind. He was seen for all of four minutes
before disappearing into the clouds.

A letter arrived in Liverpool the next day to report that Lunardi
had descended near Tarporley in Cheshire and was on his way back
to Liverpool via Chester. The perverse irony – that a crowd had
nearly destroyed a balloon with the aim of preventing it from going
up – restored Lunardi's reputation as a man of courage. He was
given a warm welcome by a large crowd: 'every Face was marked
with some pleasing *energetic Passion*; every Hand that was extended
towards me seemed a Brother's; and my Heart beat as if it would

burst my *Bosom* to mingle my *Affections* with theirs', wrote a very relieved Lunardi.[58] His ascent was immediately incorporated into the Harlequin pantomime at the Theatre Royal, where it joined a medley of Robinson Crusoe, a comic opera and an imitation of the fire-defying bulldog of Signior Scaglioni, whose dancing dogs had performed in Liverpool in October 1784. An entirely new scene in perspective was painted, showing the inside of the fort; a young boy played the aeronaut.[59] This mimicry was a compliment of sorts, not exactly heroic. Lunardi moved on to Chester, where tradesmen had collected seventy guineas in a subscription for him.

In Chester worse was to come. During the filling process, one of the casks produced gas too fast and a terrified cooper dropped the bung into it. Lunardi thrust in his arm to try to get it out, to no avail. His hand was so badly burnt by the acid it was obvious he could not fly. In order not to disappoint the spectators, he sent for his servant who ascended, made a fuss-free flight (it was a windless day), landed safely and returned to Chester that evening to reinstall the balloon in the Shire-hall. This servant was carried through the streets on the shoulders of an exalting crowd. 'Poor Lunardi! What an intrepid man he is! every body is delighted with his behaviour and sorry for the hurt he has got; I never saw a more shocking burn', wrote one spectator.[60] Lunardi's mortification was complete when Thomas Baldwin (he of the Flying Room) asked to borrow his balloon and on a hot, bright and calm day made one of the longest and most productive flights to date. Satisfying spectators with an elegantly decorated car (coloured bladders pragmatically doubled as potential buoys), aloft for two and a quarter hours over a distance of twenty-five miles, Baldwin performed a variety of modest but purposive scientific experiments, went a mile and a half high and managed the distention, hovering and descent of the balloon to land softly on Rixton-moss, a Lancashire moor where he 'alighted as gently as the falling snow'.[61]

After his flight, Baldwin published a heavyweight book, *Airopaidia*. Its title gestures to encyclopaedias and indeed it was encyclopaedic − the fullest and best of all eighteenth-century accounts. The handsomeness of the tome gave it a genteel feel; it was readable, enquiring and wondering. Its author had much to say about sensations and perceptions; he supplied measurements and descriptions aplenty. It also had innovative illustrations and aesthetic ideas, discussed further in Chapter 10 (and via Plate VI). It was more serious than Lunardi's flighty sensibility, though that had its own colourful appeal. The Liverpool newspapers noted with resentment that Lunardi held on to his impressions so as to sell an account rather than making information public through them; that Baldwin did so too may explain why his book was not better known at the time.

Lunardi's accident ironically gave others the chance to fly. Besides Baldwin, a lieutenant in the local militia also borrowed Lunardi's balloon and made a success of it, travelling for two hours and forty miles.[62] It was in a way an impossible circle to square: if Lunardi let others fly, he diminished his own aura; if he did not, he risked looking ungenerous. And he could not direct balloon madness any more than he could control the winds. The opportunity to astonish was better where he was a novelty. When he recovered, he moved on to Scotland for a series of successful if not always heroic ascents around Edinburgh and Glasgow.

The north-west, however, produced one enduring form of balloon madness. In June 1785 Lunardi was invited by a balloon-mad gentleman to ascend from Lancaster. Lunardi arrived, but the next morning pleaded an urgent engagement in London, much to the annoyance of his host who had hoped that his star attraction would bring extra business to the Lancaster races. When ten days later, he began to organise practicalities for Lunardi's promised return his fellow citizens issued a snub:

> We duly received your favour of the 16th inst. & communicated the contents to several persons of the first consequence in the town who are all of the opinion that a sufficient sum cannot be raised here to defray the expense of filling the balloon etc. as it is much greater than expected as you are so very much out of pocket by ascending from the extensive & wealthy town of Liverpool ... what can you expect from such a small place as Lancaster.[63]

Two surviving invoices to Lunardi, possibly for an actual flight, reveal costs for repairs, minor perhaps because an experienced boat-swain rigger had been hired for 13s 2¼d to oversee rope-slinging. '550 Printed Bills an Appollogy' cost nine shillings.[64] Various merchants, an upholsterer, tailor, chaise hirer, watchman and at least five labourers all benefited from balloon-related employments – as did Richard Gillow, Lunardi's admirer. It was this furniture maker who was then inspired to design a rounder, lighter-shaped back for mahogany chairs, thus adding the balloon-back chair to our reper-toire of Georgian classics. The first set of balloon chairs was sold to Sir John Brisco of Lancaster in August 1785 for £1 0s 4d. A second, refined design appeared in 1786. It is a nice instance of how balloon madness did not need actual balloons to be imaginative.

IRELAND: DUBLIN AND RICHARD CROSBIE

'Magnificent men in their flying machines': the famous phrase from 1965 has become a staple of popular aeronautic history. Richard Crosbie brought magnificence to balloons in the form of a flashy costume of his own designing, and grandiloquence from his fellow Irishmen who celebrated his achievement as a matter of national pride. Like Tytler in Scotland, Crosbie represented his country and its Enlightenment aspirations; like Tytler, he endured fickle support from a public who invested in his ambitions and punished disappointment with derision.

Crosbie's biographer, Bryan MacMahon, presents the Dublin of Crosbie's youth as a place of fights and processions that may explain Crosbie's showy side. He was also seriously curious, designing clocks before he turned to balloons. A small fire balloon had been sent aloft from Ranelagh Gardens by a Mr Riddick on 4 February 1784, and Crosbie promptly sprang into print to advertise his Aerial Chariot and his wish to contribute to the good of his country: 'He means to ascend in it himself and show the way to manage it; any subscriber who chooses can accompany him. He does not come from another country to impose on the imagined ignorance of this by exhibiting a child's bawble to the curious multitude'.[65] Noble intentions nonetheless needed financial and scientific help. Crosbie enlisted the support of Dr Henry Ussher, Professor of Astronomy at Trinity College Dublin, and James Caulfeild, first Earl of Charlemont, first President of the Royal Irish Academy and sympathiser with Irish patriots. Using a supple language of patriotism and politeness, Crosbie promoted and exhibited his inflammable air balloon at Ranelagh on 16 August. It had unusual features: not a basket but a construction akin to a two-masted boat whose sails, like the silk-covered rudder, could be managed by a seated aeronaut. Aft were fixed rotating vanes like windmills, which could be turned by hand to aid the sails in directing the balloon, even against the wind. It all looked good.

The background to Crosbie's endeavours was politically stormy. 'The affairs of Ireland come over to us in a very clouded, dark state, and seem to grow more and more confused every day.'[66] Rapacious absentee landlords, religious discrimination, famine and poverty impelled the oppressed into increasingly violent opposition – or emigration. Reformers petitioned George III to dissolve their useless Parliament and sort out their corrupt aristocracy.[67] Irish Volunteers, headed by Henry Grattan, pressed for the repeal of Poyning's Law, which decreed that all prospective Irish legislation had to be approved by the English Privy Council first. It was repealed in 1783 but Irish print culture continued to be highly political. London papers complained about 'the inflammatory prints which second the zeal of the populace against every thing belonging to this country [England]. These papers are written with such violent animosity against government and all legitimate authority, that they should be decorated with a *vignette of daggers* and the impression made *in blood.*'[68]

The anti-French sentiment which made the English so suspicious of balloons was present dilutedly in Ireland, where the old enemy's enemy was thought of as a friend. One of Crosbie's competitors, Dr Potain, was castigated by the *Dublin Journal* because all the materials for his balloon were imported[69] – a touchy subject, because the English imposed punitive duties on Irish cotton and linen. Tarring and feathering of people who sold English goods, especially textiles, was common. Nonetheless, the Dublin establishment backed Potain; his committee of supporters included many of the same names as Crosbie's. When an ascent from Dublin in June 1785 ended in a tangle near Powerscourt waterfall some twenty miles south, Potain limped to the nearest house. He could speak no English but his name was recognised[70] – helped no doubt by its similarity to *poitín* or poteen, the traditional highly potent spirit which from the 1660s it was illegal to distil.

A home-grown hero delighted the nationalists. Crosbie's intended voyage was a colourful retort to English condescension: 'Notwithstanding Ireland abounds with *inflammable matter*, much more than either England or France, it is remarkable that we hear nothing of the Hibernians amusing themselves with a balloon'.[71] More patronising still was Blanchard's comment that the Irish had hearts but not heads for ballooning.[72] On 19 January 1785, Crosbie set about proving him wrong. His balloon was adorned with paintings of Minerva and Mercury, with the arms of Ireland and symbols of the winds. It also had a motto from Virgil, much noticed by local poets: '*ausus se credere coelo*', an allusion to Daedalus, who *dared to trust himself in air* in wings of his own workmanship. The filling was difficult – the Irish Daedalus had to ditch his windmill and sails – but after nearly seven hours' striving, Crosbie rose elated above an excited crowd of tens of thousands. 'Idea cannot form anything more aweful and magnificent than his rise; ... No man ever undertook a perilous voyage with such cheerfulness', reported the *Dublin Journal.* The *Freeman's Journal* agreed: 'The balloon ascended with its courageous master, slow, perpendicular and majestic ... the MAN shone forth in all the pride of intrepidity. Yet did he seem perfectly collected, exhibiting a noble and shining picture of a real philosopher and hero.'[73] Emotions rode high. In view for three and a half minutes, Crosbie rose to about eighteen thousand feet – his barometer was broken, so he guessed – before descending bumpily on the north side of Dublin Bay.

The Irish public was ecstatic. ''Tis destined now Hibernia's favoured son/ Shall do what man as yet hath never done:/ Wrest that great boast from Albion's haughty throne,/ And rule the empire of the seas alone.' The skies were a place of no limits: Crosbie was 'the great ornament of our universe, our country, of science and of human nature'.[74] In Bryan MacMahon's words, 'It seemed to be roses, roses all the way for Crosbie as 1785 advanced.'[75] By May the national hero had repaired his balloon, but in spite of a gift of £200 and a very polite letter from the Duke of Rutland he was in financial trouble.[76] Subscriptions had not covered his costs. On 10 May a huge crowd gathered to watch his next attempt: 'Thousands on thousands were seen running, walking, hobbling, grunting and creeping through all the streets, lanes and alleys of this city to occupy every field and vacant space that could afford a front, side or back prospect of an ascent to, or above the clouds'.[77] An ineffectual fill meant Crosbie had to postpone. The disappointment was taken badly. The Irish turned on their hero with verbal ferocity. Balloon disappointment echoed national frustrations; the public's revilement of Crosbie was full of displaced bitterness.

One poet saw the crowd that headed to Ranelagh to see Crosbie in January as a rare scene of national unity:

> A motley, strange, and miscellaneous throng,
> These for reform, and these against it strong.
> A single day suspends discordant aims,
> Turn'd from low politics to higher themes;
> All to the garden, garters, rags, and stars,
> On foot, on horse, in hack, or glitt'ring cars;

Crosbie would look down on an immoral, selfish and grasping world below:

'Bove low ambition, thine the bark to steer
Above the views of *little greatness* here;
Thro' purer paths in godlike state to go,
Tir'd of our schemes and politics below.[78]

But the poet himself turns to political recrimination, sandwiching heroics into a small section in the middle of the poem. It was a sign of the fractured, factional world Crosbie also had to navigate. This poet quoted Virgil on Daedalus: if Daedalus united science and myth, the Irish liked myth best.[79]

In classical mythology Aeolus, god of the winds, and Fame are often represented with trumpets. Both governed uncertainties. Feeling the full blast of public disapproval, Crosbie swore he would ascend or die. As he struggled on 12 May to rise again, it was obvious that he was too heavy. After much agitation a lighter man, Richard McGwire, replaced him – at eight stone, half Crosbie's weight. The balloon took off successfully and its novice pilot managed to keep it up until he came down at sea, where he was fished out of the water by boatmen paid for by Crosbie's supporters. McGwire returned to a hero's welcome, a knighthood, medals, ballads of acclamation and a raft of honours that poor Crosbie was denied.

Tho' Envy, Crosbie, vilify thy name,
And strive to blast the harvest of thy fame,
'Tis virtue's common lot; nor thou repine,
The tribute due to great attempts is thine.

At least there was one sympathiser.[80]

Crosbie persisted, with a courage even greater than his intrepidity in the air. On 19 July 1785 he strode out across Leinster Lawn, aiming again to cross the Irish Sea. This time he had a cork jacket and buoyancy aids, and the balloon was designed more specifically for his weight. After an awkward ascent he stayed in view for half an hour, then rose through the clouds to the blue. He could see British and Irish shores: 'it was impossible to give the human imagination any adequate idea of the unspeakable beauties which the scenery of the sea bounded by both lands presented. It was such as would make me risk a life to enjoy again'.[81] Despite cold freezing his battered barometers and ink, and condensed gas drops wetting his notes, he wrote joyously of the moment:

My course now bid so fair for success that I experienced more happiness and transport in the idea than I believe ever before fell to the lot of man. My mind that was hitherto voluptuously fed, made me inattentive to the cravings of my appetite, which at length grew rather pressing, and with my pen in one hand and part of a fowl in the other, I wrote as I enjoyed my delicious repast.[82]

Then the weather cut in. Flurries of hail and gusting winds forced him down to just above the sea. He hoped he could rise. He sank. Throwing out all the ballast made no difference; the basket had taken in too much water. It was mortifying.

Though Crosbie was rescued and returned to plaudits, they were muted in comparison to that first moment of glory. Besides the usual difficulty of raising money, public favour for balloons was fading. His account, reprinted in Dublin and published in Britain, added a little to aerial knowledge – he reported pressure on his ears – but unlike Lunardi's it had no literary travel. Even his splendid outfit, the prototype of the aviator jacket in connecting flight and fashion, inspired no imitators. His ambitions blown out by squalls, Crosbie's heroics were rewarded only by the laurels handed to him by poets, some of whom preferred to hail McGwire. A whippersnapper had stolen his thunder.

The Irish Sea remained uncrossed during the years of balloon madness. Sadler nearly succeeded on 1 October 1812; in the end it was his son, Windham, who made the first crossing, on 22 July 1817. Debts dragged Crosbie down and he died penurious. His biographer has located a nineteenth-century American memoir which reports that Crosbie, having scraped a living as an actor, died a grand old ruin, drunk and proud.[83]

THE ISLE OF MAN: A CAT

There was a little fall-out of Irish balloons beyond Ireland, on the Isle of Man. Strictly speaking not part of the political entity of Great Britain though part of the British Isles geographically, in the middle of the sea between the north of Ireland and the south of Scotland, this small island had a taste of balloon madness thanks to the prevailing south-westerly winds. On 6 July 1784 a balloon from Ireland fell on the Isle of Man: 'It occasioned wonderful consternation in the neighbourhood'. A bold person read its ticket, took it home and was visited by almost everyone on the island 'to see the wonder of all wonders an air balloon, which few of them had any faith in previous to that event'.[84] One of Crosbie's tethered balloons was set free in September 1784; it landed just off the Isle of Man with a cat aboard. One account humorously claimed that the escaping gas terrified fishermen into farting their own odiferous gas. A comic retelling imagined the cat to be the black cat of Katterfelto, who then meets Lunardi's white cat to produce a litter of aerially-conceived kittens.[85] Even the remotest balloons produced responses of reason and humour.

When balloon madness swept through, a historian of the Isle of Man proposed a flying magician brought down by the prayers of St Patrick as Europe's first aeronaut.[86] A wish for avatars was a way to connect old stories of flight with its new reality.

OXFORD AND MANCHESTER: JAMES SADLER

James Sadler might have been as famous in Britain as the Montgolfiers were in France. He missed out very narrowly on two achievements for the record books: the first manned ascent in Britain and the first crossing of the Channel. In his home town of Oxford, it was not until the twentieth century that any monument to his achievement appeared; the Royal Aeronautical Society renewed a headstone for him in 1928, the centenary of his death. In 1784 he was usually described as the son of a pastry cook, though at some point he was employed by the University to assist in the laboratories on Broad Street. These were housed below Elias Ashmole's extensive museum of curiosities and provided a place for the practical experiments of natural philosophy and the skills that led Tiberius Cavallo to describe Sadler admiringly in 1785 as 'the sole projector, architect, workman and chymist' of his balloon activities.[87] He let off a balloon in February 1784 from a house in St Clements. In the summer he exhibited a larger hot air balloon (sixty-three feet in circumference) at the Oxford Town Hall, and sought funds for a 'large Aerial Machine'. On 4 October 1784, 'he made the first ascent by any English aeronaut with a 170-foot hot-air balloon he had constructed himself. He rose from Oxford to a height of 3600 feet, landing 6 miles away after a half-hour flight.'[88]

There is officially some doubt as to whether Sadler made this flight. Cavallo wrote that nobody saw Sadler ascend or descend, a statement at odds with a detailed account in *Jackson's Oxford Journal* featuring airborne observations of instruments, sensations and impressions: 'being disengaged from all Terrestrial things, he contemplated a most charming distant View; with Pleasure and Admiration he beheld the Surface of the Earth like a large and extensive Plain, and felt himself perfectly agreeable'. This account convinces Hodgson: 'the distinction of being the first Englishman to ascend in a balloon from English ground appears undoubtedly to belong to Sadler.'[89] Mark Davies, whose biography tracks Sadler's experiments carefully, concludes regretfully that 'a tiny element of doubt will always remain'.[90] Some source material hints that Sadler worked in secret to avoid attracting the loutish attentions of aristocratic undergraduates. It is odd there is no mention of anyone in attendance, especially when Sadler was publicly soliciting funds. His second voyage was unequivocally public: on 12 November he took off from the Physic Garden in full view of an immense crowd, with the bells of Magdalen ringing enthusiastically. After three minutes he disappeared into the clouds, to be caught in a brisk wind that took him fourteen miles in seventeen minutes, coming down at Hartwell near Aylesbury with such a bumpy landing the balloon was almost demolished.[91] But the October flight received official recognition on its bicentenary, when the Lord Mayor of Oxford laid a commemorative stone in the wall of Merton facing onto Christ Church Meadow, to celebrate the 'First English Aeronaut'.

Sadler could be described as the best English aeronaut, in terms of steadiness of attempts and achievements. He was unluckily thwarted in his hopes of being first to cross the English Channel, for which he worked night and day on a new balloon, ready at the end of December 1784 and costing more than £500.[92] He sent it to Dover by water. When it arrived, the freshly-varnished silk had stuck together. The balloon was unusable. And Blanchard had got there first, crossing on 7 January. Nonetheless, Sadler embarked on several more aerial voyages in 1785 which in different ways took British ballooning to higher levels, on a par with French achievements. On 5 May, he made the ascent with William Windham which impressed Royal Society witnesses with its manoeuvres, and in mid May he made two ascents from Manchester, aloft for an hour and three-quarters on one flight and reaching an altitude of thirteen thousand feet on the other. Local excitement led to the naming of Balloon Street next to the ground where he ascended. There was real risk involved: on the second ascent, after a rough landing the balloon dragged Sadler for two miles, inflicting injuries. He recovered to attempt another ascent from Oxford on 24 June, but the balloon could lift only one of the four intended. Colonel Richard Fitzpatrick, the lucky one, wrote nonchalantly to his friend Windham of his descent:

When I saw the shadow of the balloon increasing very fast, and could plainly distinguish objects, so small as horses in waggons and in the fields, I threw out my sixth bag [of ballast], but unluckily when I was preparing the seventh upon the anchor, it slipp'd off, and fell without it. Within a very few seconds I came to the ground on the side of a steep hill, in a corn field. The shock was trifling but the unevenness of the ground overset the Car, and rolled me gently out. Disentangling myself from the cords, I held fast the side of the car, and with some difficulty held the balloon till some country people came to my assistance. I then perceived a large rent in the lower part of it, which accounted for my descent, and which, I suppose, by a more judicious use of the valve I should have prevented. The curiosity and astonishment of the country people who flocked in by shoals were prodigious. I got Sadler's balloon, however, safe in a stable, and waited at a little publick house two hours for his arrival. We were then conducted with great triumph about 5 miles to Wantage in Berkshire, where we dined, but as I did not admire this triumphal mode of travelling, I declined making my entry in to Oxford, and got on by myself as far as Henley, and came the next morning to Oxford.[93]

Fitzpatrick added that he thought Sadler was a prodigy, and unsupported in Oxford because university Fellows were jealous of his abilities. It might explain why Sadler turned to other things. But he kept his hand in with balloons: in June 1790 he teamed up with the chemist Thomas Beddoes to send up a balloon from Pembroke College gardens. The idea was to represent the production of meteors, and to that end Sadler devised a way of using marsh gas to fill his balloon. Science became spectacle when at a great height the balloon caught fire, keeping its form to glow like the sun, much to the delight of witnesses.[94] Though he seems to have stopped aerial voyages when balloon madness subsided, he resumed flights in 1810, with high-profile ascents from London, Birmingham, Bristol and Oxford, and a failed attempt to cross the Irish Sea from Dublin. In these later years, experiments were re-described as exhibitions though nothing different was exhibited and Sadler's landings continued to incline to the violent. He could be seen as a bridge between early balloon madness and its reappearance in Victorian showmanship, with Sadler father and son bringing aeronautics to a new generation eager for tamed thrills. But in the short era of balloon madness, the First English Aeronaut did not surpass French records for time or distance. As a correspondent to one newspaper sneered a couple of days after Blanchard crossed the Channel, the French were way ahead.[95]

Besides his 'native Genius', however, Sadler's unfussed efficiency made him of interest to writers. One was Henry James Pye, who dashed off an eleven-page poem after seeing Sadler ascend on 12 November. Grandly titled *Aerophorion*, this poem hailed Sadler's 'manly enterprize' in the name of Science, and sumptuously imagined what it was like aloft:

> See Earth's stupendous regions spread below,
> To hillocks shrunk the mountains loftiest brow.
> Who now his head sublime, astonish'd shrouds
> In the dull gloom of rain-distended clouds,
> And sits enthron'd 'mid solitude and shade,
> Which human eye-sight never can pervade,
> Or rides amidst the howling tempest's force
> Tracing the volley'd lightning to it's source,
> Or proudly rising o'er the lagging wind,
> Leaves all the jarring Atmosphere behind,
> And at his feet, while spreading clouds extend,
> While thunders below, and while storms descend,
> Feels on his head the enlivening sun-beams play,
> And drinks in skies serene the unsullied stream of day.[96]

Man and the elements: Pye's version of Sadler makes him a sublime human engaging with a meteorological and metaphysical world previously home to gods – and close to God, if you note the shroud, throne and nimbus. That Sadler's reports logged pain in his ears and shortness of breath[97] was gloriously irrelevant to Pye, who defended balloons as an invention of dubious use; he argued that not everything had to serve profit and balloons were valuable for imagination.

Sadler's Oxford balloon was the anchor-point for another topical publication. In 1785 a new poet laureate was to be appointed. The job went to Thomas Warton, a Fellow of Trinity College, Oxford, famous for *The Pleasures of Melancholy*, published in 1747 when he was nineteen. A collection of verse appeared satirising the laureate contenders and getting in some digs at Pitt. The authorship of these *Probationary Odes* is now too obscure to establish the various contributors; relevant here is that the prose contribution in Warton's name is a parodic account of an ascent from Oxford in Sadler's balloon.[98]

Warton definitely had an eye for a good send-up. He published a parody of Oxford guide-books in 1762, followed in 1764 by a parody of university poems, *The Oxford Sausage*; it would be delicious if this bit of aerial fun was his self-parody. Its running joke is about ballast: the poet has to throw out his own weighty works, after which the balloon springs upward and he settles in the clouds to write an obscure and sublime ode, which he manages to finish despite his ink freezing and the nibs of his pens flying upwards. Of a five-hour flight, the self-styled first Literary Aeronaut spends four hours composing his ode on the King's Birthday, and lands safely to be met by a friend with a spare wig before returning to the city in triumph. *A Full and True Account of the Rev. Thomas Warton's Ascension from Christ-Church Meadow, Oxford* sails through literary in-jokes and smoothly rewrites the town hero as a gown one.

Sadler was just too artisan to become a gentleman hero, but he was a local and a national hero, briefly. Dragged through hedges, dashed against cottages, stones and trees, battered and bruised, he was the object of rapt attention. People followed him for thirty miles; country people were on the watch, eager to welcome him and transfigured by rapture: 'In short, the highest encomiums are due to him through every stage of the business; and the delight he gave to the multitude of spectators, can only be conceived from the fixed attention and wonder that was visible at once on their countenances.'[99] Fitzpatrick's account of his reception with Sadler is a Roman triumph: entrance into the city by generals given honours normally accorded to the powerful and rich. After his ascent from Oxford in November, the crowd compelled people to illuminate their houses for his triumphal return, an accolade for a hero.[100] Sadler made class differences immaterial: he united urban and rural people in a common project, reaching deep parts of England. One finder was moved to heroic generosity in refusing Sadler's reward of eight guineas for his balloon's safe return.[101] 'Celebrity' is not quite what Sadler was; he was 'celebrated'. His balloon became a symbolic platform for an English ideal of liberty: freedom of speech, whether in satire on establishment or utopian dream. If vision was pompous and parody was silly, nonetheless Sadler lent an elevated note to aerial aspirations, and a reminder that Enlightenment had rough landings.

LONDON: JEAN-PIERRE BLANCHARD AND STUART ARNOLD

London balloons appear elsewhere in this book, so I feature here two aeronauts who represent broadly two different strands of aerostation in the capital, one foreign, one local. Strictly speaking, the local enterprise involved three aerial voyagers – Appleby, Stuart Arnold and Arnold's son – who between them contributed eventfully to the height of balloon madness in London and further afield. Like Jean-Pierre Blanchard, they also played a part in the parachute story explored in Chapter 13. As the centre of commerce and fashion, London was an epicentre of balloon madness. It was easy to buy small balloons to send up, and there were some open grounds and pleasure gardens that could contain ascents. London had skilled chemists, physicians, artisans and intellectuals who refined designs of balloons; it was also home to opinion-formers and disseminators, the *beau monde*.[102] Metropolitan density also supplied counter-currents: the city's buildings could impede viewings, and urban rumour carried scorn as efficiently as enthusiasm. Patronage, performance, politeness, politics, print culture, royalty and scandal flowed in and out of London. With advertising, connections, subscribers, supporters and promoters, an aeronaut could be elevated to celebrity. As in France, the rewards of money and fame were elusive and tangible, and gains turned too on an element of character – what we might call charisma.[103] Character also enfolded national character, so French aeronauts faced suspicion and dislike even though the metropolis was home to cosmopolitanism.

Blanchard avoided making personality part of his enterprise. He did not have much personality to spare, perhaps. He was by far the most skilled aeronaut in that he managed smooth ascents and descents, and he appeared to be able to steer his balloon – not against the wind, but adroitly enough to perform aerial manoeuvres [Plate IV]. He was in England seeking better rewards than he had managed in France where his parentage and manners did not please. When the English did not take to him enough, he went back to Europe – later visiting Philadelphia where, on 9 January 1793, he performed the first ascent in America and his forty-fifth flight.[104] Born in 1753, he showed an aptitude for mathematics. By 1781 he had designed a 'vaisseau volant' based on the mechanics of bird flight; in 1784 he added to it a hydrogen balloon and a parachute. Drama surrounded his early ascents, and after success at Rouen in May and July of 1784, he arrived in England in August. His 'Globe and Flying Vessel' was exhibited at Christie's Great Room in Pall Mall. By now Londoners were getting used to grand foreign balloons: the Grand Aerostatic Globe of the Montgolfiers had been on show in February at the Lyceum on the Strand, wonderfully illuminated for evening viewing by candlelight.[105]

On 16 October, Blanchard prepared to ascend from the Lochee Military Academy in Chelsea. He had a passenger, Dr John Sheldon, a physician and anatomist who brought intellectual status aboard and, according to Blanchard, far too many scientific instruments, which accounted for a bumpily slow start. Clearly the hero of his own tale, Blanchard evidently resented Sheldon's presence and set down in Hampshire to offload him before re-ascending to perform a gratifyingly solo voyage. Sheldon had been enraptured, telling Blanchard: 'I am unable to confine myself to any particular observation. All that I see delights and enchants me. In this moment I possess no other power but that of admiration.'[106] Blanchard merely glanced at a heap of stones below that turned out to be the town of Chertsey. What he attended to instead were the machine's mechanics, which he boasted were capable of changing direction and speed, developments he would further test when he crossed the Channel.

Once he had got rid of Sheldon, however, he confided:

Alone among these clouds, in the midst of the most profound silence, this situation, which might be thought perfectly terrible, enchanted me. – It is in a moment of extasy, like this, in which the mind becomes elevated, that man may be allowed to exult in his discoveries. I had never before been so proud of my existence...[107]

Blanchard aloft was also surprisingly sociable. He dropped visiting cards and thank you notes over the side. He waved his flags to townspeople below, who appeared to him like puppets. He played his flute from behind a cloud to the consternation of a woman and girl who ran away in terror. He wrote a letter to a friend and sent it off by a pigeon. When he landed near Romsey people rushed to tow him to town, and Blanchard obligingly fell in with heroics:

These honest people laying hold of some cords, which hung from my boat, I threw out a few handfuls of ballast, and amused them with the sight of my globe rising above their heads... Lengthening my cordage, and diminishing my ballast, I proceeded, led on by my conductors, above the trees, the walls and the houses, in order to enter the town. I found the streets filled with spectators: the roads, likewise, were on all sides crouded; and I enjoyed, with them, the pleasure of having rendered such a multitude happy at so easy a rate. To give my extraordinary entry all the aid of fancy, I stood erect in my car, at the elevation of the house-tops, bearing my colours in my hand, with which I saluted the innumerable throng of spectators that surrounded me. This scene, so novel to the worthy people, who gave me so cordial a welcome, lasted until the close of the day. Wearied as I was, from having passed the preceding night in preparations for my enterprize, and from the exertions of my voyage, yet I could not deprive them of the gratification they so eagerly desired; and I suffered myself to be led by them, in this manner, several times about the town.[108]

Romsey was a small town but Blanchard captures its rapturous welcome for a wider readership, shaping the language of heroism and practices of acclaim. Sheldon rejoined him and there followed a triumphant public return to the metropolis, simply a larger balloon-mad place.

Blanchard had a plan. Cannily he saw that crossing the Channel would be a milestone in the regions of air, and that it would be adventitious to beat his French competitors, principally Pilâtre de Rozier who was readying on the French side. Blanchard secured a patron in Dr John Jeffries, a Bostonian physician with meteorological interests and wealth. The price was taking Jeffries along. Jeffries underwrote the costs of the whole (over £700), and paid another hundred guineas for passage in the balloon as it travelled south on 30 November, in a trip ending near Dartford in Kent.[109] Jeffries carried out some measurements and experiments, later returning phials of air to Sir Charles Blagden and a report to the Royal Society. The voyage lasted an hour and a half; as Jeffries pointed out, one could do little in that time on a winter afternoon. Still, he ascertained a few findings and enjoyed himself. They landed safely, accompanied by a half-frozen dog, and met with a warm reception:

> The neighbouring inhabitants soon flocked about us, asking thousands of questions; and finding in the bottom of our Aerial Car a few bits of chicken and morsels of bread, I, at their urgent requests, divided it almost into atoms among them; every one being eager to get some of that food, which they had seen literally descend from the clouds.[110]

On 7 January 1785 the balloon was at Shakespeare's Cliff near Dover, ready to go but stalled by a quarrel. Blanchard claimed that the balloon would not support two people; Jeffries counterclaimed skulduggery, suspecting Blanchard of wearing a heavy girdle.[111] An éclaircissement in front of the Governor of Dover Castle showed that Blanchard was not sporting lead underwear and restored speaking relations. He had compelled Jeffries to a contract in which Jeffries was to get out of the balloon should it be necessary for Blanchard's preservation and – possibly to avoid another row – Jeffries travelled light, with only barometer and compass.[112] Blanchard took letters from English nobility and a large parcel of pamphlets. Dover harbour was packed with small boats; the beach and town were crowded with spectators craning for a view [Figure 7]. The balloon rose smoothly and sailed uneventfully across the Channel until about halfway, when it lost height alarmingly. The aeronauts threw out ballast. Fifteen minutes later they descended dangerously further, barely above the waves. They threw out apples, biscuits, then the wings, then the *moulinet* or mill by which Blanchard claimed to be able to steer – to no avail. They cut off the ornaments and lining of the balloon and its basket and threw them into the sea. The balloon sank further. They threw the anchor out. They stripped off coats

DOVER CASTLE,

WITH THE SETTING OFF OF THE BALLOON TO CALAIS, IN JANUARY 1785.

Painted by T. Rowlandson, & engraved by W. Birch, Enamel Painter.

Published Aug.t 1.1789 by Wm. Birch, Hampstead Heath &fold by T. Thornton, Southampton Str.t Cov.t Garden.

Blanchard and Jeffries set off from Dover to cross the Channel on 7 January 1785. Engraved by William Russell Birch, painted by Thomas Rowlandson, published 1 August 1789.

7

and trousers and threw them out too. They put on their lifejackets of cork. The balloon steadied and rose just in time to clear the cliffs of France and rise high over Calais. They now had almost no ballast and, approaching the Forest of Guînes, needed to keep the balloon above tree-level. Jeffries brightly suggested they try shedding liquid ballast.[113] Peeing into spare bladders, they cast away five pounds of urine which made enough lift to let them descend on a spot where a commemorative column was swiftly erected. England and France shared the honours, just: a Frenchman had succeeded, but launched from the English side.

In the summer of 1785, Blanchard led developments that were speculative and practical. His interest in parachutes combined with successful balloon ascents. He was accompanied by one young lady, Miss Simonet, on 3 May, and her sister on 21 May. *'Being now hors'd upon the sightless coursers of the air*, the adventurous atmospherical voyagers' waved flags whilst in view of the *'up-turn'd wand'ring eyes of mortals'*, who applauded like mad, according to the newspapers.[114] Miss Simonet the elder was not the first female English aeronaut in Britain – Laetitia Sage has that honour. On 29 June 1785 she went up in Lunardi's balloon from St George's Fields. It should have been a threesome – and one print mistakenly shows it thus – but Lunardi gave up his seat to George Biggin, who was to supply all the ideological ballast of being an English scientific gentleman. Mrs Sage had briefly been an understudy to Sarah Siddons.[115] A rather large woman, she overcame the embarrassment of being publicly weighed to ascend with Biggin, share in his experiments and exult happily in aerial voyaging:

> Your happy sister found herself secure from disappointment and floating in the boundless region of the air. We arose in a slow and majestic manner, forming a most beautiful object, amidst the acclammations [*sic*] of thousands, whose hearts at that moment appeared to feel but one sentiment, and that for the safety of two adventurers. … I really felt no other sensation than a most pure and perfect tranquillity of soul.[116]

With all these 'firsts', public attention was still riveted on intrepid voyaging. Blanchard set up an Aerostatic Academy near Vauxhall as a base and a showcase. In the early spring and summer of 1785, he held London's attention while Lunardi toured north. He drew huge crowds but he could not command the admiration showered on Lunardi. Small, neat, insuperably French, Blanchard was grudgingly respected where Lunardi, the dashing Italian, was freely acclaimed. It probably helped Lunardi's reputation that he wrote engagingly; in contrast, Blanchard in person and in print appeared sneery and vain. The story of his alleged lead underwear fitted the cliché of French perfidy, so when he promised a second parachute experiment on 16 June 1785 and it failed, his English prospects began to dwindle.

Balloon madness was passing its peak. It was now less premised on novelty – although that's a tricky phenomenon to measure, even in the hectic world of eighteenth-century fashions. Blanchard, Zambeccari, Lunardi and a selection of fortunate others had established the possibility of safe voyaging. They had also shown that the same factors which produced intrepidity drew in chaos too. Bad weather, faulty equipment, ill-prepared balloons blew off course any Enlightenment story of progress. Analogies to sailing faded away; the regions of air were clearly less tractable. Scientific investigation of the upper atmosphere could not produce startling discoveries to fix public attention, and no new design of balloons solved the problem of navigation.

There was, however, still enormous interest in London in the summer of 1785 – enough to raise great interest and high hopes of proposals made by one Mr Arnold. Stuart Amos Arnold was a Navy purser who had lost a leg in the service of his country. In March 1785, he and a partner projected a huge balloon, ten times bigger than Blanchard's or Lunardi's, in which to make a Grand Aerial Journey from London to Paris. It was to be as wide as the new *Royal George* ship, and it too would be named the 'Royal George'. Departure would be from St James's at midnight, and astonishing: it would 'have a body of light in the centre, which will give it an appearance far more brilliant than the Moon at the Full, and will, by such splendid addition, be the most noble, grand, and sublime spectacle ever exhibited, or perhaps conceived!'[117] Delays and difficulties meant that when the balloon was finally ready, it had different ambitions: it avoided long-distance travel and promised instead the world-first of a human descent in a parachute. Dogs, cats and sheep had parachuted successfully; now so would Arnold's friend and fellow-sailor Appleby. On 31 August 1785 at St George's Fields, accompanied by Arnold's youthful son, they embarked in front of a huge crowd which poured in from all parts of the city, suburbs and villages, stimulated by curiosity, 'which seems to prevail more in this country that in any other in the world'[118] [Figure 8]. Here was the promise of a home-grown hero, a British tar. 'His intrepidity was

A View of the Royal Circus from S.t Georges Fields at the time of the Ascension of Arnolds Balloon. 1785.

8   Arnold and Appleby ascend: London, 31 August 1785.

strongly characteristic of his profession; instead of feeling the least alarm for attempting an enterprise so dangerous, and which had never been hazarded by man, he set himself as calmly in the basket as if sitting down to a customary meal.'[119]

It all went horribly wrong. The balloon over-filled so the netting broke; as it rose, the parachute was caught on a fence and the car hit a cart. Appleby was in a basket attached to the parachute and jumped out. Young Arnold was carried up holding perilously to the balloon's broken cords. The huge crowd was horrified and the father distraught – 'his cries and tears were most affectingly distressing to every heart of sensibility'.[120] The balloon burst and fell towards Rotherhithe. There it was discovered that young Arnold had miraculously fallen into the Thames and was unhurt. A few days later his father published a long hand-wringing exculpation, and rather less apologetically advertised the exhibition of his balloon at the Rotunda in St George's Fields, promising another ascent shortly. Like Icarus falling out of the sky, young Arnold showed how flight could end in tragedy. Mr Arnold's heavenly vision of a full moon balloon was scaled down to a modest globe with too-thin silk that fell apart, ignobly dashing hopes that Britons might rule the air.

Rather than see Arnold and Appleby's attempt as a failed ascent, we might see it as a catalyst for crowd behaviours. Arnold complained that congestion of several hundred carts and carriages blocked the way for spectators on foot, depriving him of £300 to £400 in revenue from what was clearly a momentous event.[121] The anguish of watching a youth about to plummet to his death showed the emotional side of a populace willing on the intrepid, entering imaginatively into dangers and offering hopes, wishes and prayers for success. The crowd bulging out from Blackfriars was united by horror, an instance of single-minded mass behaviour. Yet crowds were complex entities. Arnold noted that some people tried helpfully to recover the balloon while others tried to plunder it. The next chapter explores how ballooning brought out the complexities of people in public.

Crowds, Criminals and Charlatans

4

'Wherever those experiments have been made, persons of every rank have gazed with the greatest anxiety, and have shewn unequivocal marks of astonishment and satisfaction'

Tiberius Cavallo, *A History of Aerostation*, 1785

CROWDS HAVE ATTRACTED the interest of historians, sociologists, philosophers and psychoanalysts. British crowds in the second half of the eighteenth century get special attention from historians in relation to political unrest, and whether riots were a form of popular revolt against forms of power. What can this illuminate about crowds at balloon ascents? How did the massing of people into crowds help to shape and spread balloon madness?

Elias Canetti's landmark book *Crowds and Power* begins by cataloguing crowds: 'we discover that there are: baiting crowds, flight crowds, prohibition crowds, reversal crowds, feast crowds, panic crowds, double crowds, invisible crowds, etc. (No lonely crowds!)'[1] Charles Tilly analyses what he calls Contentious Gatherings from 1758 to 1834 and also finds a rich vocabulary: they involve 2,500 distinct verbs, he says. 'The category of verbs whose share increased by at least a third 1758–1820 were cheer, disperse, meet, petition and support'.[2] Just for that movement of gathering which creates a crowd, Tilly supplies a long index of terms: abandon, abate, accompany, accost, advance, appear, approach, arrive, ascend ... and that's just the As. The lexicon of crowds is complex.

The grammar of crowds is also complex, but it has a tendency to turn singular. Mark Harrison suggests that crowds fascinate us because many individuals seem to become one: 'the sea of faces becomes, paradoxically, a single-headed entity. ... reduced to a single, coherent, entity, they are presented, either by their spokespeople or outside commentators, as representatives of a single, coherent, *belief*.'[3] This unifying language can change fast: a crowd becomes a mob when it acts to offend. Some activities described as riots in this period were not necessarily violent; Tilly shows that food riots, for instance, were protests where fighting was uncommon. There were many shades of riotous behaviour in everyday life, and especially at elections; lobbing a brick or a stone was a common art. Violence at balloon launches usually had a trigger point, when an erstwhile peaceable and patient crowd grew restive, boiled over and attacked balloon, aeronaut and authorities – and each other. Though that behaviour was often described at the time as 'riot', the simple noun and verb can mislead us: what crowds contributed to balloon madness was much more than mob violence.

Crowds moved in distinct ways, as noticed in a court case in April 1785. On his way to Tottenham Court Road to see Zambeccari's balloon launch, William Tubb was jostled in a crowded gateway and lost his watch. 'My arms were thrown up upon other mens shoulders', said Tubb, adding: 'It was a different hustle to passing in a crowd.' Calling a witness, a sawyer who had gone with his shop-mate to see the balloon, one of the lawyers pressed questions about the nature of the crowd: 'It is not the temper of an English mob to stand very quiet, they like to hustle, they wave to and fro, do not they, that is the way, is not it? – It is too much the way.' The witness had been shoved by the press of people and lifted up over their heads: feeling neither afraid nor at ease, he described his elevation as 'foolish fun'.[4] Hustling, jostling, shoving take on distinct meanings; a crowd could be read as a mob through its energy.

By 1785 there was explicit anxiety about crowds at balloon launches. Ascents 'of no useful purpose in view which call the multitude together ought to be suppressed.'[5] Employers were indignant when workers downed tools and flocked to launches. Elizabeth Montagu, bluestocking wife of a rich mine-owner, wrote disapprovingly to her sister after she had glimpsed Lunardi's Newcastle disaster from her coach:

> I am surprised that ye Corporation of Newcastle will permit any one to play these tricks when they certainly must have ye bad consequence of making many thousand Persons idle, besides ye drunkness & expence of ye Pittmen, Street men & Sailors in Alehouses, to ye loss of the rich & distress of ye poor. Our proper business lyes much below ye Region of ye Air.[6]

A week later she wrote to her learned friend Elizabeth Carter expressing pleasure that her miners had not been diverted from their duty by idle curiosity but had kept their proper station underground.

In alarming the master class, the assertion of liberty for some in going to a balloon launch can be seen as a quiet form of riot.

At a trouble-free launch there was another issue: 'the hilarity which the sight inspires induces the company to spend the rest of the day in idleness and drinking', which left people still drunk the next working day.[7] Even when no riot broke out, crowds produced a carnivalesque energy that was easily unstable. A lampoon of a typical crowd at a Dublin launch caught that energy so well it was reprinted three times:

> Millions unnumbered, men, women, children, infants of every age, gentle and simple, nobility and mobility, townsmen and gownsmen, wool-scribblers and paper-scribblers, captains of ships and captains of men, peace officers, war officers, custom house officers, counselors and privy counselors, gentlemen's gentlemen and gentlemen at large, ladies of easy virtue, lords of no virtue, barbers and surgeons (for they are now divided), volunteers, lads of the brush and of the comb, sheriffs, tarrers and featherers and attornies all joined to see the wonderful air balloon...[8]

The crowds who went to see balloons were huge. Reporting Lunardi's ascent from Chelsea on 15 September 1784, newspapers marvelled at the numbers who gathered: 'London poured forth its myriads on this occasion. The neighbourhood of the place was crowded beyond almost all example, and we are surely within bounds at estimating the multitude at more than one hundred and fifty thousand'; by another reckoning, a tenth of the population of London could be seen, a new spectacle in itself.[9] Scaffolding appeared on the houses and windows bricked up to avoid tax were unblocked for the occasion. Pitt paid fifty guineas for his view; he could have paid a hundred.[10] A thousand spectators crammed into the Artillery Ground; thirty or forty thousand around it craned for a view.[11] In one sense the crowd was democratic, or demotically democratic, since everyone was talking about balloons:

> The general attention of the town and its inhabitants of all ranks, from the Countess to the Cobler's Wife, and from my Lady in St. James's square to my Lord, the little crooked shoe-shiner, in an alley in Shoreditch, has been for some days passed engrossed by Mr Lunardi and his Balloon. "To mount or not to mount" – that has been the question; a question this day will decide.[12]

The countess and the cobbler's wife would have different places in the crowd. Seats within the Artillery Ground cost a guinea, half a guinea or five shillings; tickets had to be bought in advance, to avoid confusion on the day.[13] It became common for balloon launches to have differently priced tickets, offering better views, seating (with straw spread below to keep out mud and damp) and music to those who paid most. Highest prices bought proximity to the filling area; some tickets also included a preview of the balloon in a different exhibition space. But this attempt to organise the event was often frustrated by freelancers and freeloaders. Local residents profited from renting viewing spots; people agile enough to climb roofs, steeples and trees evaded paying. Lunardi made a loss – any balloon sailing across the sky could be seen for free. So an event socially stratified on paper, and notionally controlled through tickets, was anarchically open to all.

Paintings and prints are not much help in considering crowds because they tend to stylise large numbers into selective types of people – presumably representatively? Prints show different ranks, both sexes and all ages, and they often include a small dog, a device borrowed from trade cards where it symbolised customer loyalty and eagerness to serve. Types of people often include a lecherous gentleman who squints at a woman's backside rather than the balloon, a visual rhyme of globes which is also a joke about the unregulatability of spectacle. Inclusion of impolite behaviours fitted balloons especially well given the wayward outcomes of ascent attempts. The genteel could easily become farce, just as a polite spectacle could easily turn into a riot.

'While the social and cultural make-up of the balloonists themselves can be identified with some degree of accuracy, attempts to analyse the audience are infinitely more problematic,' says Michael Lynn.[14] From newspaper reports, correspondence, diaries and other sources one can, as he does, find quite extensive evidence about who spectators were and what their reactions were. Lynn thinks this evidence points to 'enormously varied behaviours' because 'attending such a massive scientific spectacle would have been a new experience for most'. He sees balloons as uncontrovertibly scientific experiments: 'the audience was often treated as witnesses to an important scientific experiment in the guise of a spectacle.'[15] This model makes both science and spectacle quite fixed entities, which suits a history of science in which Enlightenment enquiry is acted out publicly through demonstrations that are also entertainments. Some balloon reports do fit this model, at least rhetorically: it was said of the Roberts in Paris in September 1784 that 'being sensible that the people of Paris would no longer countenance an aerial experiment which promised nothing more than a spectacle; it is their ambition in this instance to afford to science new discoveries.'[16] Ideas here are speculative – a sense of what crowds want and an aim to satisfy them are not exactly scientific, other than that crowd-pleasing becomes itself an experiment.

At many launches the science was elusive. To some contemporaries, it was pitiful: Sir Charles Blagden reported that Lunardi brought down a piece of ice 'to show as a curiosity, perfectly forgetting it would melt.'[17] If spectacle is a 'guise' that masks science, why is science something that is both important and in need of disguise? Lynn answers this by mentally cordoning off savants from gawpers – those in the know perform science, everyone else watches. But balloons in Britain had relatively light-weight claims to science, though it was notable that the process of filling was usually smoothed when supervised by skilled chemists. The category of 'discoveries' gestured to by the Roberts was broad. Similarly, although successful ascents did provide spectacle, in the early dizzy period of balloon madness it was all so new that spectators – and readers – did as much defining as aeronauts or savants. One observer who reported considerable suspicion of balloons as a continental plot to dupe John Bull also reported that ascents united everybody in astonishment: 'I was accompanied to these sights of amazement by a philosophical friend, who, as well as myself, gaped as wide, and stared as wild, as any of the great or small vulgar around us.'[18]

To claim aerostation exclusively for science attaches aeronauts to a specific discipline, which was in the process of sorting itself out into what became several disciplines – chemistry, physics and so on. In the mid to late 1780s, lines of thought which we identify as scientific were criss-crossing experimentally and with priorities different from ours.[19] Theories of heat, electricity and mechanics joined enquiries into the composition of air at altitude, the effects of pressure on gases, changes to bodies, and bird and animal behaviours. In practice, those aloft had to deal with the fragile machine: they had a short and perilous time to attend to sensations and aesthetics. When Pilâtre de Rozier and the Marquis d'Arlandes made the first free flight in a *montgolfière* on 21 November 1783, the Marquis, on the east side of the balloon, was fascinated by what he saw below: 'I was surprised at the silence and absence of movement which our departure caused among the spectators, and believed them to be astonished and perhaps awed by the strange spectacle' – musings which irritated de Rozier, who was on the west side of the balloon stoking the fire.

> I was still gazing when M. Rozier cried to me – "You are doing nothing, and the balloon is scarcely rising a fathom." "Pardon me," I answered, as I placed a bundle of straw upon the fire and slightly stirred it. Then I turned quickly, but already we had passed out of sight of La Muette. Astonished, I cast a glance towards the river. I perceived the confluence of the Oise. And naming the principal bends of the river by the places nearest them, I cried, "Passy, St. Germain, St. Denis, Sèvres!"
>
> "If you look at the river in that fashion you will be likely to bathe in it soon,' cried Rozier. "Some fire, dear friend, some fire!"[20]

Getting busy with a pitchfork the Marquis stoked the fire energetically, with only a glance to the view to see where they were before realising that cords overhead were bursting, and the fabric of the balloon was breaking where small fires were singeing holes that had to be extinguished at once with a sponge if they were not to plunge to earth in a flaming balloon. Survival was the point, not science.

Balloons do count as science in two ways. First, the balloon itself was an experiment, involving hydraulics and gases. As experimental object, it inspired other experiments. The discoverer of inflammable air, or hydrogen, Henry Cavendish and friends tracked the path of Lunardi's balloon with a theodolite (an instrument for measuring angles) and a clock.[21] Second, some experiments were performed in them. The results of the latter were unknown until the aeronaut sorted and reported findings back on the ground; the experimental nature of a balloon in itself was certainly uppermost in the first ascents. Here one has to distinguish between spectators with different experiences. Some of the first witnesses in Britain had read accounts of launches in Paris and had a grasp of the possibilities and liabilities. Others, enticed along by publicity and word-of-mouth, went simply to watch a human in a machine attempt to fly. Newspapers and magazines disseminated information, some of it impressively detailed but most of it pretty simple scientifically. Uncertainty about whether lifting power came from rarification or phlogiston was easily sidestepped by a simple principle of lighter-than-air. Explanations were no more complicated than those for why a ship floats, an analogy frequently offered in print.

Of course spectators included the illiterate and the uninformed. But one should be careful about assumptions. Larry Stewart quotes the Birmingham chemist James Keir, who declared in 1789: 'The diffusion of knowledge, and a taste for science, over all classes of men, in every nation of Europe, or of European origin, seems to be the characteristic feature of this present age.'[22] As evidence of cross-class interest, Stewart cites a mathematical society formed by Spitalfield weavers who clubbed together to buy instruments relevant to chemistry. Some 'savants', then, were working class. It is also useful to distinguish first-time viewers from those with previous experience, who might also be less beguiled by any guise of spectacle. Some were sufficiently savvy to perceive incompetence as they watched attempts to inflate. Spectacle too is a lumpen term if it is detached from the context of eighteenth-century public life, which offered abundant sights open to all – congregations in church; aggregations in parades, processions, pleasure-gardens; representations in print-shop windows – and visually showy events like masquerades and assemblies which had a surprisingly wide range of participants. Many in the crowds who came to see balloon ascents also saw the balloons exhibited beforehand and some were experimenters themselves, having purchased small balloons that were set off from gardens and streets. Like science kits for children now, they blurred a distinction between education and fun. 'All ranks of people seem to have found pleasure in such kinds of experiments', noted Tiberius Cavallo.[23] The majestic spectacle of a manned balloon ascending was different in scale but not entirely in degree from the little spheres whose fire-illuminated glow pleased many purchasers and endangered urban life. Expectations were various – undefined, coloured by reports, informed by provisional sciences. And being open-mouthed is not at odds with being open-minded: spectacle has ideas in it too.

The assembly of large numbers of people contributed to the disorderly potential of balloons, partially re-ordered by satire and comedy. There is a peculiar mix of wonder, scepticism and humour in many letters written by people who had seen balloons and were telling their friends and family, as if making light of the event left it open as to whether it was serious or silly. Scholars do face frustrating gaps. In the Bristol archives I came across a diary by a seaman: an entry read, 'Saw the balloon.' I leant forward in expectation but alas! That was all the diarist had to say. Evidence points to balloons being memorable – at the Old Bailey, a defendant who had forgotten his whereabouts on a particular day was pressed to recall by the judge. You must remember where you were that day, he said, because it was the day of the balloon.[24]

Especially in the gathering process, people of different conditions passed each other, mingling in movement. Some came in coaches; most came on foot. One type of person moved through crowds in deliberate closeness: pickpockets. It may seem perverse to take pickpockets as a focus point in crowds when they were the one group not looking at balloons. But they were defining agents in the drama, their presence noted with alarm and humour. The associations of disorder around balloons were aggravated by pickpocket attraction to launches. Some formed micro-societies that inverted the social macrocosm: where there were gentlemen, there were also gentleman rogues. Moreover, pickpockets were close to the rich and poor – literally, in that they stood next to them, and their facility for escaping into crowds shows how well they blended. Perhaps it is the art of pickpocketing, its artful dodges, that accounts for its ironic respect by the press. In the same week as Lunardi's Chelsea ascent, 'the populace took the horses from the coach of the Right Hon Charles James Fox, in Old-street, and substituted themselves in their places; but lest he should be too much elated, contrived to pick his pocket of a valuable gold watch.'[25] That fluid criminality swirled around balloons.

Crowds could enforce law as well as break it. Swift retribution usually followed crimes detected on the spot. At Ascot during the races, a 'gentleman of the turf' pickpocketed a gold watch. He was caught, taken to a pond and ducked, then led by a halter round the course before being kicked out. His fancy hairdo was punished: the tail of his hair was cut off and hoisted on a stick. *'What a pity that all the thieves that were there had not received the same discipline.'*[26] The volatile history of mob justice has been explored by Jerry White, who suggests that thieves were 'more deeply unpopular in plebian London', and that 'the mob' was most active in punishing injustice and informers.[27] Given the way 'mob' is readily used, then and now, to describe crowds at balloon launches, one should note how some violence was approved.

When *The Public Advertiser* complained humorously that the whole country was 'air-balloon-mad', it excepted pickpockets: 'The well-known *Slight of Hand Club*, who live by an attention to the signs of the times, take every possible advantage of this temporary delirium; and while the eyes of the multitude are soaring among the clouds, their fingers are diving with great dexterity to the bottom of every pocket within their reach.'[28] That was on 6 September 1784. The day before, it reported parodically: 'The Society of *pickpockets* had a numerous meeting last night to consider of the supplies for the coming year, when it was agreed to *transfer* the handkerchief *stock* and *reduce* the number of *pigtails* during Bartholomew Fair.'

Pickpockets frequented public places – gatherings at church, at playhouses, hangings, fairs and races – so it was natural they would turn up at balloon ascents. Newspapers warned people setting off to see balloons to secure their houses: 'the thieves and pilferers, of which there are not a few, will attend the exhibition, their harvest lies elsewhere'.[29] On 13 September, just before Lunardi's ascent from Chelsea, *The Public Advertiser* reported: 'The increase of air-balloons has considerably lessened the market for pocket-handkerchiefs in Field-Lane, &c. the shops being nearly over-stocked, owing to the facility with which the industrious manufacturers of these articles are able to work while crowds stand gaping in the street.'[30] Reports of these crimes in the press are oddly full of irony. Gentlemen, Society, Club – the polite designations make organised crime into mock-respectability, just as the industriousness of pickpockets mimicked the proper economy. An earlier model of licence proposed the world turned upside down; here was the world turned inside out, like a pocket.

By the late eighteenth century, British people – especially the English – played with irony materially through clothes. John Styles has analysed the meaning of clothes in part through thefts. He notes: 'Theft of clothing and clothing materials was one of the most frequently prosecuted offences in the eighteenth-century criminal court.'[31] Balloon launches gave pickpockets plentiful opportunities: handkerchiefs, watches and cash were spirited away with lightness of touch. Balloons had affinities with silk and linen. 'I went to see the air balloon, I was going along, there was a great mob, and I picked up this handkerchief under a barrow', pleaded Daniel Mackaney, charged with theft in June 1785.[32] Accusations and problematic identifications turned identities round in a crowd. 'I was going through Barbican, and there was a great mob of people; I went to see the balloon, like others, and got into the crowd; and this gentleman came and said I had the watch; immediately my foot slipped, and I fell down, and the gentleman picked up the watch before me, and said I took it', protested a defendant in a pickpocketing case after a launch.[33] Innocents slipping and pickpockets sly-dipping show the shadowy side to spectacle, and the protean character of crowds.

One pickpocket known to the authorities was George Barrington. He was also well known to the reading public. The stealthy and flagrant movements through fashionable society of the 'Prince of Pickpockets' were widely reported. At a ball at the Guildhall in 1784, a wag said Barrington was there, dressed in brown and gold; in that identical dress was Pitt, who was nearly removed by the marshals.[34] Lunardi's ascent from Chelsea on 15 September 1784 attracted one of the biggest crowds ever assembled in London. It also attracted a record turn-out of pickpockets. 'It is supposed that there were not less than five and twenty hundred pick-pockets, on Tuesday last, properly dispersed in the vicinity of Moor-fields, and at their labour – the notorious Count Dive, alias Smirk Barrington the pick-pocket, was within the gates, and got off safe with his plunder.'[35] Barrington was also at – at work, presumably – the Blanchard and Sheldon ascent at Chelsea a month later; there he was 'instantly handcuffed by the peace officers in waiting'.[36] One of those gentlemen thieves who captures imagination as readily as he stole property, Barrington's familiarity does not seem to have stopped him carrying on his trade. Like many gentlemen rogues, legends surround him, probably none of them true. He was born in Ireland around 1755, stabbed a fellow schoolboy in a fight in Dublin, ran away and fell in with a company of strolling players led by a swindler. There he learnt to pick pockets. After a successful career, with many arrests and releases, thanks to his ability to charm powerful patrons and many of his victims, in 1790 he was finally sentenced to transportation to Botany Bay, where he showed such good conduct he was pardoned. He became chief constable at Parramatta until lunacy overtook him. He died in 1804, notorious for years after.[37]

Barrington understood his business perfectl, and mingled with the rich and fashionable everywhere. He followed Sarah Siddons to Edinburgh and Dublin; it was wittily said 'She *entertains* the company, and he *takes* the *money* at the door.'[38] In August 1784 *The Morning Post* in Dublin warned: '*Barrington*, the *first* of his profession, is again let loose upon the public; he was liberated from Newgate on Tuesday last, and now roams at large. It therefore behoves the public for their own safety, to be upon their guard against the *polite condescension* of this *finished* pick-pocket.'[39] Let loose, liberated, at large, Barrington's movements are described in words also used for unpiloted balloons. And they, like pickpockets, were around in abundance: 'Last night, between eight and nine o'clock, a gentleman walking from Whitechapel church to the 'Change, counted no less than seven balloons, with lights to them, floating in the air, one of which fell in Whitechapel.'[40]

Pickpockets mingled with the rich for richer pickings. When Blanchard and Sheldon ascended,

> five well-dressed young men had fixed a telescope in a tree near the spot from whence the balloon was to ascend, and after having looked through it themselves, genteelly offered several well-looking spectators an opportunity of doing the same, and in helping them to get up, as genteelly picked their pockets.[41]

But it was not all glamour. John Styles observes that 'watches were stolen far more often from plebeian owners when they were out enjoying their leisure at an inn or the races than when they were at work.'[42] Lunardi's launch at Heriot's Gardens in Edinburgh on 5 October 1785 saw several people relieved of pocketbooks containing significant sums. Suspicion fell on six people, apprehended a long way off at Aberdeen. They proved to be three husband-and-wife teams, in which one was a former soldier and two were the sons of a flaxdresser and flesher.[43] There was no irony in the death sentences that awaited them.

Balloon launches occasioned frauds as well as robberies. In Birmingham a youth obtained lodgings from an old couple, saying he'd come to see Harper's ascent and it was too far to go home; in the night he beat them, robbed them and made off.[44] Two audacious robberies made headlines in 1784: in March, the Great Seal was stolen from the Lord Chancellor's house; in September, Burke's house was robbed of valuable plate. Complaining of a crime wave, one writer thought criminals should be lashed to a balloon car and sent upwards with no ballast. He was pleased with the idea as a deterrent: 'I seriously believe it would make a visible Alteration in the Old-Bailey Calendar. The Punishment would be ten Times more aweful and affecting than that of hanging'.[45]

The presence of pickpockets, criminals and potential riot in crowds made some fears well-founded. There was also a strong suspicion, crudely intellectual, that aeronauts were foreign impostors who aimed to dupe British spectators and effectively rob them of admission money. Since balloons came from France, they were possibly a treacherous means of dominance. Suspicions of French plotting were activated all the more because the first successful manned ascent in Britain might have been Chevalier Moret's. On 11 August 1784, he attempted a launch at the Star and Garter, Chelsea. Thirty thousand eager spectators assembled, their curiosity whetted by reports of ascents in France. About a hundred, including Lord

North, Fox and their Whig friends, paid for admission to the garden where they saw a large globe of canvas, a hundred feet in diameter, sagging between two poles. The Chevalier was running about tending a fire of cork and straw. Smoke going into the balloon issued almost as swiftly from its porous canvas. After three hours, the balloon was barely inflated. 'The poor Chevalier seeing this, was taken suddenly ill; the burning machine (and it was certainly warm work) had overcome him, and he threw himself on the grass panting for breath and groaning in the spirit. ...This occasioned a tumult, the fire under the Balloon was neglected, and just as it sunk the mob broke in from the neighbouring fields, and committed it, and every thing around it, to the flames.'[46] It took all of three minutes to turn the balloon into a bonfire; Moret, hiding at the end of the garden, was spirited away by some gentlemen.[47]

The conflagration had important consequences. Moret had taken out advertisements in the English newspapers promoting his genius for discoveries and the elegance of his intended balloon, a Chinese temple on a cloud lifted by four eagles, which 'notwithstanding its enormous weight and capacity will be filled in an instant'[48] [Figure 9]. If all these promises produced was a smoke-filled bag incapable of lift, then science became a kind of fraud. Gentlemen might be believed; Frenchmen were not. Some commentators took a cheerful view of the crowd's violence. 'The sport of the day was heightened by the disappointment. The humorous spirit of John Bull turned the matter to good account.'[49] British prejudice was not the only prompt to violence – a balloon in Holland the same week which failed to ascend was likewise torn to pieces[50] – but associating the French with perfidy was traditional, patriotic and an easy excuse. In the same week came a report from Swansea of two Frenchmen who meant to make an air balloon. Their first effort burnt as it went up; their second rose chimney-high and collapsed, 'so that we have met with a double disappointment from this Frenchified scheme.'[51] A satirical print [Figure 10] showed the Chevalier atop a balloon, more whoopee cushion than Chinese temple, surrounded by papers referencing old hoaxes.[52] Lord North and Fox in the corner of the print add Whig windiness. The artist prefers fraud to be local: 'Then let us if we must be bit/ Be still the dupes of British wit.' That was already happening: three days after Moret's failure, a crowd turned up to Stinchcombe Hill in Gloucestershire to behold a balloon, only to see a child's kite flown by a couple of con artists who quickly eluded furious spectators.[53]

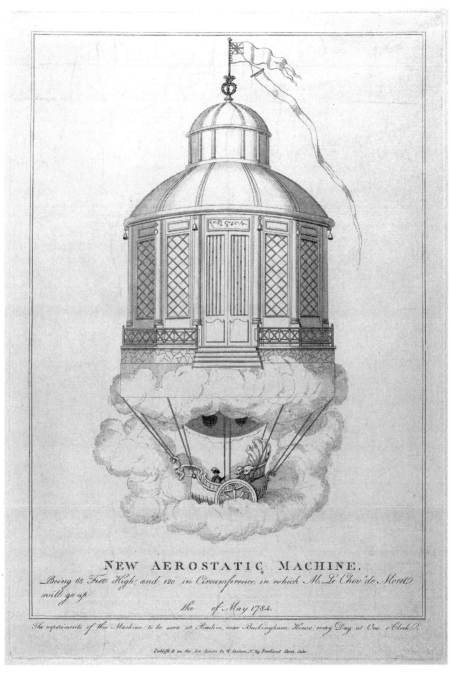

NEW AEROSTATIC MACHINE.

Being 65 Feet High, and 120 in Circumference, in which M. Le Chev. de Moret will go up

the of May 1784.

The experiments of this Machine to be seen at Pimlico, near Buckingham House, every Day at One o'Clock.

Publish'd as the Act directs by W. Skelton, N. 99 Portland Street, Soho.

Moret's balloon in the guise of a Chinese temple, August 1784   **9**
(engraving). The inscription over the 'temple' doors does not match any
oriental or masonic scripts.

10   Suspicion and cynicism in the wake of Moret's failure. Etching, 17 August 1784, published by William Wells.

Moret's disaster upped the ante for the next ascenders, who at least had the advantage of not being French. Advance publicity for Lunardi was carefully genteel. Moret is dismissed as a French 'stroke of *finesse* to raise the *wind*, at the expence of a credulous and easily bubbled people'.[54] This same credulous crowd is then appealed to as a 'discerning and unprejudiced multitude' who will naturally support the ingenious and learned in recognising Lunardi's superior abilities, connected clearly to his rank. Not everybody was convinced: Moret's intentions had been good, said some, and 'Humanity recoils at the idea of mentally wounding the man who narrowly escaped with his life for deceiving the public, rather from want of daring than of honesty.'[55] Lunardi had several competitors. Excitement focused most on a large balloon being constructed in Lord Foley's garden, which lay between Harley Street and Great Portland Street. Lord Foley was a spendthrift and racing confederate of Fox; the Duchess of Devonshire asked him to lend his grounds for experiments by Blanchard, Sheldon and Jeffries. The first effort involved John Sheldon and Colonel Gardiner, a veteran of the American war. Sheldon was an anatomist and skilled surgeon; he later became notorious for preserving his dead mistress and showing her to selected visitors.

Sheldon had been working with Keegan who had a shop on the Strand selling oiled silk and umbrellas. He could supply frame and varnish.[56] After several postponements, the balloon was allegedly ready, and admission tickets were reissued for an ascent on 25 September 1784, shortly after Lunardi's triumph, from Lord Foley's gardens in Portland Place. A graphically brutal print by Paul Sandby soon after showed the flaming balloon as an enormous arse with flames leaping from the crack, and a small balloon in the shape of a head wearing a fool's cap [Figure 11]. A quotation, '*Coelum ipsum petimus Stultitia*' (from Horace's *Odes*), mocked the attempt: *our folly reaches to the sky*.[57] After the debacle, Keegan sued Sheldon for damages. In court on 7 December 1784, three labourers testified that Sheldon had stoked the fire unwisely. Keegan had suspected a conspiracy, possibly to win a large bet. A defence by 'gentlemen of science' saw Sheldon acquitted and balloons restored to more legitimacy.[58]

Though Foley, Sheldon and Gardiner were indisputably English, and English gentlemen to boot, Londoners found something anti-French to have fun with. It was said that among the crowd who gaped at the burning balloon in Lord Foley's garden was a

11   Balloons as folly: Paul Sandby's scathing view. Etching and aquatint
showing the bursting of Keegan and Sheldon's balloon in Foley House
gardens, 25 September 1784. The fool's cap is inscribed, 'The English
balloon 1784'.

shifty-looking person who exclaimed every now and again, 'Begar, I
did ver wel to cut deir throats.' It turned out this French cut-throat
was Lord Foley's French cook, who had heard his compatriots opine
that the balloon couldn't possibly rise. Having nothing for Lord
Foley's supper, the cook seized upon the pigeons Sheldon had chosen
to fly with him, and cut their throats: they would make a compôte
that evening. 'To be sure I was ver vise, *n'est-ce pas?*'[59] Violence over
national cuisine resurfaced in October, when Blanchard and Sheldon
launched together from Chelsea. Blanchard threw out Sheldon's
instruments and provisions, a rash act he explained by words to the
effect that 'if you wanted to get rid of an Englishman, throw away
his food'.[60]

Lord Foley's enclosed garden provided some protection from an
angry crowd, clearly desirable. Moret, anticipating this, had applied
to the Artillery Company based at Chelsea for permission to use
their ground, and was refused on the grounds that their lease disal-
lowed other activities. Refusal meant forgoing military protection.[61]
Lunardi, who had been planning his venture since the spring, knew

that a secure location was important. He begged Count Bruhl, a German diplomat and astronomer and Zambeccari's patron, to help him get permission to use the nearby Chelsea Hospital's garden;[62] after Moret's disaster, that was withdrawn. Some of the subsequent correspondence, which Lunardi included in his post-flight *Account*, shows that riot and mob were words that triggered rigid panic in the authorities – here the governor of Chelsea College, Sir George Howard. Lunardi was in despair. Where else could he go so late in the day? He lobbied again, with the help of the Reverend R. Kirwan, chaplain at the Neapolitan Embassy where Lunardi was Secretary,[63] and the balloon-mad gentlemen Dr Fordyce and Mr Biggin, them-selves keen to get airborne. They went to see Sir Watkin Lewis, who had been Lord Mayor of London in 1780 and was an MP for the City of London. He was the Artillery Company's colonel. A tech-nical explanation of the different principles of Lunardi's balloon and an offer of a hundred guineas to some Artillery Company orphans persuaded him to back Lunardi, and his support was crucial. At two stormy meetings, he cast the deciding vote. Lunardi's account of this cliff-hanger period stresses two things – the power of science to persuade gentlemen, and the power of anti-French feeling to persuade an English crowd to turn violent. Lunardi's description of that was lurid: when Moret's balloon sank into the fire below it, 'the mob rushed in; tore it in a thousand pieces; robbed many of the company; levelled with the ground all the fences of the places and neighbourhood; and spread desolation and terror through the whole district.'[64]

Mob violence is frightening. 'Men, it has been well said, think in herds; it will be seen that they go mad in herds.'[65] Can the herd be mad and think? In *The Wisdom of Crowds*, James Suriewicki proposes that in some circumstances crowds may have better information and use it better than any individual. If we take the terms mob and riot at face value, we miss some complex emotions and thought processes that went on in crowds. At the first balloon launches especially, there circulated strong suspicions that the event's protagonist was a char-latan. Even Lunardi conceded that French impostors had sometimes appeared in England, and he was anxious he might be mistaken for one. On the day of his launch, it helped that he was supposed to be accompanied by an Englishman; that he was admired by the ladies; that the Prince of Wales turned up and approved proceedings; that he could see well-dressed people crowded into surrounding houses. The royal heir and Prince Caramanico, Lunardi's patron, showed apprehension – 'the whole company view us with a kind of regret, as devoted persons, whose return is at least problematical.'[66] These were all steadying, supportive reactions. Lunardi was not so sure about the main part of the crowd, which he totalled at 150,000; it was wedged into the large square around Bedlam, the insane asylum whose symbolism was all too obvious. A compressed, impenetrable, immense mass of people, it looked to him like a living pavement of human heads. They were getting impatient. The inflated balloon would not raise the weight of two people – in a last-minute drama, Biggin relinquished his place, Lunardi threw himself in, forgetting observational instruments, and the cords were cut.

'The effect, was that of a miracle, on the multitudes which surrounded the place; and they passed from incredulity and menace into the most extravagant expressions of approbation and joy.' When he waved his flag and worked his oars to signal to them, 'they literally rent the air with their acclamations and applause'.[67] Rising to a sublime calm, Lunardi sailed over London on a current of glory. While he recovered, adjusted the furniture of the balloon, ate, drank, wrote some letters and marvelled at the soft green scenery below, what did the crowd think? According to one witness, at first the mob – to him, a distinct and definable part of the crowd – thought

> Lunardi was *humbugging* them. And if, indeed, it had not risen, his life might have atoned to the savage vulgar for the disappointment. But as soon as they saw the balloon floating, like the cupola of St. Paul's moved from its base, they were lost in astonishment, and expressed a great concern for the fate of Lunardi. Many of them, however, would not suffer themselves to be persuaded that there was a living man in the gallery: They insisted that it was only the image or effigy of a man. As to the principle of motion which raised the Balloon, they seemed to consider it as a great Kite. One swore that he saw Lunardi put his night-cap in his pocket: Another that he saw half-a-dozen of shirts packed up in the gallery.[68]

What's unexpected about this description is that people don't believe what they see – the living man must be an effigy – and people see things not there – nightcaps and shirts. The savage vulgar might well not care about science, but evidently their idea of a spectacle was not as simple as the simple word suggests. Notions of time are folded with space in their fantasies of clothes; their opinions are vehement, yet debated. These 'savage vulgar' have emotions in common and different ideas.

If successful launches demonstrated scientific principles in action, why were they not more successful in defining balloons as things of science? Resistance shows an interesting tension between reasoning and belief. After landing in a meadow near Ware in Hertfordshire, Lunardi returned to London escorted by gentry. He was given a rapturous reception. 'Here circumstances of gratulation and joy crouded on me every hour.' Prince Caramanico's house was besieged with well-wishers, and people who had deprived him of income by renting their views rushed to atone: 'They had considered and treated me as an impostor. My ascension, as a charm, dissipated their ill opinion, and gave them an enthusiasm in my favour.' As a charm: science here is magic. The solicitude, admiration and applause were almost overwhelming: 'I receive the compliments and congratulations of two or three thousand persons in a day.'[69] Lunardi noted all this as a turn of the tide: the backing of royalty, newspapers, beautiful women and intelligent persons would all help to establish understanding of balloon enterprises and spread proper information. He had proved that balloons made flight possible.

The significance of Lunardi's aerial voyage was simultaneously recognised and yet not quite absorbed. Lunardi reckoned twenty thousand people had been to see his balloon exhibited before the launch at the Lyceum on the Strand. The number who would have seen his machine and gained some sense of its workings was expanded after his ascent by display of the balloon at the Pantheon. These exhibitions fuelled balloon madness and increased enthusiasm to see flights. The next big success was Blanchard's, launching from Chelsea on 16 October 1784. Roads to the site were blocked for four hours by carriages, stage-coaches and people. 'In short, there was not a single person, who had the least spark of curiosity, from *my Lord* to the shoe-black, who did not press to the scene.'[70] Again, a witness described the crowd as highly sceptical. One part was armed with bludgeons, 'to set an example to all Frenchmen of the manner in which they would be treated if they ventured to play their ballooning-tricks any longer in England'.[71] Anti-French sentiment was still directed at balloons, and here anti-intellectual prejudice is evident too. Despite the success of Lunardi a few weeks before,

> It was curious to observe, among the spectators, many declaring their opinions about Balloons, and maintaining that no man, nor men, could be wafted through the air; and that Lunardi's flight, and all the other jargon from France, about ballooning, was so incredible to the

mind of man, that none but those who had their heads filled with inflammable air could credit such reports. Lest their vast knowledge should be branded with foolishness or stupidity, they said, that they attended to laugh at the credulity of others.[72]

This crowd was not impervious to spectacle – besides the balloon, the bludgeoners treat the balloon-mad as a satirical spectacle. Blanchard disappointed them by a fine ascent loudly applauded. But their cynicism suggests that neither empirical demonstration nor spectacle were evidence enough to persuade some spectators of the value of balloon madness. It would be easy to attribute this resistance to the stupidity of bludgeoners and take them as indicative of uneducated, unenlightened opinion. But educated and enlightened people also struggled to believe what they heard and saw. On 7 December 1783, William Grant wrote to his friend Dr Gilbert Innes:

> I am inclined to believe you would not implicitly give faith to the letter I sent you respecting the Air Balloon and I must confess that at the time I sent it I did not believe One syllable of it but there is now in Town such evidence of the Truth of the material parts of it, that I am forced to acknowledge that Scepticism would be folly – Sir Joseph Banks mentioned in a Company where Sir Wm Forbes was present that he had received a letter from Dr Franklin narrating the whole affair pretty nearly in the terms of the letter I sent you, and I have been offered ten Guineas to return a hundred when a person will arrive from France in Great Britain in an Air Balloon – if you are inclin'd to trust your Money to such Airy security I believe I can do it for you to some amount. – Notwithstanding this and my having been an Eye Witness to the possibility of a Body remaining suspended in Air unsupported by any terrestrial Communication when I hear of a person or persons ascending to the height of more than a thousand yards, I am sometimes inclin'd to suspect a well Concerted Hum upon the credulity of John Bull and to recollect the story of a Man creeping in to a pint Bottle. If However I am mistaken in this supposition Good God My Dear Innes what a charming Trip to the Continent shall we have – How will all my Castles in Air at which you us'd to laugh be realiz'd and how will you be astonished to find yourself so much elevated above all the *little things* of this World.[73]

Grant's letter is a lovely instance of uncertainty of mind. He knows that learned opinion (Joseph Banks, Benjamin Franklin) supports balloons, he understands that bets make the possibility of flight a pecuniary reality, and he has actually seen flight demonstrated.

Even so, he finds it hard to shed associations with classic hoaxes (the Bottle Conjuror, from 1749, in which a man claimed to be able to climb into a bottle). Scepticism co-exists with optimism: castles in air will be realised. When Grant went to see Zambeccari's balloon the following year, he imagined himself able to fly – a vision of possibility untangled from doubt.

Given the close relationship between Enlightenment and science, it is easy to miss the continuance of magic in eighteenth-century beliefs. It shadows the investment in moral reasoning yet is neither reasonable nor moral. Or rather, magic reasons in a different way from reason and for different ends. Nonetheless, eighteenth-century rationalism recognised some power in a language of magic – as in the Bottle Conjuror. Magic was not the popular parlour pastime that it was for the Victorians; it was more public and ingenious, present in the magic of automata, waxworks and inventions. Magic infuses technology with supernatural power, borrowing from the wizard's wand and the witch's broomstick an ability to conquer time, place or shape. Satirical prints about balloons alluded to this power.

Enter Katterfelto, with his black cat attendant. Katterfelto's biographer calls him the Prince of Puff, and like his contemporary Dr James Graham, he was an artist of publicity. Where Graham sold rational self-improvement, an idea of a healthier self, Katterfelto sold the idea of magical science. 'Wonders! Wonders! Wonders!': his catchphrase amused the public. In 1782 he had become famous in London, performing different three-hour shows each night of the week in Piccadilly. 'By revealing thousands of "insects" writhing in a drop of water, he persuaded Londoners terrified of catching influenza to purchase his patent medicine at 5s. a bottle'; 'Katterfelto also owned a large hydrogen balloon, and charged people to watch him ascending with his two black servants for making astronomical observations.'[74] Although his fortunes fell and he left London in 1784, he continued to be associated with balloons. His lectures included demonstrations of balloons and he may be the figure on whom William Blake based his character Inflammable Gass in his 1784 satire *An Island in the Moon*.

Money was not always openly involved: in shifting a living, Katterfelto kept up enigmatic appearances. Mysterious notices appeared in the press, hinting at great discoveries. Masonic networks hummed. One story claimed Katterfelto had launched a balloon in St Petersburg sixteen years earlier, and before witnesses; it had travelled a hundred miles in three hours.[75] A night-time ascent at Buckingham

Palace, demonstrating 'his new-invented Night Air-Balloon' to the king and queen, no less, was also reported, with promises of discoveries for astronomy that would astonish the world.[76] 'The poem celebrating his ascent before the Royal family was regularly reprinted, always written afresh by a resident of Carlisle, Shrewsbury, Hertford, Derby or wherever he happened to be.' Such associations were opportunist. Before balloons, Katterfelto had associated himself with electricity; afterwards, with magnetism, which he demonstrated by raising four pigs and four cats simultaneously to the ceiling.[77] All these fashions built up his persona as a great and wonderful philosopher. Though his self-serving rhetoric can easily be read as charlatan marketing, it did give balloons a penumbra of magical science from which discoveries could be conjured.

Science and magic shared a vocabulary: 'to excite Admiration and produce Astonishment!' was a mutual aim. One of Philip Astley's tricks, the Magic Nosegay, involved artificial flowers made from goldbeaters' skin, dilated at will by pumping air through hollow stems. The blossoms would swell 'like little aerostatical Balloons'.[78] Other magicians made use of chemistry, mathematics and electricity to assist sleight-of-hand, describing their activities as experiments. Magicians also brought an interesting cosmopolitanism to natural philosophy. Their allure was increased by intellectual genealogies which typically featured travels around Europe, rewards from courts, high standing in occult orders, and honours from learned societies.[79] They criss-crossed countries, courts and institutions; like balloons, they travelled.

As one entertainer explained, in magic 'the Imposition of the Actor and the Credulity of the Spectator are equally necessary, and of which the Charm entirely consists'.[80] Magic is contractual – a spectator agrees to be fooled, and to forgo rational explanation of illusion. For balloon ascents, a suspicion of imposition hung around in the overlap between balloons and money, in bubbles and a language of credit, with its mash-up of the creditable and credible. These symbolic associations between balloons and financial fraud, aggravated by the activities of pickpockets in launch crowds, prepared imaginations for hoax and criminal intent, especially where French aeronauts were involved. Angry crowds rushed to destroy apparatus as a riposte to having their illusions destroyed.

Yet disbelief was also suspended. We have an instance from the end of August 1784:

The rage for Flying is so predominant, that some Wags, taking advantage of the present Furor, advertised last Saturday, that a Man in a Coat of Feathers, with a monstrous Pair of Wings, would take an aerial Excursion from Moorfields, and invited the Publick, gratis, as Spectators, in consequence of which several Thousands assembled at the appointed Time, and waited for a considerable while, diverting themselves with each other, till a young Man, being too free in his Witticisms, and hinting obliquely his Knowledge of the Advertisement, the Populace were with great Difficulty restrained from making him an Object of their Resentment.[81]

No money was fleeced, which may account for why the crowd did not become a mob. One description of the crowd watching Lunardi a fortnight later divided it into social groups: the mob, who thought of flight as the night province of goblins; the populace, who struggled to understand how anyone could fly; the middling classes, who were doubtful; men of science, who worried about the aeronaut's safety; and the rich, who just wanted to be diverted, even by death.[82] These psychological distinctions make a crowd composite and complex. And one crowd is different from another.

It is instructive to compare balloons to another startling invention of the same time: walking on water. In much the same way as balloons, it was hard to tell if public demonstrations would turn out to be enlightenments or frauds, and fraud had its own enlightenment, instructive like a collection of fakes. In December 1783, a watchmaker in Paris announced an experiment in which he would walk across the Seine in special boots.[83] This proved to be a ruse to attract a subscription. But the concept did not go away. In 1785, it was reported that a Spaniard crossed the Seine in eleven minutes, with several stops, one to scoop up a glass of water: 'He had on his feet a sort of cork buskins, and did not sink lower in the water than mid-leg.' There were a hundred witnesses, including officials from the Admiralty who attested the feat.[84] One paper was dismissive: hydrostatically, if a cubic foot of water weighed seventy pounds, the man had only to displace two feet of water to support 140lbs weight. The balancing act was no more difficult than rope-dancing. 'It may be a sort of consolation to John Bull, who is always ridiculed for his curiosity, that on this occasion there were at least twenty thousand Frenchmen assembled, and that the tickets of admission were livres.'[85] Exaggeration softened embarrassment. Then aquatic walking surfaced in London. On 7 September 1785, 'Hand-bills were distributed in the morning, that a bold adventurer meant to *walk* upon the Thames from Riley's Tea Gardens:– This was surely a wonderful sight; and gentle and simple attended in crowds; very few, however, thinking to pay the *aquatic* hero his demand for entering the gardens.'[86] Instead people crowded the water in boats, so thickly the adventurer could hardly move – and to everyone's surprise, he wore not aquatic boots but a large cork and tin machine round his middle. Wearing this he waded into the river and paddled about for half an hour, before being ushered away.

Commenting on this, one newspaper reaffirmed the value of experiment: 'Though the fellow who last week *humbugged* the public, by pretending he would walk upon or in the water, richly merits its chastisement, yet the thing itself is far from impossible. It was very lately performed with success at Paris by a Spaniard, who walked across the Seine.'[87] Another paper picked up the thread of uneasy nationalism: 'John Bull ever ready to be caught by the marvellous, was yesterday most completely duped'.[88] Exposing curiosity to the risk of failure, of fraud, and hence national embarrassment was a necessary part of British faith in pragmatism. Frenchmen were evidently amused: 'Our correspondent laughs at the incredulity of the English, who will believe nothing that they do not witness. *Aerostation* was a French chimera; and no doubt, he says, we will give *Hydrostation* the same epithet; but this experiment has been made in the presence of thousands.'[89] Walking on water, like sailing in air, was possible. Empirical proof was key to proving things true or false, but it could not completely overpower the imaginative possibility that you could believe the incredible if you saw it. The allure of balloons drew crowds as an act of faith in reason – and also in imagination.

Levity

Fashion 5

'Do not wonder that we do not entirely attend to things of earth: fashion has ascended to a higher element. All our views are directed to the air. Balloons occupy *senators*, philosophers, ladies, everybody…'
Horace Walpole to Sir Horace Mann, 2 December 1783

FASHION WAS A well-established idea and practice by the late eighteenth century. The concept, argues Hannah Greig, was a fluid one with meanings too multiple to be explained by one all-encompassing theory.[1] Some historians see the whole century as one of consumer revolution, while others identify surges towards the end of the century. 'Technical innovations in textile production were crucial in propelling and defining the Industrial Revolution. Fashion, especially fashion in clothing, was central to any remodelling of consumer expectations that preceded, or accompanied revolutionary increases in production.'[2] John Styles argues magisterially that those consumer expectations were not confined to the rich. Plebeian people took an interest in fashion and were leaders as well as followers of fashion. Literature that complained about luxury emphasised that all classes were too eager to buy and display. If the poor made do with ribbons and fairings rather than lace and jewels, they were nonetheless literate in the language of clothes – not least because many worked in textile-related trades – and contributed to making fashion an important cultural force.

Balloons played into this world in several ways. They inspired particular fashions in clothing, they promoted a new shape for women, and they accelerated the growth of fashion beyond a core category of clothing to encompass new categories including that of newness itself. For some of this there was a ready-made language: French. *Ton, beau monde, à la mode* were established terms for fashionability in the eighteenth century and applied easily to the latest products from France – of which balloons were one.

The dress of our fashionable *belles* departs, day after day, more and more from genuine simplicity and natural taste. It does not altogether yet approach the male form, but it is of that mongrel form which appears to less advantage than either male or female dress, separately. But it is *fashionable*, and whether it is *decent* or not will appear on enquiring into the *patterns* of female dress, French milliners and strumpets from France – nay, rather than not have a virtuous example to follow, our prostitutes here are deemed good authorities, and their taste quoted as the standard of elegance. *O tempora! O mores!*[3]

As more people spent more money on goods other than necessaries, more goods appeared that had decorative function or no function, and more functional goods were also more decorative. So balloons appeared on furniture, fans, handkerchiefs, snuff boxes, china and wallpaper, on delicately engraved glasses, tiles, miniatures, board games, prints and engravings, pencil boxes, patch box buttons, umbrella tops, rings, seals and medals.[4] Some were souvenirs of particular ascents, some simply celebrated the balloon as decorative object, usually aloft in a landscape with spectators. Reinforcing the idea of balloons as a thing of beauty, these goods also added stock to the idea of things as beautiful, an idea actively welcomed by late eighteenth-century consumer Britain.

Fashionable phenomena in the 1780s ran deeper and faster than superficial imagery, beautiful though much of it is. Precision in fixing the chronology of cultural change is difficult; nonetheless, changes particular to the 1780s show fashion becoming a force to be reckoned with in a way it had not been before. These changes concern dress, display and sex. The story of fashion I am tracking through balloons is a composite one of clothes, behaviours and bodies, and it touches more on gender relations than class relations, though the two intertwine in places. When in the autumn of 1785 a newspaper reported that a balloon was filled 'in front of a large concourse of persons of fashion', it used that term without distinction of sexes.[5] The word 'persons' also blurs a distinction between bodies and clothes: like celebrities in jeans, persons of fashion might be fashionable regardless of what they wore. On the other hand, expensive clothes – what eighteenth-century people called 'rich' dress – confer fashionable status. And what we might call style could create fashion, even when it was expressed through sartorial minimalism.

Take the case of Mary Robinson, who preceded balloons as a trend-setter. She caught the eye of the Prince of Wales in 1783 when she played Perdita in *The Winter's Tale*, after which she became his mistress. Royal paramours have instant cachet in London society, but Mary Robinson's dress attracted attention beforehand too. There was a turn to simplicity in her dress, a sort of anti-fashion stylishness. 'My fashions in dress were followed with flattering avidity', she noted, and though she sometimes led in richer dress, like the gold silk embroidered stockings that became a must-have item in March 1783, her taste, possibly shaped by youthful years in debt, shows that fashion was not always about conspicuous forms of consumption.[6] So 'we find 1783 to be the year of the "Perdita Hood," the "Robinson hat for Ranelagh," the "Perdita handkerchief," and the "Robinson gown," ... as Robinson continued to simplify female day dress and develop various pastoral, Quaker, and urbane personae'.[7] Adoption of a fashion through accessories was an established process by the 1780s; a French print mocked the trend of balloon-related consumables for both sexes [Plates II and III].

The 1780s saw hyperactive capitalism sell new fantasies through fashion. An amusing play satirised current taste: 'this is the golden age and every thing is bought and sold' – including the author, a lawyer who secretly informed against United Irishmen and then eloquently defended them in court.[8] The play's main character, Lady Flippant, tries to make her husband wear more fashionable underwear and other clothes she has smuggled in from Paris. Her own accessories include paint, patches, pomatum, false hair, curls, perfumes, gauze, ribbons, cork rumps, hoops, high heels and feathers. Protesting against the current fashion of hoops for women, one character exclaims: 'A hoop! No – it makes a woman appear like a walking sphere, encircled from the nadir to the meridian – and if the effeminacy of the men were not so well known, one would be apt to imagine that the women were all in a state of ---'.[9] Hoops, like the ballooning of pregnancy, associated women, fashion and balloons in triviality: 'The Soul of a Woman ... is defined by some as a kind of intellectual trifle, which, like M. MONTGOLFIER's cloud, is perpetually fluttering without any regular pursuit, in a suspended motion, and entirely absorb'd in a continual succession of aerial bagatelles.'[10] By the autumn of 1785, women and balloons were so fashionably connected that the agency involved was read in reverse, as air-headedness: 'The *balloon influenza* rages with more violence than ever; added to balloon hats, balloon bonnets, balloon caps, balloon ribbons, and balloon pins, the ladies have now *double balloon ear-rings*, and *balloon side-curls*; so that there are now no less than seven balloon articles appertaining to the decoration of the most beautiful balloon in Nature – the head of a pretty woman.'[11]

Fashion attracted much discussion in the press in the 1780s: 'whatever is most light and vapid in society as in agitated waters, usually rises to the top'.[12] It made good copy and it was endlessly topical:

> FASHION is fickle as the Wane
> Which shifts about, and back again!
> Each day some *Bagatelle* takes place
> To deck the Bosom or the Face![13]

Gender especially was changing. 'The fair sex drive four in hand … brandish their whips, cock their hats, and shew the pretty ankle covered by a boot!'[14] If the women were masculine, the men were effeminate. Such complaints were not new – there were well-worn satirical vocabularies for fops in general and for male followers of fashion, like the macaronis who sported feathers in the 1760s. '*Men ape* the *Women!* and the *Women, Men!*'[15] Men's military uniforms were adapted by women for a sharp silhouette and favoured the riding coat, taken up by the French as 'redingcote', to fill out a figure. This new 'pigeon pout' look featured a full bosom and full rump. You could puff up your bosom by a wire construction padded with gauze and wool, and you enlarged your behind with a cork rump:

> The Fair long since at Routs and Drums
> With Cork and Wool conceal their Bums;
>   To bailiffs bid defiance!
> When fore and aft you gently press
> There's so much false about their dress
>   On them there's no reliance.[16]

One aim of padding was to expand the space a woman's body could occupy. A sphere shape made a statement of presence, like a sphere of influence. A young woman in the 1780s asking a friend, Does my bum look big in this? would want the answer Yes. Traditional accusations of artifice in the construction of femininity, as in Swift's satires about the unnaturalness of women's aids to beauty, were interestingly altered, possibly because more people in the 1780s were genuinely more relaxed about women's assertiveness. It may also be that satirists were amused by the technological ingenuity that went into the enormity of this shape for women. The full-bosomed, full-rumped look was springy: it was meant to have bounce. It joined up with a technological fashion for springs in everything, including shoe heels: 'I vow and declare there's not one single thing/ That some how or other don't go with a Spring!'[17]

It's tempting to see powerful analogies between women's fashion and balloons in the 1780s. Why was an inflated shape in fashion? Were balloons themselves imaging femininity? Some historians have got excited about the roundness of balloons: it reminds them of breasts and buttocks, a pornographic rotundity. Some gush about balloons as a feminine symbol. 'It is not only an elegant shape and a gaudy silken dress that makes the balloon the most feminine of man's creations. It is feminine also in its wayward temperament and in the ephemeral quality of its beauty.'[18] Bouncy women in the 1780s might well have waved their cork rumps at this male fantasy. 'When half the world is staring to the moon,/ Buoyed up by fashion's trumpery balloon' — fashion was and is a material form of ideologies.[19] Yet overlaps between clothing fashions and balloons are intriguing. Besides a suddenly desirable filled-out shape, quivering and springy, there was a fashion for stripes — in 1785, for instance, white and buff or white and lemon.[20] Many balloons were striped and made from silk. Light materials were as fashionable as flight. For a couple of years after 1783, aerial colours of sky-blue, white and silver became more popular. The extensive fashion for feathers preceded the appearance of balloons in 1783, but balloons extended the flight properties of feathers through the resemblance of fashionable female shape to pigeons.

Balloons inspired one specific accessory: the balloon hat [Figure 12]. Like a balloon, it was space-invading; it was also known as the Lunardi hat. 'The balloon hat, chip, covered with coloured sarcenet and a large piece of Italian tiffany pinned in loose puckers very full round the crown. A plain band of ribband with a very large bow behind. The hat has a wire at the edge and curves up a little on both sides,' directed *The Lady's Magazine* of December 1783. The style stayed in fashion after 1785, when it began to acquire other names as balloon madness waned.[21] If you were unlucky enough to be behind one of these hats at a balloon launch, you couldn't see a thing. Horace Walpole craned and peered past an enormous balloon hat at one launch; he claimed hardly to have seen the balloon at all. They became a joke. A skit set in a theatre described a would-be viewer:

> on one side sat a Lady with a Lunardi hat; before him was placed one
> with a feathered headdress ... the Colonel tried to see the stage, but in
> the attempt he got such a whisk from Miss Feathers on one cheek and
> such a poke from the wires of Miss Lunardi on t'other, he gave up.[22]

THE SUPPLEMENTAL MAGAZINE.

12   Expansive fashion for women: balloon hats, false fronts and cork rumps.
Satirical print from *The Supplemental Magazine*, 1 January 1786. The
woman on the far left is being fitted with a puffed-out artificial bosom, as
held by the woman next to her. Hand-coloured etching, published by S. W.
Fores 'at the caracture warehouse, No. 3 Piccadilly'.

A form of conspicuous consumption in their excessive materials,
balloon hats also blocked the male gaze. It was considered very
obliging when Lady Derby agreed to take off her balloon hat at the
playhouse.

Large bodies and huge headgear suggest fashion was articulating
women's occupation of more space. Balloons made vertical space
newly available:

> from the waving frippery with which our females adorn or rather
> disguise their lovely heads, one would imagine they indulge the hopes
> of being wafted by the aid of what are fashionably termed balloon
> bonnets or hats, above us mortals; for it must be acknowledged that
> they are too generally ambitious of gaining the ascendancy.[23]

Occupying more space horizontally with their balloon hats, women
also moved visibly into vertical space. The public sphere was
stretched into an imaginary upwards. Since ascents began, observed
one writer, 'there seems to prevail a kind of aerial phrenzy amongst

us. The term balloon is not only in the mouth of every one, but all our world seems to be in the clouds.'[24] Elopement figured largely in people's minds as they imagined the uses to which balloons might be put; franker wits like one Patrick O'Flighty made jokes about slipping into Venus and then visiting Mercury. Elopement was a polite allusion to illicit sex. Fashionable persons were having sex – lots of it, and not with their official spouses. Some women were certainly up for it. In the 1780s, readers of public prints might have concluded half the aristocracy was in the divorce courts. That women were as much makers as takers of sexual pleasure can be seen from a *bon mot* which reported that ladies who had sex in shrubberies were describing it as 'being transported to the plantations'.[25] A mock-advertisement sought a companion to tour European cities by balloon, alighting in nunnery gardens 'to take up all such young ladies as are inclined to go to heaven'.[26] Aerial pick-ups got scripts. Balloons, being something you rode in and something that rose, were great for double entendres. Wit, much displaced by sensibility, was still enjoyed by people of fashion. *The Rambler's Magazine* reported: 'The Perdita is allowed to have wit as well as beauty: She paid a fine turned compliment to her gallant Colonel a few days ago. The Colonel observed to her, that she looked divinely in a riding habit; she assured him she would always wear that dress, provided he would always be in a riding habit when he came to visit her.'[27] Large bets were laid in London clubs and coffee-houses as to who would first have sex in a balloon.

> When a lady and gentleman are powerfully impelled by "Cupid, god of soft persuasion", to a private airing, let them only mount one of these aetherial vehicles, and they will be out of sight in a twinkling. I will then defy the most curious sharp-sighted prude, or curious keen-eyed impertinent, to find out the spot to which they have winged their flight.[28]

Balloons were a space in which the sexual double standard was suspended: the mile-high club began in 1784 [Figure 13].

Lunardi's fashionability included his appeal to women from women's point of view. A fictional Lydia Lovely went to the Pantheon to admire the enormous swell of Lunardi's balloon, which she longed to see rise:

> Let they who will with Luni ride
> Upon the air's uncertain tide
> I own I envy when I see

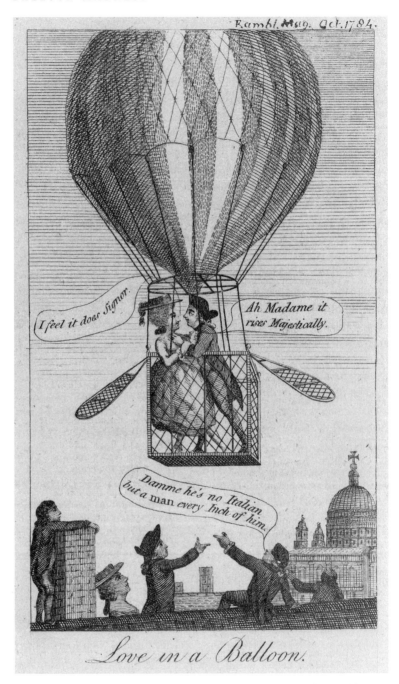

13   Up to something: balloons as vehicles for sex. Print from *The Rambler's Magazine*, October 1784, satirising Lunardi's sex appeal and the balloon as a vehicle for sex.

Him twin'd about Maria's knee:
The height of joy is surely this
To have in sight the realms of bliss.[29]

Lunardi played the game knowingly: garters signed with his name were distributed. In Scotland he begged the ladies to lend him their underwear to provide silk to mend his balloon, like a popstar who encourages his fans to throw knickers. In London he was mobbed.

> Literally speaking, Mr Lunardi was devoured; the crowd was so great about him, that he was almost in danger of suffocation; the apartment resounded with the loudest acclamations, and the clapping of hands was so violent and repeated, that for almost the space of three hours, every ear was deaf even to the shrill note of clarinet and hautboy. The very skirt of Mr Lunardi's coat was kissed by those who could not reach his hand, with an enthusiasm that bordered on idolatry.[30]

His coat may well have been the scarlet uniform of the Artillery Company who had let him use their grounds; on later flights, he changed into it. To be celebrated invited scrutiny of dress and appearance, formerly the prerogative of rank and now becoming attached to famous commoners. Royalty was robed in finery; celebrity took on its aura. Discussing a typical court circular from the *London Chronicle* of 4 January 1783, Michael Gamer and Terry Robinson read it as a 'world in which theater, royalty, and fashion mix seamlessly':

> Last night their Majesties, the Prince of Wales, the Princess Royal, Princess Augusta, and Princess Elizabeth honoured Drury-lane theatre with their presence, to see the Grecian Daughter, and appeared highly pleased with Mrs. Siddons' performance. His Majesty had on a suit of ruby-coloured velvet. Her Majesty appeared in a carmelite satin gown, with pink bows, and had on a black hat-cap, ornamented with rich brilliant plume, and a row of jewels round it, with diamond earrings and necklace. The Prince of Wales was dressed in a fashionable brown. The Princess Royal was dressed in a clay colour and white striped satin, with white bows, and had on a beautiful cap, with a braid of jewellery in the front. —The Princess Augusta had on a pearl blue silk. —Princess Elizabeth wore a white dress, with Carmelite bows. The caps of the two younger Princesses were much alike, each having a small black plume in it. The shew of diamonds, however, were in favour of the Princess Augusta.[31]

Class hierarchy had new competition from figures elevated by popular enthusiasm. Lunardi was one. 'Some of the morning papers puff the man who went up in a balloon as if he had done some signal

service to his country; and even the cloathes in which he attended
the Ambassador to Court are particularized, as if he was a person of
the first consequence', complained one writer.[32] Preceding Lunardi
were, amongst others, Sarah Siddons the actress, for whom a rage
swept Britain in 1782,[33] and Auguste Vestris, son of a famous dancer
and known as 'le dieu de la danse'. He made his debut in London at
the King's Theatre on 16 December 1780. Horace Walpole satirised
the rapture:

> The theatre was brimful in expectation of Vestris. At the end of the
> second act he appeared; but with so much grace, agility and strength,
> that the whole audience fell into convulsions of applause: the men
> thundered, the ladies forgetting their delicacy and weakness, clapped
> with such vehemence, that seventeen broke their arms, sixty-nine
> sprained their wrists, and three cried bravo! Bravissimo! so rashly,
> that they have not been able to utter so much as no since.[34]

Though Vestris' astonishing springiness secured his talent, he also
leapt into fashion: he wore a particular sky-blue that became known
as 'Vestris blue'.[35]

Fashion was important to male aeronauts too. Lunardi had rivals
in aeronautical *haute couture*. When Richard Crosbie made his ascent
from Dublin he devised an exotic costume: a robe of oiled silk lined
with white fur, waistcoat and breeches of quilted satin, Moroccan
boots and a leopard-skin turban.[36] It didn't catch on, unlike the
aviator jacket later, but it impressed. Many encomiastic poems
after his historic flight above Dublin on 19 January 1785 noted his
clothes. The longest, *The Aerial Voyage*, made them the conversion
point between hero and divine leader:

> A moment now, to love, to friendship due,
> Soft from the crowd the anxious chief withdrew,
> But buskin'd soon, in drawers, in satin vest,
> An ample stole and graceful turban drest,
> Again returns all dauntless to the charge
> Smiles on us all, and mounts the airy barge.[37]

It became *de rigueur* for aeronauts to dress up. Even Blanchard
joined in:

> Mr. Blanchard was dressed in a green frock white dimity waistcoat,
> nankeen breeches, and white silk stockings, and his shoes were
> fastened with black silk ribbons, drawn nearly into the form of cock-
> ades; his hat was covered with a gree[n] japan, and to it was affixed
> a green cockade, from which rose a small Ostrich feather.[38]

His aerial companion Colonel Thornton wore a matching costume with a pearl-colour trim to his shoe ribbons. The woman in the scene, Miss Simonet, is curiously drab. She wore a brown and white cotton gown, a black cloak and a black hat. Did she decide not to spoil the show of male finery?[39]

Even aeronauts in difficulties were conscious of their clothes. After their historic flight from Paris on 21 November 1784, when Pilâtre de Rozier landed with the Marquis d'Arlandes an excited crowd grabbed his redingote and fought over it. A politer welcoming committee awaited back in Paris. De Rozier had to borrow garments so seedy he was ashamed to appear in them, and he let the marquis go on alone to receive congratulations.[40]

Fashion has long been associated with a whirl, and fantasies of speed are part of a rhythm of increased consumption. Modern times are often seen as the world speeded up – a sense of speed that preceded balloons but was intensified by them. Two years before balloons, some comic verse letters lamented: 'Ah, John! times and seasons are alter'd, in truth,/ Since we drawl'd up to town in the days of our youth:/ 'Twas then a month's journey thro' rough, ragged ways,/ But now we were *wisk'd* here in three or four days'.[41] Speed expressed freedom of movement and freedom from social rules; many women wanted both. Lady Flippant, defiantly in the driving seat, airs a desire for speed that leaves men gasping:

> Heav'ns! How ardently I pant to be elevated in the phaeton, to take the circuit of Hyde Park, rolling in a cloud of dust, four horses, two outriders, whip in hand, flowing manes, hunters tails, sweep down Piccadilly, turn into St. James's-Street – up fly the club house windows, out pop the powdered heads of the bucks and beaux of fashion – some nod, some smile, some kiss hands, – all praise – she is a goddess, exclaims one, – a venus, ejaculates another, – an angel, sighs a third. I cut on, flash down Pall-Mall swift as lightening, rattle furiously through Charing Cross, overturn Lady Dapper's whim and cats at Northumberland House, lose a wheel in the Strand, leap from my seat as the carriage falls, and am received in the arms of some handsome fellow whom love has directed to my assistance.[42]

Lady Flippant's wild attitude to road safety anticipates the poop-poop motoring fantasy of Toad of Toad Hall, also kicking up dust. Although balloons in beautiful mode were stately and slow, philosophically they joined a fast lane of ideas that envisioned the world's future as speedy – as we might say, light years ahead. Modernity makes us imagine the future as faster, unless some disaster befalls and winds society back to the plodding ploughman. Balloons promised faster travel and fewer indignities of the road, like floods, tolls, jolting and accidents: 'Our prospects too must be so much more extensive, in consequence of the height of our elevation, and of the removal of all terrestrial obstructions, that many persons will, doubtless, be tempted, by such considerations alone, to prefer the balloon machine to any post-coach, gig, whisky, or diligence in the three kingdoms.' Usefulness to fashion would be use enough: 'air balloons will be as common, in a few months, as hackney-coaches: no man, who has the smallest pretensions to taste, will be without one; he will think his balloon flight full as necessary as his phaeton or cabriole'.[43]

Balloons were part of the exchanges between England and France in the 1780s that created a fashionable class, self-elect and self-conscious:

> The People of Fashion in France, England etc now seldom rise till after mid-day Dine at Six attend Public Diversions 'till 4 or 6 in the Morning and retire to Sleep for the Day. Even Tradesmen and People of Professions and Business ape Them in Their Hours, by laying in Bed late of Morning Dining at 3 or 4 and going to Bed at midnight. 'Tis the present Ettiquete to call it Morning till you have Din'd, and you'll often hear the Puppies biding you a good morning of a winter's day afternoon, when 'tis just Dark.[44]

Shared behaviours were supported by the exchange of goods; French aristocrats in the 1780s were keen on English guns, dogs and carriages. In this shared culture of consumption, some things – including balloons – passed into a common cultural language. The allure of things became the power to allure through things. Paul Keen argues that 'the hybridizing effects of commerce had blurred the distinctions between these different realms – the world of the mind and the body, enlightenment and fashion, science and sexuality, innovation and transgression'. Balloons represented both commercial modernity and modernity through commerce:

> In some ways, it was precisely this semiotic elasticity – the ease with which ballooning could mean so many different things to different people across a range of contexts – that made it so open to skepticism. Ballooning's endless adaptability on a symbolic level reinforced its power to evoke the fluidity of a commercial society generally; its very ubiquity amongst these sorts of satires (many of which played on the idea of ballooning as a "bubble") ... made it an easily recognized symbol for all manner of foolish or unstable or

disreputable behaviour in a social order where the very concept of value had floated free from its epistemological foundations.[45]

The special partnership of sex and fashion was entrenched so successfully by balloons in the 1780s that it produced a lasting template. In 1808 an astounding story appeared in the British press. Balloons were around still, dallying with steam. Even as the 1808 story seems to be pointing to a new fashion, it merges topicality with an amorous narrative familiar from the heyday of balloon madness:

> A very novel species of duel lately took place in Paris. Monsieur de Grandpré and Monsieur le Pique having quarrelled about Mademoiselle Tirevit, a celebrated opera-dancer, a challenge ensued. Being both men of elevated minds, they agreed to fight in balloons, and in order to give time for their preparation the duel was postponed for a month. On the 3rd of May, the parties met in a field adjoining the Tuileries, where their respective balloons were ready to receive them. Each, attended by a second, ascended his car, loaded with blunderbusses, as pistols could not be expected to be efficient in their probably distant situations. A great multitude attended, hearing of the balloons, but little dreaming of their purpose. The Parisians merely looked for the novelty of a race in the skies. At nine o'clock, the cords were cut, and the aerial machines ascended majestically, amidst the shouts of the spectators.
>
> The wind was moderate, blowing from the N.N.W., and they kept as far as could be judged about eighty yards of each other. When they had mounted to the height of about 900 yards, M. le Pique fired his piece ineffectually; almost immediately after, the fire was returned by M. Grandpré, and penetrated his adversary's balloon, the consequence of which was its rapid descent, and M. le Pique and his second were both dashed to pieces on a house-top, over which the balloon fell. The victorious Grandpré then mounted aloft in the grandest style, and descended safely with his second about seven leagues from the spot of ascension.[46]

What a story! It was entirely credible that duellists would take their quarrels to the skies, acting out in miniature a scenario of aerial warfare that was well established in plans for balloon uses. Given the hot-headedness of duellists and the flimsy pretexts for some of their fights, this persuasive story offered cool deliberation and a natural cause of contention – a doubtless lissom woman with a fine singing voice. Was it not imaginative of the contenders for her favours to rise to the skies?

There is, however, even more imagination at work here than at first sight. Look again at the names. To an English-speaking ear, they sound normally French. But Monsieur le Pique, Monsieur de Grandpré and Mademoiselle Tirevit are not quite what they seem. Pique has several definitions: a pike or long-handled weapon; the suit of spades in a pack of cards; and that state of low-grade anger for which the English language simply borrows the French word, as in 'a fit of pique'. In natural history it was the word used to describe a plunging dive of certain birds, later adopted for the plunging dive of an aeroplane. As a verb, it means to prick or needle – hence the force of pique. So Monsieur le Pique could translate as Mr Annoyed. Prick is also a term for an annoying man, metonym of male anatomy. 'Pré' means 'meadow', straightforward enough. But in the eighteenth century, according to a dictionary of 1787–88, 'sur porter de la pré' meant 'to find a spot for a duel'[47] – so the open ground of Grandpré could be a duellists' pun, subtler than the sexual slang of 'fire his piece', penetration and mounting. Mademoiselle Tirevit turns out to be a joke too, if an antique one: 'Tire-vit (Pull-Prick) had already been euphemized to Tireboudin (Pull-Sausage) by the fourteenth century'.[48]

The story stayed in circulation in Victorian literature; it has appeared in modern histories of duelling and websites.[49] All of them present it as a real event. That it is an obscene hoax is less striking but still fun: whoever thought up the verbal game would surely be amused to have continued hoodwinking English readers two hundred years on. It is also a nice instance of how the credibility of balloons demands a degree of credulity. The story's reference to 'men of elevated minds' is both sly in terms of the sexual associations of balloons, in which elevated minds substitute ironically for erect penises, and a philosophical piece of wit quite familiar in humour about science. Perfectly illustrating what Marie Thébaud-Sorger has called the ironic and authentic properties of balloons, the story also shows how balloons were part of fashion, which has ironic and authentic properties too. The association of balloons with fashion joined up clothing, designs and fantasies. It was a powerful inflation of ideas. It was also irresistible to satirists, as Chapter 6 explores.

Satires   6

'for even when reason and science make the greatest strides, folly
profits by it to extend her domain.'

Comte de Ségur, *Memoirs*

MUCH OF BALLOON MADNESS was joyous and excited.
But there was also resistance and opposition. Aerostation
seemed to move fast in its developments; in the first years, comments
on voyages note record-breaking achievements in distance, height
and time which raised expectations for other flights. Many satirists
concentrated on ineptitude in particular failures; some cast doubt
on the whole enterprise of aerial endeavour. The old trope of bubble
connected folly and politics, and balloons drew satirists in flocks.
Attacks were often personally directed. Thus *The Lunardiad, or, The
Folly and Madness of the Age* (1784):

> Vain, idle Folks, but born to gape and stare,
> To view a Monkey – mounting into Air.
> And when the Thing descends to Earth again,
> You meet the Creature – with the Hero's Strain,
> Men give him Cheers, Belles dress for him their Charms,
> And in a Furor snatch him to their Arms.
> England, alas! thou'rt Folly's foremost Heir
> To waste thy Time on Fiddlers, Fools, and Air.[1]

Balloons as a form of folly feature in another print of 1784 – *The
downfall of taste & genius or the world as it goes* – that satirised topical
amusements in popular culture, including mountebanks, performing
animals and freaks.[2] Vehicles of folly in themselves, balloons revealed
the folly in people too, in unchecked ambition, deviant escape from
norms, loose behaviour, upside-down values, greed, fraud, appetite, gullibility and credulity. This chapter explores that world in
relation to the rage for balloons – a world not simply of scandal,
politics or fashion but the intersection of all three. It was possible

to be famous for being famous – and fatuous. What historians call the public sphere included in 1783 much personal life aired through personalities and sexual affairs, especially those conducted publicly by the aristocracy. The fashionable world was also a political world; balloons contributed to fashionable politics.

An active press and print culture made politicians and the aristocracy known in new ways: caricature made faces recognisable, newspapers savoured transgressions. Political arguments were attached to personalities with a new intensity, as the differences of Fox and Pitt as persons and the differences between their politics lent themselves to colourful polarity. Balloon madness had a backdrop of other phenomena seen as signs of the times, including a rage of party in politics, intensified consumption by the moneyed classes, looser sexual behaviours and vocal assertion of opinions. All were publicly on show and in circulation. It was a world of arguments – in and around parliament, in law courts, in print – and some of those arguments were bad-tempered. Satire had ample materials and a growing audience.

Chapter 7 gives weight to poetic and philosophical responses to balloons, even in light verse; this chapter focuses on uses of balloons as a response to the follies of the age, both general and particular. Where light verse sends up, satire sends up and punctures. Satire had two main traditions drawn from the classics, smiling and savage, epitomised by Horace and Juvenal. Eighteenth-century inventiveness brought in wordplay, a gentle amusement, much enjoyed in spite of some highbrow sniffiness about puns. Jokes about balloons going to the moon invoked lunacy from the start – thus *The Air Balloon, or a Trip to the Moon*, a satirical print published on 2 November 1783, in which a Fellow of the Royal Society surveys an air-globe and pronounces: 'We shall now have a Lunatic Journal'.[3] Lunar jokes naturally intensified with Lunardi. His ascent on 15 September 1784 was delayed by a change in weather attributed to a new moon; hence a new joke, that he was moonstruck.[4] In 1785, inducted into a Freemason Lodge in Edinburgh, Lunardi sang an Italian air and a Scottish song. 'It being suggested that a second part to the song would add to its beauty, a Brother immediately began, but soon after was under the necessity of stopping, declaring that Mr Lunardi went infinitely too high for him.'[5] Another joke told of an aeronaut asking a minister if he could launch from his church; the minister replied no, because his business was to make people come to church, not fly from it.

Balloon madness was happily inverted through mock-forms. A mock court circular caught the *ton*: the king and queen set off for Windsor in an air-balloon built by Signor Vertigo and drawn by eagles; the Duchess of Flywell, taking an airing in a balloon over Hyde Park, met with an unfortunate accident caused by a pigeon and got stuck in a tree.[6] The dignity of dignitaries was comically reworked again in a parody of sporting news in 1784, futuristically set in 1785, in which sky races at Newmarket were contested by Lord Puff, Lord Blast, Sir Windy Whistle, Lord Breeze, Lord Hurricane and Colonel Zephyr.[7] Wordplay through names was a stock feature in the theatre where it signalled the lightness of comedy. Referring for once to the dangers of balloons to spectators, following the collapse of scaffolding at launches, a mock advertisement for a balloon invited interested parties to contact Messrs Trepan, Bonesetter & Co. at the corner of Break-neck Alley in Tumble-down Street.[8] A spoof of polite advertising in the name of Messrs Aether and Aeolus announced – and illustrated – a cross-Channel service of double balloons from Dover to France:

> A King's Messenger is this Minute unbasketed at the City of London, who left the Pier-head at Calais less than two hours ago. It is almost needless to say, that Sea-Sickness, and all the *Train of Consequences* which attend a small Cabin, are by the Use of these Air-Balloons avoided, and that a fine Bird-Flight View of the two Kingdoms renders the Balloon Passage one of the most pleasing Journeys imaginable.[9]

Satire was operating in a text-filled world in which argument was habitually oppositional: 'there are parties even concerning balloons'.[10] Promotional literature for balloons used this tactic, as a verse on Lunardi's publicity describes:

> Behold a windy competition
> Two puff-makers in opposition
>   The whole must end in vapour.
> By various means their puffs they utter,
> This uses water, flour and butter,
>   And that pens, ink and paper.[11]

Some of this misanthropy appears in an otherwise good-humoured poem by Mary Alcock, in which aeronauts dispense with old aerial machinery like Venus's doves, flying carpets, Pegasus and castles in the air. The last lines of the majority of the stanzas introduce a note of contempt: a gazing and enquiring multitude becomes a grovelling, stupid and senseless multitude. What's satirised is detachment from fellow-feeling, an arrogant looking down on people which becomes criminal. The advertisement warns against soaring ambition, underscored by capital letters: 'N.B. *The* Air Balloon *will be found to be of the greatest importance to those who wish* TO EVADE THE LAWS OF THEIR KING OR COUNTRY.'[12] Aeronauts and crowd were satirised as equally gullible – hence equally culpable – by *The Ballooniad*, which took Harper's ascent in Birmingham as its immediate target. Its anti-hero is Strap, a barber, echoing Harper's reported profession, and also possibly alluding to Strap in Tobias Smollett's novel *Roderick Random* (1748), a character whose foolishness periodically creates chaos. If so, the allusion invokes large-scale knockabout parody of a world view. Strap gets aloft and visits Jove:

> This bag, friend Strap! I give as thy reward,
> On earth you'll find much use for its contents,
> 'Twill serve as matter for advertisements:
> Let printers have it for a paper puff,
> They know the value of the precious stuff.[13]

Paul Keen links tropes of paper in balloon satire to anxieties about paper currency, analysed by J. G. A. Pocock:

> Balloons, "at the mercy of the wind," and as imposing and luxurious in appearance as they were hollow, evoked all too easily these instabilities of a modern commercial culture, prised free from the foundational wealth of landed wealth and subject to a fluctuating network of exchanges in which appearances frequently counted more than inherent worth.[14]

Here one can see anxieties attached to fears about writing as a commodity. The ephemerality of satire had particular value when it treated topical matters; it dealt in a currency of current affairs. Faced with competition from ephemeral literature around balloons, in handbills, advertisements, announcements and accounts, satirists fought to protect their historic rights of shape-shifting and their specialised market in levity.

Besides being objects of satire on their own account and through their inflated language, balloons moved into the mainstream of public life. They joined a world of satire which did much to create that public life through publicising how it worked. Many satirists focused on identifying errant behaviour in a society felt to be changing fast, and in which the terms of satire were also changing. Some thought satire was becoming more savage:

> The Writers of Scandal, private History and Satire seem to be daily increasing in their Numbers, and they diffuse a Species of Suspicion through the Community, which is very unfavourable to publick Happiness. According to them, there is not at this Moment a Man of real Worth and Merit in the World. A spiteful Satirist of one Party degrades a Hero of the Opposite; all good Qualities are clouded, and the Ears and Hearts of Men filled with nothing but Slander and Destruction.[15]

One essayist, the well-named Diogenes, advanced a very grumpy conspiracy theory. Why was it, he asked, that fashionable amusements appeared at times of national emergency? He had a long list: the Stratford Jubilee was all a distraction from Wilkes and liberty; the vogue for the dancer Vestris in 1780 and 1781 conveniently diverted people from an unsuccessful war; the inglorious peace settlement of 1782 was not protested against because the whole country was 'Siddonized into tears for Belvidera, Isabella, &c. when every British heart should have bled for its country's cause!'[16] Diogenes blamed politicians: they buried bad news under a rage for some new entertainment. Balloons were the latest instance. In France, faced with the disastrous failure of a major bank, the Caisse d'Escompte, which Benjamin Franklin compared to the Bank of England, ministers amused people with an air-balloon. Worse, the diversion worked:

> when the blow fell, all eyes were staring at a bladder in the *Champ de Mars*! Bankruptcy and ruin were no longer the topics; *gas* and inflammable air filled all the mouths of the fluttering Parisians! Parties to the moon were every where proposed, and *gum taffeta* cicatrized the bleeding wounds of the credulous and versatile Frenchman![17]

To Diogenes, balloons were a plot to suppress weightier concerns.

One print on the occasion of the first inflammable air balloon ascent showed Parisians scrambling up a wall for vantage views; men ogle the exposed backsides of women rather than any higher distraction.[18] Diogenes may have been mollified to see balloons take up political meanings. A pantomime, *Harlequin Junior*, represented the Caisse as a replica *montgolfière*. Newspaper reviews praised the bank-balloon as a fine satire: 'The change of the bank at Paris into an air-balloon is excellent. The clerks, &c. appear in a gallery round the balloon, which is balanced by a package of American bonds.' It ascended through clouds: 'This piece of magic had a very good effect, and was highly relished by the audience.'[19] Inflation in its modern sense of a rise in general prices is a later development, but balloons indicate inflation in the sense of being inflated, from *afflatus*, full of air – a term frequently applied to populist orators and exorbitant speculation. The associations of balloons with philosophy and commercial adventurism made them a symbol of uncertainty about speculation in both domains. Hence satirists shrilly attacked balloons for representing unsteady value.

The course and tenor of French aerostation had some influence – newspapers circulated regular and detailed accounts – but Britain was fertile ground for home-grown cynicism. As an epigram of 1784 put it:

> GREAT Men, as disappointment tells,
>   Are disappointed moons;
> Their promises but fruitless spells,
>   Addresses, AIR-BALLOONS.[20]

Ambition rose; disappointment sank. The ups and downs of politics were also ins and outs, especially in and out of government for Fox. Balloons were good images for political frustrations and disappointments because politicians were already associated with insubstantial, airy promises. Old tropes of orators as windbags acquired particular meanings in the 1780s. Lord North was often referred to as Boreas, the North Wind: 'The wise and valiant Lord of North/ In windy words did bluster forth'.[21] Most balloon satire takes an anti-Opposition view of politics – that is, North and Fox are far more often the target than William Pitt (the younger) and his followers.[22] In part this was because of Pitt's new popularity and the odium felt for the Fox-North coalition; it was also because Foxite Whigs were more closely associated with balloons and more active in making political capital out of their display. A satire published when the coalition fell shows Fox and North with ropes round their necks, attached to a runaway balloon; as it drags them upwards, a jubilant crowd cheers in speech bubbles: 'Huzza; it is a pity they were not Hang'd 7 Years ago'; 'Never did Rope fit better'; 'and never was exaltation more proper'; 'what joy to poor old England'.[23] Frederick North had been Prime Minister from 1770 to 1782, when he was forced out of office over the conduct of the American war and replaced by Lord Shelburne. He returned as Home Secretary in April 1783 in a coalition with Fox which almost everyone regarded as a sell-out of his principles, such as they were. The Coalition lasted till December, when Fox's East India Bill to reform the East India Company was thrown out of the House of Commons and Pitt was invited by George III to form a government. A general election in March 1784 strengthened Pitt's support in both parliament and the country, leaving Fox and North to oppose as creatively as they could the government from which they were emphatically excluded.

One of Fox's biographers says, 'For those who were to know and like him, Fox's personality was absolutely compelling.'[24] For those who disliked him, Fox was unprincipled, perfidious and malign. His name was synonymous with slyness, and his swarthy features and bushy eyebrows made him a gift to caricaturists. Some simply drew a fox. Others cast him in diabolical characters like Satan, Machiavelli, Carlo Khan and Cromwell. The most difficult years of Fox's life were 1782 to 1784: George III loathed him so much he encouraged Pitt to use foul means to keep Fox out of politics. In the general election Fox managed to hang on to a parliamentary seat for Westminster, narrowly surviving the humiliation of a recount. His hatred of George III for interfering with the executive, especially the appointment of ministers, combined with his loathing of Pitt as the king's creature, 'could call up astonishing bursts of energy and violence', as L. G. Mitchell puts it. But the events of 1784 also made him disenchanted with politics and he withdrew with his companion Mrs Armistead to a villa at St Anne's Hill in Surrey. 'For some, the only point at issue was whether Fox had abandoned politics or politics had abandoned him.'[25]

So the years of balloon madness were also years of extreme ups and downs for Fox. In power in 1783, out of power in 1784, in opposition to the king all the time, not always actively, Fox and his friends – a talented group including Edmund Burke, and a fashionable group including the Prince of Wales, who had his own filial grounds of opposition to George III – were highly visible in a scene that made the most of London as a city of appetite. Sex, gambling and drinking were constant diversions. Profligacy and bawdiness were just normal. They were also politicised by being the diversions preferred by the Opposition, in contrast to Pitt's restraint and the king's uxoriousness. Vic Gattrell has described this world as one of hectic social ferment, spectacular sexual liberation, outrageous behaviour, ribaldry and iconoclasm: 'In the sexual or sporting *demi-monde* high and low met promiscuously. And both found the comedies of booze, sex and body funny.'[26] We talk of heavy drinking; eighteenth-century idiom referred to deep gambling. It may be that the gesture to measure which Fox and his friends regularly pushed beyond extremes found a counterpart in balloons, in which voluminous capacity was integral to function. Balloon launches became another party political scene and another location for partying in ways that confirmed the Fox circle as leaders of fashion – their consolation for not being leaders of the country.

There is a chronological track by which to follow anti-Fox balloon satires – of which there were many – from the East India Bill, the fall of the Coalition and the general election to the West-minster Scrutiny and after. That period, from late 1783 to late 1784, is also when balloon madness got going, and it can be hard to distinguish which is the primary satirical object – balloons or Foxite politics. *Two New Sliders for the State Magic Lanthern*, a 1783 print by Thomas Rowlandson, has ten compartments. The sixth, 'Political Montgolfier', shows a balloon with the head of a fox poking up at its top. The seventh shows a fox falling from a balloon into a pit. Fox's ascendancy is ended by Pitt. The balloon is relatively neutral. In the 1784 print *English Credulity or the Chevelere Morret [sic] taking a French Leave*, Fox is associated with a failed ascent by a Frenchman [see Figure 10]. The balloon explodes out of a temple of folly; Lord North blows air towards it and Fox next to him says: 'My Dear Chevelere thou art a man after mine own heart.'[27] The scene is full of references to frauds around both Fox and the balloon.

In early December 1783 Fox put forward the East India Bill, a set of proposals to reform the East India Company which ran British affairs in India. Fox's Bill proposed the separation of political rule from trade, to restrict the enormous self-enrichment by Company employees. 'Corruption' was rife in eighteenth-century politics: few people had the probity of Lord Chesterfield who defined corruption as taking a sixpence more than your salary. But although complaints about corruption were widespread, it was so much part of the polit-ical texture of eighteenth-century Britain that efforts to uproot it rarely made headway. Any sense that Fox was motivated by idealism was damaged by his suggestions for new Commissioners to govern India: all seven were his political allies. *The Political Balloon, or the Fall of East India Stock*, published on 4 December 1783, was part of a raft of outraged jokes about Fox's East India Bill.[28] It was not as inventively comic as satires that used elephants to depict the vastness of ambition, greed and power at stake, and the imagery turns on old analogies between swelling riches and bubbles going back to the disastrous speculation of the South Sea Bubble in the 1720s. But it was creative in connecting the novelty of balloons to old metaphors of political fortunes rising and falling. Balloons were

risky things, on the rise and curiously blank. In their early days
described as 'air-globes', they were easily changed into an emblem
of the world. Global interests like those of the East India Company
sat comfortably on a balloon. So too did the worldly understanding
of Fox, now in partnership with his erstwhile opponent Lord North
and busily arguing for all sorts of things he had once denounced. In
the print, three former directors fall from a balloon, coins tumbling
from their pockets. The balloon's surface is a map of India, with
'Gold Mines' and 'Madras' marked on it. Fox exclaims: 'Thanks to
my Auspicious Stars, for now I see, the Gold & Silver mines before
me; 'tis this I am Soaring for.' Hostility to the East India Bill also
came from those who saw it as an attack on chartered rights. The
Company petitioned against it on 24 November; the City of London
on 25 November. The Bill passed through the House of Commons,
turbulently, but had to get through the House of Lords to become law.
George III sent Lord Thurlow, the Lord Chancellor, a note which
said that anyone who voted for the Bill would be showing enmity to
the king. This none-too-subtle tactic of intimidation had the desired
result: on 17 December, the House of Lords rejected the Bill. The
next day, George III had the satisfaction of dismissing Lord North
and Fox and calling in a new ministry headed by William Pitt. Fox's
fortunes were indeed as deflated as a balloon.

After Fox's dismissal, a print appeared on 23 December 1783
which moved balloons onto different satirical terrain. In *The Aerostatick Stage Balloon* [Plate V] a fully-inflated balloon about to ascend
supports three tiers of people.[29] Who were they and why were they
brought together? At the top are three scandalous ladies: Grace
Elliot, Mary Robinson and Lady Worsley. In the centre gallery,
sitting on the left is the Duke of Portland, who had headed the Coalition as titular Prime Minister, though led by Fox and North who
here hold strings attached to the duke's nose. Next are North, Fox
and Burke, dressed as a Jesuit and looking at the Pope, who balances
the Devil on the extreme left who surveys the ex-ministers with
satisfaction. The lowest gallery has an array of well-known public
characters: Vestina, who advertised the celestial bed of Dr Graham,
who sits next to her; Jeffery Dunstan, mayor of Garrat, holding his
sack of old wigs; Sam House, with a foaming tankard of beer; and
Katterfelto, the mysterious magician with his black cat. The balloon
is tethered to a platform with a tub inscribed 'Vanity', which bubbles
with soapsuds of Froth. A capering Frenchman flourishing a knife
exclaims 'O Begar dis be von fine Cargo.' Against a backdrop of St

Paul's and the Monument, and below a crescent moon, the balloon symbolises an inflation of metropolitan fashion into what we would call celebrity. M. Dorothy George reads the print straightforwardly as a satire of the Coalition or of politicians through their association with mountebanks and women of damaged reputation. But one could read the print alternatively as a satire on the overlap between sex, fashion and self-publicising, to which the perfectly inflated balloon gives visual fullness.

Looking more closely at this print helps unpack the satirical short-hand in ways that reposition the balloon. The political class occupy the middle gallery but a reader's gaze does not centre on them, nor indeed on any of the tiers; it slides between levels. Below the coalition are equal-sized figures, just as important. Jeffery Dunstan was a seller of second-hand wigs in the West End: he was 'mayor of Garrat' thanks to a ceremony held after every general election, in which the head of an association of inhabitants around Garrat Common in Surrey was elected to represent them. This was a public joke, in that the most eccentric characters were chosen at a mock election attended by very large crowds – fifty thousand in 1781, according to *The Gentleman's Magazine*.[30] Sam House ran a pub in Wardour Street near Covent Garden, 'The Intrepid Fox', so called because of his enthusiastic support for Fox in the 1784 election.[31] So Dunstan and House are not mountebanks but mock-politicians. Katterfelto, who appeared in Chapter 4 on crowds, was a Prussian conjuror who occupied a shady territory between science and magic. It was said he had a balloon – a night balloon, of course – which was demonstrated to George III, and that he would be made a Fellow of the Royal Society. He was not: he managed a living by exhibitions, shows and lectures. Both he and James Graham were consummate self-publicists and masters of flamboyant advertising: both had serious ideas which they inflated for commercial gain.[32] So the 'mountebank' tier is rather a group of populist entertainers who were also in various degrees friendly with Fox or associated with him by others as smooth-tongued deviants. 'It is reported that *Dr. Katterfelto* has sent Proposals to the *Coalition* for a Junction of his wonderful and wonderful and wonderful, and most wonderful Abilities, as he apprehends that his *Quackship*'s Presence is necessary to contrive how to poison and destroy *Britannia*.'[33] Graham and Katterfelto are purveyors of wonders, slippery characters but decidedly assured rhetoricians. One rumour reported that Katterfelto and Walker (he of the Eidouranion) were each claiming they had invented balloons; it added satirically:

Dr Graham means to put in his Claim, as a last Stake; and when he has poured out his whole Soul in a farewel Blessing on the empty benches of the Temple of Hymen, to convey himself in a balloon of sufficient Power to pass over Spunging-Houses and prisons, and to deposit all his admirable Talents in the bosom of his native Country.[34]

To dismiss these figures as 'mountebanks' or 'charlatans' slides over how they are explicitly linked to Fox and to balloons, with their own dubious 'promises of wonders'.

The women are, as Dorothy George puts it, 'notorious at that time for their amours'. As with the lower-tier figures, that's not quite the whole story. Grace Dalrymple Elliot had an exceptionally hectic sex life even by late eighteenth-century standards. Married to a Scottish doctor, she had affairs and a very public divorce in 1776. In 1782 she gave birth to a daughter, whom she called Georgina Augustina Frederica; speculation abounded as to which of her eminent lovers was the father, though the mother's choice of names pointed heavily to the Prince of Wales, one of four main contenders for her favours at the time. In 1784 she began an affair with the Duc d'Orléans, a balloon aficionado, whom she followed to Paris where she witnessed the Revolution and where her royalist views placed her in danger – she shared a cell with Madame du Barry and was nearly executed for possessing a letter from none other than Fox. In 1783, Dally the Tall, as she was known, was still captivating English society. Mary Robinson, in Chapter 5 as a trend-setter in dress, had caught the eye of the Prince of Wales whilst playing Perdita on stage; after being shed as his mistress, she had many other lovers.

Lady Worsley was more upper class than the other two. As Seymour Dorothy Fleming, she married Sir Richard Worsley in 1775, bringing him £70,000. He was a lover of art who later put together a fine collection of antiquities at his home on the Isle of Wight, where he was governor and MP for Newport. She was a lover of men: thirty-four of them, claimed Horace Walpole.[35] Worsley lost all his offices when Lord North was dismissed, but he was known to the public mostly through his broad-minded attitude to his wife's affairs, a tolerance that apparently expired in 1782 when she refused to come home and he sued one of her lovers for damages. He lost. On the grounds that he had abetted her infidelities and colluded through voyeurism, a jury threw out his claim for £20,000 damages and awarded him one shilling. An account of the trial ran to seven editions. It was full of lurid details. In 1782 nearly a dozen prints circulated salacious illustration.[36] Also in print in 1782 were two poems, neither of them written by the protagonists, in which wife accused husband of impotence and indifference, and husband accused wife of sexual insatiability, so much so that even gods would need help to satisfy her, perhaps in the form of one of Dr Graham's electrical beds.[37] The poem in Lady Worsley's name also shares imagery with *The Aerostatick Stage Balloon*. She defends her sexuality simply as free: 'Free and as common as the air we rove,/ And deal to all who ask, a share of love'.[38] Unashamed, assertive, demanding pleasure, these libidinous women joined libertine men in pursuing their appetites. Balloons helped symbolise their uncontrolled desires. 'I hate the mean, the paltry, grovelling soul/ That yields obedience, and can bear controul,' says Lady Worsley's persona. It sounded much nobler than the Attorney-General's summing-up at her lover's trial: 'This Woman, for three or four years, has been prostituted with a variety of people; that is extremely clear.'[39]

A poem beneath the image glosses the reach of the aerostatick stage. It turns to that well-established satirical ground, the moon, where fantasies can be realised:

Who choose a journey to the Moon
May take it in our Stage Balloon.
Where love sick Virgins past their prime
May Marry yet and laugh at time,
Perdita W—sley Fillies free,
Each flash their Lunar Vis a Vis,
There N—th may realize his Dreams,
And F—x pursue his golden schemes
And Father B—ke may still absolve 'em
Howe'er the Devil may involve them;
The Pope may plan his Machinations
With Panders Quacks & Polititions.
Sam House enjoy his Tankard there
And Old Wigs still be Garrats May'r
Great Katerdevil work his Wonders
Spruce Gr—ham launch Electric thunders
Vestina too – nor fear a fall
Sr [sic] Satans Net shall catch ye all
So said Monseiur [sic] in broken Brogue
And up they mounted W—e and R—e.

The characters have equal weight: *The Aerostatick Stage Balloon* is more than a satire on politicians. The print's title points to a balloon supporting a theatrically-arranged gallery of figures associated with sex, politics, fashion and rhetoric. London is behind them but they can reach the rest of Britain – hence the balloon's departure from the Swan with Two Necks at Lad Lane, a major coaching inn. The politics are notably Foxite. The balloon is not a backdrop: it is a platform for a world of fast and loose. This sublunary world is full of issues about class whose distinctions the balloon represents skimpily – high-class scandal on top, popular culture puffs below – because Whore and Rogue figure at all levels. They come together through the balloon's conflation of schemes, appetite and power.

Satirists used grosser euphemisms too, as in a print *British Balloon, or the D[evonshire] Aerial Yacht* (1784). This has a balloon of Fox and North's faces with asses' ears, from which hangs a car in which sit the Duchess of Devonshire and the Prince of Wales. He says 'It rises majestically'; she answers 'Yes, I feel it.' Below are various spectators, including the cuckolded Lord Derby and Miss Farren, who says to him: 'Aye, my dear Lord, when shall we take a flight from our Platonic Box and Jog together in the Milky-way.' For the 'high Fliers of Fashion', in the print's phrase, sex, politics and fashion came together in balloons.[40] Libido and balloons were linked by numerous innuendoes about rising parts [Figure 13]. A comparison to condoms is hinted at by this prediction:

> The world of love and gallantry owes unspeakable obligations to the first discovery of air balloons. As they will very soon be so constructed as to carry in the pockets, and use upon sudden occasions, no sooner will a *tender couple* in the *Park*, or *Kensington Gardens*, &c. find themselves in danger of being over-looked than they pull out their balloons, fill them, and *away!*[41]

Sexual licence led to fun at science's expense: 'a young man and woman, very ardent lovers, are to be sent up into the atmosphere, in order to try what sort of celestial beings may be engendered, in the first heavens, by mortal embrace.'[42] Women keen to fly understood the power of sex: a lady of reputation and fortune apparently made an offer of marriage to Harper, the Birmingham balloonist, provided he took her up in a balloon.[43] Whether or not this anecdote is true doesn't matter: a balloon was an erotic attraction and a new location for sex. And women were up for it.

> We hear there is to be a grand Sweepstake Match to be sailed for over *Maidenhead Thicket*, between Lady C—n, Lady G—r, Miss R—n, Miss E—t, and Mrs A—d, in their respective balloons, but the odds are greatly in favour of Lady C—n, she having been accustomed to soar above the clouds long before the invention of Balloons.[44]

Risqué jokes, here possibly starring Lady Craven, made fast and louche links between aristocratic women and sexual freedom. Lady Elizabeth Craven, writer and traveller, was famous as an auburn-haired beauty. Abandoned by her husband in 1783, she was said to have had many affairs. Lady Bristol warned her daughter against seeing her in Paris in 1783: 'She is quite undone, and has not an atom of character left.'[45] Like the other women named, she partied in Whig circles.

In all the conflation of politics with scandal, representation itself became a contested area. People learned how to read prints – in Cobbett's phrase of 1808, caricatures are simply 'figures of rhetoric proceeding from the pencil'.[46] That rhetoric, visual and verbal, evolved rapidly and inventively. Newspapers helped readers keep up. In January 1785 one reported: '*Twaddle*, as we have informed our readers, is the successor of *Bore*.' Politics was its arena: 'for the perfection of *twaddle*, we have only to look to the Westminster Scrutiny'.[47] The Westminster election of 1784 was so close that an official scrutiny was set up. It went on for months, costing £25 a day and £5,000 in total, it was said. It took half a day to go through the evidence for one vote; Fox meanwhile treated his supporters, referred to as independent electors, to slap-up dinners with wine.[48] He was eventually confirmed as elected. Balloon satire fed into this tension: Elizabeth Inchbald's play *The Mogul Tale*, first performed on 6 July 1784, joked about political language; the Mogul's admonitions about India got a hearty laugh.[49] Electioneering pressurised language but not everyone blamed politicians alone: 'the populace greedily imbibe any hasty opinion, and *bang* about the words *oppressive, cruel, unjust, impolitic*, with as much confidence as if experience had taught them the meaning of the words'.[50] Cynicism about language was spread by satire, using irony that was occasionally satirically explained. An amusing dictionary for 1785 included these definitions: *Matrimony* – that which precedes a divorce; *Popularity* – the huzzas of chimney-sweepers and pick-pockets; *Irishman* – a great favourite with the ladies; *Scotchman* – any person without breeches; *Englishman* – that which occasions an ague in the mind of a Frenchman; *Liberty* – a watchword for calling people together; *Money* – a substitute for every good quality; *Bon Ton* – anything perfectly ridiculous.[51] Satirical codes were at work in topical language: satire reflected it back in irony, innuendo and abuse, and increased attention to what people said.

When Chevalier Moret attempted to launch a large balloon in the shape of a temple from the Star and Garter in Chelsea in August

1784, foremost among a crowd said to be thirty thousand strong
were Lord North, Fox and others of the coalition. Newspapers took
a detailed interest in their attendance. Fox was with his mistress
(later his wife) Mrs Armistead, with whom he chatted in French. She
was modestly dressed 'but with a number of younger nymphs more
gaudily dressed in her train'. The correspondent who supplied the
public with such detail was suspicious of these 'demireps' and the air
of liberties, both social and sexual: 'The whole company in Chelsea
Gardens were free with one another. The occasion, the scene, and the
mob, levelled all distinctions of rank.'[52] On 21 August, more details
of the 'heavy—a[rse]d balloon': 'I know not how it happened, but
every body who could, chattered in French. Lord North, the greatest
wit, undoubtedly, of this country, on the failure of the experiment,
said "Voila la philosophie en bas".'[53] An adjacent item reports the
Prince of Wales constantly attended by French nobility and friendly
with the Duc de Chartres (balloonophile and Anglophile).

Here in this report are all the key ingredients of the Whig top
circle: sex, politics, fashion – and balloons. There's cleverness too,
at ease with French and philosophy. It was suspiciously unpatriotic
to lesser talents. Although the scene was local to Chelsea Gardens
it was being read as far afield as Scotland: metropolitan *ton*, set by
Whigs, accompanied balloons on paper around the country. Moret's
balloon was hugely unwieldy: with a circumference of a hundred
feet, it was 'so strong and so substantial it would have required the
force of gunpowder to elevate it'.[54] It completely failed to ascend
and Moret fled. Comparisons were made with the fallen Coalition:
'Whether the evil star which has lately influenced that political body
attended them to the garden of Mr. Moret, or the undertaking was
too great for a single man, is a question we will not decide upon.'[55]

Fashionable opposition frequently included the heir to the throne.
Balloons were one of the few interests that George III and the Prince
of Wales shared. It would be easy to say the father was interested
in the science and the son in the spectacle, but that would be to
miss political implications. The prince saw balloons up close and was
seen to view them in the company of Foxite Whigs. Where father
followed aeronauts by telescope, the son braved atrocious weather
in person. For Lunardi's great launch the prince hurried back from
Brighton, heading the rush from watering places. Whilst watching
the filling process, one of his companions told him the balloon was
likely to burst and blow them all up. The prince responded with
sang-froid that his companion had better get out of the way. He was

at the great party in the Pantheon where Lunardi's balloon was on show, and sent him handsome presents, including a gold repeater watch. (The king gave Lunardi a hundred guineas.)[56]

To some extent balloon launches were just another fashionable public diversion, even an extreme sport like the boxing matches, rowing contests and high-stakes races which the prince and his entourage attended enthusiastically in between extravagant fêtes and all-night parties. Horse-racing was a kind of flying: the unbeaten Highflyer, said to be the best horse in England, sired Rockingham, for whom the prince paid £2,000,[57] and other winners including horses engagingly named Miss Blanchard and Balloon. In 1784 George Frederick was associating very closely with Fox and the Whig opposition; they were party animals and Party animals. 'Spectacle' is too broad a term here, for what was on show contained oppositional politics. Balloons acquired specifically Whig colouring – literally so in the case of the doomed fire balloon set up in Lord Foley's garden in September 1784. Front seats cost 1/6, second tier seats a shilling, back seats sixpence – but anyone wearing blue and buff, the Whig colours, paid nothing.[58] Georgiana, Duchess of Devonshire, played an important role in this colouring. Among her many skills was an understanding of how to use public show to advance Whig interests, intertwining balloons with politics and fashion. How close they were can be seen from a note concerning a chalk sketch of her made by John Downman in 1784.[59] It describes the drawing scene at Devonshire House: the Prince of Wales is there, as are Lady Duncannon and Lady Elizabeth Forster; a French prelate arrives and goes, then Blanchard arrives, having just descended from his balloon. Royalty, the *beau monde* and an aeronaut are all in the same room and not standing on ceremony.

Georgiana flouted convention by turning out to support her friend Fox in the highly contested election for Westminster in 1784, where she kissed tradesmen in return for the pledge of their votes for Fox. Satirical prints of the day professed shock at this new *infra dig* campaigning, a shock in proportion to its effectiveness. A print by Thomas Rowlandson, *Madam Blubber's Last Shift, or The Aerostatic Dilly* (published on 29 April 1784) turned women's campaigning into a balloon joke. Albinia Hobart was canvassing for Wray and Hood. Rowlandson, using sketches by George Viscount Townshend, makes her lower body into a balloon (she was fat) bringing voters to the Covent Garden hustings. The engraving follows up a handbill published the day before, signed 'Katterfelto Junior', which promised that a distinguished lady would descend as an air balloon, having found a novel way to transport outlying voters. The text explains that she has sewn up her petticoats, filled them with gas and thanks to 'secret influence' (a form of corruption, in which the king is too close to ministers), she wafts to the election scene. A song below the image pits her comically against the Duchess of Devonshire, who successfully courts Westminster voters in the city. 'Mrs H——t has not ballooned a single vote to the Hustings since she was Caricatured,' it was reported.[60]

The association between balloons and Foxite Whigs was channelled through the Duchess of Devonshire in person. A grand masquerade at the Pantheon included a bookseller from Piccadilly who wore an enormous balloon hat hung with fox tails, a dig at the Duchess of Devonshire.[61] More subtly, it mocks a Whig taste for fashion that included balloons which Georgiana personally encouraged. She had Lunardi to dine, and turned Blanchard's ascent from the Rhedarium into a Whig party for which she bought a hundred tickets in advance. She and her female friends turned up dressed in blue and buff ribbons; she held one of the tethering cords and let off the small directional balloon. The Prince of Wales expressed the highest satisfaction, it was said, and she was suitably gratified.[62] Blanchard dipped back to earth to accept a pair of her colours and took letters for her to French nobility.[63] A balloon launch in front of her house in Bath spread the *ton* beyond London.

Satirists had to exercise some caution in representing politicians as criminals – there was libel and patronage to consider. Topical medleys laced with fantasy were suitably and safely unflattering. 'Balloon Intelligence Extraordinaire' in November 1784 masked satire in mock-myth:

A PACK of hungry Indian Hounds will soon set off from Brooke's in Balloons, on the Chase of wild Geese, whose Feathers they wish to pluck, under the Direction of those keen and sharp-set Sportsmen, the celebrated C. F. and E. B. [Fox and Burke] who loves a sublime and beautiful Prospect of distant Regions, particularly the Diamond Mines of Golconda. It is supposed that they will catch Plenty of Geese in the Fens of Westminster, having already given Specimens of their Skill in that Art in Devonshire, the now deserted Island of Portland, &c. though they failed, and by soaring too high over the Bay of Bengal, had the Fate of Icarus in their Chase of the Harpies of India, who are said to divert their Pursuers from overtaking them by the contrivance and golden Balls of Hippomanes.[64]

Foxite writers went the other way from myth, inflating banality to discredit Pitt:

> The Friends of the Coalition are indefatigable ... they pry into his very Amusements, to find Something to torture into a Crime; but what an exalted Opinion must be entertained of a Man, whose Enemies are obliged, for Want of other Matter of Abuse, to make his going to Brighthelmstone, his walking in the Fields, or his talking to Mr. Steele, a capital Crime. Then his going to see the Balloon launched in the Artillery-Ground was boyish in a Prime Minister, and a Sin never to be forgiven.[65]

That Fox and his friends had avidly attended the same launch was of course beyond satire.

Not everyone was party-pris. Fox asked one of his fellow gamblers at Brooke's what he thought of current credit policies. The reply was evenly witty – neither Pitt nor Fox were good financiers: 'He never had any debts, and you never pay any.'[66] When Pitt took power, he began to tackle the country's enormous national debt, a sum so large that if laid out in shillings it would allegedly circle the world three and a half times.[67] He introduced new taxes, the profit from which was to go to a sinking fund whose interest would eventually pay off the debt. Two new taxes were especially contentious. A tax on windows had existed since 1696, as a form of property tax. Taxes on tea accounted for 85 per cent of its price by 1784, which encouraged smugglers. Blending discretion with bravura, smugglers were spotted at tea auctions listening attentively to the rates at which tea prices were set so they could undercut them; they were recognised by their tans, their kerchiefs and their shifty gaze.

Pitt proposed to raise the window tax and cut tax on tea, his argument being that what people saved on tea would offset what they paid on windows. There were many objections to this logic, in a context of general grumbling about tax and opposition to specific taxes. 'We have reason to believe that the Taxes are working extremely to the discredit of Administration throughout the Country. The Window *Tax* is certainly becoming every Day more odious for People find their *Tax* worse or dearer than before.'[68] That same month, one of the London debating societies considered 'Would not a Tax upon Batchelors be a just and beneficial measure?'[69] They were only half joking; there was a tax on bachelors who kept servants. Although the Opposition took advantage of unpopular taxation – which had after all caused the American war – to discomfit Pitt, they were careful to keep in step with public criticism. It had a violent edge.

On 24 June, a crowd enraged by new taxes on shops pursued Pitt and his secretary. Pitt had to dash like lightning into the House of Commons; Dr Prettyman had to hide in a nearby house. It was not just aeronauts that angry mobs pursued.

New taxes were applied to horses, servants, printed linens, hackney coaches, hats, ribbons, receipts, bricks, tiles and paper. The poet William Cowper wrote vehemently on 3 July 1784 against Pitt's new tax on candles as hurting the poor:

> I wish he would remember that the halfpenny which government imposes, the shop keeper will swell to twopence. I wish he could visit the miserable huts of our lace makers at Olney, and see them working in the Winter months by the light of a farthing candle from four in the afternoon till midnight. I wish he had laid his tax upon the ten thousand lamps that illuminate the Pantheon, upon the flambeaux that wait upon ten thousand chariots and Sedans in an Evening, and upon the Wax-candles that give light to ten thousand card tables. I wish in short that he would consider the pockets of the poor as sacred, and that to tax a people already so necessitous, is but to discourage the little industry that is left among us, by driving the laborious to despair.[70]

The increase in window tax led householders to brick up windows rather than pay: it was said that four or five out of every dozen windows were blocked accordingly.[71] Light was a sensitive subject. 'Why tax the *light*, and leave untax'd the wind?'[72] Satirists turned to balloons in two ways: first, as a means of escaping a world where everything was taxed; second, as a novelty that like everything else would attract taxes. A suggested tax on water was ludicrously extended to air: 'Balloons also to pay a certain sum for the wind that guides them.'[73] Were balloons to become a viable form of transport, they could sail over the new turnpike roads, avoiding their fees. Ironists proposed these light vehicles should attract heavy taxes. Thus one periodical invented a sliding scale of tax:

	l.	s.
An air balloon going to Gretna Green with a couple of fond lovers	5	5
Ditto for carrying more than two voters for a rotten borough	10	10
Ditto going to Constantinople with female recruits for the Seraglio	21	
Ditto going over land with dispatches to the East Indies, while the new Bill is pending	100	

Ditto going to Paris with milliners, friseurs, and mantua-makers, under
pretence of studying fashions; but, in fact, to smuggle foreign trumpery   500
Ditto going to Ireland to export bulls, lame ducks from the Alley, and
import bulls from the Isle of Saints {alias one and twenty thirteeners}   1   1
Ditto going upon a trip to the moon, as the passengers must certainly be lunatic – all their fortunes, which we will suppose at   100,000
Ditto going to the devil, to discover his Plutonic majesty's dominions, as they must be in d—n'd good luck if they find them out   500.[74]

Politicians were also in the news as victims of crime. The Great Seal was stolen from Lord Thurlow's house on 24 March 1784.[75] The audacity of the theft put pro-Pitt satirists in mind of Fox. A letter from Faustus, sent by air balloon to a printer (cueing jokes about printer's devils) ran the theft, the election and the Opposition together:

> I have now before me letters from every Individual of the notorious Majority, imploring me to send one or two of my Imps, in the shape of electioneering Parsons, among their Constituents, in Order to persuade them, over a Bowl of Punch, that the Coalition Ministry were all honourable Men; that the present Administration is composed of Debauchees, Sharpers, Fools, and Pickpockets; and that Lord North, and his Colleague, Charles, spend most of their Time in singing Psalms, and reading the Pilgrim's Progress. Last Night's Post brought me an humble Petition from the Triumvirate which planned and caused to be executed a late Burglary of an alarming Nature; declaring, upon their Honour, that nothing more was intended than a Piece of Fun; that they meant only to sweat the Chancellor, and confound the *var-tuous* Ministry...[76]

Faustus says he will tell Fox and his friends to go hang themselves, and he plans to head off to Norwich, another contested constituency. Balloons are a topical device; the devilish speed of news and gossip borrows their power to circulate. The core of the piece turns on a Swiftian sense of a lie – the thing that is not, as the Houyhnhnms put it in *Gulliver's Travels*. In politics, things are presented as the opposite of what they are. Balloons had antithesis – wonderful invention, fraudulent flop – and their association with wind transferred easily to the empty promises and misleading tactics of politicians. Delicacy was not required in attacking Fox: *A New Way to Secure a Majority, or No Dirty Work Comes Amiss* shows Fox kissing the bare arses of shoemakers, tailors and barbers.[77] Balloons offered slightly more elevated imagery.

Here satire picked up old technologies of flight – the devil flies about a bit – and made links between broomsticks and balloons. Political intrigue was easily compared to black magic, though applications were more strategic than consistent. In one satire, for instance, a flying sorceress called Martha Mandrake is first anti-Fox then anti-Pitt.[78] In Elizabeth Inchbald's popular 1784 farce *The Mogul Tale*, three characters arrive in Constantinople in an inflammable air balloon: the Doctor; Johnny, a cobbler from Wapping; and Fanny, his wife. Johnny repeatedly invokes the devil: 'the devil take all balloons I say ... where the devil are we? ... it is devilish hot'. In classic farce fashion, he is inveigled into saying he is the Pope, taken to the seraglio and made very drunk, leading to more diabolical puns; he and Fanny extricate themselves and the Mogul magnanimously lets all three depart. Johnny's talk of the devil runs from colloquial oaths – 'what the devil!'– to the devil as a revelatory power: 'the devil a Pope am I'.[79] Against a balloon backdrop, even comic devilry is slippery.

One might read the liveliness of witchcraft imagery as a sign that the eighteenth century had shed actual belief in it. Or one might read it as a continuation of folk beliefs that had not entirely died out, even after the Witch Act of 1753, but which a confident metropolitan caste could use for symbolism.[80] Read one way, the aeronaut in balloon is rational man versus benighted witch or devil on broomstick. Read another way, the balloon is ambiguous: who has the greater power, aeronaut or witch? Whatever the science behind it, balloon flight was a kind of magic. A satirical print of 1783, *The new Mail carriers, or Montgolfier and Katterfelto taking an airing in Balloons*,[81] has the principals address each other amiably from twin balloons with a devil holding a broom in the space between them, gesturing slightly to Montgolfier [Figure 14]. 'Monsier [*sic*] Montgolfier let us be reconciled', says Katterfelto, and Montgolfier seems to agree: 'Let us fly up to de sun, Mr. Katterfelto.' Atop the magician-scientist's balloon, a black cat plays with white kittens; atop the inventor-aeronaut's balloon, an ape plays a fiddle. It may be significant that the ground-level scene positions a church steeple underneath Montgolfier, and that the last-to-read spectator speech

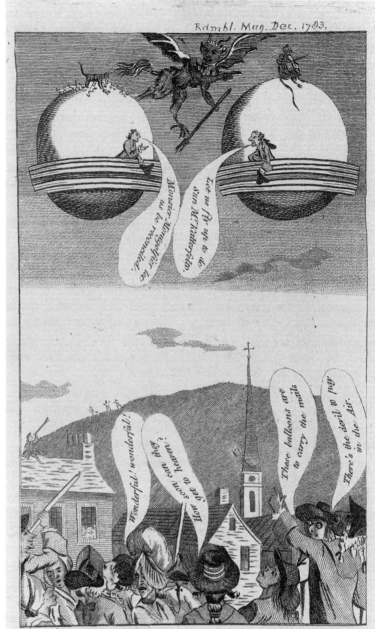

The new Mail carriers, or Montgolfier and Katterfelto taking an airing in Balloons.

14. Magic, science and religion: Montgolfier and Katterfelto meet aloft. Satirical etching from *The Rambler's Magazine*, December 1783.

balloon says 'There's the devil to pay in the Air.' The steeple is notice-
ably needle-like, as if it might puncture Montgolfier's balloon above.
The composition balances shady and enlightened even-handedly.

Dark arts brought politics and balloons together. Fox's devious
brilliance attracted more satire because his Whig circle liked
balloons: as toy, as adventure, as an invention with potential, as
emblem of crash and re-ascendancy. Like hustings, the aerostatic
stage was an acting-out place. Some applied this not just to Fox but
to all politics of the day:

> *On the late effects of Mr. Harper's Balloon, addressed to the Premier, Mr.*
>   *Fox, &c. &c. &c.*

> If it be true as learned Fellows
> Of Colleges, and such folk tell us,
> "Effects are equal to their cause,"
> How light is popular applause;
> Lighter than air, since smoke can raise
> A mob's displeasure, or its praise;
> Its praise, like smoke too, vanishes as soon,
> 'Tis all a bubble, or an Air-Balloon.[82]

The Tory and Whig addressees of the poem above show the political
significance of balloons; the author's persona, 'Ex Fumo Lux' (Light
from Smoke), hangs uncertainly in the air. Two hundred years after
this, historians were embracing a history of the hitherto unwritten
in a turn described as 'history from below'. Balloons provide a
history from above, as evanescent as smoke.

In thinking about images of air, Gaston Bachelard argues that
metaphors of height, elevation, depth, sinking and fall are more
natural and essential than any others:

> They engage us more than visual metaphors do – more than any
> striking image can. And yet language is not particularly well-suited
> to them. Language, conditioned by forms, is not readily capable of
> making the dynamic images of height picturesque. Nevertheless,
> these images have amazing power: they govern the dialectic of
> enthusiasm and anguish.[83]

The difficult visualisation which Bachelard identifies is made easier
by satirical prints; they provided a visual language for sky and flying
beings, often in partnership with speech bubbles. And that difficult
visualisation was also perhaps the very thing that made balloons
appealing to satirists: it gave graphic shape to rise-and-fall materials
of economic, sexual and political kinds, just as compelling as the

literal ups and downs of aeronauts. Deceptive language enveloped balloons – in puffs – and scandal, whether financial, political or sexual. It is difficult to visualise. We too struggle to find imagery. One might now say, smoke and mirrors. After 1783, one could say, an air-balloon.

Literature

'From Chloe's Hand, Launched forth in Fields of Air,
       Swift as the Bolt of Heaven I took my Flight,
            Child of the Wind, I flutter'd here and there
       Till Clouds obscur'd me from the Gazer's Sight.'

From a poem attached to the unmanned balloon launched by
Robert Kingscote in Gloucestershire on 15 September 1784.[1]

IN 1786 JANE CAVE PUBLISHED a volume of poems. Literally
provincial – she was from Brecon and the book was published in
Bristol – many of the poems feature air as an imaginative medium.
Balloons make an appearance:

We in these aether castles ride
With all the equipage of pride,
And in imagination rise,
Superior monarchs of the skies.[2]

The literature of balloons had a wide reach, encompassing many
amateurs and anonymous writers. This chapter explores some of
them.

Aerostation was incontestably a new science, yet the literature of
aerostation draws deeply on old genres in its fashioning of imaginative possibilities. A rare surviving handbill from a provincial press,
for instance, uses a fire balloon as a vehicle for a sermon.[3] In prose,
balloons had their own new genres, from the formal accounts of aerial
voyages (in English, using French narratives as starting points) to
the looser life-writing of aeronauts about experiences aloft.[4] These
accounts did empirical work and reflected upon imagination, especially through the sublime, but they were not leading influences on
imaginative responses to balloons. Among letter writers there was
a common fantasy of balloons shrinking distance between correspondents: 'If air balloons were as common as Hackney coaches and
as easily managed, you might call and spend an evening with me

once a week, and I could do the same with you, but 'til this new mode of travelling is more improved, we must be content to go on in the old way, and converse by paper.'[5] In different ways, different literary forms engaged with questions of distance raised by balloons.

The literature of balloons is extensive and my account of it is necessarily selective. One way to explore it is through genres, covering – appropriately – both high and low. In poetry, balloons appear in odes and acrostics and pretty much everything in between; they also run the gamut of seriousness, from attempts at epic to mock-epic and very light verse. Some of this verse is awful as poetry, but bad poetry has its charms and effort can teach us about what's being attempted. There was much occasional poetry (that is, written on or close to the occasion of flights); it circulated in print regardless of merit because it grappled imaginatively with novelty and signif-icance, and that mattered more than polish of metre and rhyme. Effort hit upon jokes, and bad jokes can be good fun.

Much of the comic verse about balloons is light in tone, as one expects in light verse, with an underlying play on the literal light-ness of mocked balloons:

> Allow me to mention the childish invention
>   Of the novel aerial balloon;
> When the people on earth, being tired of their birth
>   Had a longing to visit the moon.
> Some went round and round as they rose from the ground
> But alas! By some mistaken notion,
> No sooner *exalted*, they wish'd to be *salted*,
>   And tumbled headlong in the ocean.[6]

Doggerel's childishness suits a view of balloons as childish. The world-turned-upside-down, a trope for disorder popular in Jacobean satire, is here applied to the downside of balloons, their propensity to accident and uncontrollability. But these lines come in an ode, *The Discontented Man*, which takes a serious look at social order: 'No man on the earth, of high or low birth/ Is ever content with his station.' An extempore on Lunardi's ascent took up this theme of disturbance of placings:

> WITH Air Balloon,
> To see the Moon,
> Lunardi flew on high;
> The heavenly Orb
> Refus'd her face

And downwards bade him fly.
"Presumptuous man!
"How dar'st approach
"With art my power divine!
"Return to earth,
"Which gave thee birth,
"And I'll unclouded shine."
Learn hence to know
My friends below,
We'd better keep our station,
Than dare assume
With air or plume
To seek another nation.[7]

We still talk of social mobility as 'going up in the world'; making light of a weighty issue is one way to make it less fearful. Poets, like everyone else in the first flush of balloon madness, pondered the uncertain uses of balloons. They also considered use in relation to social strata and different types of people. Thus, *THE AIR BALLOON to the tune of Come haste to the Wedding &c.*, by one M. D. of Saffron Walden, which I give in full:

LAY down all your Coaches ye Beaux and fair Ladies
    A Way to the Regions above us is found;
In Air you may float, till you [reach] the Pleiades,
    Or vint en passant the Planets around.
CHORUS – Then deem it not madness
    When with Harts of gladness
We sit in a large *Air Balloon* at our ease
Come trace, through the vast airy Spaces
Our course over Mountains and Vallies
No Mode of Conveyance can surely be milder
    No Motion more easy than waiting in Air,
No cross Roads a Passenger here can bewilder
    No Highwayman damp his bold Spirit with care
No carriage beside but is under Taxation,
    Exepting our novel Machine the *Balloon*
Should that e'er be tax'd- from this land of Vexation
    We'll go to tam'd *Wilkin's* World in the Moon
To those who are Vers'd in chimerical Dealing,
    Redoubled Advantages hence will accrue;
Secure, at their leisure from Star to star fleeing.
    The Quixotes may safe their Wild Goose chace.
The Regions of Air to the learn'd Antiquary,

In abstruse Researches rich Fountains will prove,
To pick up old rubbish in some heavnl'y Quarry,
    Or find hidden coins in the Planet of Jove!
Astrologers fix'd in *Balloons* may unravel
    Perhaps, with more Skill, each celestial Knot;
With *Sol* in his course thro' the Zodiac travel,
    And weaken their Wine at the *Watering pie*!
The Debauchee cloy'd with terrestrial Beauty,
    May now visit *Venus*'s Nymphs in the Stars!
Drink Nectar with *Saturn*, to *Jove* pay his Duty,
    With *Mercury* Journey, or quarrel with *Mars*!
Machines of such service as this to Creation,
    Can never arrive at Perfection too soon;
And Science's Friends, with renew'd Animation,
    Will ever encourage the new *Air Balloon*.[8]

Stephen Fry suggests in *The Ode Less Travelled* that light verse assumes community between writer and reader.[9] *The Air Balloon* is quite typical of balloon verse in doing so – we'll go to the moon – but differentiates between groups – passengers, quixotes, antiquarians, astrologers, debauchees – who suggest differences within society that may not harmonise into a one-voiced 'we'. Jaunty rhythm and agile rhyme keep the form springy, but the words express the less jolly possibility that the air balloon could lead to familiar old rubbish. Utopian faith carried dystopian doubt.

The occasional verse which balloons inspired probably needs a typology (a book in itself). There were heroic and satiric poems about launches. Newspapers set epigram competitions on aerostatic themes; magazines and almanacs chose balloons for their enigmas or riddles, especially in 1784. On stage, balloons appeared in prologues and epilogues as signs of the time, a new form of madness, a mad form of novelty. Comedies – especially Frederick Pilon's *Aerostation* (1785), described as a farce – starred characters who were balloon-mad in thought and deed. They were met with great laughter and applause. There were jovial songs, new words for old tunes, fashionable airs; there were odes, like the *Ode to Dead Aeronauts* published after Rozier and Romain's terrifying crash. Verse gave form to the confusion of feelings around balloons, especially uncertainty about whether they would be good or bad and for whom. Balloons were one of many potent subjects for anxious wit – luxury, gender and nationality were others – and in the later eighteenth century versifiers made few inflated claims for their productions. Hack writers could occasionally

ride on Pegasus by writing occasional verse. It was sociable. Like
balloon launches it brought people together for the verse's occasion,
no more and no less. Light verse attracts few theorists; critics simply
agree that it offers levity and entertainment. That there were also
lengthy epics which gave gravity to balloon madness was an irony
acknowledged by writers. Their choice of persona for public letters,
fantasias, debates was often lyric, a compromise between gravity and
levity: An Aerial Wanderer, S. Skylight. Their choice of titles looked
backward with a topical spin: *The Ballooniad, Aerophorion, Airopaedia.*

Poetry was hospitable to flight because it indulged in flights of
fancy. 'Twas Melos' bard [i.e. Homer] first taught mankind to soar/
In fancy's maze, till France has taught us more', wrote a poet celebrating Richard Crosbie's ascent from Dublin in 1785.[10] Classical
myth pictured imagination as a winged horse, Pegasus, steed of
Apollo, the god of poetry. There were novelty balloons in the shape
of a horse in both France and England.[11] Several were described
as Pegasus. Though new technologies were speeding up life in the
1780s, dependence on horses was universal. The two came together
in William Cowper's poem *The Diverting History of John Gilpin*, a
comic ballad that was a runaway success in 1782. In the poem a
linen draper makes what should be a straightforward journey on
horseback to bring some wine to the celebrations of his wedding
anniversary. The horse has its own ideas and gallops through town
and country in a dash through comic incidents in which breathless-
ness drives inspiration. This fantasia of horse-powered speed anticipates balloon madness: all sorts of things in the poem are flying
– windows, gates, cloaks, horse and rider. So in 1783 imagination
took to air readily, both seriously and comically. 'Poets are the only
living Creatures, the Camelion excepted, that have any Interest, or
Real Property in Air. It is well known that they have built in that
Element; and, unpleasing Reflection! have often been condemned
to *feed* upon it.'[12] Poets were repeatedly identified with air and its
metaphysics, for instance in *The Selector*, an anonymous periodical
very probably written by a woman. No. 2 has a poet and Apollo
make a flight (by swan!) to visit Apollo's cave of learning. The poet's
'boundless soul/ Mounts to those climes, whose high-form'd clouds
condense/ The cumbrous particles of Thought and Sense'.[13] No. 3
went higher still, using a vocabulary shared with balloon accounts
and explicitly informed by them (the author recommends Faujas de
St Fond's *History of the Air-Balloon* in the first issue). Thought 'can
fly to regions which memory never knew, and explore worlds never

explor'd. It can mount on the swiftest gales, and leave every thing but itself behind.'[14]

The association between poetry and elevated thought was so strong that poets were figuratively airborne before balloons – thus James Thomson's *The Seasons* (complete set first published in 1730) attends closely to the heavens in weather, clouds, rain, winds and birds – 'My Theme ascending'('Spring', line 570). It features many sequences in which the perspective is one from above looking down, his Muse 'High-hovering o'er the broad cerulean scene' ('Autumn', line 877). So it was easy to send poetry aloft in balloons. One Scots poet wrote several poems supposing himself hovering over his neighbourhood or being visited by an aeronaut Muse with news:

> An' wha kens, Tam, some afternoon,
> When you an' your balloon's in tune,
> But ye may slip up to the moon,
>   (Braw coothie carle!)
> To hear an' see what's said an' doon
>   I' that white warld.
>
> If sae, as soon's ye tak' the air,
> (I mean when ye return frae there)
> Gif ye ha'e ony time to spare,
>   I beg ye'll light,
> An' into Ochiltree repair,
>   An' crack a night;
>
> An' tell me a' your lunar news.
> Clean daft ye'll may be think my muse,
> An' doth for too much freedom use,
>   Or's in a dream —[15]

It was also easy to send poetry up, in the sense of making that loftiness comic. A bird's-eye view could show more widespread folly. A long perspective was useful as old forms of wit combined with light verse. Thus an epigram by 'Crito', titled *Puff Pegasus*:

> Do not wonder balloons were found out in this age,
>   Now to *ride on the wind* of all mankind's the rage;
> On a puff, as on broomstick, your blockhead will rise,
>   Till he's *lost in the clouds* in attempting the skies.[16]

One feature of light verse is that it usually calls attention to its obedience to form, perhaps to offset its licence in subjects. Light free verse is rare. The limerick's obedience to recognisable rhythm and emphatic rhyme is an instance of how form carries meaning. In light verse, readers may assess with lighter judgement than usual the poetic components other than sustaining of rhythm or rhyme. An unusual poem from 1785 illustrates this in relation to line beginnings. Signed 'Colin', it was made up entirely of surnames taken from ladies and gentlemen present at a Lunardi launch in Edinburgh. Read downwards, the initial letters of the lines of its five stanzas spelled out Daring Master Vincent Lunardi:

> Livingston, Kennedy, Richardson, Wright,
> Urquhart, M'Ewan, M'Dowell, M'Kell
> Noble, Neil, Nimmo, Young, Donald, M'Fell,
> Angus, Kilpatrick, Wild, Lauchlan, M'Ghie,
> Ronaldson, Mucklejohn, Littlejohn, Lee,
> Dick, Dickie, Dickieson, Morrison, Craig,
> Irvine, Carnegy, Monro, Baillie, Haig.[17]

This is a glorious example of the community of light verse – literally! Acrostics give pleasure through vertical reading, a descending meaning which here also ingeniously reverses that ascent by the aeronaut which occasions the poem. With another nice irony, it offers the constituents the pleasure of seeing Lunardi come down which they missed in reality.

Literature explored philosophically how aeronauts represented those they left behind. Were they an advance guard of a new outlook? Did they take old verities aloft? Gods were immortals; heroes were, like everyone else, mortal. *The Air Balloon*, a poem by T. C. Mitcham published in 1787, started lightly enough:

> Oft fancy flies/ Up to the skies/ And mounts like air balloon:/ Thoughts void of weight/ evaporate/ And are dispersed soon. // A body fair/ of lighter air/ Flies through the atmosphere:/ Some years ago,/ Who could foreknow/ Such wonders would appear? // Had you told men/ 'Twould be so, then/ Your credit had been crost:/ But now 'tis known,/ That men have flown,/ The wonder is all lost. // Some think they rise/ To scale the skies/ As they sail in the air:/ Presumption great,/ At any rate,/ They loudly do declare. // So ships at first,/ No doubt, were curst,/ 'Twas look'd upon as vain,/ That men would wish/ To live like fish,/ And skim about the main. // They now for wings/ Make other things,/ Like birds, to mount the air:/ With pomp to greet,/ They mount in state,/ And make the people stare.

But the poem takes a light turn to the morbid:

> They have great need/ To take good heed,/ For sake of preserva-
> tion,/ Lest they too soon/ Should strike the moon,/ And split their
> navigation. // Those men who sail,/ They often hail/ A grave
> within the deep:/ When those on earth/ Do lose their breath/ The
> earth their bodies keep: // But those who fly/ Both may deny,/
> And leave them to the air:/ Can they contrive/ While they're alive/
> T'inter their bodies there. // Earth, air and sea/ May all agree/
> They shall have place in neither,/ Then they must steer/ Through
> atmosphere,/ And lodge dead bones in aether.[18]

Can you put bones in space? Where does elegy go? That aeronauts
risked death voluntarily made them foolish heroes to some, hubris
deserving nemesis. Accidents inspired grim prophecy. Writing
about the crash and burn in June 1785 of Rozier and Romain, one
author warned: 'Let the surviving adventurous tribe beware how
they play among the clouds; if they meet with a thundery cloud,
as probably these have done, it will do for them. Men may sport
with life as they please, but life when once lost or fooled away can
never be recalled.'[19] Fatal accident had a context. Newspapers were
full of lives cut short, violently, involuntarily, by murder, fire, war,
childbirth, poverty and disease. Why risk a fatal accident by balloon
when Death the leveller came to so many prematurely?

Uncertainty was steadied by allusive quotations as epigraphs. An
epigraph signals a frame for reading: in this one from the dependable Horace, '*Negata tentat iter vita*', Virtue, opening heaven to those
who do not deserve to die, makes her course by paths untried.[20]
The virtue of ancients had a conventional travel of emotions, which
writers had to make anew for balloons. Melancholy gives way to
uneasily godlike dispassion in a poem (c. 1788) titled *Air-Balloon*:

> In vain, since hapless Mortals try/ To shun th'unerring shafts of
> Death;/ Since all that creep, and all that fly,/ Must, soon or late,
> resign their breath: // Why should we fear t'improve the day?/ The
> fleeting day from Darkness given! – / And, where bright science
> points the way/ To range the land, the sea, the heaven! // Then
> freely mount th'expanse above,/ Fond man! Nor dread the ebon
> rod;/ On wings of wind sublimely rove,/ A great, a momentary
> God! // Behold he mounts! And deems it fable/ By gloomy Jews
> contrived of old,/ That those who rais'd the Tower of Babel/ Were
> by the Almighty's hand controul'd. // No more the Eternal rules
> in ire –/ His wondrous love is round display'd!/ He smiles to see
> weak man aspire –/ Pleas'd with the worm his breath has made! //
> And those who cleav'st the azure sky,/ Like him, with pity, shall look
> down!/ Shall view, like him, with equal eye,/ The Shepherd's Crooks,

the Monarch's Crown! // Then, plac'd above the storm's career,/ Shalt hear wild warfare rage below –/ And learn to drop the manly tear,/ To see the blood of thousands flow! // "Poor Human Race!" – I hear thee cry,/ When sailing 'twixt the earth and moon;/ "Is all this bustle but to die?/ "Ah! What is life – an Air-Balloon!"[21]

This poem mixes registers of serious and light to make balloons a symbol of vanitas. Contrast between ephemerality and eternity was also managed through the language of gods and heroes; in poems, heroes entering godly space were advised not to leave it but to avoid overstepping bounds understood to be questionable. Hence the poet puts key concerns as questions. Why should we fear progress? Is aerostation's triumph just another vanity? In both these poems, a melancholy note shows writers mourning a changing world order.

Light verse helped lighten philosophical burdens. Cheerful rhythm, steady metre and strong rhyme provided predictability of form that stood in for ideological order and withstood the disorder aroused by balloons. Similar compensatory work is done by allusion. Eighteenth-century writers used earlier literature with great confidence, adapting it to suit the present in mock forms. Confident play can air anxieties. Allusion often borrows the stability of older literature, here to counterbalance the newness of balloons. If you filtered novelty through the familiar, you could also defamiliarise it, thus acknowledging the startling and strange effects of balloons. Since balloons were so readily heroic and comic, mock epic was an obvious place to head to. English readers had great fondness for Cervantes, increased in the late eighteenth century by a growing interest in eccentricity as a character type. *The Life and Adventures of Sir Launcelot Greaves* (1760) by Tobias Smollett was a full-scale application of Quixote to British politics. The old idealist baffled by contemporary behaviours and beliefs can be an oppositional type. In France, young courtiers at Versailles hit upon knight-errantry as a way to challenge old customs. For a short while, they succeeded in introducing 'the costume most befitting a knightly, a gallant and a warlike court',[22] and so Louis XVI's court dressed in the costume of Henri IV, whose death in 1610 at the hands of a fanatical Catholic assassin falls between the publication of part one of *Don Quixote* in 1605 and part two in 1615. These chivalry-obsessed youths acted out the appeal of knight-errantry perfected in *Don Quixote*; one, the Comte de Ségur, persuaded the king their parodies were amusing rather than subversive.[23] Subversion was in the air – a light skirmish in class war influenced by Voltaire and Rousseau, notes Ségur – a subversion that is present and safely distanced in *Don Quixote*. Harold Bloom has argued that every reader makes a different Quixote, but he identifies several features relevant to eighteenth-century admirers. One is the infinite reach of Quixotic aspiration: 'Since Cervantes's magnificent knight's quest has cosmological scope and reverberations, no object seems beyond reach.' That suited high-flying balloons. So too did the looseness and sociability of quixotic narrative: 'we are invisible wanderers who accompany the sublime pair on their adventures and debacles.'[24] Eighteenth-century literature was very hospitable to conversation, formally in dialogues, a popular eighteenth-century genre in which debate was aired constructively, often with good humour. Quixote was a bookish figure – he buys and reads more books than his house can hold – and he is a talker, a combination eighteenth-century readers could identify with. Explicitly quixotic novels like Charlotte Lennox's *The Female Quixote* (1752) and Richard Graves' *The Spiritual Quixote* (1773) showed how Cervantes' world could be imaginatively updated. Both authors use Quixote as a figure for madness who is not all wrong. Quixotic characters are often right in their reasoning and wrong in their objects; their wrong-headedness may be endearing. Fictions of sensibility confirmed the value of feeling, but many showed it was ultimately a lonely business, so prone to disappointments it might be a mistake to cultivate it. Ambivalence emerges – neither feeling nor reason has all the answers. Uncertainty about how to interpret the world of dreams was also relevant to writers imagining the consequences of balloons. So Don Quixote attracted writers as a figure through whom the play of ideas was enjoyably playful, and serious questions made entertaining. Cervantean credulity had a comic logic that could agree with reason and show up its difficulties. It offered writers a respected prototype for ambition and ambivalence, with 'castles in air' easily converted to balloons, and it wrapped in gentle melancholy the insubstantiality of dreams.

An essay from November 1784 immersed itself in Quixotic imagination to grapple with the strangeness, novelty and implications of balloons. It took an epigraph from an ode by Horace, firm ground: 'On sailing wings, thro' yielding Air explor'd/ Unwonted paths'.[25] Horace's eagle hangs over the author's waking dream in the Elysian Fields, where we find Don Quixote in rusty armour and Sancho Panza appearing, very agitated because he's just heard from a ghost that people on earth have taken to the air. 'He told me that they built carriages of silk, with rooms in them, which without any conductor would fly through the air, and carry those in them wherever they pleas'd, that they could fly so high they could not see the earth, and that they could live almost whole days amongst the clouds.'[26] Don Quixote is incredulous: 'thy imagination must be strangely infatuated to suppose that men, wise men, would trust themselves to no more stable support than clouds and meteors.' They decide to go and see Newton, who is gazing at the heavens. He responds to their news 'with a smile of pity and contempt' and says gravely, 'the science of an Astronomer is not the science of building *castles in the air.*' Don Quixote conjectures: 'The people who use these airy carriages may perhaps be so many Knights errant, who, that the miserable may languish as short a time as possible in misery, have constructed these wonderful machines to fly about and do good. No other motive could have suggested the design; but then, should two Knights meet, their fighting in the air might have dangerous consequences.' Given the tension in aerostation's early days between optimism and pessimism, this moment can be read with no irony – 1780s readers were questioning balloon uses – and with much irony – 1780s readers could already suggest many uses for balloons other than doing good. Newton makes a speech recommending man to stay in his proper sphere, which Don Quixote takes as confirmation of his own view that the earth provides world enough for knight-errantry – and so the author quits Elysium.

This airy fantasy is both simple and complicated. Don Quixote here is a figure of the far-fetched, like balloons; by the comparison to romance, a synonym for fiction, air travel becomes stranger than fiction. The idealist able to fight considers a phenomenon with utopian energy and dystopian threat. Running through the piece is a current of thought about class and power. Don Quixote's world of dukes, knights, goatherds and Arcadians is benign in its class relations, not least because class distinctions are maintained: 'every worldly station has its blessings'. In leaving the earth literally, air travellers might leave that system behind. Conceding that the soul of man looks skyward, Newton recommends people look at the earth: 'behold every plant grow in its own sphere'. A quotation reinforces the point: there is no need to ask 'why oaks are made/ Taller or stronger than the weeds they shade' (from Pope's 1735 *Essay on Man*, which argued conservatively for a chain of being where man kept to his place between nature and God). For rational man, a hierarchical social system is natural. The conclusion unites the wisest of the wise (Newton) with the maddest of the mad (Quixote).

Nonetheless, just as balloons wandered between provinces of science and imagination, Newtonian moralising could not entirely tie reason to botanical order. The regularity of heavenly bodies provides an ethical perspective and model of order, but it is by wandering out of his sphere that man sees what his sphere should be. Countless eighteenth-century novels played on this paradox. Don Quixote was a wanderer with comically fixed ideas about class, and the windmills he tilts at have sails, giving dynamism to air. Also easily extendable to sailing in air were the imaginative flights of Milton. Like Cervantes, Milton supplied hierarchical worlds. His grandiloquence suited wonder; it was epic and full of spirits, which let imagination have a holiday from the classics and be baroque. Allusion helped stabilise the whirl of thought that accompanied balloons, particularly on a first or sublime sighting. Allusion is imagination's infrastructure: to those at a loss for words, it gives a starting point; to the articulate, it creates literary community. It builds bridges. Casting about for reference points is nicely illustrated by the Reverend James Lapsley, out visiting the sick in his rural parish when he heard a strange humming noise. An old woman who joined him argued it was the buzz of elves and spirits before Christmas Eve. Not best pleased by this comment, the Reverend was thrilled by the appearance of a balloon (which had Lunardi aboard). But then he was pained by a struggle to describe it. A young man helps him out with some lines from Milton:

> Nigh at hand hung high with diamonds flaming and with gold;
> Thither came Uriel gliding thro' the ev'n on a sun-beam,
> And swift as a shooting star which in Autumn thwarts the night.

Lapsley is 'not ill pleased to find that we have got some likeness, tho' fanciful, to compare it to.'[27] The allusion, which he calls a conceit, is of course nothing like old women's pagan belief in the buzz of fairies.

Milton was obviously present in literature of the sublime, which balloons joined speedily. Epic Miltonic machinery of flight used wings, but his spirit world connected to a seventeenth-century imagination around devils and witches whose broomsticks were still real to many and useful for satire. The sacred heft of Milton could also help manage dangerous ambition. A correspondent to *The Gentleman's Magazine* volunteered some lines from *Paradise Lost* for use by fellow Christians who might fall from balloons into the sea:

> upled by thee,
> Urania, with Heaven I have presum'd

An earthly guest, and drawn empyreal air,
Thy tempering, and with like safety guided down
Return me to my native element;
Lest from this flying steed unrein'd (as once
Bellerophon, though from a lower clime,)
Dismounted, on the Aleian field I fall
Erroneous there to wander, and forlorn.

The lines might be tweaked, he suggested: change 'Aleian field' to 'British sea' and make the last line 'Too ventrous – there to sink, for ever lost.'[28] Allusion could be tortured to fit.

In the world of allusions around balloons, Shakespeare is notable by his absence. This is puzzling, though there was at least a plan for a novelty balloon in the shape of Falstaff – the Aerial Colossus [Figure 15]. Samuel Johnson's new edition of the plays published in 1765 and the Stratford-upon-Avon Jubilee of 1769 organised by David Garrick helped promote Shakespeare as the national bard, yet there are relatively few Shakespearean associations with balloons. One balloon, representing a French flight of 19 October 1783, appeared in a production of *The Tempest* in Edinburgh; there may be others.[29] When Blanchard and Jeffries set off from Dover on their voyage across the Channel, English soil was given potency by evocation of the Dover cliffs in *King Lear*. In his first publication, Lunardi noted that Shakespeare was 'celebrated in all parts of the world, not excepting those where his native language was not understood', a globalism to which aeronauts and balloons might aspire.[30] Lunardi's publisher did include in the *Account* proposals for an edition of Shakespeare with implications for aeronationalism, which I discuss in Chapter 11. It may be that the mythologising of Shakespeare was still too fragile to carry the cultural complexity of balloons; it may be that Shakespeare's beauties are too grounded to be usefully airy; it may be that English embarrassment at coming late to the balloon party made Shakespeare a consolation best kept away from its cultural turbulence.

It is important to remember that for all the excitement about balloons and their implications, there was already enthusiasm among poets about air. Besides the old potency of airborne viewpoints, the years immediately preceding balloons saw new interest in the heavens through science. Discoveries about air interested poets – in 1773, Anna Laetitia Barbauld addressed her friend Joseph Priestley in the voice of a mouse petitioning for freedom from experiments in his air pump. In the 1780s new apparatus explained the heavens.

The AERIAL COLOSSUS,
A Machine of an Entire New Construction now making
By M·PROSSOR,
With which he will Ascend into the Atmosphere when finished

Pub: According to Act: March 9.th 1785 by M Prossor

15   A fantasy balloon of 1785. Coloured print, published 9 March 1785.

It caught the imagination of poets like young Eliza Knipe, aged eighteen, who penned a tribute to a man who gave lectures about the planetary system using a three-dimensional model, an Eidouranion. She responded to how it unfolded the immensity of space, her enthusiasm expressed through metaphors of air and flight:

> The heart, with sensibility endu'd,
> Alone can tell, how loth from heights like these
> The soul to sublunary objects sinks:
> But yet, while rob'd in elemental dross,
> She cannot long sustain such airy flights.[31]

Sensibility was well established by the 1780s. Its dizziest heights were arguably in the 1770s, but its privileging of feeling played a significant part in aerostation. Lunardi made use of it, possibly genuinely, as a common language of feeling that would appeal to his foreign audience. Sensibility believed in universal humanity; it could partner balloons in travel. In November 1784 several British newspapers printed a letter from Strasbourg dated 16 October.[32] 'A sublimer traveller, a new hero, enters the atmospheric theatre,' reports the writer: 'I had better tell you his story as I heard it.' He and a banker friend were strolling through a vineyard when a flitting shadow alerted their attention to an immense balloon descending ahead. A handsome young man jumped out and embraced them, exclaiming 'Am I again among men?' He sheds tears which the narrator sympathetically reciprocates. The three men share a picnic and the aeronaut, Henri de Clermont, tells his story. Wishing to participate in the improvement of aerial vehicles, 'whose invention and progress I have attended to with all the enthusiasm of a lover', he had designed a new spring-loaded valve, attached it to an inner balloon within a balloon and ascended at dawn, leaving an admiring crowd below. He rose rapidly to a great height from which Switzerland looked like a map, the lake of Geneva a pond and the Po, Rhône, Rhine and Danube mere streams. The earth 'was now a huge circular plane of a greyish green cast: the sun, a round blaze of glory, with the white ethereal lustre of the other stars, which the refractions of this thinner atmosphere no longer concealed.' Breathing became difficult and his bottle of wine exploded. He threw a pebble out to see how high he was but, terrifyingly, the pebble stuck to the gallery. He panics: "'And shall I never set foot again upon my native planet, but freeze slowly to death in the empty waste of space, far from my friends – my mother?" exclaimed I, casting myself on the floor in an agony of despair'. After gnawing the gallery in rage, it occurs to him to slash the inner balloon; then scraps of paper he throws out begin to rise – a sign he is returning to earth where on landing he sprains an ankle and falls gratefully into the arms of the narrator.

This account is gripping in its sensational events and sublime description of the earth from the air. It is almost certainly fiction. Clermont was an old aristocratic name in France and a new aristocratic name in the Irish peerage; it was a sufficiently romantic name to suit a title character in one of the seven 'horrid novels' commended in Jane Austen's *Northanger Abbey* – Regina Maria Roche's *Clermont*, published in 1798, the same year Austen's novel was written. Other eighteenth-century novels have male characters whose names end in 'mont' – Belmont in *Clarissa*, Valmont in *Les Liaisons Dangereuses* – but Clermont was a real name. The inner balloon arrangement had been used by aeronauts and ascents were often runaway. The story included recognisable features of aeronaut narratives and yet it is not quite that. So what is going on?

If you re-read the story as fiction, the classic body language of sensibility leaps out at you: youth, beauty, lots of weeping, people flinging themselves around, violent emotions. It has extravagant passions, tears shed freely as a gift or a return for a gift, especially the gift of a story. It even has sensibility's penchant for symbolically vulnerable writing materials, usually in the form of damaged manuscripts, here in the form of torn scraps of paper. Such scraps were genuinely used to ascertain altitude and in experiments, just as pebbles were, but they could also do literary work, like the stone pocketed by Wordsworth as an emblem of the French Revolution. The drama of uncontrolled flight is, I suggest, a vehicle for the author to explore uncontrolled emotions. Our hero has perfect manners on the ground: he is affable to peasants, mild-humoured to all. But aloft he is all agony, despair, fury. He shouts at heaven and bites his balloon. In short, he behaves like a child in a tantrum – and the story of the pebble mysteriously stuck to the gallery then released is a 'fort-da' story, a version of Freud's infant controlling its mother's movements. In the fiction of sensibility, a hero could invoke his mother without being seen as a mummy's boy; the balloon gives him a reason to lament the loss of earth, another mother. The story is science fiction in that it imagines what it would be like to be lost in space; what's terrifying about it is that the hyperpoliteness of sensibility disappears, leaving a primal being.

The story appeared in the newspapers as fact, uncommented on. One newspaper put it suggestively on a page with two other stories – one a report of a maroon slave rebellion, a violent uprising brutally suppressed, the other an account of North American Indians and their gender roles.[33] Savagery was not just for savages: the story of Henri de Clermont used the codes of sensibility to explore how in space, if no one can hear you scream, the most charming and polite young man could become a howling savage.

Here balloon literature joined up with another genre, fantasies about life on the moon. The moon was a popular destination for imaginary voyages well before balloon flight. If anything, actual flight focused minds more on sublunary possibilities, and even after the invention of balloons some writers preferred to stick with flying ships and giant birds as their means of space travel. There was a very rich literature of aerial travel throughout the early modern period – too big to engage with here.[34] Many fictions in the eighteenth century took up the theme.[35] Illustrations added in important ways to the repertoire of lunar life-forms. One hinge between old and new lunar fantasy can be found in Filippo Morghen's *Reccolta*, a series of engravings first published in Naples c. 1766. The first edition featured two voyagers, Cavaliere Wild Skull and Philippe de la Hire, a famous astronomer opposed to the idea that the moon could support life (an irony of which Morghen is either mischievously aware or blissfully unaware). The second edition changed the protagonist to Bishop John Wilkins; the *Reccolta* represented animals and machines unknown on earth except as described by Wilkins. The first plate shows a lunar vehicle which Brian Aldiss says 'seems to be no more than a flying chicken run': it is a rectangular box with a folding lid and two stiff pleated wings.[36] The third edition, undated, adds to this contraption an air balloon, possibly copying Blanchard's, as a nod to progress. Morghen's text was dedicated to his friend and patron Sir William Hamilton, British envoy at Naples, better known now for his interest in volcanoes, collection of antique vases and broad-minded *ménage à trois* with his wife Emma and her lover Lord Nelson. Like much lunar imagining it was appropriately transnational and timeless. It adapts existing technology in strange ways – a coach with sails, a boat with bellows and steam-powered sailing pumpkins which double as houses on land and water. The moon is inhabited by winged serpents, enormous eagles and giant rats with long snouts which are kept in check by a blade like a guillotine prototype. There are savages and sultans: as Aldiss puts it, 'Like us, the lunarians have their classes of society.'

Lunar fantasy had much to say about class, and in its politics of lower orders it touched on slavery. There may be an oblique reference to actual slavery: some sea-voyages that end up on the moon have trajectories that uncannily evoke transatlantic passage, and many stories added land travel to lunar voyaging in itineraries that took in imperial and slave-owning societies. Lunar imagination sanctioned distortion and muddling; it also mixed up literary traditions. 'The Trifler No. IV' offers a peculiar and intense aerial fantasy about an archangel who yearly traverses the globe in a large balloon. Lunardi, ascending at Naples, is suddenly whisked off by a whirlwind and seized by the Archangel, who deposits him in Fez to pick up the emperor of Morocco. In the Archangel's airy chariot, they survey the Atlas mountains below, the coast of Africa, caravans, lions, sandstorms and the golden rivers of Guinea flowing to the sea. Disgusted by the 'rough caffres' who live there, the Emperor looks towards the Cape and sees European fleets. The Archangel tells him they are mostly ships from Britannia, 'a nation that exceeds all others in courage, in power, in wealth; her sons are the favourites of heaven: Each corner of the earth is familiar to them; and they go with facility from pole to pole. Behold yonder, in the southern deep, the adventurous Cook! And hovering over him, a guard of angels!' The Emperor then looks down on Abyssinia; he sees its king and an army, 'their shining arms covered with lightening. The lion and tiger, princes of the wood, and the crocodile, the monarch of the river, sullenly retired to their dark abodes.'[37] The Emperor spots the Nile, Cairo, the Sphinx and armies of janizaries, who are described with a chunk of Milton (from *Paradise Lost* Book I, where Satan marshals his army for rebellion against God):

> thro' the armed files/ Darts his experienc'd eye, and soon traverse/ The whole battalion views, their order due,/ Their voyages and stature as of gods:/ Their number last he sums; and now his heart/ Distends with pride, and, hard'ning in his strength,/ Glories ---.

So far, you could say we have the ramblings of a writer rather carried away by imagining the earth from above. We have been here before, figuratively; jumbled echoes of Milton, Thomson and Johnson turn Africa into a landscape of beasts, empty spaces, kingdoms of violence and possibilities. But the fantasy has even grander ambitions, poetic and planetary. The Archangel takes the Emperor higher still so they can see the whole world:

The poles shook their snowy heads. Upon the right hand they beheld the day blazing over one half of the world; and, upon the left, they saw the night, with her moon and sparkling stars. The earthly voyagers remained dumb with astonishment at the vast prospect of land, and sea, and sky. The thunder burst the clouds under their feet; the raging tempest made the ocean boil, and they viewed whole navies tossed about upon the troubled element.

The Archangel alights on the Arctic Circle, then ascends to the gates of heaven so the earth becomes small like the moon: 'The universe was spread before them. They beheld every planet and every star making their revolution round the throne of Jove who sat supremely great above all height, hid amidst his own glories!' Lunardi finds it all too dizzying and begs to be returned safely to earth, but the Trifler has settled into a stride more apocalyptic than sublime:

The solemn sound of distant planets – the alternate reign of silence and thunderings – the shower which fell upon all the universe – the sudden darkness that o'erspread the worlds, whose huge orbs sparkled through the gloom of night – and that sudden universal day, blazing from ten thousand rising suns, unloosed the weak frames of mortals. The Almighty looked down with compassion. Jove rose from his throne; his glories darted through the skies –

         — He gave the nod,
The stamp of fate, and sanction of the god;
High heav'n with trembling the dread signal took,
And all Olympus to her centre shook.

The lines are from Pope's translation of Homer; they were singled out by Hugh Blair in his *Lectures on Rhetoric and Belles Lettres* (1783) as an instance of the sentimental sublime nearly spoiled (he thought) by rhyme.[38] The lines (*The Iliad*, Book I, lines 684–7) appear after Thetis pleads with Jove to act on behalf of her slighted son Achilles; Jove concedes, and gives an irrevocable sign – a nod (not to be confused with the expression 'Homer nods', meaning a continuity lapse). In *The Iliad*, Jove's nod paves the way for the Trojan Wars. It ends the Trifler's story on a reverberating allusion. 'The earthly voyagers sunk into a trance of ecstasy; and when they awakened, they found themselves under an arbour in the Imperial gardens of Fez.'

Perhaps it's disappointing that the fantasy comes back to earth with a bump, and by the unoriginal device of it-was-all-a-dream. Perhaps too you can say that the Trifler gilds the literary lily by combining an aerial fantasy with an African extravaganza. But it's worth taking seriously because eighteenth-century readers did. The printer of the *Caledonian Mercury*, John Robertson, thought well enough of it to put it on the front page, displacing half his usual advertisements for newly arrived teas, loans, liquid blacking for carriages and boots, announcements of ships departing for Jamaica, lands to be sold, notices to creditors. The Trifler was evidently worth risking revenue. The only other time in 1785 that advertisements were moved off the front page was to make way for a patriot-pleasing piece by Boswell just after Johnson's death, on Johnson's visit to Edinburgh. The *Caledonian Mercury* did print poems now and again, but it gave space to politics, business and law rather than literature. It had also been fairly hard-headed about balloons. But the success of Lunardi's Edinburgh ascent made a difference. The luckless Tytler forgotten, Lunardi embodied heroic possibilities, and so when the Trifler rose to the occasion, there was a welcoming outlet.[39]

Allusions to Milton and Homer lent epic possibilities to air by putting earth in relation to heaven – for Homer, gods and men; for Milton, God and man. Their subjects could be understood as heaven and earth, or earth and air – with Milton's blank verse establishing grounds for air that writers could adopt or adapt. In myth, gods come down to earth in mortal guise; in aerostatic literature, men venture into the realm of the heavenly. The uncertain implications of this theological temerity are kept from being too wobbly by devices of vision and dream – devices which a reader understands to offer a temporary contract of make-believe – and by cautiousness about theological identification. We have in the Trifler's story a Miltonic Archangel and a Homeric Jove. Are we in a classical or a Christian heaven? Both. His earth has mountains, rivers, stars, countries, empires, regions of mind and soul, myth and religion. Landmarks are cultural – the Sphinx – and phenomena are natural – sandstorms. This, then, is our earth. It is also described with an ideological map: there are 'caffres' disgusting to the Emperor of Morocco, and noble British tars. That would make it repellently imperialist, except the picture is not a simple binary of black and white. It moves on from that geographically to the South Seas and philosophically to the kingdom of Abyssinia, Samuel Johnson's country of the mind, where Rasselas explored questions of happiness. The point of view too is not an imperial one, or not a British one: the Emperor of Morocco, an Arab, keeps an idea of imperial power present, but located in a region adjacent to Europe, the kingdoms of Morocco and Egypt. What does a North African perspective offer? Arabs were enslavers, which may reinforce the undercurrent about slavery. A few pages

on from the Trifler's story were reports from Arabia of a warri-
or-prophet fomenting revolution, and European kings quarrelling.
Morocco was one of the four Barbary states, along with Algiers,
Tunis and Tripoli. Its emperor in 1785 was Sultan Sidi Muhammad
Ibn Abdallah, who has a place in American history for releasing the
captured brig *The Betsey* and for signing a treaty in 1786 that established diplomatic relations with the United States.[40] So the Emperor
of Morocco is a figure somewhere between piracy and diplomacy,
just as Lunardi – for Scots readers – was somewhere between
foreigner and national hero.

Archangels and emperors lent aeronauts auras of power and
dominion. Biblical and fabulous, they evoked the imaginative space
between this world and others. For the Trifler, there was still a
place for old symbols, national purpose and human skills; there
is a cheering compatibility between the Archangel's airy chariot
and Lunardi's balloon. Although America, Asia and Europe get a
mention in this story, it is Africa that dominates, positioned as a
terrain of enslavement against which imagination can be free, liberated, soaring. (As it continued to be: see Shelley's sonnet of 1812,
To a balloon laden with Knowledge.[41]) At the end, when an Italian and
an Arab are deposited in the latter's imperial gardens, one wonders
what on earth this story was for? The Trifler's story shows that
literary history was important ballast for writers on balloons. On 10
April 1786, the Trifler explained his persona:

> I am a great grandson of the famous Isaac Bickerstaff, a chance
> medley between his grandson and an oyster-wench. I resemble my
> mother more than my father. I naturally hate beaten tracks, and
> shun, as I would do an elephant, the common, heavy, jog-trot. This
> passion shows me many flights and capers up into the air.[42]

Bickerstaff was well known to eighteenth-century readers in two
forms: one as the pseudonym Swift adopted for a satirical pamphlet
announcing the supposed death of his *bête-noire* John Partridge, an
almanac-maker and astrologer; and second, as the gently humorous
character invented by Richard Steele for some papers of *The Tatler*.
Oyster-wenches were sexualised figures.[43] Without labouring the
Trifler's genealogy, it reminds us that lunar fantasy moved in a space
where astrology had overwritten the heavens – as the Montgolfiers
knew when they included a zodiac in their sumptuous air-globe
decoration. It also reminds us of literary descent: what comes down
through the ages are traditions, heroic and comic.

Writers used the moon as a place for working in contemporary preoccupations too, like religious ones. *A Journey Lately Performed Through the Air* had two French aeronauts swapping Catholicism for a more deist belief in a Supreme Being.[44] On the moon they find a perfect Christian society (with whom they can luckily converse in Hebrew!) which nonetheless reverences them as higher beings, much like a crowd for a balloon ascent. They also share mortality and a world of strong emotions. Loneliness is one: lost in space at night, the aeronauts turn to faith for comfort in otherwise unbearable loneliness. Although the moon-world attracts them so much they stay and send the text back to earth, along with the usual cargo of moral warnings is a poignant lament: they miss their families, parents, wives and children. Sensibility's ambivalence about sociability played out perfectly: space could be empty and peopled, allowing exploration of loneliness and joy. A religious equivalent focused on terror of abandonment and redemptive communities of worship.

Imaginary voyages are often described as utopias.[45] But along with ideals came painful realisations of imperfections which complicate a distinction between utopia and dystopia. Like relations later between science fiction and fantasy,[46] genres blurred. R. B. Rose separates eighteenth-century utopias into four main types: historically-based; geographical (especially islands); hypothetical constructions with no identifiable time or place; and the remote future.[47] Even this helpful filter is complicated – the moon could fit multiple categories. In post-1783 literature, balloons tended to be more than merely a means of getting somewhere fantastical; they were both a new technology of travel and a vehicle of ideas that were still at a speculative stage. Their meanings narrowed for early nineteenth-century writers who used balloons in futurist fiction as symbolic shorthand because aerostation was a stalled technology, yet still eloquent of emotions. Thus Mary Shelley's *The Last Man* (1826) and Jane Webb's *The Mummy* (1827) both use balloons in scenes of extreme emotions. In the years of balloon madness, balloons are obvious emblems of uncertain progress; they are also symbols of imagination itself.

After 1783, aerial fantasy travelled along with real balloons intermittently. *The Aerostatic Spy*, published in June 1785, included a plate of Lunardi's first ascent. Its advertisement promised 'a view of various Countries, in different parts of the World, and a variety of Characters from Real Life'. It also hoped 'to stimulate the Ingenious to bring to the highest degree of perfection this infant Mode of Travelling'.[48] Alas, one review dismissed the book as infantile: 'These volumes are altogether the most contemptible catchpenny that has been for some time crammed down the throats of the public. The whole is a confused jumble of illiberal incoherent invective, conveyed if possible in worse language.'[49] A second issue in 1786 abandoned pretence to the real and retitled the work as a novel. It certainly had weak machinery: the aerial traveller's first balloon, built after a shipwreck, is somehow constructed with no silk, cloth, paper or thread, and halfway through it changes from a fire to a hydrogen model, a transformation performed by a heavenly being, Amiel, who emerges from a cloud of aether to take the hero on a tour of the globe. But it also had a design, manifest through strong views. What the protagonist encounters are tales of oppression and unhappiness. It's a grim compilation in which happy marriages are thwarted or ruined, and decent men cheated and oppressed. A set-down in Indostan leads to a fierce critique of British rule: 'Gentoos and Mahometans complained alike of extortion, oppression and a contempt of their country laws'.[50] You could see the balloon as merely a device to get between miserable stories, but time aloft provides a narrative space for philosophical reflection. Amiel could be read as a Milton-lite derivative of Rasselas's tutor Imlac: both want their protégé to understand humanity through a survey of happiness and humanity's own obstruction of it. High-mindedness needs experience to give it substance, to make it reasonable not airy. The protagonist, Charles (named for the hydrogen aeronaut?) has a true love, Lucia, with whom he is eventually reunited: the whole tome can be read as an allegory, in which the hopes balloons inspire were mapped against a dystopian world. Real balloons drift in and out. Charles is present at several launches in London, described perfunctorily, and at a debate at an inn in the town of Reading as to whether manned flight will ever be possible. This is a scene which indeed strains credulity – regardless of whether it is clumsily written, it imagines a scene in which literary imagination is already airborne, like Charles flying with Amiel, and which also believes retro-futuristically that ingenuity could make reality airborne too. For all its moral tales and confessional sensibility, the novel invests in an allegory of enlightenment – thus Lucia, light – which is ultimately grounded in real world progress. This progress, moral as well as mechanical, is doubtful but not impossible, improbable as balloons themselves. As an ode of 1786 concluded, 'Tis all Philosophy can teach,/ That man's an air-balloon.'[51]

Balloons continued to attract writers after balloon madness declined. They go on meaningfully in other contexts, including Romantic poetry. Coleridge used a balloon to image intense love:

> The presence of a ONE,

> The best belov'd, who loveth me the best,

> is for the heart, what the supporting air from within is for the hollow globe with its suspended car. Deprive it of this, and all without, that would have buoyed it aloft even to the seat of the gods, becomes a burthen and crushes it into flatness.[52]

Goethe compared poetry itself to balloons:

> True poetry manifests itself in that like a secular gospel, by its internal serenity, by its external ease, it is able to deliver us from the earthly burdens which press upon us. Like an air balloon it raises us with the ballast that clings to us, into higher regions, and makes the most intricate mazes of earth lie before us in a bird's eye view.[53]

From Orpheus onwards, poetic *furens* was traditionally divine. Balloon madness was a fresh breath of shared air. Goethe's sense of the numinous in poetry and piety liberates reverence. In 1783 monarchy was still a focus of reverence, and the next section, Gravity, unfolds how balloons, carried upward on currents of seriousness, played into ruling ideas.

Gravity

Monarchs

'The *Moon* grows pale, in envy sighs
To view the Monarch of the skies
In triumph ride...'

Air-Balloon, or Blanchard's Triumphal Entry into the Etherial World;
A Poem (1785)

HISTORIANS AGREE THAT the institution of monarchy changed in the eighteenth century. 'The French Revolution marks the transition of monarchy as a divine institution to a monarchy legitimised by the nation. This process, which had started long before 1789, was associated with a loss of the magical, with a desacralization of the monarchy and a separation between the king and the divine.' Quite how and why the old order ebbed is 'anything but a straightforward tale',[1] though one can point to factors like the power of Enlightenment critiques of absolutism; the growth of the press, which made monarchs less important; and, in Britain, where satire of the king freely circulated, the familiarising of royalty through royal families. At the same time there was also a growth in civic organisations, friendly societies and freemasonry, all variously keen on loyalist and royalist activities.[2] Belief in monarchs as earthly representatives of divine power continued; what weakened was belief in the monarch as embodiment of divine right. In Britain, Queen Anne was the last monarch whose touch was believed to cure 'the king's evil', or scrofula; George I thought the idea abhorrent and stopped it.[3] What Antoine de Baecque describes as the transition of sovereignty from the body of the king to the great citizen body was not an even process across Europe, and to complicate matters some monarchies played better in the new order than they had in the old, laying the grounds for monarchy to re-establish itself tenaciously in nineteenth-century Europe. 'It is easier to document this apparent transformation in the monarchy's public status than account for it,' says Linda Colley, though she suggests an upsurge in royal and national spectacle in Britain was partly due to an outpouring of patriotic art by Royal Academy painters, which benefited the reputation of their patron, George III, who had encouraged it.[4] Tracking changes in France, Sarah Melzer and Kathryn Norberg also see the Bourbon monarchs benefiting from spectacle, with Versailles as its great theatre.[5]

So how did balloons and monarchs affect each other in this period of transition from early modern to modern ideas? I want to explore two ideas: how monarchs promoted balloons, or not, and how royalist imagery transferred between balloons and monarchs. This chapter looks first at how a selection of European monarchs responded to aerostation, narrowing the focus to Britain before explaining why 'majestic' was the word so widely used in descriptions of balloon flights.

Monarchs were nations when it came to peace treaties, which were made in the name of kings rather than countries. They were identified with countries symbolically in ways that ran deep in cultural imagination. After news of aerostatic experiments in Moscow and Milan in the summer of 1784, the King of Prussia, Frederick the Great, reportedly exclaimed 'Fire! must be my element, for Russia and Austria aim at universal sway on land, England at sea and France in the air.'[6] England was jittery about signs that the French were building a powerful navy: 'we may expect in the next War, to meet a Foe, in the State our Navy is in, that will drive us out of the Ocean'[7], and invested heavily in marine symbolism. In 1783 Pitt, arguing forcefully against sending English troops to defend Hanover against the French, declared that England 'was like an amphibious animal, which might live upon land, yet whose proper element is the water'.[8] When Somerset House was rebuilt for the Admiralty in 1784, its main entrance off the Strand featured a statue of George III, improbably in a toga; at his feet is a mighty lolling Father Thames, mimicking Neptune.[9] In 1781 the astronomer William Herschel discovered a new planet. In a compliment to his king, he named it 'Georgium Sidus'. European astronomers applauded the discovery but were appalled at its name. It was fine to name lands and islands after kings, but not stars: they suggested Uranus, Cybele, Neptune, anything but the name of a British monarch. Herschel had broken with the consensus that heavenly bodies should have mythological names, and pressure was applied to remove this nationalist intrusion on imaginative space. (It was eventually called Uranus.)

Thanks to French success in aerostation, however, identification of Louis XVI with air was incontestable. An epigram competition showed the idea's attraction:

> In the Pride of his Heart (says *Louis le Grand*)
> So great is my sway I can Nature command:
> The Air is my Slave – nor dares disobey.
> Guards, stop the Balloon – The Balloon flew away.[10]

French rhymes of 'loi' and 'roi' invited comparisons of absolutism with natural law; balloons provided a connective space between. Even when kings were not mentioned by name, nationalism used royal imagery. In another epigram competition, one entry elaborated regally on a French original:

> Beneath the haughty sons of Britain
> Old Ocean's sceptre vanquish'd lies;
> Gallia's light sons, their foes outwitting,
> Usurp the empire of the skies.[11]

Monarchs across Europe initiated enterprises that were identified with improvement and progress and noted across Europe. The British press reported that Louis XVI was setting up a college for experimental agriculture, supporting the building of a great new canal and raising a loan to drain marshes.[12] French royals joined in their nation's enthusiasm for chemistry and a new mineralogical school at Paris.[13] Some enlightened activities involved co-operation between countries otherwise suspicious of each other, and here monarchs could provide a hinge. A French mathematician, wanting to measure the exact distance between the observatories at Paris and Greenwich, needed some help on the English side: 'his Majesty (who is ever ready to patronize useful schemes) immediately granted a thousand pounds for the carrying it on'.[14] In a suite of presents assembled annually for the emperor of China, Louis XVI included two dozen taffeta balloons, their apparatus and full instructions: 'Without doubt, this new Spectacle will give infinite Pleasure to a Prince who loves the Arts and Sciences.'[15] Perhaps it worked: later that year the emperor, Kien-Long, published an edict ordering trade restrictions to be taken off Europeans who were now to be treated as friends.[16] Future aeronauts might even 'find themselves over Pekin, come down, compliment the Chinese emperor, on the part of the king of France, re-ascend, and return some hours after and give Louis XVI an account of his Tartaro-Chinese majesty's state of health'.[17]

Catherine the Great was particularly interested in exchanges with Britain, with whom she was an ally against the French. Having acquired Sir Robert Walpole's collection of paintings at what some English people grumbled was a knock-down price, she sent four young men to London to study agriculture; two Oxbridge youths (paid for by Lord Shelburne) returned the compliment.[18] There was goodwill towards her for having helped Cook's battered crew returning from the Pacific – both she and Louis XVI were presented with commemorative gold medals – and interest in Russia generally, fanned by the press in 1784 by extracts from a new book, *Anecdotes of the Russian Empire*.[19] The author, William Richardson, was a Scot who had resided in St Petersburg and was on good terms with Catherine the Great, who arranged his appointment to the Chair of Humanity at Glasgow University.[20] Catherine received interesting gifts from Britain: the queen gave her a model of Windsor Castle and its surrounding countryside, 'the greatest curiosity of the kind ever before attempted' – and some wild horses, for which she had a passion (it was rumoured, a sexual passion).[21]

One cultural exchange proposed by Catherine the Great could have changed the course of history. Having added extensively to her empire, finally annexing the Crimea in 1783, she ruled over dominions so vast nobody quite knew what was in it. In 1785 she commissioned a great expedition to find out. The expedition to Siberia and the north-west Pacific copied the scope and methods of Captain Cook's voyages; one of its two leaders was Joseph Billings, a British navy officer who had been on Cook's third voyage. Meanwhile, and during the height of balloon madness, the British parliament was discussing what to do with its convicts – after the loss of America, they could no longer be transported to plantations. One scheme proposed was to dump a hundred felons on a tiny island in the middle of the Gambia River.[22] There they could subsist on coconuts and whatever else they could grow. Escapees would run a gauntlet of cannibals resident along the riverbank. Edmund Burke for one was horrified at the cruelty of this plan; he protested in the House of Commons, 'the gallows would rid them of their lives more mercifully than the climate and natives of Africa would'.[23] Catherine the Great, whose remote dominions were barely populated, offered to take British convicts. She also offered to convey them at her expense.[24] British ministers were tempted by this proto-Siberian labour camp idea, though in the end they decided to expand the settlement at Botany Bay.[25]

In such gestures of alliance Catherine the Great shows how emperors were powerful individuals. It was no wonder that writers who imagined balloon voyages to the moon and beyond often imagined it ruled by an emperor, as if absolute monarchy saved space from being lawless. Catherine the Great was also typical of European monarchs in forbidding balloon activities in her dominions.[26] Such edicts sound anti-Enlightenment, with monarchs standing in the way of aerial progress, but the reality is a bit different. Catherine's edict was made in 1786, by which time aerostation was evidently not making progress. It was taking years to survey her lands, and water seemed the best way to connect them – she planned a canal between the Caspian and Baltic seas.[27] Other monarchs also turned hostile to air. 'The King of Prussia wisely forbids these experiments being made in his Dominions', wrote Elizabeth Montagu to her friend Elizabeth Carter, adding another reason for her anti-balloon views: 'It wd be very disagreable to have a flaming Balloon fall upon ye top of ones house. The newspapers on Saturday said air balloons were to be used as a conveyances [sic] for fish & indeed it is fit for such animals as frying will not destroy.'[28] As monarchs well knew, incendiary practices sometimes partner incendiary views. Putting out fires in the eighteenth century was not yet part of state infra-structure, though most municipalities organised some sort of fire service. A Spaniard ascending on 5 June 1784 was nearly burnt to death when his *montgolfière* caught fire amid houses.[29] Monarchs who banned balloons were protecting their subjects against multiple dangers. In Holland, a ban came into force after an aeronaut, one Major van den Berghen, went missing and was presumed dead:

> we have too much reason to fear that the valuable life of this brave and distinguished officer is fallen victim to his fatal philosophic curiosity. To add to the melancholy catastrophe of this tragic event, Major Van den Berghen was shortly to have been married to Madam Rossola, daughter of the Governor General of the Spice Isles, who, upon hearing of the event, became distracted, and has since utterly lost the power of speech. The States have proclaimed a reward of one thousand pounds to whoever shall bring the body or balloon of Major Van den Berghen, and prohibited on pain of death any further aerial experiments in Holland.[30]

Catherine the Great's prohibition invoked time-wasting and point-lessness as well as danger; even capable and experienced aeronauts were refused permission to fly, as the king of Prussia did politely to Blanchard in a letter printed in English newspapers.[31]

European monarchs in the eighteenth century might seem to be a forbidding lot. It was standard for monarchs to forbid duelling and normal for them to do so repeatedly because no edict eradicated the practice. It was also rational, since a duel was likely to deprive them of at least one subject. What else did monarchs forbid? In 1785 the king of Spain forbade bullfighting: he thought it was a waste of cattle. At the end of June 1784 in Madrid, a Frenchman ascending in a balloon misjudged the weighting and turned topsy-turvy; it caught fire, he jumped out and broke a leg. The king of Spain then forbade future experiments. Frederick the Great was busy forbidding too: in 1783 he prohibited the use of stays in girls' schools, nunneries and orphanages, because it impeded growth and injured health. There was equally enlightened thinking in his forbidding of the ringing of church bells in 1783's season of summer storms: evidence suggested that bell-ringing increased the risk of lightning strikes. Monarchs who readily sent subjects into battle were becoming more careful about the value of life in civic contexts. Even substituting convicts for citizens in balloon ascents was more discussed than acted on. In the winter of 1784, magnetism became fashionable in Paris as a health and slimming aid. Its proponents, Dilon and Mesmer, proposed to publish the secret (in return for a large fee). Louis XVI stepped in to forbid magnetic cures, on the grounds that magnetism deprived people of animal functions without even touching them.[32] A comparable suspicion of quackery hovered around balloons.

But monarchs were attracted to balloons, especially at the beginning and in contexts of public display. A luckless adventurer dangling upside down was unattractive, but a splendid show fitted into the theatrical staging of majesty still important to eighteenth-century monarchs. The Montgolfier story shows the ebb and flow of hopes from royalty. I discuss it here because it unfolded possibilities that were understood at the time to be important in how air-globes could develop, and because Bourbon use of balloons for spectacle set a precedent for other courts. The Montgolfiers had a family papermaking business affected by royalty in the form of privileges, subsidies and orders from government. The designation of *manufacture royale* was an honour and a commercial advantage; some of the Montgolfier family hoped balloons would land them one.[33] Their first ascensive machine was attested by officials at the demonstration on 4 June 1783 at Annonay. The next phase required more money. Joseph argued that if the state did not support their venture, they should turn to rich patrons in England. Etienne managed to get the

VUE ET PERSPECTIVE DU JARDIN DE M.ʳ REVEILLON FABRIQUANT DE PAPIER,
Fauxbourg S.ᵗ Antoine, à l'ancien Hôtel de Titon, où se font faites les expériences de la Machine Aérostatique de MM. Montgolfier freres, dans le courant de l'Eté, en l'année 1783 à la satisfaction d'un concours immense d'amateurs.

DÉDIÉE A M.ˢ LES PHYSICIENS.

A Paris, chez Renault et Bligilly, rue S.ᵗ Jacques, à la Ville de Coutances.

A successful test flight for the Montgolfiers, 19 October 1783. Coloured engraving, after Claude Louis Desrais (1746–1816). Louvre, Paris, France.   **Plate I**

Plate II   Fantastical balloon accessories: hers (companion lithograph to Plate III).

Fantastical balloon accessories: his. Anonymous French coloured
lithographs, late eighteenth century, showing a fantastical range of
fashionable balloon accessories.

Plate III

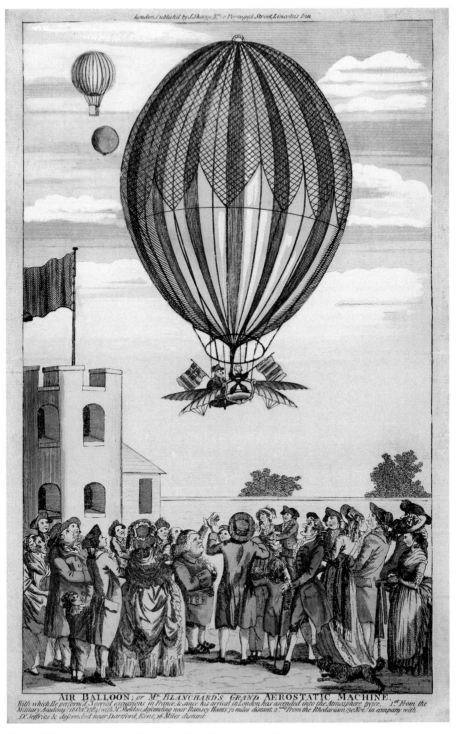

Plate IV   Jean-Pierre Blanchard's balloon, 1784. Coloured engraving.

'The Aerostatick Stage Balloon.' Etching by 'Hanibal Scratch', known also as John Nicholson; published by William Wells, 132 Fleet Street, 23 December 1783.

Plate V

AEROSTATION.

1. *Montgolfier's Balloon*   2. *Blanchards.*   3. *Charles & Roberts.*   4. *Lunardis.*
5. *Baldwin's View over the City of Chester, from Lunardi's Balloon.*

Plate VI   Coloured lithograph showing different types of balloons, with an aerial
view of Chester in the centre, reproduced from Thomas Baldwin's
Airopaidia (1785).

'La Minerve', 1803. Nineteenth-century French plate, painted by J. Siquier.   **Plate VII**
The design was based on the eighty-ton aerial vessel imagined by the
physicist and illusionist Etienne-Gaspard Robertson, able to carry sixty
people for several months with the aim of making discoveries. According
to Robertson, the rooster symbolises vigilance. The full design included
an observatory, laboratories, accommodation for ladies away from the
scholars, workshop, kitchen, storehouse – and cannon.

Drawn and Etch'd by J. Piggot, Fenton Street Walworth and Published by him and John Bellamy Nº 0. Borough Road Southwark. Augt 7. 1802.

A VIEW

Of Monsʳ. GARNERINS ascension with his BALLOON, from Vauxhall-Gardens accompanied

by his wife and a gentleman. And the experiment of the Parachute on tuesday evening Augt 3. 1802

Price, 6 ᵈ.

Plate VIII   Garnerin's descent by parachute in London, 1802. Drawn and etched by J. Piggot, published 7 August 1802, London (price 6d).

Ministry of Finance to rise to the challenge, and its controller-general set in motion what became the demonstration of 19 September at Versailles – in front of the king. For that display, a utilitarian model of taffeta was turned into a gloriously adorned object, the now classic *montgolfière* in shape and decoration, 'fit to float above a king, and still more so over the particular queen who was Marie Antoinette. The background shade was azure, and the effect that of a tent at some *fête-champêtre* with its *pavillon* and ornaments personifying the sun in color of gold.'[34] It outshone the dumpy red and blue striped *charlière* of the rival hydrogen camp, thanks to the Montgolfiers' friend Réveillon, also a papermaker, whose speciality was richly decorated wallpaper and who may have supplied the decorative bands of paper that were overlaid on the exterior. At a pre-trial on 12 September, heavy rain made these bands peel off and reduced the whole bag to a soggy mess. Etienne and Réveillon and their chemist friend Aimé Argand had to work frantically to make a smaller machine for the royal demonstration. They reverted to taffeta. It was again blue, and on its main body was repeated the king's initial, L, entwined with its mirror image.[35]

On 19 September 1783, Louis XVI and Marie Antoinette arrived at the scaffolding surrounding the air-globe. The royal party, which included the king's brothers, sister and sister-in-law, inspected the machine and Etienne Montgolfier gave the king a précis of the experiment, written at the suggestion of a Versailles official so as to provide correct expectations of the altitude and distance to be attained. Once the machine ascended, with duck, cock and sheep aboard, and landed about two miles away, Etienne Montgolfier went up to the royal apartments. 'There he found the king still engaged in observing the machine with his field glasses' and expressing satisfaction. Etienne had to criss-cross the enormous palace of Versailles to meet the queen, who had come out several times to look for him. He gave her the précis and outlined his hopes for future projects; the queen listened kindly, he wrote home.[36]

Royal interest at the Versailles demonstration accounts for the expansively grand decoration of the great *montgolfière* moment on 21 November 1783 – the first successful human flight in public [Plate I shows their earlier experiment in Réveillon's garden on 19 October]. 'Signs of the zodiac in gold were interspersed with fleur-de-lis around the dome; a belt of ceremonial royal initials alternating with flaring suns girdled the waist; a flight of eagles ringed the base amid festoons and garlands, their open wings bearing the great

sphere aloft, azure against the background of the sky.'[37] Two further
details: on the lower third of the globe, the heads of lions hold rings
in their mouths attached to painted curtains, fringed and swagged.
There are masses of theatrical swagging – another band runs round
the point where prism becomes pyramid – though the line is much
tighter than Réveillon's characteristic arabesque line on his elegant
wallpapers, as if either covering up the machine's construction or
respect for majesty required formal restraint. The obvious allusions
to French monarchy – *fleur-de-lis* and Bourbon sun – are reinforced
by kingly lions and eagles. In 1784 Louis XVI, aged thirty, had been
king for ten years. The ideology of the self-styled Sun King Louis
XIV resurges in the globe's cosmic allusions. Louis noted the decorative compliment and ensured the Montgolfiers were rewarded.
Letters patent turned the family into 'de Montgolfier'.[38]

The Montgolfiers continued to work a line of royal compliment through design, unlike the workaday striped globes of the
Académie-supported Charles and the Roberts. Etienne's vision
of worldwide aviation made little impression; Louis XVI merely
wanted to impress the Francophile nephew of Frederick the Great,
King Gustav III of Sweden, who was visiting and wanted to see a
balloon. Etienne, out of Paris, arranged for Pilâtre de Rozier to pilot
his fourth craft, named the 'Marie Antoinette'. It had a new design,
with top segments of leather rather than cloth and a tapering profile.
He was not at the Château de Versailles for the launch on 23 June
1784, and although (after a smooth flight of forty-five minutes) the
balloon was met by a royal party including the king's cousin, the
Prince de Condé, it was damaged by fire after landing. When Etienne
begged the Ministry of Finance for funds to restore it, he was given
a brush-off. His biographer implies he flattered royalty too little,
and that even flattered royalty cared little for inventiveness other
than in the service of spectacle.[39] It was said a balloon representing
the castle of Stockholm – to go up at night, illuminated – had been
laid aside as too dangerous.[40] The medusa-like bag of the 'Marie
Antoinette' may have suffered by the comparison.

A command performance laid on for the king of Sweden in
Naples three months later showed how dazzling balloon displays
could be. 'The Balloon Rage has spread itself all over Italy,'[41] and by
this account, the Italians were unsurpassable in artistry:

> His Majesty the King of Sweden having expressed a Desire to see
> the Experiment of the Air-Balloon, there was yesterday a grand

Exhibition by Order of the Court of Naples, and in the Presence of their Majesties. Perhaps it was the noblest Sight the human Eye has ever yet been regaled with. Imagine an immense Globe of 150 feet Diameter, and 200 in Height, gilt, bearing on the Top an enormous Crown, sparkling with well-imitated precious Stones of various Colours; to the Globe was annexed a Building of the most beautiful Architecture of the Doric Order, formed of Pumice-Stone, and surrounded by a Terras or Gallery, railed in, with Orange Trees and Lemon. This wonderful Machine rose majestically to the Heavens, in a clear Sky, at Noon, in Sight of an applauding Multitude, carrying with it an Orchestra of eight capital Performers, whose Musick, for the short time it could be heard, had the most sublime Effect.[42]

This kid-skin balloon and its artistic appendages were the work of Antonio Lipetti, who was rewarded with £2,000 and a patent of nobility. Besides the orchestra and citrus trees, there was international nobility aboard – three Neapolitans, three Spaniards, a Frenchman and an Englishman, each of whom was also awarded an honour from the admiring sovereigns. Most monarchs supported learned societies and academies in more than name, providing prizes for discoveries and rewarding inventors: it was natural that aerostatic experimenters looked for royal patronage.

How balloons affected monarchy in Britain is a less showy story than elsewhere in Europe, and more bound up with science. George III, the first of the Hanoverians to be born in England and to speak English as his mother tongue, spent an otherwise constricted youth developing interests in practical arts, especially agriculture. The royal children had a miniature farm to run at Kew; they were expected to run it efficiently. 'Farmer George', as the king later became known, knew his oats from his wild oats – of which he sowed none. British monarchs have rarely been readers: nonetheless George III built up a handsome library and a fine collection of scientific instruments. Patron of the Royal Society, he asked its president Sir Joseph Banks if money was required for balloon researches and expressed willingness to fund it. Balloon madness touched him too: in 1783 the chemist Aimé Argand was invited to Windsor to demonstrate the properties of air-globes. A print of the occasion shows small-scale showiness before an attentive royal audience, including the queen and children [Figure 16]; a partner print shows a similar demonstration given to some genteel Georgians [Figure 17].

Like Louis XVI, George III got out his telescope to follow the progress of balloon flights. He saw Lunardi's historic flight through

The King, Queen, & viewing a Baloon let off in the Garden of Windsor Castle.

16   Royalty takes a close interest in ballooning. Hand-coloured engraving, published 30 January 1784.

A Professor Filling, & Explaining to an Audience, the Nature of a Baloon.

17   The sciencey bit: a professor explains inflammable air (companion print to 16).

his telescope with 'infinite Satisfaction' and sent him a hundred guineas afterwards.[43] In return, at an audience at court, Lunardi presented him with the manuscript account of his voyage.[44] The king and queen, in Windsor Great Park when Blanchard's balloon was spotted overhead, hastened to the observatory to view it. George III specifically asked that Blanchard's flight path pass over Windsor: Blanchard obliged, and *en route* dropped a letter addressed to M. le Roi – unfortunately not on Windsor Castle but on Winchester Castle.[45] 'It is an indication of the fact that the "theatre of state", with the royal family in the principal role, does not work unilaterally from above.'[46] Indeed; it was joked that the air-bladder attached to Blanchard's letter burst like a fart over the mistaken royal residence.[47] In what later became a staple of nineteenth-century royal celebrations, pantomimes staged balloons and fireworks together – for instance at Astley's in the summer of 1784, featuring a salamander[48] – but George III favoured a different style, unequivocally majestic, as in the grand and stately celebrations for the centenary of Handel's birth. Handel had provided spectacular ceremonial accompaniment for George I with his Water Music and for George II with his Royal Firework music, both composed for extravaganzas on the Thames, which in 1775 was also the stage for the grandest regatta ever seen in Britain. The Handel concerts in Westminster Abbey gave George III an association with performing arts in a context of architectural and historic splendour; they were widely praised as illustrious and a source of national pride. In comparison, balloons seemed to offer little.

But balloons were a symbol of George III's other affinity – with science. He was not a monarch given to building but he did care about royal institutions. The Royal Society, founded in 1660, was of less interest to him than the Royal Academy, created by him in 1768 to encourage design and create a national school of art. The new poet laureate in 1785, Thomas Warton, penned an *Ode on His Majesty's Birthday* which noted science as a way to transfer greatness from king to society:

> Fair Science to reform, reward, and raise,
> To spread the lustre of domestic praise,
> To softer emulation's holy flame,
> To build Society's majestic frame
> Mankind to polish and to teach,
> Be this the monarch's aim.[49]

But the transfer faced various difficulties, relevant to balloons. One was that in 1784 the Royal Society was convulsed by a row. The president, Sir Joseph Banks, was too autocratic for some members who suspected him of keeping out brilliant men from humble backgrounds. A small pamphlet war broke out. One charge against Banks was that he authorised some expensive chairs, suitable for royalty to sit on should they come to visit, and which might in the absence of king and queen be sat on by the titled. These chairs (which cost £20) looked suspiciously elevated, even like thrones to some untitled members. Proud of their intellectual standing and independence of court patronage, they denounced these chairs as *de haut en bas* furniture, another proof of unfair science. Enquiries established that elsewhere in Europe monarchs were perfectly happy to sit on regular chairs in equivalent academies. As one disgruntled member wrote, 'every man leaves his rank at the door of the Royal Society ... we do not wish to see it a *monarchy*'. Defiantly he declared, 'it becomes crowned heads to bow to science, and not science to bow to crowned heads.'[50] Potential royal patronage did not ensure deference: so Blanchard wrote grandly to Frederick the Great, 'The man who devotes himself to the progress of the sciences belongs to the universe'.[51]

In society's majestic frame, balloons connected to monarchs through practices of naming. Not all balloons were given names though an inclination to do so may be seen in the Prince de Condé's order that an unnamed *montgolfière* should be called 'Pilâtre de Rozier' after its pilot.[52] French aeronauts were patriotic, naturally, since they understood the cultural force of this invention. Two aeronauts who went up from Dijon felt a surge of patriotism 'when we saw the clouds floating beneath us, and secluding us in a manner from the earth. We then jointly repeated the motto fixed to our aerostats, *Surgit nunc Gallus ad aethera*.' Now soars France to the skies: the motto invoked country, not king.[53] Mottoes and devices on French balloons, often described as 'rich', replicated the heraldic accoutrements of nobility, some of whom were lesser royals, some not. Aeronauts themselves were widely acclaimed as heroes but not associated with the elevation of monarchy. A rare exception comes from 1785 when 'little' Blanchard, successfully demonstrating before the Stadtholder, his court and a huge crowd in Holland, was referred to as 'the Prince of Aerostatic Adventurers'.[54] Even so, he is prince not king – some sacral element is missing.

Numerous balloons, on the other hand, acquired royal names and royal imagery. Foreigners turned to nationalism as a prophylactic

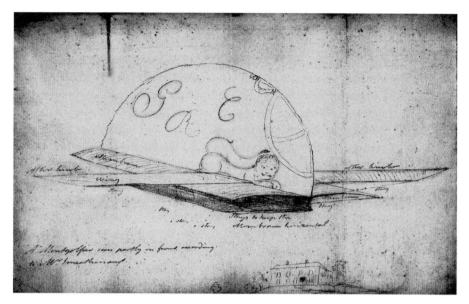

18. Design for a *montgolfière* by Henry Smeathman, 4 March 1784. Front
view, showing a membrane around the balloon held horizontal by stays,
with fixed wings attached. The balloon is decorated with royal insignia
and the king's initials.

18

against crowd violence. Zambeccari promoted his 'British balloon';
Lunardi's second balloon was designed like a British flag; even
Blanchard waved an English ensign when he crossed the Channel.
Royalty also mattered to English balloon-minded subjects. An
amphibious balloon was designed by Henry Smeathman, who had
consulted Banks about its mechanics. Elongated rather than globular in shape, it had a membrane skirt connected by stays to single
wings on each side. His sketches show some artistic decoration: the
balloon has royal initials, GR, a homely-faced lion as figurehead, a
unicorn and a St George's Cross[55] [Figure 18]. Smeathman obviously thought it desirable to add insignia to what were otherwise
technical drawings; it made his machine majestic. Others invoked
majesty directly: the balloon promised in York by Deeker and Weller
was 'The Royal Balloon'. It may be that relatively few balloons in
Britain picked up royal names because of what happened in 1782
to the Royal Navy's first-rater, the *Royal George*. On 29 August,
moored up at Spithead for minor repairs, she began to take in water
and capsized. Women and children aboard on visits all drowned, bar
one little boy who survived by clinging on to a sheep.[56] The disaster

was a tragedy. It was also a national embarrassment. In 1783 a commemorative monument to Admiral Kempenfelt and the more than nine hundred who perished when the *Royal George* sank was unveiled at Portsea near Portsmouth.[57] Other memorials followed. Efforts to raise the ship throughout the summer of 1784 had mixed success – the anchor was recovered but the wreck remained a danger to shipping, despite £11,000 of government money being spent on salvage.[58] When Stuart Arnold advertised his balloon in London in 1785, he ignored these unhappy associations. His 'Royal George' was to fly from London to Paris: departing from St James's at midnight, illuminated by lights that would make it more brilliant than a full moon, it would arrive in France at dawn.[59] It was another disaster. Far from carrying twelve passengers the balloon could barely hold three, and it burst over the Thames.[60] Naming ships after royalty proceeded cautiously after the loss of the *Royal George*, but there were vessels of all sizes, merchant and military, named for the king. In excise, naming was clearly ideological: a lugger called *The Flying Devil* of Dover was caught by an excise cutter named the *Royal George*, and found to be smuggling casks of spirits.[61]

In this mixed picture one can see royal symbolism in the 1780s moving in two different directions. On the one hand, 'in the 1770s and 1780s a pleasant, voluntary simplicity ... was part of a European-wide royal aesthetic, which rarely implied limited royal ambition'.[62] One story in circulation concerned Joseph II at Ostend. He sent for six English merchants, who found him sitting in his waistcoat. 'He rose at their entrance, desiring they would be seated, and sat down with them ... The enlightened and glorious Monarch desired they would divest themselves of all embarrassment at his presence, and speak freely, considering themselves as in company with a merchant like themselves.' To everyone's amazement, one of the most powerful monarchs in Europe deliberately behaved like a merchant. (On the basis of their opinions, he decided to make Ostend a free port.)[63] Samuel Johnson, at work in the royal library, was visited by his king who chatted with him about books in a conversation Johnson later described as a nearly overpowering act of condescension, meaning an act of crossing class boundaries that suspended normal hierarchies.[64] Yet monarchs were also figureheads in courts where hierarchy was expressed through clothes – Joseph II's invitation to *divest* points to that symbolism. Descriptions of court clothes in the press underlined how monarchs were meant to commandeer the most expensive, fabulous stuffs and exquisite workmanship in dress. However much a new consumer capitalism was changing the world, monarchs were still its glittering leaders.

A futurist court circular imagined His Majesty travelling from St James's to Windsor in a balloon designed by 'Signior [*sic*] Vertigo'. The conveyance would be drawn by suitably regal eagles (the travelling time of fifteen minutes would be halved once they got used to drawing a balloon). They would surpass nobility like the Duchess of Flywell, whose balloon would be drawn by sparrowhawks.[65] Symbolic pecking order put monarchs firmly above, in a space with ideological competition only from ideas of divinity, to which monarchs had established connections. The power of this system is evident in the furore around Herschel's choice of 'Georgium Sidus' as a name for his new planet: it disrupted the mythological system of heavenly bodies, which in British culture revolved around planets as metaphors – thus Venus for love, Mars for war. What could George III possibly symbolise compared to classical gods! And yet people constantly described balloons as a majestic spectacle. The word derives from the Latin *major*, comparative of *magnus*, great: monarchs had to be greater than their people.

Majestic seems a cliché to readers now but it was clearly fresh to users then. At a point where newspapers told of monarchs in shirtsleeves, why was majestic so appealing? If one follows the historians who see eighteenth-century royalty becoming less extraordinary yet more appealing to a growing bourgeoisie, it might be explained as nostalgia – majestic was what royalty had been. Or what it should be – a platonic constant. Patriots sang 'Hearts of Oak' less and 'God Save the King' more.[66] Majesty was emphasised through new pageantry like Trooping the Colour, introduced by George III, in which the king publicly reviewed troops. Eighteenth-century music had a term *maestoso*, 'to play or sing with majesty, pomp, and grandeur, and consequently slow, though with strength and firmness of the hand or voice'.[67] It was unrushed, unlike the world of fashionable speed. London aristocracy in the 1780s was looked up to as a source of wealth and fashion but not much else; the Prince of Wales was an exemplar of why. Positions at court were still important but the king was openly attacked and mocked in the press. Vilification can of course co-exist with loyalty: when Margaret Nicholson stepped out of the shadows in St James's Park in 1786 to stab George III, *The Gentleman's Magazine* carried a report that combined old concepts of sacred majesty with a very modern metaphor: 'The Noise of the Attempt on the sacred Life of His Majesty circulated through the

Metropolis with electrical Speed'.[68] The king was unhurt, and the sigh of relief breathed by loyal subjects was fervent but not particularly deep. In 1788, a young hairdresser got into the royal apartments to declare his passion for the Princess Elizabeth; again, the political fuss was over quickly, though endured longer by the youth who suffered five weeks in a straitjacket. Loyalty was combined with hostility at times surprisingly extended to the royal family: when Princess Amelia died in 1786, it was cruelly noted her death would provide savings on the civil list, which George III had overspent.[69]

What other words were in the lexicon of royalty? 'Progress' no longer meant a royal tour round dominions: it meant social improvement, by all for all. 'Condescension' is interesting: it evoked body language in its import of bending down, graciously. It was courtiers' bodies on which royalty's codes were most rigidly inscribed in codes of dress and deportment.[70] Condescension might have been a word to use for a descending balloon, but nobody did. A balloon descended with no hint of monarchical condescension; it simply came down. Neither transitive verb nor noun appealed to writers as much as the adjective 'majestic', a word invoking monarchy without reference to specific monarchs. Slow, stately, placed high above: balloons like monarchs were a spectacle in which looking enabled feeling, a feeling of admiration and reverence that connected kings, queens and balloons

Gods and Heroes

'the present Age will be for ever Distinguished as being productive
of one of the boldest Efforts of Human Genius, to obtain what all
Ages of the World have ardently wished for.'

Felix Farley's Bristol Journal, 26 April 1785

ENLIGHTENMENT THOUGHT is usually characterised as
having a drive to secularism, most obviously in the writings
of those anti-clerical French philosophers – Voltaire, Diderot –
who redrew the era's intellectual maps. The 1780s were a decade
in which Enlightenment was as widely and explicitly pursued as
it ever would be, before the implosion of the French Revolution
turned secularism into an aggressive ideology determined to throw
out old institutions and overthrow old class relations. What, then,
is the significance of descriptions of aeronauts as gods? Is it a way
of instating classicism as an alternative to clericalism? Is it a lightly
allusive language that playfully creates a category of social actors
for whom there needs to be distinction? Is it a carry-over from the
ancient world, one of many that Enlightenment revivified, in which
mythology appeals because it provides an explanatory system that
is both secure and remote? What sort of ironies are at work in the
metaphor? And how does the idea of aeronauts as gods fit with belief
in God, which was upheld by much Enlightenment activity even as
rationalism loosened the grip of piety for many? Why too did people
evoke gods when they had a perfectly serviceable alternative, both
classical and contemporary, in the term heroes?

Some light is shed by comparison to the language used about
aeronauts in a later period. It has been suggested by a scholar of
Victorian balloonists, Elaine Freedgood, that ballooning provided
an escape from 'the new social world created by industrial capitalism
with its suddenly too-numerous and too-contingent object relations', and that by the mid nineteenth century ballooning offered a
way to enjoy silence and space, increasingly rare commodities. What

she describes as 'a necessary pause from the tearing pace of produc-
tivity and progress' could equally apply to the 1780s, which felt
hectic to people at the time.[1] Even after fifty years of ballooning, the
exceptionality of aeronauts was remarked on: 'A person who makes
an ascent in a balloon will become, at least in his own estimation,
a person of consequence.' Discussing the parachutist Cocking in
1837, this same writer commented: 'What extraordinary exertions
and fatigue must this great personage have undergone merely to
delight his fellow-creatures.'[2] But note that 'in his own estimation';
an element of scepticism appears, which for all the satire, mockery
and doubt attendant on balloons in the 1780s was rarely generalised
into an idea of inflated egotism. In contrast, Victorian opposition
to ballooning as pointlessly risky was extraordinarily vituperative.
After Cocking died in a crash in 1837, although twenty thousand
visitors flocked to the spot where he fell, the queen gave his widow
£50, and parliament agreed to buy his aeronautic collection, unsym-
pathetic views were vocal. A would-be successor to Cocking was
denounced by *The Morning Post*:

> Is money, or notoriety, or are both, the aim of this person? Is Mr.
> Hampton tired of his life? If he be, let him go hang himself, and not
> call upon the public to pay for a silly suicidal exhibition in a para-
> chute. We must trust that the good taste and feeling of Englishmen
> will not be parties to a scheme for the perpetration of self-murder.[3]

Staying with the Victorians briefly, we can see how terms have
hardened. Balloons in the 1830s have shed claims to science and the
excitement of imaginative possibility:

> Still must we ask, what is the advantage of those exhibitions?
> – Human curiosity naturally turns to them with strong interest –
> philosophy sees in them a tantalising spectacle. Of all the discov-
> eries of mechanism, this machine seems at once to be the nearest to
> perfection – and yet separated from that perfection by an obstacle
> hitherto unsurmountable. The Nassau balloon [flown by Charles
> Green from Vauxhall to Nassau] shows us what might be effected
> by this great instrument. In that instance, five or six hundred miles
> of sea, plain, mountain and valley were swept over in a night. Before
> another sunset Europe would have been traversed – four-and-twenty
> hours in addition would have brought them in sight of the frontiers
> of British India. The aeronauts tell us that the balloon might have
> been kept up at this rate for six months. Such are the powers of the
> balloon, but those powers depend upon an element which hitherto no
> man has been able to master, and the invention still remains a toy.[4]

The tone of impatience comes from frustration: imperial applications are just out of reach. Since 1783, progress has stalled: as in the early days, crowds had to wait for ascents that never happened or which ended in a crash and whose failures led to riots. But now balloons had become explicitly part of an entertainment business, with aeronauts as showmen. For all that aeronauts of the 1780s supplied spectacle and needed to raise money, there was a nimbus of philosophy around balloons which has simply disappeared a generation later. In the 1840s the development of steam power and the railways made progress evident, and reductively so for balloons. If they were ever to be any use, it would be as a form of transport running alongside the railways, modernity with a future. Dreams of going to the moon persisted but they were less playful; imaginative voyages became journeys of imperial ambition. Even the romance of the moon invoked by Jules Verne's fantasies in the second half of the nineteenth century was to be compatible with its exploitation. There was a different emotional context too: less tolerance of risk, more assumption of spectacle, and more contempt for both risk and spectacle. Aeronauts were not acclaimed as brave adventurers; they no longer carried universal ambition aloft. Nineteenth-century news reports showed interest in the mechanical innovations of particular assemblages – thus in 1840, G. B. Gale's balloon has two small side balloons like ears that take excess gas, and a new grappling iron with five points[5] – but the attention paid to parts is accompanied by indifference to the philosophic whole.

Writers on balloons in the 1780s do invoke both mastery and toys, but with respect for play. Toys were moving into the world of children, often in the form of miniaturised adult tools, and trifles could still be philosophic.[6] If balloons were ludicrous to some, they were ludic too. The wild enthusiasm that balloons generated was not complacent: 'we live in a century of wonders!' exclaimed one writer on aerostation, but promptly noted, 'we labour under a horrid degree of ignorance'.[7] Promoting balloons from a miscellaneous section in 1783 to their own special section the following year, the *London Magazine* declared 'every one will perceive, in this wonderful effort of human invention, a certain means of extending commerce ... we have, without a doubt, an evident right to make public our ideas on the means of perfecting this discovery, and bringing it into use; nay, it is a tribute which every thinking being owes to society'.[8]

Rights, use, the public, perfection: here in a nutshell are key Enlightenment terms. Capitalism, not yet fully industrialised, encourages effort in the forms of work, invention and discovery that are as much attached to emotion – wonder – as to labour. Here is a psychosemantics of heroism: the hero achieves something recognised by reason as extraordinary exertion, for which the element of extra in extraordinary is rewarded in a commercial language. Paying tribute was one way of paying for it. We make heroes out of people who have done something we acclaim as valuable, a value converted into praise, a gift paid through language.[9] The process is quasi-economic; paying tribute allows the public to confer value freely. The idiom accounts for why people denied this gift transaction describe themselves as feeling cheated. It also informs the common description of failed aeronauts as frauds upon the public. It isn't just that aeronauts have taken money and failed to deliver; they have failed to deliver on the gift economy too.

The developing psychology of capitalism in the 1780s explains a language of heroes but not so obviously that of gods. One might simply say gods are one step up from heroes, as they are in classical mythology, and that gods more naturally occupy that heaven which is figuratively and literally located somewhere up above the clouds. Gods can fly and gods hang out in places; it helps that in French, *dieux* rhymes with *lieux*. Leaving nature literally below, aeronauts ascending to the heavens entered a place traditionally associated with the supernatural. Gods are loosely epic, suiting the more-than-heroic adventurism of aeronauts. They are also subtly divine: not God. The history of late eighteenth-century relations between reason and religion is too big to go into here: what's relevant is that Enlightenment thought largely avoided impiety in its public questioning of unthinking reverence. Gods was a useful trope for evoking new human powers without unseating the power of God. It was obvious to many that balloons could lead to secular appropriation of a symbolic realm previously held by God. After Etienne Montgolfier demonstrated the animal-manned balloon at Versailles, he was given a poem which included the line 'The creator of this globe is still merely a mortal man'.[10] An account of a hydrogen balloon flight in December 1783 by Charles and Roberts showed a little inset scene in which Jove and Mercury hand laurels to the three aeronauts.[11] Immortals bestow something extra on mortals; they pay tribute, in lieu of us, and as symbols of *lieux* which aeronauts visit on our behalf. The secularising Enlightenment enjoyed allegorical tendencies, drawing up pantheons of figures with numinous functions. In this way people could borrow divinity without

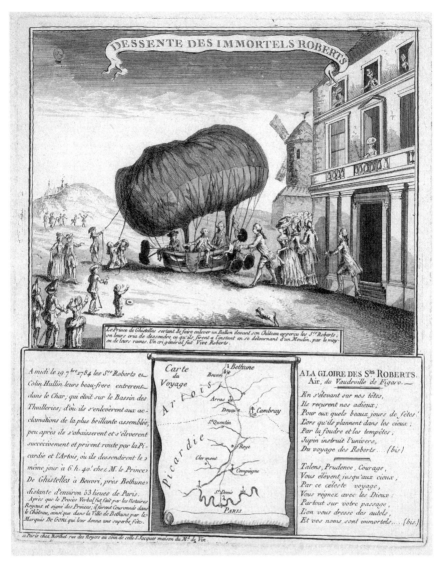

A descent by immortals: partly-coloured print commemorating a flight
by the Roberts on 19 July 1784. 'Le Prince de Ghistelles sortant de
faire enlever un Ballon devant son Château apperçu les Srs Roberts, on
leurs cria de dessendre ce qu'ils firent a l'instant en se détournant d'un
Moulin, par le moyen de leurs rames. Un cri générale fut Vive Roberts.'
[The Prince of Ghistelles, setting out to launch a balloon in front of his
château, sighted the Roberts; they were called on to descend, which they
did straightaway, managing to avoid a windmill by means of their oars. A
general cry went up, Long live the Roberts!] Paris [1784]. Note the tiny
balloon top left, also coloured.

necessarily usurping it. Three-fold immortality is conferred in a print celebrating the Roberts again, descending with their brother-in-law in 1784 [Figure 19]: in the title, in the laudatory verses and, eloquently wordless, in the tribute of colour given to balloon, aeronauts and car, landing before an uncoloured prince in a black and white landscape.

One of the happiest instances of numinosity features a trio who made a successful flight from Norfolk in the autumn of 1785. Back on the ground they wore laurel wreaths and referred to themselves as 'the favoured of heaven'. The Reverend Mr Peter Routh (who built the balloon), Mr Robert Davy and Mrs Hines (who replaced an unfortunately too corpulent Miss Fanny Shouldham) were described as 'gods' by a report that bet both ways, on secular and religious inferences, explaining that the trio were gods for 'this singular act of courage, and instance of divine protection'.[12] Rather more mundanely, protection was provided by a Dutch fishing boat whose crew scooped up these gods, one of whom could speak a little Dutch – a goodwill act possibly stimulated by an annual festival at Yarmouth celebrating fraternity with Dutch fishermen, who visited in yellow boats for a weekend of socialising.[13] One of the fillers of this balloon was a Reverend Houlden, who remitted a year and a half's tithes to farmers whose crops were damaged by spectators. God's employees were part of the property economy; 'gods' takes us back to the gift zone. It may also be no coincidence that near-divine metaphors attached readily to trios of aeronauts, as if allegorising trinities unconsciously mirrored a Trinity it would be blasphemous to invoke directly.

A language about gods was a means through which an educated class used allegory and metaphor to manage ideological complexity. Joseph Montgolfier incorporated this verse on a balloon design:

> Le genie est du ciel le don le plus parfait,
> Montgolfier l'obtint, maitre de l'Empiree
> M'entraine sur ses pas a la voute Etheree;
> Et je rapporte aux Dieux le tribute de bienfait.

> [Genius is the greatest gift from heaven/ Montgolfier obtains it, master of the Empire/ Following in his steps to the Etherial way/ And I carry to the Gods the tribute of making.][14]

Montgolfier offers a virtuous circle in which the source of invention is carefully located as coming from above, to whence his balloon returns the credit.

Balloons showed that the intersection of commerce, religion and invention in the 1780s is complex. Commerce encourages invention, religion does not. One reason Count Zambeccari came ballooning in England was that it was a country where he was safe, following a brush with the Inquisition. That Zambeccari was in danger of arraignment for heresy testified to the still real risk of punishment for blasphemy on the continent. A language of gods evoked piety whilst keeping gratitude for invention neutral rather than Christian. The gift economy of praise left room for inventors to take credit. Here we bump into a tangle of meanings around the word credit. Etymologically from the Latin *credere*, to believe, credit gives us the core statement of Christian belief, the Creed. In the late eighteenth century, this religious discourse co-existed with a broad Enlightenment economy of knowledge in which truth was described as something creditable, and with a flow in capitalism towards turning material invention into intellectual property. Paul Keen has applied a version of this model to Lunardi, reading him as an instance of commercial modernity in which commodification, science and fashion spun interdependently.[15] Arguing for the co-dependence of science and technology in this period, Larry Stewart suggests 'The seeking of recognition in the marketplace was one of the singular marks of the modernity of eighteenth-century scientific practitioners.'[16] Etienne Montgolfier was terrified that the credit for inventing balloons would not revert to the Montgolfiers: 'we are surrounded by hornets ... and they will not hesitate to steal our work and appropriate the credit.'[17] Hornets invert that metaphor of bees producing honey in the hive of industry which eighteenth-century writers liked as a descriptor of commerce that served social progress.[18] What balloons exposed was a tension between an enlightened economy of knowledge open to all and reward for the individual inventors. That tension is eased by a concept of intellectual property which enables individuals to claim credit and secure financial gain, but this was still in development in the 1780s. The patent system went some way to formalising a relationship between ownership and profit from design, but then as now it was often a murky business. What we call Arkwright's spinning jenny, for instance, was highly contested, with numerous lawsuits brought by people who reckoned Arkwright infringed their designs. Invention must catch on to be profitable but in doing so is at risk of running beyond the control of its inventor. Etienne Montgolfier kicked himself for making information too freely available in the états particuliers published after flights; his brother Alexandre counter-argued that doing so was what made Etienne famous and that publication secured him credit.[19] How freedom of information beds into intellectual property is an issue still with us in the internet age. Talk of gods, tribute and gifts from gods was one way to air the problem without committing to a solution.

The realisation of the dream of flight put reason at a threshold of new powers; a language of gods acknowledged its potential to displace divine omnipotence. This idea was significantly and paradoxically represented as a feeling. Present at the first ascent of a hydrogen balloon on 1 December 1783, the Comte de Ségur described it feelingly:

> The kind and feeling heart of Louis XVI, terrified by this rash attempt, wished to oppose it at first. At the moment when every eye was fixed on a frail skiff, bold enough to brave the winds, immensity of space, and so many other perils till then unknown, an order of the minister arrived to prevent their departure; but the courage of the aeronauts, and the impatience of an immense crowd assembled to enjoy this effort of genius, triumphed over every interdiction. The ropes were cut, the balloon ascended majestically from the earth, and we soon beheld the aerial navigators intrepidly traverse the vault of heaven.[20]

The earthly power of kings, and an absolutist monarch at that, submits to aeronauts and their tribute-paying crowd. In this whirl of feelings, language reaches a frontier:

> On that memorable day, and after this triumph of genius over nature, each of the spectators felt as if his dignity had increased, and the word impossible seemed no longer to exist. One would have said that every barrier had just disappeared before the pride and ambition of the human mind.[21]

Spectators become first kingly, then free of any earth-bound definition. In a remarkable flight of imagination, humans no longer need any higher belief system. It was a brief glimpse of visionary possibilities. Nothing was impossible.

Nonetheless, a language of gods persisted because it did important emotional work. Classical gods are stable as personifications: Jove always represents power, Minerva wisdom and so on. But they do not always behave rationally. Many stories of gods turn on occasions of emotion – a goddess slighted, a god moved to anger. Although a biblical God has emotions too – anger in the Old Testament, compassion in the New – there was more decorum in aligning

passions with a pantheon of gods. That decorum was also compatible
with humour, including potentially indecorous innuendo, as a verse
of advice to Lunardi slyly suggests:

> It was the custom, long ago
> For Gods to visit us below;
> But now the case seems alter'd quite
> For we in turn now take our flight,
> To spy what's going on above:
> But have a care, lest angry JOVE
> Your visits bold should disapprove.
> So be advis'd, don't mount so often,
> His Highness may be hard to soften;
> If you persist again to fly,
> He'll look on you with jealous eye,
> And doubtless think, not without reason,
> Against his state you plot high treason:
> His Ladies he may think in danger,
> At sight of such a handsome stranger,
> And may, who knows? For deed so hardy
> Repel with *thunder* poor LUNARDI.[22]

Mythology manages the sense of temerity, that boldness which
in eighteenth-century parlance often meant crossing a social line,
whether making sexual advances or advancing into the skies. Since
Lunardi did both, a discourse of gods readily attached to him,
perhaps reinforced by his Roman-descended nationality and by his
having exhibited his balloon in classically-named places of display in
London. In 1785, one satirist especially had fun with mythology of
all sorts in a mock-biblical account of his rise and fall:

> *Lunardi* an Italian hired the *Lyceum*, and shewed the marvelling
> multitude of unbelievers his balloon, with which he was to raise
> himself above his fellow mortals. ... And he arose into the regions
> of the air, in the sight of the great assembly, who shouted aloud,
> and cried in the English tongue, Surely this man is greater than
> Daedalus, and more adventurous than Phaeton. ... Lunardi is fallen
> ... yea, the false God of the Pantheon shall ascend no more for ever![23]

Moving classicism into the aeronautical scene also provided a
way to negotiate emotions which witnesses could express unham-
pered by theology. As Richard Holmes has explored, wonder was
one.[24] Astonishment, even stronger, was another. They were rather
different emotions. Astonishment renders a spectator dumb: the
astonished say nothing and need say nothing because astonishment

says it for them through a body language of immobility and open mouths. Conversely, a language of gods could be very articulate. Planets to which aeronauts might sail had gods' names and qualities which set off puns and naughtiness:

> I am just come down in an air balloon from all the planets I have visited them one by one; and though Jupiter gave me a very strong invitation to stay, after slipping into Venus and touching Mercury for the benefit of my health, I thought it as well to come home again...[25]

But the language of gods also made silence expressive, like the zone of inarticulacy on which the sublime turned. Lunardi evoked this most strongly for spectators in Britain, and Crosbie in Ireland. Seeing a human being in flight for the first time produced intensely strong emotions: 'Nothing could equal the surprize and amazement, the pleasure and concern, the fear and expectation that appeared through the altogether astonished multitude.'[26] Spectators of early ascents showed rich and contradictory body language: tears of joy and fear; shouts and awed silence; hands clasped in tension and prayer. Their body language copied that physical oratory of eight-eenth-century theatre and religion which made gesture emotionally expressive.

There was one other important word in the vocabulary around aeronauts: intrepid. Used so frequently one might notice it only as a cliché, it attached itself to minor aeronauts as well as obvious heroes. Poole, for example, who made a flight in October 1785, was 'our intrepid Aeronaut, who during the whole time showed a degree of coolness scarcely to be paralleled'.[27] The word, relatively new, was coined by Dryden to mean fearless, inverting *trepidus*, alarmed or agitated, from the Greek *trapein*, to tread. What's underfoot gener-ates an emotion; not to have anything underfoot shows the more courage in going forward. Intrepid had a nautical chime: there were at least three ships named *Intrepid*, one of which saw active service between 1780 and 1782: under Admiral Rodney at Martinique in 1780 (a draw); in 1781 at the battle for the Chesapeake (a defeat); under Admiral Hood at St Kitts (a win on points). Intrepid heroes ventured where, in Alexander Pope's phrase, angels feared to tread.

At the same time as gods and heroes supplied a stabilising clas-sical framework, and intrepidity a modern one, there was also a language about balloons and the lower classes that slotted in at the bottom of the social order. There were some differences between that social order in England and France, although in both countries it suited the enlightened to associate ignorance with superstition. It is also difficult to disentangle native forms of class condescension, since the British press printed verbatim aeronautic reports from France and the continent. One matter of English pride was that its labouring class was to all appearances not as benighted as the French peasantry. English chauvinism prided itself on not having an under-class who were barefoot and starving (even if some were). Cultural stereotypes affected higher classes: when French manufacturers engaged in espionage and tried to lure over skilled workers, English industrialists were keen to tell those tempted that if they went to France they'd have to eat frogs and snails.[28] Ordinarily, French peasants were assumed to be ignorant by virtue of both class and religion, since Catholicism was by definition a superstitious religion in the eyes of Anglican rationalists and deists. But balloons united people. A pair of aeronauts, Morveau and Bertrand, who took off from Dijon and landed at Auxonne, found two men and three women kneeling to their balloon. Reverence to balloons was rational, given their universal power to astonish. When Blanchard and M. Boby descended from a flight from Rouen on 23 May 1784, they were met by people (Blanchard's term would be *paysannes*) who cried, Are you men or gods?[29] At the frontier of humanism, aerostation adopted a universal language significant not just for its elevation of aeronauts but also for its universalising of spectators.

Like reverence, intrepidity was also open to all classes and both sexes – and all ages, like the old woman who was the only one of forty people not to flee when Sadler descended in a cornfield at Burford in 1785.[30] The courage of intrepidity was particular: cool not fool-hardy, it gestured to a rational assessment of risk both in the air and on the ground. The young woman who alone of her fellow-labourers came to Lunardi's aid when he descended in a field at South Mimms was admired for her courage; it was not seen as exceptional in class or gender terms, though her companions are stereotypically fearful. A print of 1784 [Figure 20] claims in its rhymes that 'The clowns are frighten'd at the sight', but at the same time it is doing its own reassuring work to explain what an air balloon is. Discussing a print of the *montgolfière* balloon which fell at Gonesse showing peasants attacking it with pitchforks, one British magazine commented that even an intelligent or learned person would hesitate to approach a thing on the ground moving in leaps and bounds.[31] The intrepidity of aeronauts was set against fear not always dependent on super-stition and ignorance; rural people frightened by balloons were not

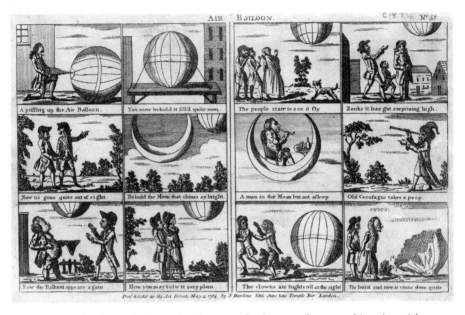

20   Staring at balloons by clowns and other people: a graphic print with
            rhymes. Engraving published 4 May 1784.

necessarily stupid peasants. Thus the fear of one farmer confronted
by a thing in his field arose from the thing's glinting; another was
able to turn monster to object by reading its label. As with UFO
sightings now, those unable to classify objects raised consciousness
about how things are classified. A balloon sent up from Bristol was
found at Wells by a man who thought it was a wild animal. My
point is he is thinking. Once he was told it was a balloon, he (rather
cleverly!) reinflated it with bellows and exhibited it at tuppence a
head.[32] A farmer's servant at work in a field in Kent was scared by
a balloon descending and ran away; he told people he had seen a
dancing devil in the shape of a meat pudding, a description that draws
intelligently on what he knows. Returning to the scene, he calmly
collared this devil and exhibited it for a profit.[33] Paul Keen notes
the 'entrepreneurial savvy' of such exhibitors;[34] 'savvy' shows that
knowing how to process concepts and define objects was not exclusively the preserve of a savant class. Learning was often described in
the eighteenth century as something one profits from. These stories
of yokels who wise up are sometimes in contrast with an elevated
language of gods and heroes but, very importantly, they are also
its lower-order counterpart. Miniature narratives of enlightenment,
they show commerce as an instrument of reason; if commerce was

open to all, so reason would be. What Pierre Bourdieu perceives in the evolution of capitalism to be a drive in which the citizen becomes the consumer is here manifested in how the balloon reconciles the citizen and consumer in simultaneous transaction.[35] There was also morality in it: exhibition created and shared cultural capital, in contrast to the French peasants who opportunistically stole valuable gold gauze from Blanchard's balloon on its landing after an ascent from The Hague in 1785, a theft described in startlingly strong terms as 'audacious and inhuman'.[36] Again one can see continuities and changes by the 1840s. When Hampton wanted to tether his balloon next to gasworks that would provide a reliable fill, he came up against ruffians who blackmailed him with a threat of cutting his ropes.[37] An urbanised underclass had invented new ways of making capital out of balloons.

The circulation of 'stupid peasant' stories in the press was doing much more than the work of class condescension. It was sharing rational management of balloon madness by all classes. Such stories are also about managing the unknown and emotions around it. That the educated drew more on myth and literature to do so makes them different in degree rather than kind from the less educated who thought they saw devils, which after all also have sources in myth and literature. There were plenty of overlaps: educated people used workaday comparisons, like the gentleman in Lincolnshire reporting the capture of a diabolically hissing and crackling balloon which, once tamed, was 'much in the Shape of a Petticoat'.[38] Educated people also played with diabolism. Mary Eleanor Bowes wrote in 1786 to a friend about a balloon at Farningham whose arrival was announced by a cry of 'flying Devil' just alighted there, 'who had come prancing through the air on Horseback; we were not without some hopes that it might be a supernatural Bailiff come from Lucifer to arrest his long devoted Creditor, but alas! It only proved an ethereal Man & Horse, wch had taken its flight from the Pantheon'. She went to see it but a frightened miller had kicked the phantom and let out the gas, 'so there was nothing but a painted Oilskin to be seen'.[39] The Darwin Awards now which feature astonishing acts of stupidity similarly evoke astonishment in the not-so-stupid, but they too make you think about not thinking – and in relation to a classifying system, Darwinian evolution. Moreover, the intelligentsia recognised ignorance as a reasonable factor in the reception of balloons. In the first phase of air-globe experiments, the French authorities issued warnings of impending flights by notices sent to the countryside. That precaution still turned on literacy, a limited skill. Here farmers came off better than peasants, though anyone might be baffled by the appearance of an airborne horse and woman, as happened in October 1785 to a French labourer in the fields. The peasant could not read the letter in the mouth of the horse, but nonetheless took both to a neighbouring château where he was rewarded. The woman-shaped balloon descended at Gentvillier among a rural crew 'who all mistook the figure, that then stood still, for a real living creature in distress. None, however, dared to advance towards it, except the farmer, who took it up in his arms, but to his great surprise found he was hugging an inflated bladder.'[40] An inflatable woman falls from the sky – when the real was so surreal, invoking the supernatural was rational.

The language of gods and heroes was an important resource in the cultural absorption of balloons. It also had a shelf life. Widely used during the height of balloon madness, it tailed off. The novelty, honour and hazard of air-blown enterprises are past, claimed a letter-writer in print in April 1785.[41] Classificatory work shared by rural people also changed, as an account from 1808 makes clear. Describing a flight made by James Sadler from Oxford on 3 July, the writer dwelt on ignorance and misunderstanding of aeronautics.[42] If one thinks of Enlightenment as a way of thinking in which practices of observation, experiment, reason and enquiry are uppermost or privileged, and spread by intellectual networks and the press interested in informing readers, then Enlightenment was not unstoppable. It was clearly not reaching the inhabitants of rural Oxfordshire:

> It would be a ludicrous description could one detail the remarks of the *gentes rusticae* at the time of this ascent, or the strange reports we heard from the country, over which the wondrous machine floated. One party were expressing their surprise, how the aeronauts could get into the balloon, after filling it so full. Another more learned expected to see them mount the distended sphere. In its progress it scattered terror unutterable, and those ill-informed of what was going on about them, took it, at least, for an angelic visitation, if not for the approach of the *very* last day. The dismay spread for thirty miles, and was beyond description.[43]

Commentators in the 1780s similarly report alarm, fear and supernatural associations, but they do not on the whole express contempt. Ignorance of balloons in the 1780s is read as relatively rational and misunderstandings, however comic, are taken as efforts to under-stand balloons within available frameworks, including religious ones. Twenty-five years later, class differences had hardened. *Gentes rusticae* are separated into a foreign language; the play of ideas has moved to ludicrous description.

The Sublime

'But what Scenes of Grandeur and Beauty! A Tear of pure Delight flashed in his Eye!'

Thomas Baldwin, *Airopaidia*

THE SUBLIME WAS CRUCIAL in giving balloon madness some cultural respectability. What was it and why did it matter? An idea with a long history, it had been refreshed in the mid eighteenth century and applied to a range of situations in which a viewing or feeling subject encountered something from which a powerful aesthetic charge resulted. This chapter explores how the sublime shaped thinking about balloons, how it paired and competed with ideas of the beautiful in the making of new aerial aesthetics, and how this reworking fits in to modern ideas about the aerial gaze.

As Michael R. Lynn notes by the title of his book, balloons themselves were described as 'The Sublime Invention', and 'sublime' is a regular fixture in accounts of aerial voyages. One example shows the frequency and typical variations of its use. When Richard Crosbie ascended from Dublin on 19 January 1785 to make the first successful ascent in Ireland, the sublime accompanied him: 'Mr Crosbie himself assures us that his voyage throughout was perfectly smooth, tranquil and sublime'.[1] What spectators felt was also sublime, with a theological colouring:

> It is but truth to affirm, the business of that day was the most awfully magnificent that can engage the human mind; that in common with the aerial traveller himself, and every feeling spectator in that immense crowd, we have experienced the most grateful, benevolent, and sublime sensations; since, while He sees us occupied in search of truth, and the enlargement of science, it would seem that Omnipotence hath scarcely set any limits to the bold enquiries, and the high aspiring views of man.[2]

Boundlessness associated with the sublime meant its effects outlasted the event which gave rise to it. So sublime was Crosbie's achievement, according to this writer, that the grateful nation which held him in the highest esteem now would continue to look up to him in the future. The celebratory poem – itself an outworking of the sublime ascent – began with the sublime:

> Th'increasing Throngs, from morn to highest noon,
> To view th'elancement of the First Balloon,
> To view th'aerial voyager in triumphal car,
> Sublimely traversing the fields of air;
> The strong emotions, and the pangs that rise
> In feeling bosoms, as he gains the skies;
> These, the mixt prospects of that signal day
> Arrest our wonder, and invite my lay.

In this poem of fifteen pages, 'sublime' makes five appearances; balloon flights are described as 'This highest species of the *great sublime.*'[3] So entrenched it needed no glossing, the sublime could be relied upon to convey emotions otherwise overpowering. It gave a philosophical frame to aerial aesthetics, helping to inscribe recognisable process and effects onto new experiences of air.[4]

The sublime had a long and respectable history going back to Longinus in the first century AD. In early eighteenth-century Britain, the sublime had been discussed at length by Addison in *The Spectator* as part of his project to take philosophy to coffee-houses and tea-tables, and it had been variously taken up by poets – especially Edward Young, whose long poem set in a churchyard, *The Complaint, or Night Thoughts on Life, Death and Immortality* (1742–45), was wildly successful across Europe. Part VII of that poem takes a key turn to the sublime:

> To lift us from this Abject, to Sublime;
> This Flux, to Permanent; this Dark, to Day;
> This Foul, to Pure; this Turbid, to Serene;
> This Mean, to Mighty!

Permanent, day, pure, serene and mighty: Young gave the sublime a metaphysical vocabulary that fitted the boundless skies encountered by aeronauts forty years later.[5]

The sublime was paired with the beautiful and given full treatment in Edmund Burke's *A Philosophical Enquiry into the Origin of Our Ideas of the Sublime and Beautiful* (1757). Burke wanted to sort out what he saw as a philosophical muddle and clarify origins, process and effects. His elegant, popular analysis was influential especially in its typology of sources of the sublime and beautiful, and how they affected the body and the passions. 'The passion caused by the great and sublime in *nature*, when those causes operate most powerfully, is Astonishment; and astonishment is that state of the soul, in which all its motions are suspended, with some degree of horror.'[6] Burke described how certain objects or situations – vast, dark, infinite, difficult and magnificent – gave rise to the sublime. The ocean, for instance, is feared because it seems infinite. Though terror is the more memorable emotion in sublime encounters, pleasure arises too: in feeling overwhelmed, we touch our limits and the thrill strengthens us. Beauty, on the other hand, was simply pleasing. It was to be found in small, smooth, round objects, ones of gradual variation of colour, like a drake's head or a dove's breast. Burke associated sublimity with rugged objects, though roughness of outline was acquiring its own aesthetic: the picturesque, formalised by William Gilpin and Uvedale Price. 'Picturesque' originally meant painterly composition, especially in landscape painting. In 1782 William Gilpin took it explicitly outdoors to apply it to picturesque beauty in the countryside.[7] All these terms were variably relevant to description in aerial voyages.

The sublime's aesthetic of powerful effects made it first choice for aerial descriptions; even so, making it airborne needed imagination. As Tiberius Cavallo put it:

> If we consider for a moment the sensation which these first aerial adventurers must have felt in their exalted situation, we can hardly prevent an unusual sublime idea in ourselves. – Imagine a man elevated to such a height, into an immense space, by means altogether new, viewing under his feet, like a map, a vast tract of country, with one of the greatest towns existing, the streets and environs of which were crowded with spectators, attentive to him alone, and all expressing, in every possible manner, their amazement, and their anxiety. Reflect on the prospect, the encomiums, and the consequences; then see if your mind remains in a state of quiet indifference.[8]

Cavallo gives us an aerial gaze and spectatorial empathy, a double form of the sublime. Witnessing heroism produced the sublime in spectators, according to the philosopher Hugh Blair:

> Wherever, in some critical and dangerous situation, we behold a man uncommonly intrepid, and resting solely upon himself; superior to passion and to fear; animated by some great principle to the contempt of popular opinion, or selfish interest, of dangers, or of death; we are there struck with a sense of the sublime.[9]

Collecting a lifetime's thoughts on retirement, Blair's publication in 1784 at the height of balloon madness uses terms suggestively like balloons: heroic entities 'produce an effect very similar to what is produced by the grand view of objects in nature; *filling the mind with admiration, and raising it above itself*' [my italics].[10] It was typical, notes Michael R. Lynn, for an audience at an ascent 'to express some sort of astonishment, surprise and awe'.[11] That 'sort' was invariably described as sublime, and one reason it fitted was that strong emotions produced a moment of arrestation that began the sublime trajectory of imaginative travel. It is as if our 'Wow!' began with the exclamation mark: '! Wow...'. So it suited the moment of pause just before a full balloon began to ascend.

Andrew Ashfield and Peter de Bolla have argued that 'the aesthetic is not *primarily* about art but about how we are formed *as subjects*, and how as subjects we go about making sense of our experience.'[12] Aeronauts took up the established sublime of the sea, calling themselves aero*nauts* and borrowing oars and rudders from ship technology. Even so, aerial aesthetics were relatively unformed: 'In the History of Airostation, each Event is yet new and *uncompared*'.[13] Aeronauts could be a sublime subject; they could also be an object of enquiry, a changeable point of spectacle, a hapless failure, even a fraud. Ballooning also involved comedy and bathos, which circumscribed the sublime's evocation of limitless possibility, and satire punctured the sublime by parodying its excess: you could be sublimely drunk.[14] Scientific experiment introduced a language of empiricism which also ran counter to the poetics of the sublime, though it was possible for texts to combine them. 'Publications such as Thomas Baldwin's *Airopaidia: Containing the Narrative of a Balloon Excursion from Chester, the Eighth of September, 1785* fortified themselves with endless tables of statistics that emphasised their scientific rigour', says Paul Keen.[15] Baldwin's *Airopaidia* also fortified itself with a long lyrical disquisition on what its author saw, thought and felt whilst aloft, testing his perceptions against notions of the sublime and beautiful. Just as science and the sublime were not opposites but partners, so too the sublime and beautiful were in dialogue with each other.

In representations of balloon ascents, the sublime had competition from the beautiful. As Baldwin described it, grand emotions 'will long continue to accompany a Spectacle so novel interesting and awful, as that of seeing a Fellow Mortal separated in a Moment from the Earth, and rushing to the Skies.'[16] The sublime's register of infinity, expansiveness and dizzying self-disarray suited because it conveyed in established ways ideas of daring and proximity to divinity. But the spectacle had beauty too, especially with striped or decorated balloons. Female passengers were hailed as heroic, like mythological goddesses moving through the air, but they were predominantly described as beautiful objects rather than sublime subjects. Thus a song commemorating the ascent of Miss Simonet with Blanchard on 3 June 1785:

> In pink and in white the sweet girl she was drest,
> Like Venus she look'd I declare
> And as Juno when drawn by her peacocks so gay,
> She sailed in the regions of air.[17]

The sublime and the beautiful harmonised in exhibitions of a *montgolfière* which had a shining design of stars and planets overlaid with gold: 'in fine, the whole exhibits the Appearance of a Huge World floating in the incomprehensible Infinity of eternal Space.'[18] Many inflammable air balloons had light netting over the top half of the inflated part to regularise differences in pressure between upper and lower areas; this netting resembled meridian lines on a globe and made balloons simultaneously beautiful, a miniature of the earth, and sublime, an image of a planet evocative of galactic space.

The sublime tended to describe the emotions of spectators, but it often gave way to beautiful in descriptions of balloons in the process of ascent:

> Beauty, next to Sublimity, affords, undoubtedly, the highest pleasure to the imagination. The emotion which it raises, is easily distinguished from that of sublimity. It is of a more gentle kind; more calm and soothing; does not elevate the mind so much, but produces a pleasing serenity. Sublimity excites a feeling, too violent to be lasting; the pleasure proceeding from Beauty admits of longer continuance. It also extends to a much greater variety of objects than Sublimity.[19]

Both Burke and Blair associated beauty with smoothness, regularity and gliding motion – motion upwards was intrinsically more beautiful than motion downwards, said Blair – so it was easily applied to a smoothly-ascending balloon. Ticking all these boxes, *The Morning Post* praised Lunardi's first successful flight in London for its 'regular and most beautiful ascension'.[20] In practice, high winds, faulty equipment and restive crowds often disrupted regularity, which made beautiful ascents all the more impressive. Practical challenges also introduced an idea of difficulty, which Hume for one thought sublime:

the idea of ascending always implies the notion of force exerted in overcoming this difficulty; the conception of which invigorates and elevates the thought, after the same manner as a vast object, and thus gives a distance above us much more of an appearance of greatness, than the same space could have in any other direction.[21]

Descents were often not smooth enough to be simply beautiful, and the sublime of difficulty was harder to apply because the balloon was notionally working with gravity, not against it. Besides, the sublime usually assumed a static object in the distance, not an object getting larger and closer. So the sublime hovered uncertainly around descents. Crash-landings in the country, where many people didn't know what a balloon was, had all the terror of the sublime, and the rushing noise of a descending balloon frightened many.[22] Even educated spectators were unsure how to describe what they saw. A clergyman who saw Lunardi's balloon come down through a Scotch mist struggled to find an image: 'I laboured, as it were, under the grandeur of the object, and strove to compare it to some thing I had seen, but I failed.'[23] Part of what disorientated this clergyman was the difficulty of reading the sublime off a moving object. Usually it worked around a fixed object like a mountain, whose immensity was constant, and the beautiful worked around littleness. Ascents and descents confused this. In ascents, the balloon looked smaller as it rose towards the empyreum, but the aeronaut's daring proportionately increased. Visual and emotional aspects of the sublime were thus at cross-purposes.

Once a balloon was out of view, a spectator was free to accompany it into an untrammelled sublime. As a would-be female aeronaut wrote in an ode to Lunardi:

My Spirit rose along with you!
I saw the grand, the glorious, View!
For, soaring High, the freer Mind
May mount upon the fleetest Wind.[24]

Free-minded aeronauts found precise aesthetic thinking liable to interruption: 'whilst we were admiring the beauty of the sublime prospect, three of the cords which held the boat gave way'.[25] Not many aeronauts were philosophically exact and their idea of the sublime was mostly a populist one. A modern analogy might be with the word 'cool', for which one could provide an exact intellectual history but to do so almost certainly would be at odds with how people actually use the word. Indeed one could argue that the cultural purchase of ideas like sublime or cool is precisely because they flourish in popular imagination regardless of philosophy.[26] Burke's 1757 *Enquiry* was probably the default source although the word 'sublime', available since the sixteenth century, means 'raise to a higher state', so etymology had already seeded an easy transition between balloons and what Sir Richard Blakemore described in 1716 as 'raised thoughts'.[27]

Elevation was of course a commonplace of the sublime long before actual flight. As Blakemore wrote: 'the epic poet should not grovel in the dust ... but keep above, and inure himself to lofty contemplation, till ... he gets a habit of thinking in the great and elevated manner ... By this he will be able to rise to the heights of heaven.'[28] Once above, however, all aeronauts looking down invoked the beautiful. Loftiness of viewing position took second place to miniaturisation of prospects. Towns were Lilliputian; fields were fairyland; buildings were like tea-caddies. Such similes unfixed the normal relativity between the sublime and the beautiful. As one poet put it: ''Tis the points whence we view things which fix, or create/ Our imperfect conceptions of Little, or Great!' Littleness thus paradoxically and pleasurably aggrandised the beautiful. The same poet apostrophised Lunardi:

> Ah! Tell me LUNARDI, – hereafter you may!
> What new scenes of wonder your flight must display?
> How awful the feel, when through new regions gliding,
> Through currents untry'd, and from cloud to cloud sliding?
> With what new ideas your mind must o'erflow!
> With what new sensations your bosom must glow! –
> How little, how trifling must then in your eyes
> Have seem'd what *below* we look up to and prize!
> No more than a molehill, the TOWER's old walls,
> A Hop-pole the MONUMENT, – Bandbox, ST. PAULS.[29]

Capital letters and lower case make the point about relative size – and a joke about it.

Aeronauts were uncertain about how useful the sublime was once they were passing through the heavens. Like people on earth, Baldwin put the sublime at a distance. The horizon was a 'grand Source of the Sublime' which helped organise views *across* the sky. Clouds were the main feature here. Clouds *below* were conventionally beautiful in seeming smooth, dazzling in sunshine like a polished crust of snow, or soft, like white tufts of cotton. Large clouds level with the aeronaut but at a distance were sublime, towering cliffs of cumulus. Through the white floor, reported Baldwin, 'uprose in splendid Majesty and awful Grandeur ... a vast Assemblage of Thunder-Clouds' which effortlessly fitted into a Miltonic sublime. Some, with 'conglomerate and fringed Tops' looked like gunsmoke solidified; others, 'dense, tonitrous Masses ... greatly resembled steep and rugged mountains seen in Perspective.'[30] Though Uvedale Price argued that thunderclouds were picturesque, most balloonists settled for the sublime.[31]

The sublime figured in aeronauts' self-consciousness. The extrovert Lunardi felt a sublimely boundless affection for his friends and Britain's first female aeronaut, Laetitia Sage, felt after her return to earth 'a species of terror' at the idea that 'I was daring enough to push myself, as I may say, before my time, into the presence of the Deity.'[32] This conformed to ideas of the sublime as something above low passions. But no critic had anticipated that experience of calm to which all aeronauts fervently testified as the emotional high of ballooning. Lunardi insisted on it: 'The critics *imagine*, for they seldom speak from experience, that terror is an ingredient in every sublime sensation. It was not possible for me to be on earth, in a situation so free from apprehension.'[33] Lunardi thought of this calm as sublime – 'The stillness ... rendered it highly awful' – and others remarked on its sacred overtones. Baldwin thought of Olympian divinities in the stillness of Renaissance frescoes: 'An universal Silence reigned! an empyrean Calm! unknown to Mortals *upon Earth*.'[34] This stillness was attributable to sound not reaching the upper atmosphere, combined with a contrary flow of air currents which arrested motion. Ashfield and de Bolla argue that:

> The sublime, in fact, is constantly understood via reference to the arrestation of movement, sometimes figured quite literally in the progress over a mountain top, or more figuratively as in the notion that the eye 'moves' through a landscape and is suddenly arrested in its movement by a specific 'eye-catcher'. This notion of suspension, of hanging in mid-air, will be well-developed in the romantic tradition, most especially in Wordsworth's poetry.[35]

It is perfectly illustrated by Blake in *Jerusalem* (c. 1821): 'silent, calm & motionless, in the mid-air sublime,/ The family Divine hover around the darkened Albion.'[36] The confluence of physical calm and mental serenity was so powerful that Baldwin tried to find a better word than sublime for it: 'an ENVIABLE EUROIA. An idea of which it is not in the Power of Language to convey, or to describe.'[37]

The challenge to articulate a new aesthetic was dramatised in a physical struggle to speak. 'He tried his Voice, and shouted for Joy. His Voice was unknown to himself, shrill and feeble. There was no Echo', reported Baldwin.[38] Echoes were to become important in Gothic novels where resonance of sound provided aural doubleness useful to plots like Ann Radcliffe's *The Mysteries of Udolpho* (1794). As a sound wave returned back to a listener, it mimicked and distorted the sublime pattern of self-possession returning to self. In his history of sound and listening, David Hendy describes how rock art around the world appears on places with echoes: 'It is hard to resist this thought: that places which echoed were special – 'labelled' by these painted images as being full of spirits, as sacred places.'[39] One of the revelations of the sky was that it had a sublime soundscape. When Crosbie ascended he too tried his voice: 'to his surprise and delight, it was re-echoed from all the surrounding clouds'.[40] What was described at the time as a scientific experiment was also a deeply intuitive reach for the numinous. The sublime is usually understood in terms of visual powers; it had an aural capacity too.

Aeronauts were the first to experience views of the earth from the air, and it is tantalising that they didn't make more of it. 'Balloon-Voyagers have ... been particularly Defective in the Descriptions of aërial Scenes and Prospects' wrote Thomas Baldwin, but even he had to interrupt his lofty contemplations. Caught by sudden gusts he wrote to himself in mid-air, 'NO MORE REMARKS, MIND THE SHIP.'[41] Nonetheless Baldwin was highly attentive to aesthetics. Enraptured by circling clouds, intense colours and the miniature world below, his written account tests exact notions of the sublime and beautiful against what he saw and felt. He also included three illustrative plates. Each contributes in new ways to aerial aesthetics: I discuss them in detail here in terms of eighteenth-century aesthetics, and at the end of the chapter in terms of their continuing influence.

Baldwin's first plate showed an aerial view of Chester, where he lived in a handsome house beyond the outskirts, which still stands. The town, in the centre, is surrounded by concentric rings of clouds like little mushrooms getting flatter towards the horizon, which curves like a bowl [Plate VI]. The original plates are hand-coloured: a red river (the Dee) and a yellow road cut through a blue town. Burke argued that indeterminacy of colour was beautiful, but Baldwin saw a contrast of simple colours which he argued was beautiful. The prospect reminded him not of a miniature but of a coloured map, and trying to describe the distinct and (to an eighteenth-century mind) new representation, he used the image of a Turkish carpet, whose colours were both vivid and distinct and whose pattern 'is made to exhibit NO EXACT *Resemblance* to the Works either of Art or Nature'.[42] Writers on the ground had also thought of Turkish carpets as analogues for flying powers. In a popular poem about ballooning, Mary Alcock joked: 'no longer will I seek (by Persian wrought)/ A carpet, to transport me by a thought.'[43] The carpet, familiar from *The Arabian Nights* as an emblem of transported imagination, was imaginatively reconceived as the earth's beautiful covering. Aerial aesthetics made more of this than anything from the sublime because the sublime had limited paradigms for looking *down*. As Baldwin put it, 'the Beautiful among the Objects below was still more attractive than the Sublime among those around'.[44]

The unsettling effects of aerial perspective are shown by Baldwin's second plate. It shows steep-sided Helsby Hill, a landmark on his flight, in a standard topographical scene. In its book-bound form, you have to unfold the page to see the top third of the engraving, where darkly grand clouds flank a tiny balloon in what has now become portrait format rather than landscape. Once you notice the balloon, the perspective seems to sweep you up as if landscape was no longer the thing to look at, towards the tiny speck which completes the composition but also unsettles it. Three registers co-exist: smoothly beautiful foreground, roughly picturesque middle ground, and sublime overhead which has as its centre a serene but active beauty, as if the balloon brought to life a spot which would otherwise be aesthetically inert.

Baldwin's third plate mapped both his own track and the countryside in a way that, like a carpet, used conventions not of art or nature but of both. The balloon track is marked by a thin black line like a squiggle from a Miró painting; the terrain is a mosaic of green patches; the town's black patches are intersected by a red meandering river, and the whole is overlaid with grey and white clouds. Clouds partially obscure the view but also act like picture frames:

> the Land, one while covered with a WHITE *Veil*; then *caught* thro' Openings for a few Seconds; the Objects appearing more distinct and *coloured*, from being seen in detached Groups and single *Pictures framed* and *enshrined* in fleecy VAPOUR; now again discovered by a Glance of the Eye, and *then* repeatedly escaping from the Sight…[45]

This evanescence (which of course is fixed in the print, so you have to imagine it) made aerial picturesque unstable. Like land-based picturesque it required active construction, but it could take no fixed perspective, for instance from immobile rocks. On land, the picturesque could be captured in a Claude or prospect glass, a device that turned scenery into stable painterly compositions. John Jeffries took one with him on his cross-Channel flight with Blanchard, though an eventful flight gave him no opportunity to use it. Baldwin's pictures are mutable and escape. Frances Ferguson has suggested that picturesque travel writing applies art to nature to bring out what she calls 'not ... particularity but ... a kind of typical particularity – the mannerism of individuality or signature'.[46] The balloonist's journey was always individual, dependent on the vagaries of wind, and Baldwin's attempt to mark his route is a picturesque signature. So too is his representation of clouds in both the plate and the text. A system of naming clouds was not regularised until Luke Howard published his *Essay on the Modification of Clouds* in 1803; Baldwin has names for some types but a stronger sense that clouds are one-offs, unrepeatable shapes, typically particular.[47]

Like other aeronauts, Baldwin was struck by a new sense of colour, especially the earth's greenness. Green was the colour of renewal, of pastoral and gaiety, and easily assimilated to what Kames called the emotion of beauty.[48] Blair thought colour gave pleasurable associations to beauty: white gave innocence, blue gave serenity. Burke thought clear colours were beautiful if not too strong: 'Those which seem most appropriated to beauty, are the milder of every sort; light greens; soft blues; weak whites; pink reds; and violets.'[49] Baldwin's analysis of what he called 'a CROMATIC *View* of the Earth, an Appearance peculiar to the Balloon' insisted on the strength of colours seen from the air. The river Dee looked red and the slate-roofed town of Chester blue. For Baldwin, primary colours supplied beauty: 'viz. RED, YELLOW, GREEN, and BLUE: all which seemed to GLOW, tho' in a *less* Degree, like the Colours of the Prism'.[50] According to Kant, pure colours were beautiful and mixed colours were not, and each pure colour was associated with an idea. In the case of green, it was friendliness – so, as Ferguson puts it, 'the notion of nature seeming to speak to us could, thus, seem to be bound up in the friendliness of that green'.[51] The sublime was mostly associated with dark colours and tones made darker by distance, so its colouring made it less use to aerial aesthetics than ideas of the beautiful and picturesque.

Aeronauts' insistence on colour was working to fill a complex ideological space. One effect of aerial foreshortening was to remove

landmarks: from the air, eminences like crags and churches were
reduced to one level. This geographical democratising was repeated
in the democratising of aeronautic spectacle. Commentators noted
anxiously how social distinctions disappeared as lower-class people
sought out high vantage points. *The Morning Post* reported of
Lunardi's first ascent:

> perhaps the English nation never witnessed upon any occasion
> whatever, such a number of persons collected together, and so *loftily*
> displayed, as were to be seen in the environs of Moorfields; not a
> plain, or an eminence, a window or a roof, a chimney or a steeple ...
> but were prodigiously thronged.[52]

A massed crowd involved a homogenising that was levelling, a
perception reinforced by views of it from above. Here French aeronauts set precedents. Of Giroud de Villette and Pilâtre de Rozier's
ascent over Paris on 19 October 1783, it was reported that 'The
gardens about Paris appeared to them like *bouquets*, and the people
passing and re-passing (according to the strong expression of Mons.
Rozier) *"like so many mites in a cheese"*. No bad situation to humble the
pride of Man.'[53]

Littleness in this not entirely beautiful form appealed to earth-
bound writers for whom the balloon became a vehicle for a lofty
moral vision from which earthly vices – such as sexual hypocrisy,
economic parasitism, even colonialism – could be surveyed with new
clarity. Satirists were fascinated by ballooning's potential to transform economies. Dystopian prophets suggested that as balloons
replaced horses, the price of grain would plummet, roads would
become obsolete, aerial piracy and war would become widespread,
and crimes such as trespass and sedition would increase. Mary
Alcock's poem was headed by a note warning that balloons would
be used by law-breakers and one of her stanzas imagines balloons
becoming a new getaway vehicle for criminals. The crimes most
commonly anticipated had an economic bent, too literal to allow in
the metaphysical transactions of the sublime.

Aeronauts confirmed a view of the world below as various,
literally and figuratively: 'as we sailed slowly over the metropolis, I
was entertained by a variety of objects which seeing, whilst unseen,
imparted a most pleasing sensation'.[54] The aeronaut joined spy
fiction, a genre especially lively in the eighteenth century. Aeronautic spies did enjoy the pleasure of panoptic control – the pleasure
of seeing whilst unseen – but we should not miss the significance

of variety. What such fictions share with actual aerial voyagers is a delight in variousness: the variety of human lives makes good copy for fiction, especially the wandering or rambling kind. Baldwin's articulation of variety – 'ALWAYS CHANGING YET STILL THE SAME'[55] – pointed to beauty, though his striking contrast of simple colours was not Burkean beauty.

> The endless variety of Objects, minute, distinct and separate, tho' apparently on the same Plain or Level, at once striking the Eye without a Change of its Position, astonished and amazed. Their beauty was unparalalled [*sic*]. The Imagination itself was more than gratified; *it was overwhelmed.*[56]

There's no panoptic control here; there's a risk of loss of control. Philosophically, variety offered the prospect of harmonising differences that would otherwise be belittling or chaotic. As Alexander Pope memorably put it:

> Not *Chaos*-like together crush'd and bruis'd,
> But as the World, harmoniously confus'd:
> Where Order in Variety we see,
> And where, tho' all things differ, all agree.[57]

Where the sublime offered a viewing subject complexity through disunity reunited, variety offers a viewing subject a simpler unity which nonetheless recognised complexity.

The sublime is still with us and modern theories continue the essence of what it meant in the 1780s. Simon Morley explains it thus: 'The sublime experience is fundamentally transformative, about the relationship between order and disorder, and the disruption of the stable coordinates of time and space. Something rushes in and we are profoundly altered.' Following Burke, he sees the sublime in the eighteenth century 'applied in relation to the arts to describe aspects of nature that instil awe and wonder, such as mountains, avalanches, waterfalls, stormy seas or the infinite vault of the starry sky. Today, however, rather than nature the incredible power of technology is more likely to supply the raw material'.[58] Let us not forget balloons are an early or even the first instance of technology supplying the sublime.

A long history of the aerial gaze also skips past early ballooning and its literature. 'After nearly four decades of visual theory dominated by a panoptic model of power in which seeing has become synonymous with controlling', says Paula Amad, 'the view from below has come to signify an intimate, embodied, local perspective

of those who are subjugated, that from above has acquired the status
of a distant, dehumanising, transcendent perspective of those ultimately in power – or so this particular myth of vision goes.'[59] To
unravel this myth in relation to aerial photography, Amad tracks
back to biblical models in which God's eye looks down on the world.
What she calls 'the ocular showdown between God and humans' was
gradually secularised:

> The distance between the gaze of God and the gaze of man became
> further abbreviated in the eighteenth and nineteenth centuries in a
> range of cartographic and panoramic extensions of human sight,
> many of which served colonial and militaristic purposes, while
> others offered popular spectacles and entertainments.[60]

Eighteenth-century balloons don't figure explicitly in Amad's
magisterial analysis of the aerial gaze, though they may implicitly
be included among her popular spectacles. But they were important
for several reasons. One is that despite the potential of balloons for
warfare, aerial voyagers promoted human endeavour and discovery.
They added enlightenment by way of science; they also reflected
on what humanity was and should be. Narratives were critical of
corruption below. The poem about Crosbie's ascent, for instance,
takes the opportunity of an imaginary view from above to moralise
in favour of better behaviours between humans.[61] Dystopia and
utopia are shifty categories here. A lofty view of a messy world was
also an aspiring vision of a better world. The aerial gaze encouraged
by balloon narratives was a social one.

Secondly, balloon narratives should be important to historians of
the aerial gaze because they expanded aerial aesthetics. They did so
in writing rather than visual forms, which is frustrating for us now
in our much more visual world. Nonetheless, in that writing was new
thinking about what the aerial gaze saw and how to represent views
from above. All the emphasis on sublime and beautiful encouraged
human connection by assuming that viewing subjects were capable
of feeling, and capable of feelings which could be communicated and
shared. The emotions spectators felt in identifying with the vulner-
ability and heroism of aeronauts are emotions we recognise now
in relation to astronauts. Lost-in-space films like *Marooned* (1969),
Gravity (2013) and *The Martian* (2015) stage philosophical questions
about co-operation; astronauts additionally channel feeling into
the emotion of caring about our planet. Aeronauts preceded them,
extending the geographical range of human capacity to feel pain and

pleasure, beauty and art. The aerial viewpoint of balloons shrank the distance between God and man. It also brought people closer together.

Interest in the aerial gaze has increased in recent years. Several exhibitions testify to its fascination for us in historically imaging our world and in opening up a new domain for art to shape.[62] Thomas Baldwin's aerial voyage has been given new life by 'Arpeggio', a video installation made in 2010 which follows Baldwin's balloon track, adds a (beautiful!) soundtrack, and mixes dissolves in and out of Baldwin's plates with eighteenth-century maps and mapping from Google Earth.[63] Miniaturisation and loftiness are simultaneously evident; engraving, aerial film and satellite imaging are blended in gentle motions to create a mobile medium of beauty. A curator observes 'we are fascinated by this bird's eye view as much for the beauty of the landscapes it reveals as for the feeling of omnipotence it inspires'.[64] Why are we fascinated? If we occupy the God's-eye view, what do we make of it?

'Flying was ... associated with the sublime because it transcended the limitations of earthly existence,' says Sam Smiles.[65] His idiom of liberation is echoed by another curator: 'When Nadar took his first aerial photographs from a hot-air balloon in the 1860s he freed the gaze.'[66] Like Thomas Baldwin, Nadar compared the earth to a carpet: 'The earth unfolds into an enormous, unbounded carpet with neither beginning nor end'.[67] Nadar's photographs took the aerial gaze away from Baldwin's hand-made, hand-coloured representations, to begin a history in which photographs of the earth from aeroplanes introduced a schematic element to representation. Robert Wohl and others have shown how the abstraction in aerial images influenced modernism and attracted cubists and surrealists.[68] What many of them were interested in was how the aerial gaze defamiliarised objects of the gaze and the gaze itself: 'Divorced from habitual modes of seeing and representing, aerial images mean nothing to the untrained eye.'[69] As Amad explains, big arguments about what the aerial gaze means tend to assume that the aerial camera's physical vantage point is also a position of advantage in securing information. The camera becomes an information pipeline, conveying a depiction. Yet the high-flying vantage point creates images that then need the close-up gaze of a human, a boffin with a magnifying glass, who knows how to interpret the maze of lines and contours. Aerial images from a lower height, like the levels balloons occupy, fill out the middle between micro and macro, and they do so with little or no strain on the human eye. They admit some abstraction, in which the human eye sees both nature and art – thus the pleasurable mystifications of subject in Yann Arthus-Bertrand's 'Earth from Above' photographs.[70]

Creative tension between abstraction and pattern invites us to look for meaning. In a late short story, 'The Figure in the Carpet' (1916), Henry James made gentle fun of critical investment in the revelatory power of meaning. In the story, a great writer, Vereker, lets slip to a critic that all his works have an element in common that explains the writer's artistic intention and passion. It is 'a beauty so rare and so great ... The loveliest thing in the world!'[71] The narrator spends the rest of his life in a haunted quest to discover it. What haunts the reader too is the idea of aesthetic completeness which connects and unites ostensibly different things and meanings: the figure in the carpet. When Baldwin and Nadar compare the earth from the air to a carpet, their metaphor familiarises the unfamiliar of what they see: a potentially confusing view is made comfortably recognisable. It is also sublime, in its dizzying union of multiplicities into metaphor. And, grimly, sublimely applied in modern war: saturation bombing from the air became known as carpet bombing – a term first used in 1943, according to the Oxford English Dictionary. The aerial gaze looks to make meanings from multiplicities, and in doing so suggests the quest for making meaning that haunts the aesthetic. As Henry James teasingly puts it: 'they fell, in all their superb intricacy, into the one right combination. The figure in the carpet came out.'[72] The superb intricacy of views from above fascinates us because it promises to reveal the figure in the earth's carpet.

Aeronationalism

11

'Fancy with airy flights my Noddle crouds,
I'm like the Nation, wholly in the Clouds'
Edward Topham, Epilogue to *Deception*, 1784

IN NOVEMBER 1784 three plays were reviewed by *The Universal Magazine*. One, Frederick Pilon's *Aerostation*, explicitly jokey about balloons, had a cast of characters with European interests. A second, John O'Keeffe's *Fontainbleau*, included a comic character called Colonel Epaulette, a French fan of England who came on stage humming 'Britannia rules the waves'. The third, a farce by Thomas Linley called *The Spanish Rivals*, included a Cumberland boy speaking in broad dialect who had been taken prisoner at the siege of Gibraltar and thereafter kept in Spain. In each of these plays people crossed national borders and still kept local identities. Comedy staged inter-nationalism while recognising national characters and conflicts. Comedy also questioned simplistic ideas of British national character:

> A well-educated British gentleman, it may truly be said, is of no country whatever. He unites in himself the characteristics of all different nations: he talks and dresses *French*, and sings *Italian*: he rivals the *Spaniard* in indolence, and the *German* in drinking: his house is *Grecian*, his offices *Gothic*, and his furniture *Chinese*. He preserves the same partiality in his religion, and finding no solid reasons for preferring *Confucius* to *Brama*, or *Mahometanism* to *Christianity*, he has for all their doctrines an equal indulgence.[1]

The self-styled Lounger who penned this portrait is thinking humorously about patriotism. Just as balloons were both serious and comic, national character was solid enough to survive ironies – or, looking the other way round, national character was solidified by irony. (The British are still inclined to be defined through their sense of humour.) Satirical prints showed that people were perfectly used to reading a language of exaggeration in which truth could be found. Truth might even be easier to recognise when it was dressed in exaggeration. But for all the playfulness about national character, in 1783 and the years immediately following there was a seriousness in discussions about the state of the nation that reflected deep uncertainties and worry about Britain's prospects.

Scholars have argued about how nationalism appeared in the late eighteenth century:

> most theorists of nationalism have argued for the manufactured and "modern" quality of all national identity, that nations are "constructed" and "imagined" out of a very diverse collection of polities and that nationalism is a fairly recent phenomenon that dates to the late 18th and early 19th centuries, although debate continues on this historical narrative.[2]

Nations are usually thought of in relation to land: at its simplest, a nation is the conjunction of a people and a place. Balloons and the development of air travel challenged conventional configurations of nation. People had thought of air in broadly spatial terms; they spoke of 'the regions of air', referring to an Aristotelian model in which air was supposed to consist of three layered regions.[3] These layers were defined vertically, whereas 'regions' on earth evoked places in relationship to each other in the same horizontal plane and distinguished from each other by political borders or differences in terrain or climate. Because the regions of air had no fixed features like seas, mountains or rivers to act as natural frontiers, terrestrial distinctions were little used in describing aerial voyages. Instead, many saw aerial achievements in terms of time. Those who had mastered the art of flying 'will leave to posterity a lasting, and perhaps useful, memorial of the genius of the present age',[4] said Tiberius Cavallo in 1785, and even in the 1840s Carlyle was celebrating balloons as a 'beautiful invention ... Emblem of much and of our Age of Hope itself'.[5] This universality was reflected in the early terminology for balloons themselves. Although 'ballon' became the dominant term in French from early 1784, copied by English soon after,[6] the word first used to describe the inflated airbag was 'globe', by itself and in combination (air-globe, aerostatic globe), as if it shared the roundness of a planet and any markings of countries were provisional.[7]

The story of ballooning is the story of an invention that has an international application – from the balloon, one ends up at the aeroplane, the airship and the helicopter and an era of mass travel. Inter-nationality becomes internationality; we name key hubs international airports. And internationality is also inter-nationality; national airlines fly between international airports. The tension is nicely illustrated in a plan submitted by Citizen Campenas to Napoleon, proposing that the capital of every country should have an aerostatic port where foreign vessels could put in to refit and trade. Since balloons would be carrying at least two hundred persons, they could send down pavilions on buoys to take up kit or supplies. An extra buoy could receive the capitulations of fortresses belonging to France's enemies or, in peace, intelligence.[8] Campenas's plan ended with an Atmospheric Code, drawn up for the peace and happiness of all the people on earth. If the common project of Enlightenment dissolved nationalism a little, it was also intensified by the waves of war that crossed Europe and its dominions.

'The celebration of the inventive citizen has been an important part of modern nationalism', says David Edgerton.[9] The location, the makers and protagonists of the first balloons were all French so the invention was surely French too. Or was it? The Montgolfiers were paper manufacturers but they both kept up with scientific developments. Etienne had read Joseph Priestley's work and Joseph had got some of his knowledge of gases from a cousin who had taken a course in Paris which featured the work of other British scientists including Cavendish. Although the lifting power of hot air pointed towards flight, there was some evidence to suggest that the Montgolfier brothers had been working on how to use hot air to move loads, a matter of mechanics. Priestley had identified hydrogen as a gas lighter than air; the Montgolfiers had considered this but decided that hot air was cheaper and easier to pursue. Their achievement came out of experiments performed across a community of natural philosophers which disregarded national boundaries in its pursuit of knowledge.

The amazement with which the early balloon flights were greeted, however, left Englishmen feeling that *la gloire* had been unduly appropriated by the French. A few reminders were due. One writer reviewed the study of air as something surely 'coeval with mankind';[10] notable discoverers of its properties known to date included Bacon, Galileo, Torricelli, Pascal, Boyle, Hales, Cavendish and, most recently, Watson, Kirwan and Priestley. A Dr Black of Edinburgh had tried to raise animal bladders filled with inflammable air; he didn't succeed but it showed he had understood lighter-than-air principles. Experiments were a combination of idea and result: the Montgolfiers had clearly triumphed in outcome, concluded this writer, but 'whatever uses may in the end result from these experiments, it appears fully, from the foregoing recapitulation, that all the discoveries which have led to them have been made by ENGLISHMEN.'[11] This put the English in the rather unusual position of casting themselves as theoreticians, a position at odds with a widespread view of the British national character as pragmatic. Benjamin Franklin, who was interested in balloons, wrote to a friend shortly after watching a successful flight: 'It is a pity that any national Jealousy, should, as you imagine, have prevented the English from prosecuting the Experiment, since they are such ingenious Mechanicians, that in their Hands it might have made a more rapid Progress towards Perfection, & all the Utility it is capable of affording.'[12] Yet not all English responses were sour grapes. When one poet resorted to cliché – 'hence France, in trifles skill'd, her talents tries,/ And forms her spheres to navigate the skies'[13] – a reviewer was severe: 'We wish the ingenious Author had spared this reflection. The philosophic researches of our rival neighbours ought less to excite envy than admiration and emulating ardour.'[14] The English could always produce Newton as a trump card, but the point about a trump card is that it depends on a hand preceding it, and those intellectual turns could be argued too: 'if France had never produced Descartes, the great and immortal Sir Isaac would perhaps have been no more than the first scholastic sophister of his time.'[15]

As aeronautics went from strength to strength in France, English writers continued to try and find antecedents who were not French.[16] Bishop Wilkins had designed a copper balloon in 1648. Francesco Lana had designed a flying ship in 1670. Archytas, a disciple of Archimedes, had designed a hollow wooden pigeon.[17] That none of these had taken off was thought unimportant. Alternatively, French success was explained by the airiness and lightness of the French national character. A Francophile writing in 1784 praised the French as enlightened and amiable, but added: 'they are passionately fond of novelty, easily elated, and strongly national'.[18] This idea was reinforced by balloons like one that ascended from Dijon on 25 April decorated with the motto 'Surgit nunc Gallus ad aethera' [Now soars France to the skies].[19] Nationalism in space fitted awkwardly with cultivation of universal knowledge modelled through the classics and the utopianism of Enlightenment:

> Happy would it be for both nations, if we might indulge the Utopian wish that all other rivalry between them might cease, except that of mutually striving to go beyond each other in promoting those

sciences on which the welfare of society depends! Let us throw away the mean and interested ambition which prompts us to decry the merit of men who happen not to have been born on our island; and while we enjoy the produce of their industry and abilities let us allow them their share of fame.[20]

It was indisputable that Britons were well down the league tables of flights significant for time, distance or height. Both the first British flight (Tytler in Edinburgh on 27 August 1784) and the first witnessed flight by an Englishman (Sadler from Oxford on 12 November 1784) lagged behind activities in France. Public interest was certainly high in Britain, as it was across Europe, but only consolation prizes could be hoped for. 'Though the French can claim the Honour of the new Invention of Air-Globes, there is little doubt but the English will be the Men to make a rational Use of them', opined a writer who wheeled on Priestley as the great white hope: 'Dr Priestley is said already to have made some collateral Discoveries on the Subject, which will create greater Astonishment than the original Invention itself!'[21]

One might read these views as simply the usual British ambivalence about their nearest neighbours and rivals, but in 1783 the English were smarting from unsuccessful war and inglorious peace. 'Great Britain dwindled to Little Britain,' as one newspaper put it: 'The common exclamation is that England is ruined.'[22] In this climate of gloom, French success increased the English sense of failure, especially in relation to the American colonies. Satirists in 1783 noted George III's mixed fortunes:

Six thousand Times thro' Glass enlarg'd,
A new Star late from Air emerg'd;
Herschell, of telescopic Fame,
Georgean, the novel Star did name:
Ah, luckless George's Stars have been!
He gains one, but has lost thirteen.[23]

Stars, an old heraldic template for national honours (like the Star and Garter), were topped up with symbolism from new appearances on national flags. In political skies, stars were mobile symbols.

Balloons promoted nationalism most obviously in their decoration. The earliest *montgolfières* were decorated with emblems from the zodiac and designs linked to the French monarchy, embodiment of the nation. Though admission tickets commonly showed a balloon with sun, moon and stars, celestial imagery free from nationalism, in the many engravings which celebrated Lunardi's success British flags were visually prominent, and for his second ascent Lunardi had a new balloon which looked like a vast British flag. It may be that red and white striped balloons picked up the colours of St George's Ensign deliberately. Three sent up by Astley on 12 March 1784 were launched from St George's Field, and a union flag flew among the trees to mark the launching spot.[24] Some aeronautic heraldry was civic rather than patriotic – thus Richard Crosbie's balloon was adorned by the arms of the city of Dublin, from where it ascended on 19 January 1785. Some emblems were aristocratic, like the Duchess of Devonshire's colours given to Blanchard for his ascent from the Rhedarium in 1784. But flags were the simplest devices to express national loyalties of aeronauts and connect patriotism to crowds below.

Celebrations of successful voyages drew on existing verbal, visual and even musical vocabularies of nationalist sentiment. When Blanchard and Sheldon ascended together from Chelsea, Blanchard waved a French flag; Sheldon, a union jack. Their procession from Hampshire back to London was marshalled as follows: 'constables; colours flying; a band of wind instruments; drums and fifes; then followed the car, supported by several gentlemen with colours in their hands. Next to them appeared Mrs. Sheldon in a chariot and four, preceded by the union flag.' Then came various gentry coaches and finally, letting down the tone in the rear, a common-or-garden hackney coach with a beadle inside. 'The band, in the course of the procession, struck up *God save the King*, before the palace-gate, and the favourite tune of *Briton's [sic] strike home*, as they passed Carlton-house,' residence of the Prince of Wales.[25] Music supplied patriotic cues.

In the air, aeronauts were representatives of the human race and the endeavours of mankind, and nationalism was set aside in some collaborations – French chemists helped to fill English balloons, for instance. An aeronaut functioned as a hero more easily when passengers took from him the burden of national representation. So Lunardi revived his flagging fortunes by taking up an English actress, Laetitia Sage, on 29 June 1785; though she was an attraction on account of the novelty of her sex, she stressed her nationality emphatically. Yet just as class difference could be subsumed into the term 'crowd', nationalists could not differentiate a balloon-agog crowd in one country from that in another.

One of the goals of early French aeronauts was to cross the

Channel. 'We speak somewhat arrogantly of the English Channel, although only one shore of it is English', observes James Williamson, who explains that topography favours the English side for shipping movements. The French side has more outlying reefs and sands, more fierce and variable tides and, in the eighteenth century, fewer harbours for ships of war, which were also more likely to be driven east by winds and bad weather.[26] English outlay of large sums to fortify their Channel ports had implications for balloons, discussed in Chapter 12; it meant that any aerial crossing had a context of anxieties about invasion by sea and land. 'The sciences are peaceable,' said some[27] – but at the same time others were imagining aerial 'Men of War, calculated to sail through Seas of Aether, and treat the World with Sights of aetherial Combats'.[28] A fantasy print of 1784, for example, showed two pairs of balloons lined up against each other, armed with cannon and filled with men firing muskets [Figure 21]. Two balloons sport flags with *fleur-de-lis*; the other two sport union jacks.

> Behold an odd Fight, two odd Nations between,
> Such odd Fighting as this was never yet seen;
> But such fights will be common (as Dunce to feel Rod)
> In the Year of One Thousand eight Hundred and odd.

The caption's stress on oddity seems to be offset by the symmetry between British and French aerial forces. On closer inspection, the nations are not using exactly the same design: the French balloons have rounder, boat-shaped cars versus the squarer British baskets, and their netting, guns and flags are mounted differently. Rather like 'spot the difference' pictures for children, a visual image which seems similar turns out to have many differences; incremental details suggest that though the French and British would share a belief in ballooning as a military technology, they would pursue competing designs – like the competition in aviation later, say between Mirage and Tornado jets.

Another common fantasy of the balloon-mad concerned cross-Channel balloon services. Writers foresaw an attractive prospect, as regular as coach travel yet still with risks:

> The only objection that has been made to this most commodious, easy, safe, and expeditious Passage is, that it may teach the French how to invade us in any future War, in flat-bottomed Baskets, but when the aerial Lightness and volatile Spirit of a Frenchman is considered, the Idea must fall to the Ground.[29]

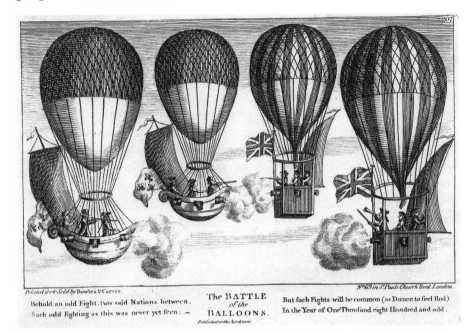

Behold an odd Fight, two odd Nations between,
Such odd Fighting as this was never yet seen; —

The BATTLE
of the
BALLOONS.
Published at the Act directs

But such Fights will be common (as Dunce to feel Rod)
In the Year of One Thousand eight Hundred and odd.

Printed for & Sold by Bowles & Carver.

N.° 69 in S.t Pauls Church Yard, London.

21   Aerial combat in the future. Undated engraving.

Later designs considered by Napoleon for the invasion of England
by air gave these fears substance. Prints depicted the French landing
at Dover, weightily squashing stereotypes. Religious difference
played a small part in shaping responses: in October 1784, one
report muttered darkly that there was secret jubilation among
foreigners that no Protestant balloon had yet got above British
chimney pots.[30] The first attempt to cross from the French side saw
English and French spectators share ascents in a tethered balloon
whilst the aeronauts waited for a favourable wind; when it came, on
15 June 1785, the flight ended in disaster. The balloon caught fire
and exploded and the two French aeronauts plunged to their deaths.
They had carried both French and English flags; Pilâtre de Rozier
had an English fiancée. People in both countries lamented the loss of
life; mortality highlighted the human endeavours at stake.

When the Channel was first crossed by the Frenchman Blanchard
from the English side, accompanied by an American, Dr John Jeffries,
on 7 January 1785, English honour was satisfied by the location,
because they ascended from what was known as Shakespeare's
Cliff in Dover. Some written accounts reported that Jeffries was
carrying an American flag; prints showed him waving a British one.
Shakespeare, fast becoming the ultimate trump card in England's

culture wars with France, played a symbolic part in framing Lunardi's voyage. The publisher of Lunardi's account of the voyage was John Bell, then based on the Strand. He used it to advertise a new edition of Shakespeare in proposals placed at the end of the text. There is an ironic twist to Bell's nationalism: the fine edition was to be modelled on a splendid edition of Voltaire, with Paris ink and specially cast Burgeois lettering, and designed to attract the admiration of Europe. Nonetheless, the bard, like ballooning, was acquiring universal appeal: he was 'celebrated in all parts of the world, not excepting those where his native language was not understood'![31] This puff by Lunardi had extra resonance given that many aeronauts had language problems; Blanchard solved these in a very French way by taking bottles of wine aloft and offering a drink to people he encountered on landing.

Both Lunardi and Bell described the forthcoming edition as beautiful, a term to mirror balloon ascents. What made it so was its visual apparatus. Every play was to be prefaced by a newly commissioned print of a famous performer and illustrated by a scene. Some would be engraved by English artists or artists effectively naturalised by working in England, such as Bartolozzi, Delattre and Heath; the rest would be produced by the most eminent artists of France. Bell explained the logic of having foreign artists depict the national poet in terms which curiously echo and reverse the relationship between England and France in relation to ballooning: 'Reward is the spur to *Emulation*, and *Emulation* the parent of *Merit*; it is therefore the Publisher's intention, to call forth, on this occasion, the GENIUS and ABILITIES of the *greatest* and *most rival* nations on earth.'[32] French success in aeronautics should stimulate English competition; English poetic success should stimulate French painters and lead to international co-operation. Bell's proposals were literally and figuratively the last word in Lunardi's *Account*, in which English writing had been associated with plainness. In the text, a correspondent advised Lunardi, 'You must be sensible that the *façon de parler* here and in France are extremely different, and that truth has never received advantage from unnecessary ornament.'[33] Understanding his market, Lunardi gratified English prejudices by calling the French vain, and played up to the idealised image held by his English contemporaries: the English are liberal, enlightened, sincere and generous. Though a note of dissent crept in – the English are also sometimes a little sullen, and some of them have ripped him off – he praised England enthusiastically as a land of opportunity.[34]

International rivalry between French and English played to the advantage of the Italian in England.

Nation and nationalism, however, were concepts that did not stay still and were not uniform; they changed shape like clouds. When he went to Scotland, Lunardi praised the Scots he had met in England as 'his *real* friends ... men of science and liberality', and he praised national pride: 'the *Amor Patriae* glows in every CALEDONIAN'S BOSOM'.[35] To evade the complications of Scottish nationalism within British patriotism, he used sensibility to dissolve powerful sentiment into borderless sensitivity. Commiserating for instance with James Tytler's failure to ascend in a fire balloon in Edinburgh, he offered a sympathising tear (as if it would put out Tytler's fire). Sailing above Liverpool, he described *terra firma* as 'the land below', in which only natural boundaries – rivers, mountains, sea – were identifiable. The precision of English fields viewed from above provided Lunardi with an image of national order in a compliment to his English hosts. Nothing was said about enclosures, the forcible privatisation of previously common land which took away rights of use from common people. Instead, England was represented as a serene pastoral. Likewise, when Lunardi sailed over Liverpool harbour he enthused about the congregation of ships as evidence of Britain's trading power. He either did not care or did not care to say that many of those ships were vessels of the slave trade. Ironically, reports of his aerial voyage were printed in newspapers hosting heated debates about the slave trade. One might read Lunardi's silence as strategic ignorance – why rock the aerial boat? – but the upper atmosphere was also a region where nationalist frictions could be left below. Elaine Freedgood reads Lunardi's account as a laconic narrative in which social lacunae create a foundation for British stiff-upper-lip repression. For the Victorians, she argues, the nation is homogenised from the air; England and Empire mesh in the upper atmosphere.[36] But in the 1780s, aeronautic escape from sublunary society also escaped contours of nationalist thinking.

Literal ascents into the upper atmosphere stimulated thinking about elevated ideals. When Lunardi's attempt to ascend at Liverpool was prevented by an accident during filling in which his hands were burnt by vitriol, the newspaper which reported those details ran an editorial on the same page. It began as a meditation on America, a new nation that could break free of narrow horizons and rise to higher concepts of nation. The imagery is clearly aeronautic and the ideas expand to envision a newly inter-national world:

there perhaps never was a period in which the powers of human nature were so generally and so effectually exerted, as in the present times; or when such important and such various objects pressed upon the attention of men, whether in the active or speculative walks of life. In this situation of the world, when avenues of correspondence and various intercourse are opened between different parts of the globe, the statesman who aspires to the government of a nation must have his eyes open on [*sic*] a variety of circumstances. His views ought not to be confined within the bounds of one state or kingdom.[37]

Balloons aided understanding of world order in global terms; they opened up wider aerial views and the horizons of the skies. Enlargement of ideas about human relations turned on a sense that the old order was dissolving; its boundaries no longer made sense in an increasingly global world. The French Revolution was to put that enlargement into fast reverse, ironically eventually replacing its repressive *ancien regime* with an old-order nationalism that Napoleon promoted fiercely. But after 1783 there were glimpses of enlightened alternatives for the future of the world.

Two of the ways in which inter-nationalism was remodelled at first glance seem contradictory. One was to stress the enlightening responses of the educated to balloons. A report on Lunardi's ascent in London described it as merely a novelty to the untutored mind. But 'to the philosopher and the man of letters it was an occasion of the most rational delight – thus to see a new element subdued by the talents of man'.[38] A language of heroes helped locate that human achievement as transnational, timeless and epic. Lunardi was quoted as saying 'I have Alexander's hope'; a charmed witness described him as 'the Columbus of Britain'.[39] The other way was paradoxically to stress balloon-mad foreignness and make that a transnational category, a late eighteenth-century character type of Johnny Foreigner. In Pilon's play *Aerostation*, a subplot features a bluestocking, Mrs Grampus, who is balloon mad. A suitor arrives, Baron Bubblebergen, who has been corresponding with her equally balloon-mad brother. Luckily Mrs Grampus is suitably attired – 'I have my balloon hat, my balloon sack, and my balloon apron on'[40] – and they talk excitedly about balloons. The Baron is a farcical caricature who talks in a jumble of Franglais and cod German: 'me be von Foreigner'. An international comic language doubles up with the inter-national symbolism of balloons. In an amusing twist, the Baron is unmasked as a valet: less tutored minds could understand – and parody – the rational delights of the man of letters.

Philosophers, moreover, could apply their talents less nobly to exploiting inter-national aeronautics for profit. Mrs Grampus's brother corresponds madly about balloons with the baron across borders. He is first seen in his library, surrounded by globes, loose papers and mathematical instruments, musing to himself about how he can persuade the government to give him and his heirs an exclusive patent for the bombardment of Algiers – by balloon. This military application of ballooning is at odds with patriotism because although he could pay off the national debt by this deal, if the government refuses he will sell his aerial armaments elsewhere: 'The King of Spain would pay me treble the sum for the business.'[41] Like Montgolfier, he is an opportunist patriot. Balloon entrepreneurs were only precariously protected by the system of patents – a recognition of intellectual property within the borders of the nation-state whose government regulates the patent process. Proliferation of patents for inventions in Britain in the 1780s shows a system straining to keep up.[42]

Comedy, war, heroism and philosophy offered transnational prospects for balloons, transected by patriotism and economics. They joined an international language of sensibility spread by English, French and German writers around Europe in fiction, poetry and travel writing. Sensibility insisted there were sensitive minds in sensitive bodies regardless of nationality, and it acquired a politics in how it contributed to the recognition of subjectivity for women and slaves. Even more universalising was a language of benevolence: it stressed the helping hand rather than the sensitive body, and it translated simply into human kindness, by everyone everywhere. The process is nicely illustrated by the Scots Society in Norwich. Initially set up to help Scots who did not qualify for relief under English poor laws, it widened its remit to help a wide range of nationals far beyond Norwich, paying special attention to soldiers and sailors who fell on hard times. In 1784 it took on a new name, The Society of Universal Good-will, and a new aim, to be 'stewards for the whole world'. Arguing that foreigners made important contributions to any nation's commerce and culture, it insisted that community mattered more than nation. Humanity, its governors wrote hopefully, was the characteristic of the age. A local charity that became global, its universalising tendency was mirrored in the way national-based aerial voyages offered representations of people as people, regardless of nation. As one poet wrote:

O what a grand display such science yields,
Beaux from Pye-Corner – Belles from Spital-Fields!
Jews, dogs and dustcarts nobly intervene,
And Ministers on scaffolds close the scene![43]

Views from above could turn local specificities into exportable generalisations.

People imagined the future uses of balloons in different and contradictory ways. Some thought it would transform international relations peaceably – indeed Etienne Montgolfier sketched out trade routes and even timetables for a fleet of balloons trading between France and America. Others thought it would catalyse national interests through war: countries with airpower could expect to win battles. Of course in the eighteenth century people were conscious that commerce created wars: balloon-led trade could create balloon-led war, especially since, as Benjamin Franklin and others pointed out, balloons could be cheaper to build than warships. Although the French government supported various aeronautic ventures financially, when it seemed indifferent to Montgolfier he threatened to take his invention to England where there were plenty of wealthy patrons.[44] To some extent, nationalism bowed to capitalism: 'we are already become entire citizens of the world, governed by interest alone', said an American in 1782 who wanted to forget war and make trade with Britain prosper.[45]

The ownership of technology determines its use, up to a point, and although there was at least one successful flight early on in Constantinople, the initiative in aeronautics lay with Europe. Horace Walpole, a sceptic about the value of balloons, saw this as a reason to be gloomy about their implications: 'The wicked wit of man always studies to apply the results of talents to enslaving, destroying, or cheating his fellow-creatures. Could we reach the moon, we should think of reducing it to a province of some European Kingdom.' New technologies simply pointed to 'how much more expeditiously the East, West, or South, will be ravaged and butchered, than they have been by the old-fashioned, clumsy method of navigation'.[46]

Others saw progress rather than exploitation, and co-operation rather than rivalry. Balloons, they hoped, would provide a platform for science in a way that served humanist interests. Montgolfier planned a balloon which would hold seven or eight people staying aloft for long periods, studying wind patterns and eventually mastering the elements. He offered this idea to the Ministry of Finance at half the price of his other idea, a balloon big enough to carry goods from one end of France to the other.[47] Neither idea was taken up. Nonetheless, people kept imagining the technology bene-fiting humanity regardless of nation – as in a Swiss artist's vision of a balloon functioning as an international space station, an idea so attractive it decorated china decades later [Plate VII]. Those aboard could eat, sleep and study chemistry; there were also parts allocated to a chapel, a hospital, an outhouse and quarters for women (who may be prostitutes, hardly an advance). In one version of the print, the balloon was surmounted by a Gallic-looking cock; in another, it has a lion adorned with a crown. In both it has the legend 'Pro Bono Publico', as if traces of one nation's advances would co-exist with a benevolent social entity not confined to the category of nation. The drawing also showed cannon aboard. The common good brought about through international co-operation would still face enemies – unknown, unnamed.[48]

Writers, artists, satirists and ordinary people tried to imagine whether balloons would be put to utopian or dystopian uses or both. In doing so they engaged with how cultural identifications shape understandings of nations. In the words of Willem Bilderdijk in 1811, balloons would bring:

> an infinite range of benefits, as yet incalculable, for the mutual understanding and coexistence of nations and peoples … the advan-tages and disadvantages of the geographical location of countries will no longer apply, the manning of frontiers will be pointless, and dominion of the seas will either lapse or be useless, when airborne fleets, carrying goods, arms and troops, can bring prosperity or war to the furthest corners of the earth, without touching on either water or land.[49]

Even for the balloon-mad, it was clear that balloons could alter the world order. The next chapter investigates how balloons joined up with fears of war in one of the deepest currents of national identity for the British: the sea.

War

'It was said even in those days [of King Alfred], that the navy of England exceeded all others in beauty, strength, and security; for strength they were compared to floating castles; for beauty to moving palaces; and for security, to the only walls of the land. Time has not, we trust, altered this distinction, and that it never may, must be the wish of every Briton.'

Universal Magazine, 1784

THE EIGHTEENTH CENTURY was a period of nearly continuous wars between European countries. Monarchies realigned, changing alliances and altering definitions of nation. As nations established, contested and extended empires, nation acted as a term that encompassed more ground than simple geographical identities. This was not a new process but its particular components in the eighteenth century included new elements. What defined Britain included four countries, a Hanoverian monarchy and overseas dominions; British interests were therefore also simultaneously European and global, spread across continents and oceans, manifested through conflicts with peoples and treaties with nations. Making the case for Britain as physically and politically European, a historian in 2006 commented: 'I took the trouble to ask the Map Librarian at the British Library whether he knows of any map of Europe which does not contain Britain. His answer was no. He knows of no map of Europe that does not contain the British Isles.'[1] Physical maps co-exist with mental maps in complex ways. What difference did it make to add air to land and sea as a place where nations operated? How did a new aerial dimension map on to a world in which European nations jealously guarded interests and zealously extended possessions whenever they could?

In exploring the role of balloons in eighteenth-century war, one must try to understand the world as it was when they appeared. English minds were full of uncertainty about peace. 'It has been easy for later historians to underestimate the instability and insecurity of eighteenth-century Britain,' says N. A. M. Rodger, who argues that 'The motives which first created a dominant English navy in the 1650s, and which kept the British fleet the largest in Europe, were overwhelmingly defensive. The navy's primary function was to guard against invasion, for which purpose the bulk of the fleet was almost always kept in home waters.'[2] This line of argument helpfully reminds us just how close and persistent was the threat of invasion – and how often that threat was French. How deeply and long-held were the stand-offs between England and France can be seen even today: a twenty-first century postcard of one of Vauban's magnificently sturdy forts at Ambleteuse in the Pas-de-Calais announces: 'Face à l'Angleterre depuis trois siècles.' Although the Act of Union in 1707 brought Scotland and England together, a Stuart and Catholic pretender to the British throne meant the English had reason to be suspicious of potential alliances between the Scots and the French, suspicions doubly confirmed by the Jacobite rebellions of 1715 and 1745.

One way to think about invasion fears in eighteenth-century Britain is to think about islands. Islands are terrestrial wholes: a fragment of land, surrounded by sea, complete in itself. Anthropologists and literary critics have seen islands as places particularly hospitable to ideas of origins, dominion and singularity[3] – all perfectly combined in the archetypal island tale of *Robinson Crusoe*, which by the 1780s had started to turn into a children's story, a myth even for the young.[4] What Timothy Garton Ash calls 'this "Island Story" grand narrative'[5] is deeply imprinted in British national consciousness, and though politicians, scholars and the public may now be impatient with it as a too-forceful cliché, in the eighteenth century it had vitality as an idea. When Winston Churchill revived the motif of the British as the Island Race, he drew on a long context of resistance to continental tyranny.[6] Being an island was conducive to liberty, thought Louis XVI's finance minister Jacques Necker: 'the waves of the ocean free you from the imperious yoke of disciplined armies'.[7]

In a popular phrase, Britain's naval superiority was attributed to its 'nursery of seamen', variously located by commentators in the north-to-south colliery trade and in fishing fleets all round the country.[8] Where the figure of John Bull represented British determination on land, his cousin Jack Tar represented Britain's self-determination at sea. The navy was an expression of nation that included all classes and appeared to be open to merit, perhaps more than the class-bound army.[9] One writer who reeled off a list of distinguished British admirals – Howard, Blake, Russell, Boscawen, Anson, Hawkes and Hood, for starters – freely admitted there were Dutch and Iberian equivalents:

> And yet, without indulging the extreme of national pride, which is but national folly, we may be allowed to assert, that as our situation as an island is more advantageously maritime than the greatest extent of continental coast, we have undoubtedly been more distinguished, both for skilful navigators, and great and excellent Commanders.[10]

Islands are also mythical and magical. One small island, little more than a rock, was held on to by the British as a dislodged fragment of national interest and, eventually, symbolic miniature of Britishness. This island was Gibraltar. It was captured in 1704 by Admiral Sir George Rooke as part of an Anglo-Dutch campaign to support the Archduke Charles of Austria as heir to the throne of Charles II of Spain, against the Bourbon Philip whose claim would see France and Spain come together as one kingdom – a fusion too powerful for other European nations to tolerate. The War of the Spanish Succession rumbled on for Britain until 1713, when the Peace of Utrecht ended fighting with France, recognised Philip as King Philip V of Spain (he gave up his place in line for the French crown) – and conceded Gibraltar to the British in perpetuity. Early governors of Gibraltar concentrated on lining their pockets, but gradually a combination of better administration, free trade and some freedom of religion meant Gibraltar began to thrive. In 1769 Britain spent an estimated £50,000 on new guns for the island's frontal defence; with these batteries and bastions, according to a Spanish historian writing in 1782, 'the city is unrecognisable from the one lost in 1704'.[11] The physical closeness of Gibraltar to Spain and its psychological importance meant the Spanish wanted it back: in 1770 the king of Spain offered a reward to any military adviser who could devise a plan for its recapture. Britain's forces were overstretched in the American colonies, but anticipation of Spanish activity led to the appointment of General Eliott, who was in charge as governor when the Spanish declared war on Britain in 1779.

It's important to understand why the British were so transfixed by Gibraltar, because in the history of balloons it became an invisible pivot. Gibraltar was strategically significant, a vantage point from which to view competitors' trade; it gave Britain a toe-hold on the ancient, rich and complex world of the Mediterranean. The island was naturally impregnable from one side, which made it a nice symbol for British security, hopefully also rock-like. When France and Spain teamed up to get back territories ceded to Britain, the Spanish anticipated a speedy recovery of Gibraltar; bombardment of the pregnable side of the island and blockade to the point of starvation would surely be successful in forcing a British surrender. But General Eliott was an exceptional soldier: vegetarian and teetotal, impervious to corruption and meticulously attentive to detail, he managed resourcefully the technical challenges of siege warfare. His defensive measures included ordering soldiers to leave their wigs unpowdered in order to economise on flour; his offensive tactics featured ingenious and arduous tunnelling to open up embrasures, known locally as 'old woman's teeth', from which his troops could fire down on to the enemy below. The townspeople of Gibraltar, caught in the crossfire, had some respite in the afternoons when the Spanish stopped their bombardments to take siestas.

As deaths ran high from fire-power, disease, starvation and a shortage of water, Eliott organised a counter-attack. On 27 November 1781, on the eve of a planned Spanish assault, the British made a surprise sortie. Within an hour they blew up supplies, destroyed enemy cannon and entrenchments and captured large numbers of troops. Their general appeared heroically through the smoke to inspire his men, before organising the collection of armfuls of cabbages and cauliflowers in abandoned gardens between the lines. It wasn't quite enough to turn the siege, even with the help of blockade-running small boats and a relief convoy in the spring of 1782 headed by Admiral Rodney. Conditions grew desperate. On 19 August the Duc de Crillon wrote with exquisite politeness to Eliott, offering him fresh vegetables. The general replied equally graciously that he could not possibly accept, since he had vowed to share both plenty and scarcity with his soldiers, and that they were all growing vegetables during intervals of rest from fighting.[12] The crux came on 13 September 1782 when the Spanish and French unleashed their own surprise, a secret weapon of 'Floating Batteries'. These were built of timbers packed with wet sand, backed by reservoirs of water to keep the sand damp and hence fire-proof. But the vegetable-minded Eliott responded with a ferocious counter-bombardment of 'hot potatoes', pre-heated cannonballs, more than forty thousand rounds, which 'peppered the advancing ships. Many were doused but invariably a rogue hot potato would lie asmouldering in the bowels of the ship and the burning cavity unexpectedly would explode into an inferno. One by one the unsinkable flotilla sank.

Planks from the wrecked floating batteries were made into tables for the Governor'.[13]

Private letters written on the day reported that the garrison blasted eight hundred barrels of gunpowder into the batteries, producing 'the most awful and grandest spectacle that ever was exhibited by military men'.[14] Four hundred pieces of artillery were in play at the same moment, confirmed Captain John Drinkwater in his eyewitness account of the most powerful force ever assembled against any fortress: forty-seven sail-of-the-line; ten battering ships deemed invincible and carrying 212 guns; 'innumerable frigates, xebeques, bomb-ketches, cutters' and other small boats assembled in the bay. On the land side, there were 'strong batteries mounting two hundred pieces of heavy ordnance, protected by an army of nearly forty thousand men commanded by a highly-reputable general and animated by the presence of royalty and nobility'. The extraordinary reversal was witnessed by about eighty thousand of these Spanish and French worthies, who had come to see what they thought would be an easy victory. Sublimity and terror turned to pathos as crews of ships on fire near the floating batteries were left by their own commanders to drown.[15] Eliott sent his *aide-de-camp* Captain Roger Curtis to their rescue. The siege – three years and seven months – was finally lifted on 5 February 1783.

The Siege of Gibraltar entered deep into British consciousness in the 1780s. Self-conscious pride in what 'is justly regarded as one of the epic episodes in eighteenth-century military history'[16] was expressed in the House of Commons in a vote of thanks to the defenders of Gibraltar. The nations of Europe, it was said, were struck with admiration for their gallant behaviour.[17] A medal was issued at Berlin showing General Eliott as *'Jupiter Tonans,* directing the thunderbolts of heaven'.[18] The date – 13 September – was added to Britain's rich calendar of political celebrations, and jubilation passed into popular culture in the form of pantomimes which gloriously re-enacted the siege with terrific explosions and fireworks.[19] Sir George Eliott was invested with the Order of the Bath in Gibraltar on St George's Day 1783;[20] patriotic delight was increased by more symbolism, in that the Gibraltar victory neatly improved on 13 September's other anniversary, the battle of Quebec in 1759 in which British victory against the French had cost the life of General Wolfe. Celebrations passed percussively through national culture. The *London Gazette* printed special editions of letters from the key players, filling out the details of heroism and benevolence.

At his one-man show in 1785, the fashionable artist Joseph Wright made an unusual foray into history painting to present his *View of Gibraltar* during the siege as the exhibition's centrepiece. It eventually sold for 420 guineas.[21] Wright's flaming drama was in turn praised by Cowper's friend William Hayley in an ode that further aimed 'to gild th' embattel'd scene with art's immortal light'.[22] Gibraltar was a sure-fire subject in the arts market.

But following the peace treaty in 1783, there was a furious debate about Britain's place in the world, and a very uneasy sense that the nation had declined. The peace treaty was criticised, in part for political gain by the Opposition, and in part because it seemed to some to be a mere plaster over a wound. 'There is not an infant that does not know, that France ever was, and ever will be, the enemy of England. The making a peace is not making a friendship,' wrote one commentator.[23] The great British victory at Gibraltar was open to revisionism, frighteningly so, from no less direct a source than Joseph Montgolfier himself. He told a philosopher friend that the origin of hot air balloons had come about one November evening in 1782 when:

> he was idly contemplating a print on the wall of his sitting room depicting the long siege of Gibraltar. ...Impregnable by land, impregnable by sea – might not Gibraltar be taken from the air? The evenings were growing cool in Avignon. A fire burned in the grate. Surely the force that carried particles of smoke up the flue could be confined and harnessed to lift conveyances and float men above the surface of the earth.[24]

The scholarly biographer of the Montgolfier brothers believes this story is plausible, and corroborates it with a letter from another brother, Jean-Pierre, written to Etienne who was *en route* to Paris to exploit the sensation of the Annonay balloon. This brother suggests 'Etienne could say that "in principle" the attempted conquest of Gibraltar had motivated the machine' – and that one might be supplied to the Turks, to increase French influence.[25]

On 2 March 1784 a political print was published in London, showing that the British understood exactly that the new airy invention could serve French ambitions. Called *Montgolfier in the Clouds*, with a subtitle 'Constructing of Air Balloons for the Grand Monarque', it shows a figure seated in clouds, blowing bubbles from a clay pipe. Some cod-French text below puts paid to any childish implications:

O by gar! dis be de grande invention – Dis will immortalize my King, my country and myself; we will declare de War against our ennemi: we will make des English quake, by gar; we will inspect their Camp, we will intercept their Fleet, and we will set fire to their Dock-yards: And by gar, we will take de Gibraltar in de air balloon, and when we have conquered d'Eenglish, den we conquer d'other countrie, and make them all colonie to de Grand Monarque.[26]

This fighting talk was serious, its intentions more aggressive than a print from the previous autumn, titled *The Montgolsier* [sic] *A First Rate of the French Navy*, in which an aeronaut sits on a globe with a cannon, above the stern of a man-of-war with more cannon; the armaments are offset by designs on smaller globes that include a bare-bottomed child, an ass, a fool's cap, a monkey's head and a blank, all reflected in the inscription below the title: 'A F---t---An Ass---A Fool---A Monkey---A Nothing'.[27] Representing balloons as insubstantial was consoling – and deluding.

Accounts from some of those present at the Siege of Gibraltar appeared in print while balloon madness was growing. Like narratives from Captain Cook's voyages, also published in 1783 to 1784, they intensified an ideology of national interest. Whether in the Pacific, where Louis-Antoine Bougainville nearly reached Australia before Cook, or in the Mediterranean, where Gibraltar was key to trade and information about ship movements, England and France competed for power. The French were allegedly sneaking troops into garrisons abroad, passing them off as members of regular crews in what one British newspaper reported disapprovingly as a very 'artful' method.[28] The year 1784 also saw reports that for the first time because of the disruptions of war, English merchants had to use foreign vessels to convey goods.[29] Leading personnel linked war and peace, air and water. The same paper reported the death of the Comte de la Porte, drowned in the River Niester escaping from *banditti*; he had escaped from one of the floating batteries at Gibraltar and ascended with Montgolfier at Lyons.

It would be simple to say that British citizens were anxious about their place in the world and that the possibility of air power increased that anxiety. So it was. But that anxiety had an intricate texture, layers of deep imagery combined with topical developments. The new invention of balloons fanned anxiety already agitated about other nations playing catch-up at sea. Imagination ran wildly ahead:

Every Power in Europe is taking uncommon Pains to encourage
maritime Adventurers. The Russians have been for some Years indefatigable; the Emperor and the King of Prussia are striving against
Nature to make Sea Ports in their Dominions, and Sailors of their
Subjects. Even the slothful Spaniards explore what a few Years ago
was to them unknown, the Regions of the Baltick. In all Mediterranean Ports also, the Powers belonging to them are busier than
ever in fitting out Vessels; and the very Turk relaxes in his religious
Prejudices, in Order to compass this End; so that it is possible in
another Twelvemonth we may see, without Surprise, the Maho-
metan Colours flying on the Thames.[30]

The years 1783 and 1784 brought in new areas of turbulence:
there was war on the northern and eastern borders of Europe, and
in the Mediterranean an escalation of skirmishes between Spain
and the fleet of Algiers. Again the chronology of news reports,
running slightly behind events, meant that reports of battles from
months ago overlapped with the latest news of aerial developments.
Historically distinct events became imaginatively simultaneous.
The Algerine case had sinister elements. French engineers were
busy assisting resistance to their former Spanish allies: 'they were
indefatigeable in the improvement of their artillery, and in endeav-
ouring to introduce the European model of discipline, cloathing and
arms, in their armies'.[31] The Spanish bombarded Algiers in July and
August of 1784 in an attempt to destroy the pirates harboured there.
In a reprise of the bombardment they had effected at Gibraltar, they
adopted the British technique of using red-hot cannon balls. French
assistance made the outcome close: 'The Algerine corsairs were now
built upon the model of the best European frigates', and their sailors
as intrepid as any of the maritime powers.[32] What if French aerial
technology spread to pirates?

Inventiveness in the 1780s devised machines that paralleled
balloon characteristics. Some were designed to 'improve' the process
of war. Lighter, faster, defying the elements – new rapid-firing guns
and new waterproof boats for transporting infantry showed the turn
to speed and manoeuvrability.[33] The British invested heavily in a
technology designed to tackle how wooden ships were slowed down
by weed and barnacles on their hulls, and shipworm, which ate away
at timbers. The Admiralty tried various tar-based substances, first
alone and then in conjunction with copper sheathing. The combination worked well and led to all British warships being copper-bot-
tomed, or protected by copper plates, with corrosion further reduced

by using copper bolts (rather than iron ones) to secure those plates.[34] Smelting all this metal increased demand for British coal, accelerating industrialisation. The costs were considerable: the fourteen tons of copper needed to treat a Third Rate, 74-gun ship of the line cost £1,500.[35] Nonetheless, the benefits were evident: as one French officer ruefully noted, 'the English sail much faster than us, especially now that they are sheathed in copper and we in oysters.'[36] Although the technical challenges of copper-bottoming persisted (enough to attract Sir Humphry Davy's interest later, when he established cast iron as the best material for bolts), it looked like invention and investment could maintain Britain's naval supremacy.

But balloons introduced the possibility of war in an element hitherto understood only in terms of favourable winds for ships. If aerial warfare happened, what use would hearts of oak be? That unofficial national anthem, with music by William Boyce and words by David Garrick, presumed that sea-power and valour, metaphorically united, would see off French invasions:

> Heart of oak are our ships, hearts of oak are our men,
> We always are ready, steady boys, steady, we'll fight and we'll
> conquer again.
>
> We ne'er see our foes but we wish them to stay,
> They never see us, but they wish us away;
> If they run, why we follow, and run them on shore,
> For if they won't fight us, we cannot do no more.[37]

Commentators were divided about the implications of balloons. In 1784 the *Universal Magazine* ruminated on themes of humanity and peace. With the arrival of flying vessels and flying men:

> That wonderful secret, for which every age has sighed, is found out at last! Man will now traverse aërial regions, and unite in himself the full perfection of the animal reign! Lord of earth, water, and the skies; fire is now the only element he cannot inhabit! – Others, with a graver aspect, observe, that every thing in the civil, moral and political world, seems to be reversed. Already they behold hostile armies in the air, and blood raining on the earth.[38]

Balloons went to the heart of Enlightenment: was progress possible or would human nature spoil it? Would universal good prevail over national ambition? This commentator was doubtful, settling for modest expectations of balloons contributing to aesthetics, science and hydraulics. Reports that balloons were being steered pressed the question of whether they would replace ships.

In tandem with tracking practical developments, Britons felt a profound unease about the place of war in a world aspiring to progress. The idea of aerial war had appalled an earlier philosopher, Robert Hooke. Reviewing designs for flying vessels in 1681, Hooke reflected: 'the Mind of man is naturally desirous of Novelty. What gratifies it, is pleasant; if innocent, good and useful.' Aware of scientific objections to the possibility of flight, Hooke thought the greatest objection was a moral one: 'For who sees not, that no City can be secure against attack, since our Ship may at any time be placed over it...?' A ship in the air could let down soldiers; it could descend to cut rigging of ships at sea, or throw down grapples, or balls of fire. It could also use these means to attack castles, cities and private houses, while staying out of reach of defensive power. The unfairness of it shocked Hooke. He wrote hopefully, 'God will never suffer this Invention to take effect, because of the many Consequences which may disturb the Civil Government of Men.'[39]

In the 1780s, philosophers were referencing Mammon rather than God. Some big questions were being asked about the relations between war, commerce and nation. Richard Watson, for instance, author of a volume of essays on chemistry, thought it perfectly proper to consider national prosperity: 'the inestimable advantage of an insular situation', he wrote, '[is] closely connected with the Number of our Seamen; and every child in Politics must know, that the Number of our Seamen will ever be proportioned to the extent of our foreign, and domestic Commerce.'[40] Adam Smith's great work of economics published in 1776 had as its full title *An Inquiry into the Nature and Causes of the Wealth of Nations*. How did nations prosper and how could they protect prosperity from the effects of war? The author of *Traité de l'administration des Finances de la France* (1784), Jacques Necker, pointed out that war had two sorts of costs: loss of revenue from commerce and expenditure on the forces of war. There was also, he pointed out humanely, a cost to people that couldn't be measured in monetary terms. Circulating in Britain, Necker's very readable analysis outlined a paradox: lately wars had been undertaken to protect commerce, yet the cost of war damaged national economies.[41] What else might nations spend the money on? He outlined some suggestions for civil projects in France, including reducing taxes, regularising the price of salt, building canals, improving prisons and creating jobs for the poor. Necker lamented the human cost of war – 'What unfeeling survivors we are! ... we walk over mutilated bodies and shattered bones,' he mourned – but even he proposed expenditure on armies and navies as legitimate, and allotted it nearly half of his imaginary fund for national investment.[42]

Readers interested in the philosophical aspects of political economy had some very real figures to mull over too. Newspapers and magazines eagerly published details of budgets, which in the mid 1780s consisted of sums of expenditure and lists of new taxes. There was thus a clear context for balloons, in that what was obvious to every child in British politics was the exorbitant cost of the navy. Six years of war under Pitt had cost the country six million pounds, more than was spent on all the preceding wars of the century, but the expense had paid for an empire. Readers were reminded of it in 1783, in journals which printed extracts from newly-translated memoirs by Francesco Algarotti. A great admirer of Pitt the elder, Algarotti described an illumination in London to celebrate the glory days:

> in a certain house in London, in which every quarter of the globe had its particular window decorated with an inscription: the taking of Gorce and Senegal for Africa; that of Surat for Asia; the victories at Minden, Cadiz and Quiberon, for Europe; the conquest of Cape Bretton, of Quebec, &c. &c. &c. for America; an illumination the Romans never could have made, for want of a window.[43]

Political possessions of the 1780s meant facing uncomfortable economic facts. Victory at Gibraltar – like the Falklands in the 1980s – had not come cheap: running the garrison was calculated to cost £500,000 a year.[44] Dominion abroad was important to British national pride, but could the nation afford this? Facing a trio of nations building up maritime power – France, Spain, Holland – what did Britain need to do to strengthen its coastal defences against attack? Throughout the years of balloon madness, the House of Commons debated defences at Plymouth, Portsmouth and other naval bases along the south coast. Large sums were approved to fortify them. By the spring of 1786, it was estimated £300,000 had been spent – in vain, if they were vulnerable to attack from the air.[45] Pitt had said Britain 'was like an amphibious animal, which might live upon land, yet whose proper element is the water'.[46] But how could an amphibian engage with air power?

It may seem unusual to approach the history of war through its poetics, but national interests in the 1780s were so often presented in terms of elements – earth, water, fire and now air – that the unsettling potential of balloons in warfare agitated currents of symbolism.

22   A duel for the empire of the sky. Engraving published in London by J. Barrow, December 1783.

These run deep: we still organise fighting forces and narratives of battle around elements. Thus the Imperial War Museum in London organises its collections into sections titled 'Land Warfare' and 'Air and Sea'.[47] One print from December 1783 [Figure 22] presented Jack Tar and a French opponent improbably levitated by balloons fighting for the Empire of the Sky, above ships whose diminutive scale suggests diminished relevance. The verses below begin with balloons breaking a bond with the sea: 'Some think we shall soon,/ By the help of Balloon,/ Be able to fly in the Air,/ And go where we please,/ Without trusting the Seas/ With our Bodies and mercantile ware.' A defiant analogy could hardly restore them: 'And as it is right,/ For the Ocean to fight,/ Why should we not fight for the air?' The imagining of balloons as viable weapons was frustrated by as-yet primitive mechanics. One might arm a balloon with cannon or fill balloon cars with infantry, but actual flight was still so unsteady there was an obvious imaginative gap. Into that empty space flowed old symbolism, trying to adapt to new circumstances.

Fables and the classics provided some simple emblems: eagles commanded air, salamanders survived fire. In his educational treatise *Emile* (1762), Jean-Jacques Rousseau wondered why young men were taught to ride but not to swim: 'Emile shall be as much at home in the water as on land. Why should he not be able to live in every element? If he could learn to fly, he should be an eagle; I would make him a salamander, if he could bear the heat.'[48] The salamander was naturally aquatic but, like the phoenix which rose from ashes, might be lifted into air by heat. 'The sprites of fiery termagants in flame/ Mount up, and take a Salamander's name', wrote Alexander Pope in Canto I of *The Rape of the Lock*. Symbolically the salamander condensed power over elements into mastery of different environments.[49] Pliny's account of the salamander was linked by Jonathan Swift to war,[50] and it continued to enchant enlightened imaginations:

> As agreeable fables readily gain belief, every one has been eager to adopt that of a small animal, so highly privileged, so superior to the most powerful agent of nature, and which could furnish so many objects of comparison to poetry, so many pretty emblems to love, and so many brilliant devices to valour.[51]

Imagery around General Eliott developed this swirl of associations between fire, war and command. Eliott, it was said,

> has given the combined forces of the House of Bourbon, a very *brilliant* proof that Gibraltar is not to be taken by either Squibs or

> Crackers ... After promising, and thereby setting all Europe agog,
> to hear of their capturing the British Salamander, and his handful of
> brave Associates; they have only proved that after meeting a warm
> Reception, they burnt their Fingers, and made their Retreat in a
> *Blaze* of Confusion, Horror and Disgrace.[52]

The destructive power of fire is transferred to a humiliated enemy.
Such symbolism should be understood to inform events too readily
dismissed as mere popular spectacle, like the new display at Astley's
in July 1784. It was titled 'The Air-Balloon, or All the World in the
Clouds; in the second Scene will be presented the Manner of travelling through the Air in the Triumphal Car, and a most beautiful
Firework, in which will be introduced a Salamander.'[53] A French
invention could be open to 'All the World'; French command of air
could be checked by the fireproof salamander.

Britons, however, had another card up their sleeves – a flying
admiral. Nautical heroes were national heroes. When Blanchard and
Sheldon made their ascent from London in the autumn of 1784, they
shared front page limelight with Lord Hood on a visit to Liverpool.
There he was fêted in grand style in a hall adorned with Neptune
imagery and decorated with a motto: 'ON THE STRENGTH OF
OUR NAVY AND THE VIGILANCE OF OUR COMMANDERS
WILL DEPEND THE SUPPORT AND CONTINUANCE OF
OUR COMMERCE'.[54] In the spring of 1785, a season of prolonged
cold weather, Rear-Admiral Sir Edward Vernon joined the Italian
aeronaut Zambeccari in an ascent from Tottenham Court Road in a
pea-green and orange striped balloon. Vernon had seen action in the
Mediterranean and at Pondicherry. Very conveniently he was easily
confused with an Admiral Vernon of the previous generation, who
beat the Spanish in the War of Jenkins' Ear and whose capture of
Portobello is commemorated in the name of Portobello Road. The
older Admiral Vernon at the height of his popularity was hailed
as a Drake or a Raleigh; his distant relative was rather less distinguished.[55] But no matter ... he was going to ascend in a balloon.
The tearful disappointment of a young woman, Miss Grice, who had
been promised a passage, was brushed aside. People of fashion were
spared the crush which killed one woman and led to scuffles:

> The mob were very outrageous on yesterday some time before the
> balloon went up, from an apprehension of being disappointed, and
> threatened to tear the machine; but on Count Zambeccari assuring
> them he would ascend immediately after the storm of snow and hail

was over, they behaved tolerably quiet, and on the globe arising, burst into loud acclamations, declaring "Sam. Buckerry, [Zambeccari] was an honest fellow, and had kept his word with the public".[56]

'Sam. Buckerry', grouchy with a sprained wrist, blamed difficulties on a slow fill by 'foreigners'. Vernon had paid him £300 for expenses providing he could join the flight; in return, on 23 March, Zambeccari got a publicist's dream of the company of a British naval hero, who nervously survived an ascent which went dangerously to ten thousand feet and landed near Horsham after an hour's flight. It narrowly satisfied a nationalist prophecy of aerial success:

Albion once more her drooping head shall rear,
And roll her thunders through each distant sphere;
While, led by future Rodneys, British tars
Shall pluck bright honours from the twinkling stars.[57]

'Admiral Vernon is the first Admiral who has ever navigated the atmosphere,' trumpeted the *Annual Register*[58] – but there was a hint of something unheroic about the episode, whether it was Vernon's being ungallant to Miss Grice, complaining of cold, or paying for his seat with what some said was ill-gotten East Indies prize money. Nonetheless the idea of flying admirals was still a hopeful levity in 1786:

We've admirals who plough the briny deep,
Through azure skies and rolling clouds they sweep,
Invade the Planets in an Air Balloon,
And fright from her propriety the Moon.[59]

One historian of winged warfare thinks it is not until 1859 in Hermann Lang's *The Air Battle* that air is first imagined as the decisive arena of war, and that before then, 'most speculation … was visual rather than literary… During the Revolutionary and Napoleonic Wars a number of such prints appeared, visualising balloons in a variety of military roles: as troop transporters; carrying out bombardments on the battlefield, or in combat with other balloons.'[60] Though historians of aerial warfare often start with *montgolfière* balloons, it was not until 1796 at the Battle of Fleurus (on 26 June, when the French defeated an Austrian and Dutch force) that a balloon saw action, and then from a lofty tether from which intelligence was relayed to generals below. The small *compagnie d'aérostiers* (founded in 1794) who manned this balloon had three roles: reconnaissance, signalling and the distribution of propaganda.

Though part of the corps survived reformation to be absorbed into Napoleon's army in Egypt, its practical contribution was minimal. One might explain the cul-de-sac as technical – balloons were too visible, vulnerable and unmanoeuvrable to play any significant part in war. Similar arguments were played out again with the development of those rigid and dirigible airships, Zeppelins, around 1900.

Following Mercier, the optimism of futurists in the 1780s encouraged more thinking about aerostatic development as a technology of civil progress.[61] Balloon historians are understandably attracted to Horace Walpole's vision of Salisbury Plain full of balloons, as if it was an aerodrome (a word first used to mean an airfield in 1908). But Walpole self-confessedly wrote letters as tragicomic balancing acts,[62] and he fantasised about balloons coming and going like ships:

> I chiefly amused myself with ideas of the change that would be made in the world by the substitution of balloons to ships. I supposed our sea-ports to become *deserted villages*; and Salisbury Plain, Newmarket Heath (another canvass for alteration of ideas), and all downs (but *the* Downs) arising into Dockyards for aerial vessels.

He continues with a parody of ship news:

> The good balloon Daedalus, Captain Wing-ate, will fly in a few days for China; he will stop at the top of the Monument to take in passengers. Arrived on Brand Sands, the Vulture, Captain Nabob; the Tortoise snow, from Lapland; the Pet-en-l'air, from Versailles; the Dreadnaught, from Mount Etna, Sir W. Hamilton, commander; the Tympany, Montgolfier; and the Mine-A-in-a-bandbox, from the Cape of Good Hope. Foundered in a hurricane, the Bird of Paradise, from Mount Ararat. The Bubble, Sheldon, took fire and was burnt to her gallery; and the Phoenix is to be cut down to a second-rate.[63]

Topical jokes and puns map a world interconnected in the future by air much as it was by sea, and in much the same way. Walpole concludes what he calls 'fooleries' with militarism and mercantilism evenly balanced: 'There will be fights in the air with wind-guns and bows and arrows; and there will be prodigious increase of land for tillage, especially in France, by breaking up all public roads as useless.'[64] When Walpole saw the balloon carrying Sadler and Windham aloft on 5 May 1785, he wrote again to Sir Horace Mann: 'Three more balloons sailed to-day; in short, we shall have a prodigious navy in the air, and then what signifies having lost the empire of the ocean?'[65] Even Walpole, whose imagination was playful and agile, thinks in ideologically continuous terms. Erasmus

Darwin, another lively imaginer, went the same way, taking balloons underwater: 'Led by the sage, Lo! Britain's sons shall guide/ Huge sea-balloons beneath the tossing tide.'[66] English writers found it hard to move away from the sea.

Paul de Virilio has theorised that people tend to imagine a war in terms of the last one, at least until it acquires its own character.[67] An overlap between nautical language and aerostation, the art of sailing in air, kept imaginations more fixed. The political writer Mirabeau, in England during 1784 and 1785, grumbled that 'these nautical islanders are eternally reminding one that they "rule the waves".'[68] The peace treaty of 1783 between Britain and France was not one of diplomacy's great successes; neither side was thrilled by it. But it did enable a peace, albeit a suspicious one, in which believers in progress continued to have faith in the future by not second-guessing it.[69] Michael Lynn observes that 'The call to wait and see how aeronautics developed over time appeared often in the first few years of ballooning.'[70] Balloon madness encompassed the sensible view that it was too early to tell. As a witness of a balloon ascent in 1784 in Philadelphia wrote: 'What Garrison can remain unconsumed? What Region unexplored? &c. &c. To what amazing perfection these Globes may be brought Futurity alone can unfold.'[71]

The hope in futurity tended to assume a story of progress, or the Whig version of history, in which things get better. By 1786 balloon madness had passed the peak of craze, though enthusiasm took two or three years more to dwindle to near-extinction. Meanwhile, a parallel story about parachutes came briefly into being, in which animals relocated balloon symbolism into uneasy parody. If balloons could too easily serve war, balloons and parachutes very easily served silliness. Miniaturising and doubling the feats of flight enacted by balloons, parachutes turned the force of gravity paradoxically into levity, freighted with jokes. The next chapter looks at how attempts to fall downward got imperfectly off the ground.

Back to Earth

Parachutes and Balloons in 1785 and 1802

13

'Mr. Blanchard and Chevalier D'Epinard ascended from Lille, and alighted at a village in Champaigne, near 300 miles from the place of their departure. In the course of this voyage, they let down a dog by means of a parachute from a great height, which descended safe about two miles from Lille.'

The European Review and London Magazine,
'Remarkable Events of 1785', 20 July 1785

THE IDEA OF THE PARACHUTE is conventionally attributed to Leonardo da Vinci, who in 1485 sketched a pyramid-shaped canopy attached to a wooden frame, with a pole from the apex and cords from the corners to which a person could hang on. Its purpose was to enable anyone to let themselves down from a height without danger; its particular application would be to persons escaping from buildings on fire. But Leonardo's design stayed unpublished until the end of the nineteenth century,[1] and although some early experiments by Joseph Montgolfier made use of the idea of using resistance to slow descent in air in ways common both to balloons and parachutes, the development of parachutes as separate entities proceeded slowly. There were successful tests at Avignon, it was said, using first a sheep, then a condemned prisoner.[2]

Inspiration – and explanation – came from the umbrella, commonly in use as a protector against rain. In October 1784, Thomas Martyn published a design for a globe balloon that explicitly included an 'Umbrella to afford easy descent' should the balloon burst.[3] It was dismissed by Blanchard, who said Martyn was welcome to take what little credit there was in such a useless device.[4] Despite this fart in Martyn's general direction, Blanchard was himself experimenting with designs of ribs attached to a silk canopy, and by June 1785 he was making test drops above his Aerostatic Academy in Vauxhall. One was to have starred a sheep – but just as the balloon launched, a lady tripped over the cords which connected sheep and parachute to the balloon, which shot off and burst.[5] Another event in July was heralded by an announcement of a surprising artistic performance. An Italian intended to waft to earth from a parachute while flowingly playing a violin. An expectant crowd assembled, joking about high notes. The Italian was supposed to begin his descent at forty-five feet. He got nervously to twenty, expanded his parachute, launched himself into the air – and ignominiously fell ten feet without scraping a note. The parachute lay broken; the violin was shattered. It was time to get away quick. 'The conjurer crawled off with the greatest alacrity, whilst John Bull, after a vacant stare of a few minutes, could only wreak his revenge on the machinery and railing of the enclosure, both of which were in a short time demolished.'[6]

Parachutes had materialised, imperfectly. The failure of this demonstration made them look like another imposition on public credulity,[7] yet attempts to launch parachutes from balloons continued, using animals as involuntary passengers. Some died. In June 1785 from a tethered balloon Colonel Thornton threw out a dog in a parachute. It crashed, and broke the dog's legs and back. The colonel was swiftly hauled down. Blanchard got in. At 4.15 he took off, heading south. While still in view, he:

> detached a large silken umbrella, having a cat suspended to it. Its descent was beautiful beyond imagination, hovering more gently than a feather; it seemed to be wafted by the wind to about a mile from the place whence it was detached, and gradually descended as it flew. We have not heard where the cat was found...[8]

The cat descended gradually into a tree, where it was netted to live – and fly – another day. Londoners were not sentimental about dead cats and dogs, but they were capable of showing feeling for a live cat or dog. Blanchard's happily alive cat – which joined the growing corpus of aerial feline literature – could not wholly expunge Colonel Thornton's wretched killing of a dog. People were not insensitive to the sacrifice of animals but many put pragmatism before pathos: as with balloons two years earlier, better a cat or dog should die than a person. Nonetheless, there was concern about a white-coated Pomeranian dog who went up in a balloon in October 1784, and returned spotted thanks to acidic drops from the valve.[9] Unease permeated witticisms: 'A petition from the dogs and cats of Great Britain, against the use of the parachute, is preparing, and will shortly be presented to parliament.'[10] Animal deaths, especially that of Colonel Thornton's dog, reinforced ideas of foolhardiness. '"There is a *puppy*

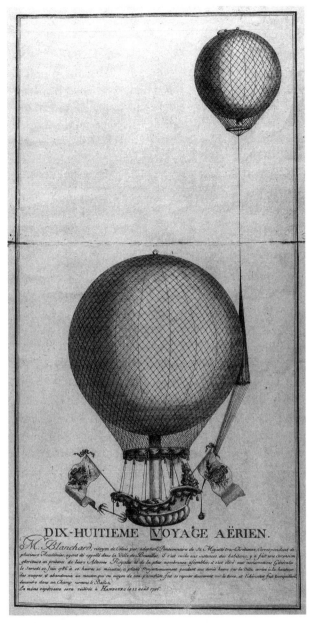

An airborne sheep accompanying Blanchard: 'Il abandonna un mouton, qui au moyen de son parachute, fut se reposer doucement sur la terre' [he let drop a sheep, who by means of his parachute was able to come to rest gently on the earth]. The sheep is hard to spot: look just above the letters GE in Voyage. Commemorating Blanchard's eighteenth aerial voyage on 10 June 1786 from Brussels.

23

going up," said a lady, as the Colonel stepped into the balloon car. "Yes," observed another lady, "there is a *pair* of them.'"[11]

Confidence was slightly restored by Blanchard's evidently gentler technique. In Lille on 26 August 1785, his plans were delayed by bad weather. Suspecting his motives, the city magistrates kept him under guard until he finally got aloft, accompanied by the Chevalier d'Epinard. Seriousness was proven by a successful parachute flight, thanks to a dog who descended gradually to make a safe landing two miles away. Blanchard went on for three hundred miles, and on returning to Lille was met with a guard of honour – a pleasant change from his military send-off. In subsequent performances round northern Europe, he finally got sheep airborne [Figure 23].[12]

In London, the combination balloon-and-parachute event promoted by Arnold and Appleby drew a huge crowd to St George's Fields on 31 August 1785 for a double fiasco. One person at least profited: an enterprising soldier got hold of the parachute and made five guineas by selling bits of it at twopence and threepence each to an avid throng.[13] A few years later, Arnold was cited in a book of science for children as a demonstrator of principles of air resistance; at the time, many wrote him off as a charlatan.[14]

That autumn saw parachutes established in people's imaginations. One satirical print published on 8 September 1785 depicted a parachute with Fox and North standing on each end of an anchor of Hope, with a canopy of 'Irish Propositions', attached to a balloon representing Fox's East India Bill.[15] The satire, on Opposition politicians for equivocating about legislation to restrict trade for Irish manufactures, assumed that the public recognised parachutes as an emblem of instability. In fashion, huge 'parachute' hats appeared: 'the milleners [*sic*] are now all at work on *parachute hats, parachute bonnets, parachute caps,* and *parachute petticoats*'.[16] Not everyone was impressed:

> It is really cruel in the fair sex to continue to use parachute hats; formerly it was a pleasure to walk the streets, and through the fields, to contemplate that infinite vanity of beauty which the English ladies may boast of. But now the whole is hid from the chastest eye, under a villainous congregation of wire, straw and crape. No man need be jealous now of his wife, for she is as effectually hid from gallants as if she was the wife of a jealous pated Spaniard, and shut up for life.[17]

Parachute escapes became an applauded feature of pantomimes – often, ironically, after displays by dancing dogs. Many cats used up some or all of their nine lives in the parachute's flighty cause, so that in a comic opera of 1785 a parachute was defined as a 'mathematical instrument, vulgarly called an umbrella, into which if you put a cat, you may toss her from the top of a house without breaking her neck'.[18]

Yet for all the feline, canine and ovine pioneering, parachutes made little progress. Like balloons, they raised imaginative hopes only to disappoint. Blanchard's consistently commanding voyages established a pattern thrilling to those who had never seen a balloon before, but increasingly predictable. All he does is go up and down, grumbled a French memoirist. Talk by Blanchard of a balloon made up of five mini-balloons, with a parachute able to support four people, was just talk.[19] Aerial voyaging seemed to have reached a point of stasis. 'The exhibition of air balloons has been discontinued in England for some years', it was said in 1800, for the obvious reason that balloons seemed to be going nowhere. 'The invention as yet has only afforded amusement to the marvelling million, and, till it can be stamped with utility the public appear inclined to rest satisfied without the sight, however curious.'[20]

Aeronautics also stagnated because the French Revolution caused massive disruption to the old network of ideas that made up the Enlightenment. News was forbidden, censored, disguised, distorted; private correspondence was intercepted. In France, the country keenest on aerial explorations, conditions for invention were confined to a tiny part of the army. Members of the nobility who had rewarded aeronauts and followed aerial progress were arrested, imprisoned and executed, like the Duc d'Orléans, who went to his death on a winter's day in 1793. Places that had seen triumphant balloon ascents were turned into sites of execution, in delicate acts of cruelty at which revolutionaries excelled. So Bailly, the first mayor of Paris, was executed in the Champ de Mars, where Charles and Robert had launched the first hydrogen balloon. A secret report assessing the chemist Antoine-Laurent de Lavoisier concluded: 'Citizen Lavoisier deserves to be placed among the men whose work, in pushing back the boundaries of human knowledge have done most to advance the arts and glory of the Nation.'[21] It made no difference: Lavoisier, a significant financier for the old regime, was condemned. Shortly before his death Lavoisier wrote peaceably to his wife, reconciled to his fate and trusting he would be remembered with some glory.[22] Others less famous had ideas cut short. A former army captain, Millin Labrosse, found guilty of irascible comments on a newspaper article and sentenced to death, wrote to the public prosecutor, Citizen Fouquier, to offer a cardboard model of an entirely new aerostat to his local Revolutionary Committee. He asked for a twenty-four hour stay of execution so he could explain the theory behind its construction: 'I am not trying uselessly to prolong my life, but I admit that I am still thinking of what might be done so that my name may be remembered, when the time of anger is past.'[23] His request was ignored. Who knows how many other aeronautically-inclined citizens were guillotined?

Yet even without revolutionary upheavals, would aeronautics have had a lull anyway? At the end of the eighteenth century, a comic poet looked back on its achievements:

> Now wild *ambition* soar'd on high,
>   Now vaulting, mounted a BALLOON!
>   Like *Phaeton*, to touch the sky,
>   Or pay a visit to the Moon!
> So great was the sight, it was confest,
>   All met from North to South,
> From East to West,
> *John Bull* beheld with open mouth;
>   Nay, every one did stare –
> To see a man ascending high,
> Till hid from every mortal eye –
>   And when above,
> What was his great dominion there?
>   He needs must go where the wind drove –
>   And so come down at last to prove
> That he was building *Castles in the* AIR!
>
> Presumption went on further still,
>   In order to attain repute –
> Contriving a descent at will,
> And falling with a PARACHUTE!
> But any man can fall with ease,
>   Indeed we have a document –
> For some poor madman once did please
>   To jump off from the *Monument.*
> Then how came men so wise as these,
>   To overlook a greater point,
> For sure a greater they did lack,
>   Whenever to return they'd want,
> They should have learn'd how to jump *back.*[24]

Several things are puzzling about the revival of interest in balloons and parachutes at the end of the eighteenth century. The most baffling is why parachute history disappeared from public awareness. However technically imperfect the 1785 designs used by Arnold, Blanchard and others, they were still more than blueprints, yet it was as if they never existed. How did people effectively forget an invention? Why, when progress was desirable, was there a silence about previous efforts? And over a gap of barely a decade?

Revolutionary stories about prisoners who planned escapes by parachute supplied a slender thread of continuity,[25] and one became credible because its protagonist, an aeronaut before the Revolution, took up aerial adventuring again with a display in Paris in October 1797 which put parachutes back in circulation. André-Jacques Garnerin had been imprisoned in a fortress where he had had plenty of time to plot ways of evading sentries, ten-foot thick walls and high ramparts. 'Blanchard's idea of presenting large surfaces to the air to increase its resistance, and the known acceleration of move-ment in all falling bodies, appeared to me only to require a careful mathematical comparison to be employed with certain success', he explained. 'After deciding on the size of the parachute or descending from a rampart or a precipice, by natural sequence I devised the size and form of parachute for a descent of several thousand feet by an aeronaut.'[26] The trial was made in a freer world, at the Parc Monceau in Paris on 22 October. Garnerin's parachute, twenty-three feet in diameter when open, had ribbed segments of canvas attached to a circle of wood at the top like an umbrella; the ribs connected to a wooden hoop below. Silence and anxiety filled the crowd. Garnerin, in a basket attached by a pole to the netting above, took his balloon to three thousand feet, then cut the cords which attached the para-chute to it. Oscillating violently, 'the parachute began to descend with such rapidity that a cry of horror escaped from the spectators and several ladies fainted.'[27] [Plate VIII: note the reappearance of pickpockets in the right-hand foreground.] The principle of air resistance worked: Garnerin reached the ground sick but safe. The parachute was proven.

Like balloons, this invention came to England and, as with balloons, by the time it arrived it had form. Garnerin had made several descents and so too had a woman who became his wife – Jeanne-Genevieve Labrosse, who in 1798 made her own contribution to aeronautic history with an intrepid jump at the Tivoli Gardens. Garnerin came over to England in the spring of 1802, and set about demonstrating his prowess through balloon-only voyages at first. To appreciate how he catalysed aerial interest, one must reunite parachutes to the story of balloons, which in England had come to a halt. Garnerin's successes had a two-fold import: first, that he filled an empty space; second, that his achievements took place at the same time as a tragicomic series of failures by an Englishman. It was all very galling – or gauling.

His credentials were heavyweight. When the French authorities banned night flights with fire balloons, they made an exception for Garnerin, who had been exclusively permitted to organise illuminated night displays. His showpiece was an imitation of a meteor seen by Napoleon over Dijon, an auspicious omen of what proved to be his victory in the battle of Marengo on 14 June 1800. Audiences were thoroughly impressed by Garnerin's show, in which a balloon at great height exploded in a whirl of starry fireworks and flames. Yet associations with Napoleon roused suspicion among the English: was Garnerin tainted with infamous revolutionary activity? Garnerin responded robustly: he had played 'no other part than that which honour may avow in all countries, and at all times', simply serving his country in its army. He had honourably surrendered to the Duke of York at Marchiennes in October 1793, and then spent thirty-one months in an Austrian prison. Besides, the French army had not paid his salary.[28] A nation of shopkeepers didn't quarrel with that. Moreover, articles of peace between France and Britain in 1802 encouraged hope of a resumption of normal relations – normal meaning a mixture of admiration and mutual conviction of superiority.

Like Blanchard before him, Garnerin looked to gain money and reputation. The Pic-Nic Society, organisers of fêtes at Ranelagh that year, paid Garnerin £500 to make his balloon part of the show. A passenger would supply extra funds and patriotic ballast, and so on 28 June 1802, Captain Sowden of the navy prepared to ascend with Garnerin. A young lady in the crowd rushed forward to try to deter him, but love lost out to money. There had been complicated negotiations over costs. Originally Garnerin was to have taken up a Colonel Greville. Beating off a rival bid of fifty guineas for the chance, Sowden offered Greville £200 to go in his place, plus a half share of the profit or loss of the Ranelagh fêtes. Since they made a loss of over £1,000 that year, a seat for three quarters of an hour cost Sowden £800, as the newspapers reported with astonishment. Sowden also made his will in favour of Greville, in a ghoulish move.[29]

Sowden's extravagance was made possible by a recent inheritance of £6,000 from his father, a patrimony he ran through all too quickly before taking to the provincial stage and meeting a dissipation-hastened death in London in 1811, aged fifty-one.[30] Garnerin attached conditions: on no account would he stop to land Sowden anywhere. They were in it together to the end.

The day was very wet. Nevertheless the balloon was filled by one o'clock. Then for several hours the wind blew fiercely. Garnerin was keen to have a British success but anxious not to have a dead Englishman, so he tried to persuade Sowden to let him go alone. After all the hard bargaining Sowden would not be deterred – so, in spite of dangerously high winds, at five o'clock the aerial travellers mounted the car, each waving their country's flag as a symbol of alliance and amity. They rose above St James's, passed over St Paul's and above the clouds over London. 'Dinner was then introduced, and eaten with pleasure and appetite.'[31] They flew for half an hour, when passing over the sea made Garnerin mindful of pressing danger, so he prepared to descend and told Sowden to retrieve the valve rope. In climbing up to do so in near gale-force winds, Sowden was whacked round the head by the tin gas tubes; both aeronauts clung on as the balloon bounced through fields, trees and bushes. The anchor caught briefly in a hedge near a house: its inhabitants came out frightened, guns in hand. Just then the anchor broke and the balloon smashed into a tree where Sowden got another blow to his head. Still, they were alive, and at last out of the car. In pouring rain they found the balloon nearby, threw themselves exhaustedly on to it to squash out the last remnants of gas and limped to the nearest house. Its owner, seeing two strangely dressed people, one in a French hat with a tricolour, one in sailor's garb, decided they must be something to do with the election and announced he wasn't going to vote for anyone. It was probably a less *outré* idea than that two people could come from London in three quarters of an hour, but it took the exhausted aeronauts nearly as long to enlist his help in retrieving the balloon and getting to Colchester, four miles away, where, very bruised, they arrived to a tumultuous welcome. Sowden dashed off a note to Greville: 'Dear Greville, After a delightful voyage of three quarters of an hour, we landed safe at Colchester. Our landing was extremely difficult, on account of the high wind. You may suppose what a devil of a rate we came at.' Garnerin wrote briefly to his friends in London, with less elation: the voyage was very pleasant but had ended in 'the most dangerous descent I ever made... We ourselves are all over bruises.' Sowden recovered high spirits, happy to return with interest Garnerin's compliments on his courage: 'I cannot help admiring the coolness and presence of mind M. Garnerin preserved, even in the most immanent danger; and I am so confident of his great talents and skill in conducting a Balloon, that I would go to the end of the world with him.'[32]

This glowing testimonial, exactly what Garnerin wanted, didn't entirely allay public doubts. For one thing Sowden's account, published in the next day's papers, begged questions. Even though Sowden seemed to know this – 'I have observed, that almost every sensation I experienced while in the upper regions was exactly contrary to what is the general opinion of the Public' – his powers of observation came across as strange. Disdaining the usual drink of heroes, Sowden and Garnerin had washed down their dinner – ham, fowl, cake – not with brandy but with orgeat, an almondy syrup, so he wasn't drunk. But altitude affected him in peculiar ways. Normally a man of weak eyesight, he reported that he could see the earth for fifty miles around, its roads, its paths, even furrows in the fields. Equally oddly, he said that at fifteen thousand feet he could hear the sound of carriages, of cattle, of people shouting below, though he and Garnerin could hardly hear themselves speak. Where he had been led to expect cold to increase with height, he found it so warm he took off his greatcoat and jacket. He felt no giddiness on looking down, whereas while looking around him his eyes went dim. Readers were sceptical. Neither Garnerin nor Sowden had reported anything to gratify curiosity or enrich science, said commentators:

> The Balloon seems to be considered as a subject of unbounded admiration, and certainly it is entitled to our surprise and wonder. Hitherto, however, men of science have viewed it more as a raree-shew than as an apparatus by which they could make experiments. Telescopes are not employed in commerce, yet their utility has never been called in question, because they have fallen into the hands of those who were actuated by philosophical research, and have conse-quently contributed to the enlargement of human knowledge.[33]

Sowden's account added to the feeling of disappointment about balloons, and to suspicions that they were entertaining but simply not useful.

Sowden's unusual findings attracted satire as well as scepticism. His experiences were wonderfully parodied in a letter written by Madame Garnerin's cat, who carefully concealed his intentions to ascend lest it alarm those tabbies fearful for his safety, like Sowden's inamorata at Ranelagh. 'The Captain could not but know, that I had his narrative particularly in my eye; and, that if he had dealt in the marvellous, he had everything to dread from a person of my sagacity, vigilance, and activity.' Restraining his chill-whetted appetite, the cat abstained from chicken and devoted himself to physical observations, especially ones of sight and sound. Where Sowden said the earth looked brighter because altitude made his eyes stronger, the cat attributed aerial glow to the reflection of the sun's rays and, with a political dig, mocked Sowden's minuteness of vision:

> Hovering over Westminster, St. Stephen's Chapel appeared to me like a *rat-trap*. I could distinctly see the inside; and round the Treasury Bench it was strewn with *cheese-parings* and *candle-ends*, and the *rats* assembling from all sides fighting and quarrelling for a mouthful...[34]

Another catty parodist reported that London's three biggest prisons – King's Bench, Newgate and Fleet – looked like mousetraps.[35] Other writers were scornful of Sowden's literary efforts, especially his comparison of Epping Forest to a gooseberry bush: no doubt 'he would have amused us by describing Greenwich park as a *hawthorn*, the muslin gowns being the *blossom*'.[36]

For all its drama, then, Garnerin and Sowden's voyage brought disappointments. There were some positive outcomes. Garnerin gave the balloon car to Astley junior, who continued his father's business of horse showmanship and spectaculars and incorporated balloons into a successful pantomime, *The Phoenix, or Harlequin and Lillipo*. A second pantomime, *The Aerial Candidates, or Both Members Returned*, made light fun of the election ironies and combined them with beauty, representing the scenery and changing perspectives of flight in satisfying effects said to excel even the 'Eidometropolis' by Thomas Girtin, a walk-through panorama of London, 1,944 square feet large, exhibiting at Spring Gardens at the same time. Another positive impression was that of speed, calculated to be at least thirty miles an hour, double that of Lunardi's. 'At the rate at which M. Garnerin's Balloon proceeded, it would go round the globe in 13 days and a half'. That it had been swept along uncontrollably mattered little; it reawakened some sense of possibility.[37]

Garnerin's next ascent was on 5 July, from Lord's Cricket Ground at Marylebone. Rumour said Sowden would fly again; the ego-bruised Sowden denied it. The place was won on the toss of a coin by Edward Locker, who initially described himself as 'Mr Brown' so as not to alarm his family. He complained that the mob was 'as usual, both troublesome and officiously impertinent'.[38] But the crowd also included an aristocratic circle which was very familiar with balloons: the Prince of Wales, the Duchess of Devonshire, Lady Dungannon, Lords Bessborough and Cathcart, and Sir Richard Fox. Mindful of his experiences at gunpoint on his last landing, Garnerin asked his royal admirer to sign a piece of paper certifying his ascent. The prince agreed and got his friends to add their signatures.

Locker proved to be a more discerning passenger than Sowden. He had read up on ballooning literature, including Baldwin's *Airopaidia*, though he thought earlier descriptions of the countryside viewed aerially were inadequate: 'I think a map is an incorrect comparison, as the various objects are not as in nature delineated with sufficient minuteness'. Instead he suggested it was 'more like a prospect seen to a camera, when placed in a very elevated situation'.[39] Locker listened carefully to sounds, and reported that above three thousand feet neither he nor Garnerin could identify earthbound noise. Garnerin too made an effort to contribute something to science, pontificating that attention to the evaporation of noise from the earth 'proves the use of trifling philosophical experiments on the constitution of the upper atmosphere, where so many changes are felt in rapid succession'.[40] He proposed that inexperienced aerial travellers – unlike himself – could be misled by the way that cavities in the lower part of the balloon reflected sounds from the earth's surface. Some sounds thus appeared to come from somewhere else, an effect exploited by magicians of the day in a trick known as the Invisible Girl. This explanation tactfully, if belatedly, accounted for Sowden's errors. Aeronautical dignity was a little restored.

It was not a trouble-free day. Pressure of the crowd led to injuries. A woman's arm was broken, and a tobacconist from Liverpool ended his day out with a broken leg. An overloaded scaffold collapsed, injuring fifty people and crushing a child to death. It was said that the scaffold had been sabotaged by people frustrated at it blocking their view of the balloon. A gang of pickpockets started a rumour that a mad bull was coming, and turned the ensuing panic to good account. A nearby farmer, furious at having his grass trampled, railed up the field gates, impounded horses and riders and demanded release fees, much to the amusement of the pedestrian crowd. But the worst problem was, as ever, the English weather. The nobility had a tent to shelter in; wind and torrential rain lashed down on everyone else.

An estimated crowd of 150,000 people sheltered under umbrellas, as close as the scales on a tortoise shell, said observers, who compared them to an army of Roman shields in testudo formation. Two hours of drenching led to four minutes in which the balloon could be seen before it disappeared behind clouds for a flight of less than twenty minutes. The departing crowd was so thick that even the Prince of Wales's carriage couldn't get through, leaving the heir to the throne and the Duchess of Devonshire to slog through mud to reach it, wet to the skin.

The next outing put forward a parachute, cautiously. Back at Ranelagh on 3 August, Garnerin appeared with his wife. 'Curiosity was excited to the utmost degree, it being the first time, for fifteen years, since a lady had ventured to soar the empyrean height.'[41] Madame Garnerin was animated, pretty and dressed in white muslin, English-style, all of which elicited enthusiastic applause from the spectators. With them went the literary cat, which was launched from a miniature parachute two hundred yards up. It landed in a garden whose owner demanded three guineas in recompense for its trespass. Feline perspective added fun to pastiche: it was said the cat mistook the Rotunda at Ranelagh for a Gloucester cheese, 'and soon after shewed a great inclination to dart at a *mouse* which she saw in a haycock *six thousand feet* below her'; there was even a song, 'Puss in a Parachute'.[42] The cat was returned to its owners thanks to a label round its neck, but without its parachute which had disappeared – no doubt, said one wag, 'not from *a degree of plunder*, but from *pure politeness* in the English, that he might not expose his life to so much peril again.'[43]

The parachute's reappearance revived interest in aerial possibility. 'Much wonder was excited by the first ascension of a man in a balloon; but surely the descent of a man from an exalted balloon to the earth, without harm, is more wonderful' said one commentator, admiring of 'an experiment as daring as it is terrific!'[44] Yet enthusiasm was fainter than in the heyday of balloon mania. *The Gentleman's Magazine* declared sniffily in September 1802: 'The experiment was in this country *nouvelle*, and by many believed to be impracticable, with safety as to the person of the aeronaut.' Another magazine's editor thought its 'utility is confined to an exhibition of personal courage', and a *terra firma* patriot questioned even the value of that: 'let us look to another element, and enquire whether an English sailor does not display more courage in one voyage, than all the aeronauts have ever displayed since balloons were invented?'[45]

One other factor troubled observers. Aeronauts were presenting themselves as engaged in a contract with the public, which gave a quasi-legal legitimacy to their activities. Not everyone approved: 'I am old fashioned enough to think that the public ought not to form *engagements* which may encourage men to hazard their lives wantonly'. That Garnerin offered a public prayer for safe conduct was also a step too far: 'I do not think we are justified in praying to be delivered from the *perils* of the *parachute*.'[46]

The simplest balloons were still capable of attracting spectators from far and wide; even after eighteen years of aerial voyaging, balloons could draw huge crowds. In the summer of 1802, two paper balloons let off at Margate drew people from all over Kent. They didn't get much of a show: one was torn by trees on ascent; the other flew for twenty minutes before landing in the sea.[47] But Margate had become the most fashionable spa town, and the launches showed that balloons were back in fashion again.

Bad weather obliged Garnerin to postpone his parachute display, and he headed down to Bath for a quick balloon ascent on 7 September. 'The anxiety it occasions is incredible,' wrote a witness.[48] It provided 'the most sublime spectacle that was ever exhibited here', said *The Historical Chronicle* with florid astonishment. 'Upon his ascent the thermometer was 30 degrees and the barometer 62.10 when his feelings were sensibly affected by the tears of interest which trickled from the eyes of the fair, and were only relieved by the beautiful and picturesque scenes that developed as he rose majestically to pursue his voyage.'[49] All went well. Garnerin's willing passenger, a Mr Glassford, enthusiastically suggested they pass through a dark cloud, but Garnerin suspected it would attract electricity to the balloon and declined. Nonetheless they went high and returned with a long list of barometer readings. A very large crowd went home thrilled and Garnerin, recovered from his emotion, headed back to the metropolis.

On 21 September 1802, Londoners witnessed a parachute flight at last. The day was fine, with a light south-westerly breeze ruffling the trees. After a five-hour fill, at five minutes to six Garnerin – in blue jacket, white waistcoat and nankeen trousers – climbed into the drum-shaped basket and bowed. Ten minutes later his balloon was over Russell Square. 'The sky was clear, the moment favourable, and I threw down my flag to show the people assembled that I was on the point of cutting the cord that suspended me between heaven and earth.'[50] Mentally measuring the vast space that separated him from the rest of humanity, with a firm hand, a clear conscience and a touch of melodrama, Garnerin cut the cord. 'This was, perhaps, the most interesting moment of the whole', said *The Monthly Chronicle* with masterly understatement.[51] Those below saw the balloon ascend out of sight and the parachute plummet, then steady as the wind caught and spread the canvas. As it came closer to the earth it began to roll alarmingly to nearly forty-five degrees from the perpendicular, swinging Garnerin from side to side like the pendulum of a clock. At twenty feet off the ground, the capsule occupant cut away a weight, which broke his fall. He landed at 6.25 in a field belonging to a cow-keeper, within fifty yards of St Pancras churchyard.[52] 'The first person who came to see me pressed me in his arms; but without losing any time, I employed myself in detaching the principal circle of the parachute, anxious to save the instrument that had so well guaranteed me'.[53] Surrounded and swept up by a well-wishing crowd that included the Duke of York and an MP carrying his dropped tricolour, Garnerin was seized with a vomiting fit. *The Times* commented churlishly: 'Monsieur Garnerin declares, that his descent in the Parachute operated as an emetic; and if we may judge of the popular pulse, those who witnessed the experiment were heartily *sick* of it!'[54]

The parachute went on display at the Pantheon, alongside a strange installation of Garnerin's own devising – a head of Napoleon, eerily lit by a hydrogen thermolamp, which reminded spectators that innovation had an uneasy political context. As in 1784, aeronautics inspired astonishment and attracted immense crowds. But the laurels all went to a foreigner: 'the accomplishment of a safe descent in a Parachute is considered the *chef d'oeuvre* of all aerial exploits', noted *The Times* with faint irony, following its blunt conundrum: 'Mr Garnerin is paid for going up into the measureless space. The English Gentleman pays. Which has the better bargain?'[55] Garnerin had successfully added parachutes to balloons. Yet the problem of directing balloons still had no solution, the enormity of massing crowds created social unease – and Garnerin was French. In 1802, aggressive nationalism replaced Enlightenment open-mindedness.

Crossing Garnerin's path was an English aeronaut whose very different story shows the vagaries of aerial fortune. Francis Barrett described himself as 'Professor of Chemistry, Natural and Occult Philosophy, the Cabala, etc.'[56] Posterity describes him as an apothecary and 'The Unsuccessful Aeronaut'. On 12 August 1802 assembled one of the biggest crowds ever seen in London. From Blackheath to Greenwich and all along both sides of the Thames thronged people on foot, in boats and in 'conveyances of every description, from the post-coach and four to the Kent-street sand-boy mounted on his donkey'. They turned out to see an English balloon, hoping patriotism could match Garnerin's feats. Barrett had been offered assistance by a Mr Andrade, who liberally resolved 'that the genius of an Englishman should not be lost for want of a patron' and lent his gardens in Greenwich for a launch site.[57] By the afternoon it was clear that the filling process was insufficient, and by handbills and bellmen Barrett apologetically announced a postponement. Andrade was nervous about whether the crowd would turn riotous, but they took it well – since the weather was fine, many took the opportunity to get drunk, have small fights and stumble home satisfied. Next day they returned, doubly expectant. Barrett had an energetic assistant, none other than Captain Sowden, now a ballooning enthusiast. In an ironic twist, Garnerin and Madame Garnerin turned up to inspect. After a couple of hours they left, smiling mysteriously.[58] By the late afternoon it was clear why: the balloon was in no way able to ascend with an aeronaut. A very nervous Mr Andrade laid on a band to pacify a crowd that at last grew unruly and decided to amuse itself by large-scale fights. Several thousand people outside the gardens, who had not bought admission tickets and quite possibly had violent entertainment in mind from the start, took on the constables with great success, liberating fellow-bruisers from custody. At eight o'clock Barrett decided to abandon his flight and send the balloon off by itself. The car was replaced, surreally, by a child's cradle, and the cords cut. For ten pleasing minutes spectators were delighted, with Mr Andrade more ecstatic than anyone even though his gardens were completely trampled.

Afterwards there was shame. If Garnerin's enigmatic smile was one of contempt, Barrett's embarrassment was deserved. It was also possible that he was a victim of foul play: two holes were discovered, cut in the neck of the balloon, which explained the failure to fill it. Even contemporaries accepted that among the thousands who went to Greenwich there were many more who were interested in fighting and wagering than in balloons. It was a perfect opportunity for pickpockets, who got very close to the action – Andrade had his pocket picked of five guineas on the balloon scaffold itself. A criminal element might well want to sabotage a balloon in order to win bets on its failure. An unsuccessful aeronaut was again a shade too close to a culture of fraud. A cloud of suspicion attached itself to Barrett.

Nonetheless the English aeronaut had another go. He headed down to Swansea, and in early October vigorous advertising allured twenty thousand people to a promised ascent: 'the town was never so full'.[59] Fields, hills, houses, ships, harbour were packed out. The day was fine and from eight in the morning, filling seemed to proceed. But at eleven the vitriol ran out and the chemist who supplied it refused to deliver more unless he was paid. 'Time was now getting on; the Balloon had no appearance of anything in it; messages and messengers now passed between Mr. Barrett and the Chemist till three o'clock, when the assemblage of persons on the spot (at least 8000) began to be unruly. Mr. Barrett now came forward on the stage to make an apology, when just as he said – "Ladies and Gentlemen" – down fell the stage with a most tremendous crash, and Mr. Barrett and his Balloon with it, with a great number of persons. Many were severely hurt.'[60] In the ensuing chaos, Barrett harangued the crowd and the chemist, but his promise of another attempt another day was greeted with hootings and howlings.

Newspaper accounts made Barrett seem yet another fraud. But appearances of deception were deceptive. Barrett published a lengthy apologia which suggests he did have a clue about what he was doing. Arriving in Swansea, waiting for his servant to bring his balloon, he had knocked up a couple of *montgolfière* balloons using local printing paper, rather too heavy, one of which copied Garnerin's cylindrical shape. He also prepared knowledgeably a parachute for a cat and dog. To his chagrin, one of the fire balloons had caught fire from a muddle with block and tackle, and his big balloon had arrived damaged. His predicament was exacerbated by running out of money; the costs of site hire, workmen and materials were not covered by spectator fees or an attempted subscription. He contemplated 'whether it would not be more profitable to cut up my balloon, and set up a manufactory of bathing caps, umbrellas, and hat-covers, of which I could soon have produced a plentiful stock'. Bitterly he wrote of 'the daily flagellation of the Gentlemen of the Type': it was the local press who fanned expectations and doubts and maliciously misrepresented his intentions. 'I consoled myself as well as I could with the old adage, "that a bad beginning often makes a good ending;" and that there is "a time for everything under the sun;" and though that time was yet to come, it might not be long before I should be able to rise above the clouds of adversity, and hold my head as high as any other aeronaut, either French or English.' What was more powerful, Barrett's dream or his impracticality? He made a final attempt to fill a balloon, this time in the open fields. Nipping back to his lodgings for a leg of mutton, he returned to find the balloon no fuller and decided to try anyway. Throwing out mutton, bread, brandy and flags, he wobbled to hedge height. Obligingly people gave him a hoist, and for a quarter of an hour he zigzagged between trees and fields. With no more lift forthcoming, he got out, mortified, opened the valve and saw the balloon sail off, looking like an acorn, until three hours later it fell to a field where the country people promptly cut it in half, 'to let me out, as they alleged, whom they supposed nearly or quite dead.'[61]

After the Swansea debacle, Barrett disappears from aeronautics, reappearing briefly in history as a biographer of alchemists.[62] Plaintive, poignant, his story shows how aerial achievements kept beginning again rather than making progress. Though science – basic science, in making gas and calculating lift – was needed, just as important was the determination of dreamers. Why did balloons persist in their imaginative pull? The next chapter explores some ways of thinking about aerial imagination which link the eighteenth-century balloon-mad to their descendants and inheritors: us.

Ascending Again   14
Balloons in Flights of Imagination

'Le vol est le premier et le dernier objet théoretique, il est la condition même d'une définition de l'esthétique, mais aussi d'une impasse
de l'esthétique.'

[Flight is the first and last theoretical object, it is the precondition
of a definition of aesthetics, but also an aesthetic dead end.]

Walter Franck, *Tentative de vol*

FRENCH INTELLECTUALS have continued to be fascinated
by air and to write about the history of aerial culture and the
culture of aerial history. Some Enlightenment rationalists mocked
this affinity as typical of an airy nation: in Britain, 'airy' becomes
'airy-fairy' very readily.[1] That expression, meaning insubstantial,
superficial, impractical and foolishly idealistic, carries fears about
effeminacy and witchcraft, yet its lightness gestures to a good-humoured enchantment with air too. The British are a nation enthusiastically engaged with air now: seafarers and shopkeepers have
become frequent flyers. The French remain the boldest explorers
of the aesthetics of air, though artists, photographers and architects
worldwide have played with air to see in it new things, subtle forces,
expansive and shaped freedoms. Balloons still cross our imagination
in particular and colourful ways. Among these are many instances
which contain traces of meaning carried over from the eighteenth
century, airborne ghosts which help explain why we still love
balloons. The aesthetic work balloons do for us has adapted to meet
modern ends, made possible by long memories that reach back to
the beginnings of balloons in the late eighteenth century. Air has a
culture rich, various and persistent.

We know balloons best as toys, little airy spheres that have
shed the apparatus to carry humans aloft, except in spirit. They're
affordable and disposable – too much so, since cast-away balloons
contribute significantly to marine litter. Filled with human breath or
by the simplest pumps, they eliminate all dangers other than the way

they make us jump when they burst loudly; they expire by withering away, as if naturally. Toy balloons came about because new materials enabled cheap, safe mass production. Rubber balloons, first devised by Michael Faraday in 1824, were sold as toys in 1825; vulcanised rubber balloons, the prototype of toy balloons, were manufactured by a London company in 1847.

Helium balloons, safer than hydrogen-filled ones and better able to carry imprinted advertising, took multiple commercial messages to the skies in the 1920s. In 1931, latex balloons were launched by the Tillotson Rubber Company in the form of a cat with a printed whisker face, the first of modern novelty balloons.[2] Then came the bub-a-loon, a cross between a bubble and a balloon created by blowing air through a short tube to turn a blob of goo into a float-able entity.[3] In 1947 *Life* magazine reported the Bub-O-Loon as a new craze, 'a favourite pastime for children and for nightclubbing grownups who choose to act like children'.[4] Imperial Toy Corpora-tion launched its Bubb-A-Loon in 1973, shipping fifteen million sets in its first three years.[5] Foil balloons, sometimes known as mylars, came by way of NASA, which developed anodised mylar to make satellites more reflective and space suits better insulated.[6]

> The toy balloon remains very alive and active on the world's scene. Balloons are manufactured by the millions daily in a number of coun-tries. They start as liquid from a rubber tree. Balloon manufacturing companies send the liquid through treatment processes and then through shaping and coloring operations. The liquid winds up as a balloon which provides a splash of color and a burst of excitement at private parties, fairs, carnivals, circuses, store sales, trade exposi-tions, and at any other place that people gather for relief from work and routine. Silver mylars perform the same function. The world is better off because of the toy balloon.[7]

Now balloons come in a glorious rainbow of colours, patterns, shapes and materials fillable with gas or air. We give them to children as toys, an object safe for them to control; we use them as a light-hearted symbol of expansiveness at festivities. Eighteenth-century purchasers of small balloons that could be sent aloft would find counterparts on sale today, flammable wicks ready to light up night skies with their flames of inspiration. They might also recognise the anxiety of watching something very flammable waft danger-ously close to other people's property. Elizabeth Bishop's poem on fire balloons catches their sense of threat: 'Too pretty, dreamlike mimicry!/ O falling fire and piercing cry/ and panic, and a weak

ASCENDING AGAIN

mailed fist/ clenched ignorant against the sky!'⁸ Local councils in Britain have discouraged balloon releases, like eighteenth-century authorities, and farmers now as then are opposed to fire balloons as a particular source of danger, and to ballooning as a general threat to animals and crops.⁹

A distinctly climate-change era language of marketing gives balloons a greenwashed story of happiness:

> Tilly Biodegradeable Natural Rubber Balloons, produced from the highest grade Hevea tree latex, are decayed by natural exposure, into soil nutrients as fast as tree leaves. One gross of balloons represents the daily tapping of a healthy rubber tree for 8 to 10 weeks during which time it replaced 10 lbs of greenhouse gas with life giving oxygen, gave steady income to a small farmer in a developing country, and provided a happy home for songbirds.¹⁰

Reading this, you might well forget that balloons could have a parallel story as a completely unnecessary commodity from agribusiness that wastes energy in shipping and chokes turtles to death. Such is the bond between happiness and balloons, reinforced by the magical transformations of cigar-shaped balloons into animal shapes by children's entertainers. Balloon modelling uses standard sizes like two inches by sixty inches, according to manufacturer Qualatex: from this uniformity may be twisted any number of inventively-fashioned objects, in which what evidently balloons is imagination itself, a power of mimicry. Perhaps there is a complementary link to inspiration: its etymology of breathing in naturally partners the out-breath enclosed in toy balloons.

There is a special association between small balloons and children which the eighteenth century did not have because it incorporated the psychodynamics of balloons into a space shared by all ages – although there are late eighteenth-century graphic alphabets for children that feature balloons, and children are frequently and explicitly included in prints of crowds watching balloon ascents. The development of toy balloons mirrored a growing investment in childhood as a distinct and special phase [Figure 24]. The child holding a balloon has become a classic image, recognisable around the world. We don't worry about words when we see it: a balloon sails, it flies away; like life, it carries on until it stops somewhere, or not, in a beyond. Balloons with labels still make random connections between people, just as they did in the eighteenth century. A four-year-old schoolgirl from Manchester let loose a balloon picked up

Drawn by James Fillans.   Eng.ᵈ by W.West. Margaret Sᵗ.

24   Trade card associating children, play and balloons. Undated engraving
            [c. 1840].

six thousand miles away by a thirteen-year-old Chinese boy, in a
story that readers found heartening.[11]

   Balloons' association with childhood has been intensified by film,
so much so that now a balloon can simply represent childhood or
a child's point of view, as in numerous films including *The White
Balloon* (1995), *The Yellow Balloon* (1953) and *The Black Balloon*
(2008). That symbolism was powerfully established by *Le Ballon
Rouge*, made by Albert Lamorisse in 1956. It stars a small boy and
a red balloon that follows and leads him inquisitively and lovingly
around the places of his life in Paris, to the disapproval, hostility and
envy of insensitive others. Critics responded enthusiastically to the
sentient, mute drama. One said 'To see *The Red Balloon* is to laugh,
and cry, at the impossible joy of being a child again'.[12] Another said:

> people's occasional, playful efforts to grab the floating, carefree balloon
> become grasping and destructive... The film's ballooning sense of
> hope and freedom is deflated by a fierce, squabbling mass. Then, fortu-
> nately, Lamorisse's film floats off, with the breeze of magic-realism,
> into a feeling of escape and peace, *The Red Balloon* taking hold of
> Pascal, lifting him out of this rigid, petty, earthbound life.[13]

The transcendentalism is simply childlike; it speaks to adult complexities precisely through that simplicity.[14] It still appeals to children around the world: *The Red Balloon* was part of a handful of films shown at a mobile cinema to divert children traumatised by the Haiti earthquake in 2010.[15]

Anyone who has ever been a child who lost a balloon or tried to comfort a child who has will know there is desolation in that loss. Why? A balloon on a string expresses a bond of trust, like being hand-in-hand; to lose it, to have it escape, is proof you are not worthy, like a junior intimation of original sin. It brings back to you how tied to earth you are, grounded, unable to dance in the freedom of air – yet it also redeems you by insisting you can follow invisible things in your imagination. 'Flights of fancy' is too weak a phrase for that emotional relationship between balloons and humans: the child's balloon indicates our drive to connect, and our ambivalence about letting go.[16]

At the end of *The Red Balloon*, Pascal's grief for the murder of his balloon by a mob of vicious boys is lifted by the unexpected appearance of other coloured balloons flying in from across the city. They form a protective cluster around him in the thick of which he ascends to the skies. We do not see him come down. In a curious case of life imitating art, an American truck driver, Larry Walters, attached forty-five helium-filled weather balloons to a patio chair to make a flying machine he called 'Inspiration 1'. On 2 July 1982, he rose in this contraption to a height of 4,600 metres. Since then, cluster ballooning has become a strange psycho-descendant of eight-eenth-century ballooning: aeronauts attempt higher, longer flights in pursuit of what the boldest to date calls 'the dream that has held me, and generations of dreamers, rapt for ages'.[17] This chaironaut, Jonathan R. Trappe, made a record-breaking flight on a standard office chair; he crossed the English Channel on 28 May 2010 and has attempted an Atlantic crossing.

Cluster balloons form a rounded pile, sometimes pyramidal. In an animated film of 2009 produced by Pixar and released by Disney, *Up*, they explicitly echo the shape of an eighteenth-century balloon. An elderly widower ties balloons to his house and with a stowaway small boy sets off for the wilds of South America. Imaginative jour-neying invokes menace and threat to enhance balloon escapology. In Ian McEwan's novel *Enduring Love* (1997), a balloon crash sets in motion a story of persistent and paranoid pursuit. The UK first edition cover used Odilon Redon's smoky-toned 1882 lithograph of a balloon in the form of an eye, titled *L'Oeil comme un ballon bizarre se dirige vers l'infini*. The eye like a strange balloon mounts towards infinity: by way of Edgar Allen Poe, whose translation by Baudelaire allowed Redilon to pay homage, balloons in art sustain their symbolic power for us.[18]

In eighteenth-century Britain, really only Thomas Baldwin's aerial views of Chester and his flight path engaged directly with the challenge of translating actual aerial perspective, although the panoramas so popular as walk-through entertainments may have been affected by aerialism's senssurround effect of wide skies, high viewpoint and miniaturisation;[19] we may suppose none of these would have caught on so well without balloon flights. Actual views from above were in the forefront of the nineteenth century's new art, photography. Gaspard-Félix Tournachon, better known as Nadar, was both a balloonist and a photographer. A studio self-portrait in sepia shows him tucked into a cramped balloon basket, its ropes stretched like guitar strings behind him, eyes upwards as if to the sky. He wears a top hat, which in a lithograph by Honore Daumier entitled *Nadar élevant la Photographie à la hauteur de l'Art*, or *Nadar Elevating Photography to Art*, is tossed by winds that buffet the man and the balloon, showing the perils of art aloft.[20] It was in Nadar's airy studio at 35 Boulevard des Capucines in Paris that the first exhibition of Impressionist works was hung in 1874. Nadar, a great connector of people, made direct connections between light and air. In 1858 he took the first aerial photographs from a tethered balloon; they do not survive. His aerial photograph of Paris from 1866 does, beaten into the record books by James Wallace Black's photograph of Boston in 1860. The development and deployment of aerial photography is a subject too big to cover here, but tiny cameras mounted on the breast of pigeons deserve a mention. Designed by Julius Neubronner in 1903, they produced excellent avian photographs, crisp and all the more compelling for bringing the age-old aesthetic of 'bird's-eye view' up to date.

In 1907 Neubronner filed for patent, using the terms 'Vogelperspektive' (bird perspective) in Germany; 'des vues … de haut en bas' in France; 'landscapes from above' in England. Although they all mean practically the same thing, the difference indicates some aesthetic uncertainty. How high is above? What height is the 'haut'? Pigeons sometimes flew higher than balloons. Eighteenth-century aeronauts reported pigeons who were down-to-earth minded, and they also described how some pigeons clung on to balloon cars and refused to fly off. 'Above' is a loose measurement, just as the 'aerial' in aerial photography gives you no sense of either the altitude or the machine from which the photographs are taken. Does it matter? Eighteenth-century poets were able to assume a position of 'above' without specifying exact altitude or even a plausible vehicle – so no, in one sense it doesn't matter. We now have a vocabulary for the regions of air that allows us to delineate the atmosphere in different ways: for instance, in layers differentiated by temperature, we have troposphere, stratosphere, mesosphere (also known collectively as the ionosphere), thermosphere and exosphere. Human imagination seems reluctant to refer much beyond the stratospheric, nor does ordinary-usage English take in much of the scientific distinction. Neubronner's 'bird', 'height' and 'above' gesture loosely to something relatively low, below the normal cruising height of aeroplanes on short-haul flights, say. In the early twentieth century, aerial aesthetics were reshaped by expressionist painters inspired by aeroplanes.[21] Our visual vocabulary now includes satellite view, in Google Earth (public release 2005), Google Sky (2007) and Google Street View (2008), aerial-view resources that also mix up aesthetics. Google Earth, for instance, uses a combination of perpendicular and oblique perspective; it also mixes two and three dimensional images. Again, ordinary usage need not bother much about the distinction; one can just marvel at these means of viewing the moon or Mars – and not by balloon! – or the Mariana Trench (Google Earth 2010; Google Ocean 2009). Digital natives will be unfazed by these programmes' variability between 2D, 3D, animation, visualisation, simulation and real-time and snapshot footage; mash-up does not make us troubled by the simultaneity of what one semiotician calls perceptographic codes.[22] Lest we loftily assume a story of progress or sophistication, let's also remember that the eighteenth century had some complex visual codes in the way its printers enthusiastically mixed up fonts.

The uses of aerial photography, like balloons, were immediately obvious to the military, who avidly took up aerial reconnaissance and intelligence. Even Neubronner's pigeon-photographers were pressed into action (where the great technical challenge was not how to deploy them on battlegrounds, for which they proved quite trainable, but how to get them to return to a necessarily mobile dovecote). Perhaps because of this history in the service of war, views from above also invite us to love. In the late twentieth century, the earth-from-the-air photography of Yann Arthus-Bertrand and earth-from-the-moon photography have been credited with inspiring environmentalism. We also have aerial phonography, making a poetics out of the sounds of balloons.[23] Yann Arthus-Bertrand uses helicopters and balloons to take his inspiring photographs: it isn't always obvious from each image what type of vehicle is the platform, although his work with lions in the Masai Mara reserve in Kenya is explicitly credited to a hot air balloon. 'Earth from the Air' was immensely popular: the original exhibition in 2000 reached a global audience of 130 million by 2008, with more encountering it through a book of still photographs. In 1991 Arthus-Bertrand set up the Altitude Agency for professional photographers. It holds a bank of more than half a million aerial images. He made a film, *Home* (2009), which explicitly puts aerially-viewed beauty at the service of environmental awareness and activism. Underlying his projects is the philosophical premise that to see the world is to appreciate its beauty, hence wish to protect and conserve that beauty. With a nice irony for the environmental movement, the richest colours on earth are put at the service of a green message. For Arthus-Bertrand, that beauty is brought out through extreme pattern and intense colour. This combination reveals the world in abstraction which is then particularised into context, often with a micro-narrative that says, look how humans impact on the planet. The process is primarily wordless, although versions of the visual work have captions and accompanying essays.

Many viewers and reviewers report a common process when looking at Arthus-Bertrand's earth-from-the-air views – an initial sense of wondrous delight followed by a curiosity-driven effort to make out the subject. 'Wow – what is that?' An absorbing aesthetic of pattern, like eighteenth-century comparisons of aerial views to Turkish carpets, needs to do no more than invite you to trace pattern: it can feel effortless as your eye simply follows contours, wavy lines, geometric shapes.

Like Turkish carpets whose traditional designs include symbols with a narrative meaning, Arthus-Bertrand's embedding of human activity often involves symbolism too, of two kinds – of destruction and havoc, and of creativity and art. Take two of his most reproduced images: vats of dye of different colours evoke tapestries-to-be; sacks of richly coloured spices evoke culinary masterpieces.[24] Dyes and spices are halfway between nature and art – part plant, part pigment. They take up a position perfectly between materials and finished work; they speak to process. The process that runs through so many of Arthus-Bertrand's photographs is stilled, in the sense of still photography, and moving, in that whatever may have been stilled for the photograph continues its life in a timeframe outside the moment of its perception by photographer or viewer. Arthus-Bertrand's photographs are widely marketed in merchandise like calendars and diaries associated with time; they also now come with accompanying educational text that warns time is running out. His version of wonder makes us see temporality and permanence, particularly the permanent effects of human impact through agriculture and industrialisation. Bachelard might say this is like air itself: we experience it as still, an element all around us (and in us); we see and feel it only through movement, in the form of the wind. Eighteenth-century prints of balloons typically show a balloon ascending above a crowd so as to depict the invention leaving behind its social context to head for the regions of air. In other words, a little earth and a little sky help to depict flights of imagination. Similarly, in Arthus-Bertrand's photographs, earth includes ocean and air, the latter visible in winds that ruffle the seas, clouds reflected in water and dust-clouds that rise golden behind combine harvesters. Where perspective is bird's-eye oblique (rather than pure perpendicular), you can also see clouds in the sky. Certainly in viewing a sequence of these earth-from-the-air marvels, air is included as a subject, not only that elemental place from which earth is viewed.

Arthus-Bertrand's aesthetic shows how ideas around balloons have carried on from the eighteenth century, and he enables millions of people to see the earth from a balloon without necessarily flying in one. His celebratory use of balloons as the principal vehicle by which he obtains his images returns slowness, or slower-ness, to an aesthetic centre. Colour proves a medium that binds nature and culture to each other, although earlier black and white examples show that aerial views enable a perception of pattern independent of colour, albeit present in tonalities, that also speaks to relations between nature and culture. For example, in 1916 *Popular Science* printed a photograph of vertiginous vertically-terraced rice fields in the Philippines, commenting: 'The work appears to be too vast to be the work of human beings. In fact it might better represent some upheaval of the earth's crust.'[25] Arthus-Bertrand's 'culture' is also sometimes an animal or bird one; in his 'from above' photographs, humans are diminutive (traditionally compared to ants, as Harry Lime does in the 1949 film *The Third Man* when viewing people from the top of a Ferris wheel in Vienna). In Arthus-Bertrand's 'above', the altitude range of balloons provides an ideal point of view to comprehend nature and culture and relationships between them. His avowed purpose is entirely contemporary in its environmentalism, but it is also human-centred in a way that continues eighteenth-century reflections on the meaning of balloons for human society. '"Home"' calls for a new awareness, because as we observe ourselves from the air, we see our world in a whole new light.'[26]

From 1783, balloons prompted new observations of ourselves and our world. 'From the Air' is an expansive aesthetic that inspires others, like the artist Philippe Pastor, whose 'Le Ciel Regarde la Terre' turns earth-from-the-air photography into fine art. In Pastor's series, pure pigments represent earth; additional materials like clay, sand, wood and cardboard represent pollution; metal grids represent human limitations superimposed on a brightly coloured world.[27] Eighteenth-century aeronauts were not attuned to pollution or human limitation (though nineteenth-century ones were, especially over London), but they presented the world as explorable in new ways. Poets warmed to this. So Charlotte Smith introduces a spider, whose waverings in air she compares to a poet:

> Small viewless aeronaut, that by the line
> Of Gossamer suspended, in mid air
> Float'st on a sun-beam — Living atom, where
> Ends thy breeze-guided voyage?[28]

Poets' interest in balloons is too big a subject to do more than touch on here, and tether it by way of Emily Dickinson (who had seen Black's aerial photographs of Boston). She is one of many who takes up balloon symbolism to represent imagination and its flights: 'I bet with every Wind that blew,/ Till Nature in chagrin/ Employed a Fact to visit me/ And scuttle my Balloon.'[29]

The symbolism of balloons has been important in bringing metaphysics to television. The motto of the British Broadcasting Corporation is 'Nation shall speak peace unto nation.' It appears below a coat of arms designed in 1927, featuring a nationalist lion holding a thunderbolt, and two supporter eagles who flank a coat of arms with a globe surrounded by seven stars which represent planets. In 1963, the BBC adopted a spinning globe as its active symbol or ident (the trade word for a company's identification symbol). The globe changed slightly over three decades – it became elongated, globular again, transparent. In 1997 the BBC designed some new idents. The spinning globe reappeared as a balloon, which became the star of a series of forty-seven short films showing it floating above various locations around Britain. The balloon still imaged the world as globe, in that its red silk showed a map of the world, with countries in orange.[30] None of the original sequences showed people. Yet human activity was present, just not in narrative. The balloon floated over mountains, trees, lochs, cityscapes ... green fields and water provided nature; stone walls and bridges spoke of culture. Docks, ruins, lighthouses, seen from the balloon, became symbols of humanity, isolated, runic, communal.[31] The balloon ident had been 'clever, infinitely adaptable, and loved by presentation enthusiasts. About time it was replaced by something inferior, then', wrote one media commentator.[32] The balloon's success came from how it supplied a narrative of connection in an aesthetic effort that felt easy. The viewer's point of view was not that of the balloonists in the globe-covered balloon, but that of an aerial observer from a parallel invisible balloon, usually above the globe-balloon, so what you were looking at was a double representation of the earth: its actual surface (of fields and streets) and its schematic surface (of the map on the balloon). Chromatography clashed with cartography, in that the actual world had natural colours of blue, green and brown – the classic tones of landscape painting – and the map world was cheerfully unnatural – the oceans were red and the land masses orange. The contrast, and the whole series of idents, shows that the aerial imaginary continues to develop.

What the BBC's globe-balloon carries is a sense of imagination, a comprehension of the world. Its swelled interior evokes an ideal full-ness to that comprehension; its surface-like skin is a filter, a medium for inscription, a place of exchange. So powerful is this image that it can withstand anachronism. In Julien Temple's 2001 film *Pandae-monium*, a drama about relations between the Romantic poets Coler-idge and Wordsworth, the airy notions of Coleridge are imaged through a scene in which he ascends in a hot air balloon while an aeroplane passes overhead. Balloons gesture to timeless imagina-tion too, often through the irony of their time-specific conjunction with timelessness. A subculture of Steampunk takes balloons as a historical turning point, a pivot into a future that never happened, an old-fashioned, Jules Verne-inspired vision of what might have been. In Steampunk, balloons are mostly steam-powered, with wind-mill rudders and mechanical sails. Joining curious contraptions of brass and leather with levers, goggles and dials, they give human industry and mechanisation a place not bound by conventions, a place of fantasy in which high tech gives way to slow tech. 'Yet it is not a nostalgic recreation of a vanished past: its devices are both imaginative and contemporary.'[33] Balloons here do double duty: as a real invention that could have become steam-powered, and more symbolically, as an image of the adaptability of inventiveness in any and all eras. The symbolism of invention can even replace the ingenuity of inventors: at the end of *The Wizard of Oz* (1939), when the Wizard is wafted away by the balloon which has taken him to the Land of Oz, he exclaims 'I don't know how it works!' Balloons can image the supreme magic of invention itself.

One other invention is like balloons in performing such symbolism so economically. The light bulb is instantly recognised as shorthand for an idea. Elaine Scarry has suggested that this association is reinforced by the way a traditional light bulb echoes the shape of a human head.[34] Eco-friendly bulbs don't yet do this; maybe their default spiral will lead somewhere else. Balloons echo skull shape more loosely than traditional light bulbs, but enough to admit a symbolism. If the light bulb expresses 'bright idea', a balloon expresses 'imaginative idea', a slightly different thing. The work of Terry Gilliam, animator in *Monty Python's Flying Circus*, proposes an aesthetic in which flying – as in Flying Circus – is synonymous with imaginative activity: inventive, subversive, liberating. The fourth season of the *Flying Circus* included an episode, 'The Golden Age of Ballooning', in which the brothers Montgolfier are visited by a Glaswegian-accented 'King Louis' who tries to steal their balloon designs to sell on to George III. The illogical logic of this narrative is averted at every step by surrealist preoccupations such as the brothers' revelations of how little they wash, the appearance of a film crew in the middle of eighteenth-century arguments, a party political broadcast by the Norwegian party, partly in Norwegian, and a voice-over parody of BBC-marketed ballooning spin-offs and merchandise. A riff on hygiene reinserts bodies as an antithesis to imagination and pastiches the factuality of eighteenth-century accounts of balloon launches:

> So, on June 7th, 1783, the Montgolfier brothers had a really good wash ... starting on his face and arms, Joseph Michael Montgolfier went on to scrub his torso, his legs and his naughty bits, before rinsing his whole body. That June night, he and his brother between them washed seventeen square feet of body area. They used a kilo and a half of catholic soap and nearly fourteen gallons of nice hot water. It was indeed an impressive sight.

The episode ends with a sequence in which a Victorian couple take off in a balloon; superimposed captions announce that this is 'The Mill on the Floss, Part 1: Ballooning'. Actual balloons hardly appear: they don't need to, because the constant verbal references to them allow imagination to take any course, as wayward as an actual balloon journey. Ending up at the start of a George Eliot novel makes as much sense as getting into balloons in the first place. A harnessed semi-dirigible Antoinette complains that her fiancé Joseph Montgolfier is balloon-mad; an enraged Count Ferdinand de Zeppelin is unable to make people understand that his airship is not a balloon.[35] The jokes play with how balloons can't be dislodged from imagination – how, like passions, they obsess.

Like Steampunk artists' use of obvious anachronism to evoke the timelessness of imagination, Gilliam applies Victoriana to madly modern comic ends. He re-worked balloons in many ways – he gave a drawing to Carol Chapman for her fiftieth birthday of the six male Pythons in a balloon shaped like a busty woman[36] – and balloons turn up regularly in his animations and drawings, some with Steampunky additions of mechanical paraphernalia. His 2009 film *The Imaginarium of Dr Parnassus* features a balloon with twelve faces in the narrative. As a gesture to time passing its fabric is distressed, but its boat-shaped car, sails and anchor come hot from the eighteenth century. Gilliam's film *The Adventures of Baron Munchausen* (1988) was a loose adaptation of an eighteenth-century memoir by a trickster fantasist; the original book has some episodes in which balloons are put to fantastical uses, which Gilliam condensed into a marvellous sequence in which a balloon made from women's underwear lands on the moon, making ripples of gold in the dark. Gilliam may also be drawing on Edgar Allan Poe's story 'Hans Phaall', in which a balloon with a huge hat in the place of the car returns an adventurer to Rotterdam. The film's poster again makes an equivalence between balloon and human head [Figure 25], and the tag line articulates how fantasy airily connects them: 'Remarkable. Unbelievable. Impossible. And true.'

The impossible-made-true is one staple of what advertising sells – and so we find balloons in British advertising, where they often represent the power of wishing made true by buying a product. Roland Barthes observed in *Mythologies* (1957) how deep and allusive metaphors make advertising work – thus ads for detergents dazzle us through a language of purification borrowed from myth. Balloons offer a similar dynamic. Gaston Bachelard explains it thus:

25   Flights of imagination: poster designed by Lucinda Cowell for *The
          Adventures of Baron Munchausen*, dir. Terry Gilliam 1988, loosely based
          on *The Surprising Adventures of Baron Munchausen* (1785) by Rudolf Erich
          Raspe. http://www.impawards.com/1989/posters/adventures_of_baron_
          munchausen.jpg [fair use via en.wikipedia.org 01.12.2015]

'Anyone who can imagine can will. To the imagination that informs our will is coupled a will to imagine, a will to live what is imagined. By suggesting images in the right order, consistent behavioural patterns can be accurately determined.'[37] Though Bachelard here is discussing Robert Desoille's thought, which emphasises the power of images to piece a self together anew psychoanalytically, suggestiveness is prized by advertisers precisely because it's a good bet for changing behaviours, including buying a new product. Bachelard continues: 'Anyone who tries to raise his life to the same level as his imagination will feel a sense of nobility welling up within him as he dreams of something rising, or as he experiences the aerial element in its *ascension*.' Leaving aside the theological ramifications of ascension – though one devout blogger reads an ad for Nimble bread as a parable enjoining us to get into the basket of faith and eat the bread of God, a communion-lite reinterpretation[38] – at least one British bank has recently used balloons as symbols of wishes. So powerful is this image that it can block out alternative associations, such as rising levels of debt or bubble-related fraud: balloons are light, debt has the heaviness of burden. The bank's slogan 'for the journey' goes metaphysically straight for nobility, dream and one of the oldest metaphors in books: life as a journey. Balloons feature as a simple instance of businesses the bank claims to have helped – a company selling balloon rides, whose shop front is adorned by small coloured balloons. They also feature as a metaphor for other businesses the bank has helped get 'off the ground', and as a symbol of wishes that the bank helps people save up for.[39]

Manufacturers of 'light' products turn to balloons to advertise the supposed 'lightness' effect of calorie-reduced stuff. One advertisement for bread aimed at slimmers had a memorable and long-lasting run (it came eighty-sixth in one 'Top 100 Adverts' poll).[40] In it, a young woman in a yellow trouser suit – so 1970s! – dangles from a harness under a balloon marked Nimble, travelling across a landscape to the song of 'She flies like a bird'; after a point-of-view shot down to a town on the ground, she alights and bites into the bread. That bread also rises is a neat overlap of symbolism, although much of Britain's bread is made using the Chorleywood Bread Process, developed in 1961, which makes that rising preternaturally quick, hence an aid to industrial-scale production. A film by Nick Park – the fourth Wallace and Gromit adventure – plays with associations between balloons, bread and lightness. Originally titled 'Trouble at t' Mill', Park's final title – *A Matter of Loaf and*

Death (2008) – throws in for good measure a punning pastiche of Powell and Pressburger's film *A Matter of Life and Death* (1946). A number of balloon preoccupations from the eighteenth century show up almost unchanged. The plot involves Piella Bakewell, a former advertising model for the Bake-O-Lite bread company. She courts Wallace, a baker, ostensibly for love but really to complete her baker's dozen murder of bakers, a grisly plot of revenge for their bread ruining her figure and hence her career. Wallace's dog Gromit cottons on to the plot and with help from Fluffles, Piella's poodle, he attempts to protect his master. Both the dogs and the villainess use the balloon as a means of escape; in the end Piella's weight means the balloon crashes into a crocodile pit at the zoo where she is eaten and her thin ghost bids farewell to Wallace. Piella is effectively punished for over-consumption of bread, whose desirable lightness does not transfer from dough to woman. Is that conclusion reactionary or revelatory? In all the fun of puns about cereal killers and exploding cakes, the balloon escapes being a commodity because it assists so much in escape.

You might agree with Gaston Bachelard that it is really air that set imagination moving, and our fascination with balloons comes from their being the easiest thing through which to see the movement of air. Other airborne materials can be eloquent too, like the feather which opens the film of *Forrest Gump* (1994). It wafts slowly to earth: we don't know what, if anything, it stands for, but we watch, compelled, caught by the rhythmic to-and-fro of something feather-light. The existential possibilities of airborne entities are further explored in Ramin Bahnrani's 2009 film *The Plastic Bag*, in which a plastic bag voiced by Werner Herzog ponders its Maker on an epic journey to the Pacific Garbage Patch. But in the aesthetics of air-filled movement, balloons retain a distinctive symbolism of slow time. The reflective ending of *American Beauty* (1999) features a plastic bag being blown about: 'The wind carries it in a circle around us, sometimes whipping it about violently, or, without warning, sending it soaring skyward, then letting it float gracefully down to the ground.' In a voice-over, the depressed suburban father who has got over his mid-life crisis celebrates beauty in the world, imaged by the air-dancing bag: 'my heart fills up like a balloon that's about to burst'. Script directions for the camera follow this image of barely-contained joy: 'We're FLYING once again ... ASCENDING SLOWLY.'[41]

Elation in balloon flight remains full of calm. Though the enormous visual bulk of Zeppelins made them a powerful signifier of slow movement, airships – another story[42] – also figured faster speed for travellers. Balloons move unrushed. In an unreleased 1997 PlayStation sim, players explore tranquil spaces, described in familiar terms as 'majestic realms', with no apparent objective: 'the game doesn't want you to worry about what you're supposed to do. It just wants you to relax, let go, and put your mind at ease.'[43] Diane Ackerman links the drift of balloon flight to mental peace: 'What a treat to stroll through veils of twilight, to float across the sky like a slowly-forming thought.'[44] The slow and steady movement of balloons has come to signify relaxation and escape, a return to reflectiveness.[45]

The uptake of balloons aroused great debate in the late eighteenth century; in the twenty-first century, we still have a powerful relationship with balloons which draws on their beginnings. Through their aerial movement we shape dreams for our species as well as our individual selves. Balloons carry hopes, our messages: like bottles riding the waves, they survive without our direction; they show our control is tenuous. They carry on into the infinite, untrammelled, losing any sense of being lost. In this symbolism, we find through balloons a miniature of transcendental meaning, direction and purpose. In their close associations with children, they come to represent simplicities of existence, uplift and freedom. Here then is the line of affect and affection which Rita Felski urged us to acknowledge and celebrate in connecting with subjects from the past. The attraction of poets, artists, film-makers and children to balloons renews their mysterious ascensional power, and affirms their enduring capacity to carry us on flights of imagination.

Notes

Place of publication is London unless specified otherwise. For simplicity, I give tri- or bi-weekly newspaper dates by their last date: thus *St James's Chronicle*, 14–16 September 1784, issue 3671, is 16 September 1784.

Sonnet by Hester Lynch Piozzi from *The Florence Miscellany* (Florence, 1785), p. 59.

BEGINNINGS

[1] Blagden Papers, Royal Society Archives, CB/1/1.
[2] [Charles Johnstone], *The Adventures of Anthony Varnish; or, a Peep at the Manners of Society* (1786), 3 vols, vol. 2, p. 1.
[3] *Morning Post and Daily Advertiser*, 4 January 1785.
[4] *St James's Chronicle*, 29 November 1784. Mark Davies, Sadler's biographer, speculates persuasively that Harper – whose Christian name remains elusive – may have been related to the Mary Harper of Abingdon who married Sadler in 1775. Mark Davies, *King of All Balloons: The Adventurous Life of James Sadler, The First English Aeronaut* (Stroud, 2015), p. 64.
[5] *Bristol Courant*, 11 January 1785.
[6] *WLA*, 6 January 1785.
[7] *London Chronicle*, 6 January 1785.
[8] Ibid.
[9] *WLA*, 13 January 1785.
[10] *St James's Chronicle*, 3 February 1785.
[11] *Town and Country Magazine*, 1784 supplement.
[12] J. E. Hodgson, *The History of Aeronautics in Great Britain* (Oxford, 1924), pp. 187–9; *Hibernian Magazine*, January 1785.
[13] Sir Charles Blagden to Sir Joseph Banks, 14 October 1783, *Scientific Correspondence of Sir Joseph Banks, 1765–1820*, ed. Neil Chambers (2007), 6 vols, vol. 2, p. 173.
[14] Tom D. Crouch, *The Eagle Aloft: Two Centuries of the Balloon in America* (Washington DC, 1983), p. 34.
[15] Richard Holmes, *The Age of Wonder: How the Romantic Generation Discovered the Beauty and Terror of Science* (2008), p. xviii.
[16] Rita Felski, 'Context Stinks!', *New Literary History*, vol. 42, no. 4 (2011), pp. 573–91.
[17] Ibid., p. 587, p. 585.
[18] Ibid., p. 590.
[19] For further discussion see my article, 'Philosophical Playthings? Balloons and the Play of Ideas', in *Sich selbst aufs Spiel setzen. Spiel als Technik und Medium von Subjektivierung*, eds Christian Moser and Regine Strätling (Munich, 2016), pp. 327–46.

20 Mi Gyung Kim, '"Public" Science: Hydrogen Balloons and Lavoisier's Decomposition of Water', *Annals of Science*, vol. 63, no. 3 (2006), pp. 291–318.

21 Paul Keen, '"The Good Things Above": The Commercial Modernity of Vincent Lunardi', http://www.18thcenturycommon.org/c18ballooning/.

22 Siobhan Carroll, *An Empire of Air and Water: Uncolonizable Space in the British Imagination, 1750–1850* (Philadelphia, 2015), pp. 115–45, p. 16.

23 Sarah Tindal Kareem, *Eighteenth-Century Fiction and the Reinvention of Wonder* (Oxford, 2014), pp. 16–17.

24 *Symposia, or Table Talk in the Month of September 1784* (1784), p. 85.

25 Louis-Sébastien Mercier, *Memoirs of the Year Two Thousand Five Hundred* [sic] (New York, 1974). Quoted by I. F. Clarke, *The Pattern of Expectation 1644–2001* (1979), pp. 29–30.

26 The Baden-Powell Collection at the National Aerospace Library (hereafter B-P).

27 David Spadafora, *The Idea of Progress in Eighteenth-Century Britain* (New Haven, 1990), p. xi.

28 Ibid., p. 62.

29 *Universal Magazine*, March 1784, p. 127.

30 *The Volunteer Evening Post* (n.d.), quoted by Bryan MacMahon, *Ascend or Die: Richard Crosbie, Pioneer of Balloon Flight* (Dublin, 2010), p. 122.

31 Michael Lynn, *The Sublime Invention: Ballooning in Europe, 1783–1820* (2010), p. 164.

32 *The Berwick Museum, or Monthly Literary Intelligencer* (Berwick, 1785–87), 3 vols, vol. 1, p. 600.

33 Happily there are new discoveries: thus Mary Hamilton's 'A Manuscript', to be edited by Nicole Pohl and Jane Rendalines. Pohl discusses Hamilton's contribution to intellectual debates in 'Of Balloons and Foreign Worlds: Mary Hamilton and Eighteenth-Century Flights of Fancy', Utopias: The Un-Placed in Language and Politics, *Azimuth: Philosophical Coordinates in Modern and Contemporary Age*, vol. 2, no. 3 (2014), pp. 61–90.

34 For further discussion see Jayne Elizabeth Lewis, *Air's Appearance: Literary Atmosphere in British Fiction, 1660–1794* (Chicago, 2012).

35 B-P.

Chapter 1: MADNESS AND BALLOONS

1 7 June 1782, E-Enlightenment: http://www.e-enlightenment.com.

2 William Griffiths, *A Practical Treatise on Farriery* (1784), n.p.

3 James Burgh, *The Art of Speaking* (Dublin, 1784), p. 32.

4 John Clark, *Observations on Fevers* (1780), p. 116.

5 Abel Boyer, *Anglo-French Dictionary* (1780).

6 See Jane Darcy, *Melancholy and Literary Biography, 1640–1816* (Basingstoke, 2013).

7 Clement Hawes, *Mania and Literary Style: The Rhetoric of Enthusiasm from the Ranters to Christopher Smart* (Cambridge, 1996), p. 2; John Mee, *Dangerous Enthusiasm: William Blake and the Culture of Radicalism in the 1790s* (Oxford, 1994).

8 Thomas Frewen, *Physiologia: or, the Doctrine of Nature, Comprehended in the Origin and Progression of Human Life…* (1780), p. 335.

9 *An Heroic Epistle* (1780), p. 10.

10 6 October 1780, E-Enlightenment.

11 Duplaix, 4 October 1738, E-Enlightenment.

12 James Henry Leigh, *The New Rosciad, in the Manner of Churchill: Containing a Judicious, Humourous* [sic] *and Critical Description of our Present Dramatic Characters* (1785), p. 37.

13 *Annual Register*, 1775, pp. 188–9.

[14] Frewen, *Physiologia*, p. 143.

[15] Ibid., p. 331.

[16] The doctor was William Hunter; *WLA*, 5 August 1784.

[17] *WLA*, 12 March 1787.

[18] Sir James Fergusson of Kilkerran, *Balloon Tytler* (1972) and Davies, *King of All Balloons* provide biographical studies.

[19] *Caledonian Mercury*, 8 September 1784.

[20] *Caledonian Mercury*, 15 September 1784.

[21] Ibid.

[22] Ibid.

[23] Miss Delessert to Blagden, 31 August [1783], Royal Society Archives, CB/1/3/262.

[24] *Caledonian Mercury*, 31 March 1784; letter dated 11 February.

[25] Elizabeth Greg to Blagden, 8 June 1784, Royal Society Archives, Elizabeth Grey [*sic*], CB/1/4/76.

[26] Banks to Blagden, 22 September 1784, Royal Society Archives, CB/1/1/102.

[27] Banks to Blagden, 18 October 1784, Royal Society Archives, CB/1/1/104.

[28] Berthollet to Blagden, 6 September 1784, Royal Society Archives, CB/1/1/215.

[29] Banks to Franklin, 9 December 1783, *Scientific Correspondence*, vol. 2, p. 230.

[30] Louis-Sébastien Mercier, *The Nightcap* [1785], 2 vols, vol. 2, p. 270.

[31] *Caledonian Mercury*, 8 August 1784.

[32] *Caledonian Mercury*, 30 November 1784.

[33] *Caledonian Mercury*, 20 December 1784.

[34] *Caledonian Mercury*, 14 December 1784.

[35] Prompted by Arnold's balloon, *Caledonian Mercury*, 21 May 1785; 15 June 1785.

[36] B-P.

[37] Paul Keen, '"The Balloonomania": Science and Spectacle in 1780s England', *Eighteenth-Century Studies*, vol. 39, no. 4 (2006), p. 509.

[38] 'The Dolphin carried off. A dream' [1784], *Scrapbook of Early Aeronautica* [assembled by William Upcott, mid 19C], 3 vols, vol. 1, pp. 8–11.

Chapter 2: ONE MAN'S BALLOON MADNESS

[1] *The Diary of the Right Honourable William Windham, 1784–1810*, ed. Cecilia Anne Baring (1866). Further references are to this text, by date rather than page.

[2] *Diary*, 30 October 1790, p. 211.

[3] Heather McPherson, 'Picturing Tragedy: *Mrs Siddons as the Tragic Muse* Revisited', *Eighteenth-Century Studies*, vol. 33, no. 3 (2000), p. 408.

[4] See Mrs Clement Parsons, *The Incomparable Siddons* (1909), pp. 59–62.

[5] *Diary*, 17 February 1784, p. 6.

[6] James Trail, letter to Jeremy Bentham, 16 September 1784: text from E-Enlightenment.

[7] Oppian, *Halieuticks, or the Nature of Fishes*, trans. John Jones (Oxford, 1722), lines 25–8.

[8] *Diary*, 29 November 1784.

[9] *Public Advertiser*, 11 May 1785, as part of a 'Letter from Oxford'.

[10] Papers, in *Diary*, pp. 75–6.

[11] BL MSS 37925.

[12] BL Add MSS 37843, folio 9.

[13] *Diary*, 1 September 1788, p. 148.

[14] Carolyn Marvin, *When Old Technologies were New: Thinking about Electric Communication in the Late Nineteenth Century* (Oxford, 1998), p. 22.

[15] Ibid., p. 5.

Chapter 3: PEOPLE AND PLACES

[1] Benedict Anderson, *Imagined Communities: Reflections on the Origin and Spread of Nationalism* (1983).

[2] For the Bristol area, see John Penny, *Up, Up and Away! An account of ballooning in and around Bristol and Bath 1784–1999*, HA Pamphlets, no. 97 (Bristol, n.d.); for Norwich, see [Edward Rigby], *An Account of Mr. James Deeker's Two Aerial Expeditions from the City of Norwich* (Norwich, 1785).

[3] 'Copland, whilst retaining the title and higher salary of Professor of Mathematics, built up a large collection of apparatus and established a reputation as an outstanding teacher of Natural Philosophy.' Betty Ponting, 'A History of Mathematics at Aberdeen', *The Aberdeen University Review*, vol. 48 (1979–80); ; part 3.

[4] Anita McConnell, *Jesse Ramsden (1735–1800): London's Leading Scientific Instrument Maker* (Aldershot, 2007), p. 88.

[5] Letter to Dr James Beattie, Peterhead, from James Mercer, 3 August 1783; quoted in J. S. Reid, 'The Castlehill Observatory Aberdeen', *Journal for the History of Astronomy*, vol. 13 (1982), p. 90.

[6] *Aberdeen Journal*, 15 March 1784.

[7] Ponting, 'History of Mathematics'.

[8] Reid, 'Castlehill Observatory', pp. 94–6.

[9] *Aberdeen Journal*, 11 October 1784.

[10] *Aberdeen Journal*, 29 March 1784.

[11] Fergusson, *Balloon Tytler*, p. 97.

[12] Meg Russell, 'Tytler', DNB; see also L. T. C. Rolt, *The Aeronauts: A History of Ballooning 1783–1903* (1966), pp. 62–6.

[13] *Glasgow Herald*, 27 April 1784.

[14] *York Courant*, 14 May 1784.

[15] *Edinburgh Courant*, 29 September 1784.

[16] *Edinburgh Courant*, 11 October 1784.

[17] Ibid.

[18] 'To Mr. Lunardi, on his Successful Aerial Voyages from Edinburgh, Kelso, and Glasgow', by Mr. James Tytler, in Vincent Lunardi, *An Account of Five Aerial Voyages in Scotland* (Edinburgh, 1786), p. 107.

[19] Lunardi, *Five Aerial Voyages*, p. 108.

[20] Ibid., p. 111.

[21] Miollan and Janninet, with the Marquis d'Arlandes helping. The king of Sweden was present, sitting gravely on a bale of straw; he withdrew, along with many of the twenty thousand subscribers. The remaining crowd tore the balloon to pieces and set fire to everything. *London Chronicle*, 3 August 1784.

[22] *York Courant*, 16 March 1784.

[23] *York Courant*, 13 February 1784.

[24] *York Courant*, 16 March 1784.

[25] *York Courant*, 23 May 1784.

[26] *York Chronicle*, 27 May 1785.

[27] *York Chronicle*, 19 August 1785.

[28] *York Courant*, 23 August 1785.

[29] *York Chronicle*, 2 September 1785.

[30] *York Chronicle*, 9 September 1785.

[31] Ibid.

[32] Ibid.

[33] Ibid.

[34] Ibid.

[35] *York Courant*, 13 September 1785.

[36] *York Chronicle*, 9 September 1785.

[37] *York Courant*, 13 December 1786.

[38] Leslie Gardiner, *Lunardi: The Story of Vincenzo Lunardi* (Shrewsbury, 1984), pp. 155–6.

[39] Ibid., pp. 156–79.

[40] *Gove's General Advertiser*, 21 July 1785. The fare was £3 13s 6d.

[41] Richard Brooke, *Liverpool as it was during the Last Quarter of the Eighteenth Century* (Liverpool, 1853), pp. 37, 158, 165, 233, 257, 302.

[42] *WLA*, 26 June 1783.

[43] *WLA*, 11 November 1784.

[44] *WLA*, 24 March 1785.

[45] *WLA*, 16 September 1784.

[46] *WLA*, 27 May 1784.

[47] *WLA*, 15 July 1784.

[48] *WLA*, 5 August 1784.

[49] Brooke, *Liverpool*, p. 286.

[50] For full and fascinating details see Lydia Syson, *Doctor of Love: James Graham and his Celestial Bed* (2008).

[51] *WLA*, 21 July 1785.

[52] *WLA*, 4 August 1785.

[53] Ibid.

[54] *WLA*, 11 August 1785.

[55] Vincent Lunardi, *Mr. Lunardi's Account of his Ascension and Aerial Voyage, from the New Fort, Liverpool, on Wednesday the 20th of July, 1785, in Three Letters Addressed to George Biggin, Esq.* ([London?] 1785).

[56] *WLA*, 11 August 1785.

[57] Ibid.

[58] Vincent Lunardi, *Mr. Lunardi's Account of his Second Aerial Voyage on Tuesday 9th August 1785* ([London?] 1785), p. 30.

[59] *WLA*, 11 August 1785.

[60] *WLA*, 25 August 1785.

[61] *WLA*, 15 September 1785.

[62] *European Magazine*, 1785, p. 134; Lt. French of the Royal Cheshire Militia, on 1 September 1785.

[63] S. E. Stuart and W. T. W. Potts, 'Richard Gillow and Vincent Lunardi: Early Balloon Flights', *Contrebis*, vol. 24 (1999), p. 29.

[64] Ibid., pp. 31–2.

[65] Quoted by MacMahon, *Ascend or Die*, p. 60.

[66] *Whitehall Evening Post*, 15 August 1784.

[67] *Morning Herald and Daily Advertiser*, 17 August 1784.

[68] *Morning Post*.

[69] MacMahon, *Ascend or Die*, p. 157.

[70] *WLA*, 30 June 1785; see also MacMahon, *Ascend or Die*, pp. 155–61.

[71] *Morning Post*, 9 September 1784.

[72] Quoted by MacMahon, *Ascend or Die*, p. 57.

[73] Quoted by MacMahon, *Ascend or Die*, p. 95, p. 97.

[74] *The Aerial Voyage, a Poem. Inscribed to Richard Crosbie, Esq.* (Dublin, 1785), p. 2; quoted by MacMahon, *Ascend or Die*, p. 100.

[75] MacMahon, *Ascend or Die*, p. 104.

[76] *York Courant*, 8 February 1785.

[77] MacMahon, *Ascend or Die*, p. 106.

[78] *The Aerial Voyager* (Dublin, 1785), p. 4.

[79] Ibid., p. 9.

[80] Samuel Whyte – the identification is Bryan MacMahon's: *To Richard Crosbie Esq. on his attempting a Second Aerial Excursion, in which he proved unsuccessful* (Dublin, 1785).

[81] MacMahon, *Ascend or Die*, p. 130.

[82] Ibid.; also *European Magazine*, 1785.

83 MacMahon, *Ascend or Die*, pp. 167–85.

84 B-P (both quotations).

85 MacMahon, *Ascend or Die*, p. 71; B-P.

86 Richard Townley, *A Journal Kept in the Isle of Man, giving an Account of the Wind, Weather and Daily Occurrences* (Whitehaven, 1791), 2 vols, vol. 2, p. 74.

87 Tiberius Cavallo, *The History and Practice of Aerostation* (1785), pp. 176–7; H. S. Torrens, 'Sadler', DNB.

88 DNB.

89 Hodgson, *Aeronautics*, pp. 141–2, quoting *Jackson's Oxford Journal*, 9 October 1784.

90 Davies, *King of All Balloons*, p. 53.

91 Graham Midgley, *University Life in Eighteenth-Century Oxford* (New Haven, 1996), pp. 151–2.

92 Hodgson, *Aeronautics*, p. 145.

93 Ibid., p. 148, quoting *Windham Papers* (1913), vol. 1, p. 76.

94 *The Times*, 17 June 1790.

95 *Morning Chronicle*, 9 January 1784.

96 Text from the reprint in Henry James Pye's *Poems on Various Subjects* (1787), 2 vols, vol. 1, pp. 157–8.

97 *York Chronicle*, 27 May 1785, about the second Manchester ascent.

98 *Probationary Odes for the Laureatship* has Sir John Hawkins' name on the title page, a surreal joke: Johnson described him as unclubbable, with a degree of brutality and a tendency to savageness. Two odes (xvi and xxxi) have been attributed to French Laurence, a lawyer friend of Burke's; the memoirist Nathaniel Wraxall said General Burgoyne had a hand in the production too. The whole collection is also attributed to Andrew Macdonald, a Scottish clergyman, poet and playwright, in a volume of his *Miscellaneous Works* published in 1791. An attribution to Macdonald is possible – he used the pen name Matthew Bramble, a comic character from Smollett's novel *The Expedition of Humphry Clinker* (1771), and he also wrote some poems in the manner of the satirist Peter Pindar, whose speciality was comically plodding bathos.

99 *York Chronicle*, 27 May 1785.

100 *St James's Chronicle*, 12 November 1784.

101 *York Chronicle*, 27 May 1785. His name was T. Frood.

102 See Hannah Greig, *The Beau Monde: Fashionable Society in Georgian London* (Oxford, 2013).

103 For further discussion see Tom Mole, ed., *Romanticism and Celebrity Culture 1750–1850* (Cambridge, 2009) and Graeme Turner, 'Approaching Celebrity Studies', *Celebrity Studies Journal*, vol. 1, no. 1 (2010), pp. 11–20.

104 Jean-Pierre Blanchard, *Journal of my Forty-fifth Ascension, being the first performed in America, on the Ninth of January, 1793* (Philadelphia, 1795).

105 *Public Advertiser*, 18 February 1784.

106 Jean-Pierre Blanchard, *Journal and Certificates on the Fourth Voyage of Mr. Blanchard...* (1784), pp. 4–5.

107 Ibid., p. 13.

108 Ibid., p. 18.

109 Hodgson, *Aeronautics*, p. 167.

110 John Jeffries, *A Narrative of the Two Aerial Voyages of Doctor Jeffries with Mons. Blanchard; with Meteorological Observations and Remarks* (1786), p. 25.

111 Ibid., p. 40.

112 Ibid., p. 41.

113 Ibid., p. 48.

114 *York Chronicle*, 27 May 1785.

115 Gardiner, *Lunardi*, p. 84.

116 Mrs. [Laetitia] Sage, *A Letter Addressed to a Female Friend. By Mrs. Sage, The*

first English Female Aerial Traveller (1785), pp. 10–11; p. 16. Discussed further in my article, '"I will carry you with me on the wings of immagination": Aerial Letters and Eighteenth-Century Ballooning', *Eighteenth-Century Life*, vol. 35, no. 1 (2011), pp. 168–79.

[117] Hodgson, *Aeronautics*, p. 190.

[118] *York Chronicle*, 9 September 1785.

[119] *Aerostation Displayed* (1802), p. 35.

[120] Ibid., p. 32.

[121] Hodgson, *Aeronautics*, p. 191, n. 4; *New London Magazine*, December 1785.

Chapter 4: CROWDS, CRIMINALS AND CHARLATANS

[1] Elias Canetti, *Crowds and Power* (1962); William Phillips, 'History on the Couch', *New York Review*, 1 February 1963.

[2] Charles Tilly, *Popular Contention in Great Britain 1758–1834* (Boulder CO, 2005), p. 395, p. 99. For a full analysis of crowd theory, see also Susan Renee Stockdale, 'An Interdisciplinary Review of the Crowd at Eighteenth Century Hangings in England', MSc thesis 2007, University of Iowa State.

[3] Mark Harrison, *Crowds and History: Mass Phenomena in English Towns, 1790–1835* (Cambridge, 2002), pp. 4–5.

[4] Old Bailey Online, JOHN FOSTER, Violent Theft > highway robbery, 6 April 1785; t17850406–3.

[5] Quoted by R. G. Auckland and K. B. Moore, *Messages from the Sky over Britain* (Leeds, 1998), p. 10; see also B-P for a notice on Sadler attracting a crowd of 170,000: 'In fact, public curiosity was never manifested in a greater degree since the ascension of Mr. Harper, in 1785, when it was calculated 150,000 people were present.'

[6] Huntington Library, MO 6136, 24 September 1786, EM to SS; MO 3612, 1 October 1786, EM to EC. My grateful thanks to Elizabeth Eger and Nicole Pohl for these references, and to Vincent Quinn for pointing out Montagu's censoriousness.

[7] *London Chronicle*, 1 September 1785.

[8] *The Volunteer Journal*, quoted – in full – by MacMahon, *Ascend or Die*, pp. 77–8.

[9] *General Evening Post*, 16 September 1784; *London Chronicle*, 16 September 1784.

[10] *Caledonian Mercury*, 17 September 1784.

[11] *St James's Chronicle*, 16 September 1784. Balloons drew large numbers later too: Harrison, *Crowds and History*, p. 4 instances a crowd of eighty thousand for an ascent in 1819; compare George III's coronation in 1760, watched by fifty thousand.

[12] *Morning Chronicle*, 15 September 1784.

[13] *Whitehall Evening Post*, 9 September 1784.

[14] Lynn, *Sublime Invention*, p. 68.

[15] Ibid.

[16] B-P.

[17] Blagden to Banks, 3 October 1784, *Scientific Correspondence*, vol. 2, p. 311.

[18] The Man in the Moon, *London Unmask'd: Or the New Town Spy* [1784?], p. 136.

[19] See my article, 'The Progress of Knowledge in the Regions of Air? Divisions and Disciplines in Early Ballooning', *Eighteenth-Century Studies*, vol. 45, no. 1 (2011), pp. 77–86.

[20] Account quoted in full in Rolt, *Aeronauts*, pp. 46–8.

[21] Christa Jungnickel and Russell McCormmach, *Cavendish: The Experimental Life* (1999), p. 361.

[22] Larry Stewart, 'A Meaning for Machines: Modernity, Utility, and the Eighteenth-Century British Public', *The Journal of Modern History*, vol. 70, no. 2 (1998), p. 293.

[23] Cavallo, *History of Aerostation*, p. 136.

24 Old Bailey Online, JOHN GODFREY, Theft > burglary, 29 June 1785; t17850629–84.

25 Duncan Sprott, *1784* (1984), p. 227; *Public Advertiser*, 18 September 1784.

26 *York Chronicle*, 10 June 1785.

27 Jerry White, 'Vengeance and the Crowd in Eighteenth-Century London', Birkbeck College, backdoorbroadcasting.net, 21 February 2011.

28 Sprott, *1784*, p. 212; *Public Advertiser*, 6 September 1784.

29 *Caledonian Mercury*, 2 May 1785.

30 Sprott, *1784*, p. 221.

31 John Styles, *The Dress of the People: Everyday Fashion in Eighteenth-Century England* (New Haven, 2007), p. 327.

32 Old Bailey Online, DANIEL MACKANEY, Theft > petty larceny, 29 June 1785; t17850629–110.

33 Old Bailey Online, WILLIAM M'GINNIS, Theft > pocketpicking, 11 May 1785; t17850511–4.

34 Sprott, *1784*, p. 275; *Morning Chronicle*, 11 November 1784.

35 Sprott, *1784*, p. 226; *Morning Chronicle*, 17 September 1784.

36 Sprott, *1784*, p. 253; *Public Advertiser*, 20 October 1784.

37 *Australian Dictionary of Biography*. See also Nathan Garvey, *The Celebrated George Barrington: A Spurious Author; The Book Trade, and Botany Bay* (Sydney, 2008), especially ch. 2 for the spurious publications attributed to Barrington.

38 Sprott, *1784*, p. 151; *Morning Herald*, 1 July 1784.

39 Sprott, *1784*, p. 180.

40 Ibid., p. 218; *Public Advertiser*, 11 September 1784.

41 Sprott, *1784*, p. 275; *Public Advertiser*, 20 October 1784.

42 Styles, *The Dress of the People*, p. 105.

43 *Caledonian Mercury*, 1 November 1785.

44 *Felix Farley's Bristol Journal*, 12 February 1785.

45 *St James's Chronicle*, 7 October 1784.

46 *York Chronicle*, 20 August 1784.

47 *WLA*, 26 August 1784. They included Sir Harry Englefield, a Catholic antiquary with scientific interests.

48 *Gazetteer and New Daily Advertiser*, 12 January and 6 April 1784; *Morning Herald*, 4 August 1784.

49 *WLA*, 26 August 1784.

50 *Public Advertiser*, 20 August 1784.

51 B-P, 14 August 1784.

52 *English Credulity, or the Chevelere Morret taking a French Leave*, published 18 August 1784 by William Wells; BM 1868, 0808.5367.

53 *Public Advertiser*, 18 August 1784.

54 *Morning Herald*, 16 August 1784.

55 *Gazetteer and New Daily Advertiser*, 24 August 1784.

56 Listed as Kugan, T., in *Bailey's British Directory ... for 1784* (1784), 4 vols, vol. 1, p. 149, though others identify him as Allen Keegan.

57 Paul Sandby, 'Coelum ipsum petimus Stultitia' (our folly reaches to the sky); BM Satires 6702.

58 The mercer who supplied the cloth had to sue Sheldon for payment. *Morning Chronicle*, 17 December 1784. Sandby print in BM 1868, 0808.5399.

59 B-P.

60 *Aerostation Displayed*, p. 23.

61 *Gazetteer and New Daily Advertiser*, 18 September 1784.

62 Lunardi to Count Bruhl, 21 April 1784, National Archives of Scotland, GD 157/3369/1.

63 Possibly a relation of the Irish chemist, mineralogist and meteorologist Richard Kirwan, FRS 1780, Copley medal winner 1782 and theorist of inflammable air.

⁶⁴ Vincent Lunardi, *An Account of the First Aerial Voyage in England* (1784), p. 15.
⁶⁵ Charles Mackay, *Memoirs of Extraordinary Popular Delusions and the Madness of Crowds* (1841), 3 vols, vol. 1, p. 2.
⁶⁶ Lunardi, *First Aerial Voyage*, p. 29.
⁶⁷ Ibid., p. 31 (both quotations).
⁶⁸ *Caledonian Mercury*, 25 September 1784.
⁶⁹ Lunardi, *First Aerial Voyage*, pp. 39–42.
⁷⁰ *Caledonian Mercury*, 20 October 1784.
⁷¹ Ibid.
⁷² Ibid.
⁷³ Papers of George Innes, National Records of Scotland, GD 113/4/157; 136. The Bottle Conjuror refers to a hoax of 1749 at the Haymarket Theatre, where a man supposed to be able to climb into a wine bottle failed to appear. The audience rioted. Sir William Forbes was, like Innes, a Scottish financier – leading lights in Coutts and RBS respectively.
⁷⁴ Patricia Fara, 'Katterfelto', DNB.
⁷⁵ David Paton-Williams, *Katterfelto: Prince of Puff* (Leicester, 2008), p. 107.
⁷⁶ *York Courant*, 25 April 1786, on 12 March 1785.
⁷⁷ Paton-Williams, *Katterfelto*, pp. 117–18; p. 122.
⁷⁸ Philip Astley, *Natural Magic or Physical Amusements Revealed* (1785), p. 38.
⁷⁹ See e.g. Signor Giuseppe Pinetti, *Physical Amusements and Diverting Experiments* (1784), title page.
⁸⁰ Astley, *Natural Magic*, p. 5.
⁸¹ *St James's Chronicle*, 2 September 1784.
⁸² B-P.
⁸³ Also discussed by Robert Darnton, *Mesmerism and the End of Enlightenment in France* (Harvard, 1968), p. 23. He sees it as an instance of limitless, hence gullible, public enthusiasm for science.
⁸⁴ *Whitehall Evening Post*, 6 August 1785; *London Chronicle*, 15 September 1785.
⁸⁵ *Morning Herald*, 14 September 1785.
⁸⁶ *Whitehall Evening Post*, 10 September 1785.
⁸⁷ *Whitehall Evening Post*, 15 September 1785.
⁸⁸ *London Chronicle*, 10 September 1785.
⁸⁹ *York Chronicle*, 25 August 1785.

Chapter 5: FASHION

¹ Hannah Greig, 'Leading the fashion: the material culture of London's beau monde', in *Gender, Taste, and Material Culture in Britain and North America, 1700–1830*, eds Amanda Vickery and John Styles (New Haven, 2006), p p. 293–310.
² Styles, *The Dress of the People*, p. 11.
³ *York Chronicle*, 19 September 1784.
⁴ All seen by the author in various archives. Grateful thanks to Nicola Buckley for finding glasses – viewable in Norwich.
⁵ *Caledonian Mercury*, 26 October 1785.
⁶ Mary Darby Robinson, *Memoirs of Mary Robinson*, ed. J. Fitzgerald Molloy (Philadelphia, 1895), p. 153; *Morning Herald*, 11 March 1783.
⁷ Michael Gamer and Terry F. Robinson, 'Mary Robinson and the Art of the Dramatic Comeback', *Studies in Romanticism*, vol. 48, no. 2 (2009), p p. 219–56, citing *The Lady's Magazine, or Entertaining Companion for the Fair Sex* (1783), p p. 187, 268, 331, 650–1.
⁸ Leonard MacNally, *Fashionable Levities, A Comedy in Five Acts* (Dublin, 1786), p. 13.
⁹ Ibid., p. 44.
¹⁰ *The Selector*, no. 1 [1783–84], p. 1.

11 *York Chronicle*, 3 September 1785.

12 *London Magazine*, August 1783, p. 19.

13 'On seeing the LOCK and KEY superceded by a BUTTERFLY in Less than a Month', in [George Villiers], *Flights of Fancy* (n.p., n.d.), p. 31.

14 *London Magazine*, August 1783, p. 212.

15 'What's the Whim', in [Villiers], *Flights of Fancy*, p. 4.

16 'The Brandy Cask, or Cork Rumps Detected', in [Villiers], *Flights of Fancy*, p. 13.

17 'On Inventions and Patents', in [Villiers], *Flights of Fancy*, p. 15.

18 Rolt, *Aeronauts*, p. 23.

19 George Keane, Prologue to *Cymbeline* (1786).

20 Mrs Papendick's *Memoirs*, quoted in C. Willett Cunnington and Phyllis Cunnington, *Handbook of English Costume in the Eighteenth Century* (1957; rev. 1972), p. 322.

21 Cunnington, *Handbook*, p. 361.

22 *The Lounger* (1785), quoted in Cunnington, *Handbook*, p. 361.

23 The Man in the Moon, *London Unmask'd*, p. 137.

24 Ibid.

25 B-P.

26 *An Aerial Dialogue between a Male and a Female Traveller above the Clouds* (n.d.).

27 February 1783; quoted by Gamer and Robinson, 'Mary Robinson', n. 16.

28 B-P.

29 *Morning Herald*, 15 September 1784.

30 *Morning Chronicle*, 19 October 1784.

31 Gamer and Robinson, 'Mary Robinson', p. 2.

32 *Parker's General Advertiser*, 24 September 1784.

33 See Judith Pascoe, *The Sarah Siddons Audio Files: Romanticism and the Lost Voice* (Ann Arbor, 2011).

34 Horace Walpole to Lady Ossory, 17 December 1780, *The Correspondence of Horace Walpole*, ed. W. S. Lewis (New Haven, 1937–83), 48 vols, vol. 33, p. 254.

35 See Martin Postle, 'Thomas Gainsborough's "Lost" Portrait of Auguste Vestris', *The British Art Journal*, vol. 4, no. 1 (Spring 2003), p p. 64–8; also http://www.adam-williams.com/DesktopDefault.aspx?tabid=5&tabindex=4& objectid=198385&categoryid=0&page=0&keyword=&sol

36 MacMahon, *Ascend or Die*, p. 94.

37 Ibid., p p. 101–2.

38 *York Chronicle*, 27 May 1785.

39 Ibid.

40 Charles Coulston Gillispie, *The Montgolfier Brothers and the Invention of Aviation 1783–1784* (Princeton NJ, 1983), p. 57.

41 *Modern Manners: In a Series of Familiar Epistles* (1781), p. 13.

42 MacNally, *Fashionable Levities*, p. 60.

43 Letter from S. Skylight, *The Delineator*, November 1784 (both quotations).

44 William Goodwin of Street Farm, Earl Soham, diary, 27 June 1785; transcribed by Mrs J. Rothery of Soham, 2001.

45 Keen, "The Good Things Above", n.p.

46 B-P; also *Dean's Yard Magazine*, quoted in Lord William Lennox, *Percy Hamilton, or The Adventures of a Westminster Boy* (1851), 3 vols, vol. 1, p p. 186–7.

47 Jean-François Féraud, *Dictionnaire Critique de la Langue Française* (Marseille, 1787–88).

48 Priscilla Parkhurst Ferguson, *Paris as Revolution: Writing the Nineteenth-Century City* (Berkeley CA, 1994), p. 22.

49 Including Robert Baldick, *The Duel: A History of Duelling* (1970), p. 161, and Richard O. Smith, *The Man with his Head in the Clouds: James Sadler, the First Englishman to Fly* (Oxford, 2014), p p. 38–9.

Chapter 6: SATIRES

[1] *St James's Chronicle*, 16 October 1784.

[2] *The downfall of taste & genius or the world as it goes*, BM AN 82865001.

[3] *The Air Balloon, or a Trip to the Moon*, 2 November 1783; BM Satires 6335.

[4] *Caledonian Mercury*, 18 September 1784.

[5] *Caledonian Mercury*, 12 October 1785.

[6] *London Magazine*, January 1784.

[7] B-P.

[8] Ibid.

[9] *St James's Chronicle*, 25 November 1783.

[10] *Annual Register*, 1783, p. 65.

[11] B-P.

[12] [Mary Alcock], *The Air Balloon; or, Flying Mortal* (1784).

[13] *The Ballooniad*, 2nd edn (Birmingham, 1785), p. 14.

[14] Keen, 'The "Balloonomania"', p. 509.

[15] *St James's Chronicle*, 10 August 1784.

[16] *London Magazine*, 1783, p. 534.

[17] Ibid.

[18] *Aux Amateurs de Physique*, 1783; image viewable via the Library of Congress.

[19] *Morning Herald*, 8 January 1784; *General Evening Post*, 6 January 1785; *Parker's General Advertiser*, 8 January 1784.

[20] *London Magazine*, April 1784, p. 297.

[21] *Gentleman's Magazine*, 1785, p. 103.

[22] Though Mary Hamilton's 'A Manuscript' is one anti-Pitt instance. My thanks to Nicole Pohl for pointing this out.

[23] *The Coalition Balloon*, February 1784; BM Satires 6399.

[24] L. G. Mitchell, *Charles James Fox* (1991), p. 4.

[25] Ibid., pp. 72–3.

[26] Vic Gattrell, *City of Laughter: Sex and Satire in Eighteenth-Century London* (2006), p. 110.

[27] Published 16 August 1784; BM Satires 6652; AN82843001.

[28] BM Satires 6275; also in Lewis Walpole Collection, Yale.

[29] BM Satires 6248; AN80705001.

[30] *Gentleman's Magazine*, 25 July 1781.

[31] E. F. Rimbault, *Soho and its Associations* (1895), pp. 190–1. From 'Broadwick and Peter Street Area', *Survey of London*, vols 31 and 32: St James [*sic*] Westminster, Part 2 (1963), pp. 219–29.

[32] See Syson, *Doctor of Love*, and Paton-Williams, *Katterfelto*.

[33] *St James's Chronicle*, 8 January 1784.

[34] Ibid.

[35] Gattrell, *City of Laughter*, p. 4.

[36] Ibid., p. 2.

[37] *The Answer of Sir R—d W—y to L—y W—y* (1782), p. 9.

[38] *An Epistle from L—y W—y to Sir R—d W—y* (1782), p. 5.

[39] *The Trial with the Whole of the Evidence, between the Right Hon. Sir Richard Worsley, Bart … and George Maurice Bisset, esq.*, 7th edn (1782), pp. 26–7.

[40] BM Satires 6668; AN150054001.

[41] *Caledonian Mercury*, 15 September 1784.

[42] *Caledonian Mercury*, 27 September 1784.

[43] *Felix Farley's Bristol Journal*, 22 January 1785.

[44] *Symposia, or Table Talk in the Month of September 1784*, p. 25.

[45] George Paston, *Little Memoirs of the Eighteenth Century* (1901), p. 144.

[46] Gattrell, *City of Laughter*, p. 221.

[47] *York Chronicle*, 14 January 1785.

[48] *St James's Chronicle*, 11 June 1784. The Westminster election of 1784 is

also discussed in my book, *Eighteenth-Century Letters and British Culture* (Basingstoke, 2006), pp. 196–208.

49 *St James's Chronicle*, 6 July 1784.

50 *York Chronicle*, 20 May 1785.

51 *York Chronicle*, 15 July 1785.

52 *Caledonian Mercury*, 18 August 1785 (both quotations).

53 *Caledonian Mercury*, 21 August 1785.

54 *Caledonian Mercury*, 18 August 1784.

55 Ibid.

56 *Caledonian Mercury*, 27 September 1784.

57 *York Courant*, 11 August 1786.

58 B-P.

59 BM AN797749001.

60 BM Satires 6561.

61 *St James's Chronicle*, 1 June 1784.

62 *London Chronicle*, 2 December 1784.

63 *St James's Chronicle*, 2 December 1784; Amanda Foreman, *Georgiana, Duchess of Devonshire* (1998), p. 45, pp. 173–4.

64 *St James's Chronicle*, 2 November 1784.

65 *St James's Chronicle*, 23 September 1784.

66 *St James's Chronicle*, 6 July 1784.

67 *York Chronicle*, 30 September 1785.

68 Richard Brinsley Sheridan to Thomas Graham, 23 October 1784; E-Enlightenment. See George Kearsley, *Tax Tables for 1784*, for full details of Pitt's taxes.

69 28 October 1784, Coachmakers Hall; Donna T. Andrew, ed., 'London debates: 1784', *London Debating Societies 1776–1799* (1994), pp. 157–64; http://www.british-history.ac.uk/source.aspx?pubid=238.

70 To William Unwin, in *The Letters and Prose Writings of William Cowper*, eds James King and Charles Ryskamp (Oxford, 1979–86), 5 vols, vol. 2, p. 258. See also to John Newton, 5 July 1784, p. 261.

71 *York Courant*, 10 December 1784.

72 Frederic Pilon, *Aerostation; or, The Templar's Stratagem. A Farce* (1785), Prologue.

73 *Caledonian Mercury*, 13 March 1786.

74 *Town and Country Magazine*, n.d.; B-P.

75 *St James's Chronicle*, 8 April 1784.

76 Ibid.

77 BM Satires 6572.

78 'Confucius the Sage', *The Oriental Chronicle of the Times: Being the Translation of a Chinese MS...* (1785).

79 Elizabeth Inchbald, *The Mogul Tale, or, The Descent of the Balloon* (first performed in 1784; first published in 1788), pp. 4, 16, 19. See also Michael Tomko, '"All the World have heard of the Devil and the Pope": Elizabeth Inchbald's *The Mogul Tale* and English Catholic Satire', *Tulsa Studies in Women's Literature*, vol. 31, nos. 1/2 (2012), pp. 117–36.

80 See Jonathan Barry, Marianne Hester and Gareth Roberts, eds, *Witchcraft in Early Modern Europe: Studies in Culture and Belief* (Cambridge, 1996).

81 *Rambler's Magazine*, December 1783; BM AN00082863; BM Satires 6705.

82 [Ex Fumo Lux], 'Aura Popularis; or, The Air-Balloon', *Public Advertiser*, 12 January 1785.

83 Gaston Bachelard, *Air and Dreams: An Essay on the Imagination of Movement* (1943), trans. Edith R. Farrell and C. Frederick Farrell (Dallas, 2002), p. 10.

Chapter 7: LITERATURE

[1] Quoted by John Baron, *The Life of Edward Jenner, with Illustrations of His Doctrines...* (1827), 2 vols, vol. 1, pp. 70–1.

[2] Jane Cave, *Poems on Various Subjects, Entertaining, Elegiac and Religious* (Bristol, 1786), p. 58.

[3] T. T. Hook-Norton, Oxfordshire [*sic*], *A Description of the Fire and Air Balloon: With a Spiritual Use of them Both* (Banbury [1785?]). Hook Norton is a place – but appears here to be the *nom de plume*. My thanks to John Carney for this item.

[4] See Holmes, *Age of Wonder*, ch. 3, and my article, "I will carry you with me on the wings of immagination".

[5] Reverend Jeremiah Belknap to Reverend Manasseh Cutler, 18 November 1785, from Dover; *The Pennsylvania Magazine of History and Biography*, vol. 37, no. 4 (Philadelphia, 1913), pp. 491–8.

[6] 'The Discontented Man', in [Villiers], *Flights of Fancy*.

[7] *Gentleman's Magazine*, January 1785, p. 55.

[8] *WLA*, 12 May 1785.

[9] Stephen Fry, *The Ode Less Travelled: Unlocking the Poet Within* (2007), p. 250.

[10] *The Aerial Voyage*, lines 17–18.

[11] *Edinburgh Courant*, 7 November 1785.

[12] Pilon, *Aerostation*, p. 5.

[13] *The Selector*, no. 2, 4 September 1784, p. 7.

[14] *The Selector*, no. 3, 11 September 1784, p. 9.

[15] James Fisher, *Poems on Various Subjects*, 2nd edn (Dumfries, 1792), p. 82.

[16] B-P [1785].

[17] 'An ACROSTICAL List of few surnames of Ladies and Gentlemen selected from the vast number who appeared in Heriot's Gardens, at Mr LUNARDI's last aerial exhibition', *Edinburgh Courant*, 26 December 1785.

[18] B-P.

[19] *York Courant*, 1 July 1785.

[20] 'Virtus, recludens immeritis mori/ Cælum, negata tentat iter via', Horace, *Carmina*, III.2.21 [1788]; B-P.

[21] B-P.

[22] *Memoirs of Louis Philippe Comte de Ségur*, ed. Eveline Cruickshanks (1960), pp. 26–8.

[23] Ibid.

[24] Harold Bloom, 'The Knight in the Mirror', *The Guardian*, 13 December 2003.

[25] *Odes*, Book IV, Ode IV, *Drusus and the Claudians*; translation by Philip Francis, 1743, in a ninth edition by 1791. See Peter France, *The Oxford Guide to Literature in Translation* (Oxford, 2001), pp. 517–18.

[26] *The Selector*, no. 11, 6 November 1784, p. 42.

[27] Lunardi, *Five Aerial Voyages*, pp. 88–90.

[28] *Gentleman's Magazine*, 6 January 1785.

[29] *Caledonian Mercury*, 4 March 1784.

[30] Lunardi, *First Aerial Voyage*, p. 48.

[31] Eliza Knipe, *Poems on Various Subjects* (Manchester, 1783), pp. 102–3.

[32] *Morning Chronicle*, 1 November 1784; *London Chronicle*, 2 November 1784; *WLA*, 4 November 1784.

[33] *WLA*, 4 November 1784.

[34] See Marjorie Hope Nicolson, *Voyages to the Moon* (1948); Clarke, *The Pattern of Expectation*; Clive Hart, *The Dream of Flight: Aeronautics from Classical Times to the Renaissance* (1972); on voyages to the moon see also Pohl, 'Of Balloons and Foreign Worlds', *Azimuth*, pp. 61–90.

[35] E.g. Robert Paltock, *The Life and Adventures of Peter Wilkins* (1751).

[36] *Life on the Moon in 1768: Ten Fantasy Engravings of the 18th Century by Filippo Morghen*, introduction by Brian W. Aldiss (Hythe, 1990), n.p.

37 All quotations from 'The Trifler No. IV', *Caledonian Mercury*, 29 November 1785.

38 James L. Golden and Edward P. J. Corbett, *The Rhetoric of Blair, Campbell, and Whately: With Updated Bibliographies* (Carbondale and Edwardsville, 1990), p. 60.

39 'Trifler' seems to be a resonant word in Scotland; it's much used about school infractions in Donald Robert Farquharson, *Tales and Memories of Cromar and Canada* (Chatham, Ontario, n.d), ch. 12. Cromar is 30-odd miles inland from Aberdeen.

40 http://www.jstor.org/pss/3181936.

41 See Carroll, *An Empire of Air and Water*, for further discussion of air and politics in what she calls the long Romantic Century.

42 *Caledonian Mercury*, 10 April 1786.

43 See John Gay, *Trivia, or the Art of Walking the Streets of London* (1716), Book III, lines 192–4.

44 *A Journey Lately Performed Through the Air* (Litchfield CT, 1784).

45 Thus *Modern British Utopias, 1700–1850*, ed. Gregory Claeys (1997), 8 vols; vol. 5 includes several balloon voyages.

46 See Patrick Parrinder, *Learning from Other Worlds* (Liverpool, 2000), pp. 1–19.

47 R. B. Rose, 'Utopianism', *Encyclopaedia of the Enlightenment*, ed. Alan Charles Kors (Oxford, 2003), 4 vols, vol. 4, p. 216.

48 An Aerial Traveller, *The Aerostatic Spy: or, Excursions with an Air Balloon* (1785), advertisement.

49 *Morning Herald*, 6 June 1785.

50 An Aerial Traveller, *The Aerostatic Spy*, vol. 1, p. 111.

51 Ode 'To Edward Malone, Esq.', 1786, in *Annual Register … for 1786* (1788), pp. 142–4.

52 Samuel Taylor Coleridge, 'The Blossoming of the Solitary Date Tree', *Sibylline Leaves* (1817).

53 Goethe, *Aus Meinem Leben, Dichtung und Wahreit* (1811–33), Book I, lines 478 ff; translation from *Foreign Quarterly Review* (1841), p. 276. I am very grateful to Matthew Bell for this reference.

Chapter 8: MONARCHS

1 Jeroen Deploige and Gita Deneckere, eds, *Mystifying the Monarch* (Amsterdam, 2006), p. 15, p. 20.

2 See Sarah Melzer and Kathryn Norberg, eds, *From the Royal to the Republican Body: Incorporating the Political in Seventeenth- and Eighteenth-Century France* (Berkeley CA, 1998); Antoine de Baecque, *The Body Politic: Corporeal Metaphor in Revolutionary France, 1770–1800*, trans. Charlotte Mednell (Stanford, 1997); Linda Colley, 'The Apotheosis of George III: Loyalty, Royalty and the British Nation 1760–1820', *Past & Present*, no. 102 (February 1984), pp. 94–129; Richard Sugg, *Mummies, Cannibals and Vampires: The History of Corpse Medicine from the Renaissance to the Victorians* (2011).

3 Colley, 'Apotheosis', p. 95.

4 Ibid., p. 96, p. 100.

5 Melzer and Norberg, *Royal to Republican*, p. 3.

6 *London Magazine*, June 1784, p. 452.

7 *St James's Chronicle*, 21 August 1784.

8 *Universal Magazine*, February 1783, p. 74.

9 The statue, erected in 1780, was designed by John Bacon the elder.

10 *St James's Chronicle*, 10 February 1784. Translation of 'Le Roi Chretien pense qu'il a le droit/ A toute la nature de donner le loi,/ Le balon s'envole maigre de par le Roi.'

11 *Universal Magazine*, March 1784, p. 153. The original is a much crisper epigram:

'Les Anglois, nation trop fière,/ S'arrogent l'empire des mers:/ Les François, nation legère/ S'emparent de celui des airs.'

[12] *St James's Chronicle*, 20 March 1784; see also *Universal Magazine*, 1786.

[13] *St James's Chronicle*, 22 May 1784.

[14] *Universal Magazine*, 15 July 1784, p. 53.

[15] *St James's Chronicle*, 20 January 1784.

[16] Ibid., 10 August 1784.

[17] Mercier, *The Nightcap*, vol. 2, p. 275.

[18] *British Magazine*, May 1783; *St James's Chronicle*, June 1784; *St James's Chronicle*, October 1783.

[19] *Annual Register*, 1784; *Universal Magazine*, February 1784.

[20] H. J. Pitcher, 'A Scottish View of Catherine's Russia: William Richardson's *Anecdotes of the Russian Empire* (1784)', *Forum Modern Language Studies*, vol. 3, no. 3 (1967), pp. 236–51.

[21] *Universal Magazine*, March 1785, p. 161.

[22] *Universal Magazine*, April 1785, p. 217.

[23] *The Parliamentary History of England, from the Earliest Period to the Year 1803* (1815), vol. 25, p. 431.

[24] *St James's Chronicle*, 3 August 1784.

[25] http://botanybaymedallion.com/?page_id=8 [16 May 1785].

[26] *Annual Register*, 1786, p. 56.

[27] *Annual Register*, 1786, pp. 139–40.

[28] Huntington Library, MO 3587, June 1785, Elizabeth Montagu to Elizabeth Carter (4 pp.), p. 3; my thanks to Elizabeth Eger for this reference.

[29] Cavallo, *History of Aerostation*, p. 151.

[30] *York Courant*, 16 December 1785.

[31] *York Courant*, 5 December 1786.

[32] *Annual Register*, November 1785; *St James's Chronicle*, 1 July 1784, 7 October 1783, 16 August 1784, 11 September 1783, 7 December 1784.

[33] Gillispie, *Montgolfier Brothers*, p. 26, p. 48.

[34] Ibid., p. 37.

[35] Ibid., pp. 36–7.

[36] Ibid., pp. 42–3.

[37] Ibid., p. 46.

[38] Ibid., p. 68.

[39] Ibid., p. 92.

[40] *St James's Chronicle*, 1 July 1784.

[41] Ibid., 27 May 1784.

[42] *St James's Chronicle*, 27 March 1784; letter from Naples 19 February.

[43] *St James's Chronicle*, 18 September 1784.

[44] Ibid., 2 October 1784.

[45] Ibid., 19 October 1784.

[46] Deploige and Deneckere, *Mystifying the Monarch*, p. 20.

[47] *York Courant*, 26 October 1784.

[48] *St James's Chronicle*, 6 July 1784.

[49] *WLA*, 9 June 1785.

[50] Andrew Kippis, *Observations on the Late Contests in the Royal Society* (1784), p. 115; *An History of the Instances of Exclusion from the Royal Society, which were not suffered to be argued in the course of the late debates. By some members in the minority*, 2nd edn (1784), p. 22. One of these chairs still survives at the Royal Society. I have sat on it.

[51] B-P [1788].

[52] Cavallo, *History of Aerostation*, p. 144. The flight was 23 June 1784.

[53] *London Magazine*, May 1784, p. 450.

[54] *New London Magazine*, July 1785, p. 47.

[55] Royal Society AP/5/12, 4 March 1784. Smeathman's design uncannily

anticipates some features of the Airlander 10, a hybrid airship successfully tested on 19 August 2016. See https://www.hybridairvehicles.com/.

[56] *An Account of the Loss of the 'Royal George' at Spithead, August 1782* (1842). See also C. A. Deane, *Submarine Researches on the Wrecks of His Majesty's Late Ships Royal George, Boyne and Others* (1836; reprinted 2001).

[57] *Universal Magazine*, April 1783, p. 222.

[58] *St James's Chronicle*, 7 August 1784.

[59] B-P, 1 February 1785.

[60] *New London Magazine*, December 1785, p. 300. Flight was 30 August.

[61] *York Courant*, 8 August 1786; see also 14 November for an excise cutter named for Admiral Rodney.

[62] Colley, 'Apotheosis', p. 108.

[63] *WLA*, 4 August 1785.

[64] James Boswell, *Life of Johnson...*, ed. George Birkbeck Hill, rev. L. F. Powell (Oxford, 1934–50), 6 vols, vol. 2, pp. 33–40, February 1767.

[65] *London Magazine*, January 1784, p. 45.

[66] Colley, 'Apotheosis', p. 104, notes more than ninety performances of 'God save the King' between 1786 and 1800.

[67] John Hoyle, *Dictionaria Musica* (1770), pp. 55–6. I am grateful to Cliff Eisen for confirming *maestoso* as a term indicating slow tempo.

[68] *Gentleman's Magazine*, 8 August 1786.

[69] *York Courant*, 21 November 1786.

[70] Meltzer and Norberg see a loosening of this rigidity in dance: *Royal to Republican*, p. 10.

Chapter 9: GODS AND HEROES

[1] Elaine Freedgood, *Victorian Writing about Risk: Imagining a Safe England in a Dangerous World* (Cambridge, 2000), p. 82.

[2] B-P.

[3] B-P.

[4] B-P; see also Joseph MacSweeny, *An Essay on Aerial Navigation* (1845).

[5] B-P.

[6] See my article, 'Philosophical Playthings?'; on miniaturising, see Susan Stewart, *On Longing: Narratives of the Miniature, the Gigantic, the Souvenir, the Collection* (Baltimore MD, 1984).

[7] *London Magazine*, 1783, p. 328.

[8] *London Magazine*, 1784, p. 567.

[9] On gift theory and practice in the late eighteenth century, see Sarah Haggerty, *Blake's Gifts: Poetry and the Politics of Exchange* (Cambridge, 2010).

[10] Gillispie, *Montgolfier Brothers*, p. 43.

[11] Ibid., p. 65.

[12] B-P.

[13] *London Magazine*, October 1785.

[14] Gillispie, *Montgolfier Brothers*, p. 84.

[15] Keen, "The Good Things Above", n.p.

[16] Stewart, 'A Meaning for Machines', pp. 259–94, p. 279.

[17] Gillispie, *Montgolfier Brothers*, p. 21.

[18] Thus Bernard Mandeville, *The Fable of the Bees* (1716).

[19] Gillispie, *Montgolfier Brothers*, p. 35.

[20] *Memoirs of ... Comte de Ségur*, ed. Cruickshanks, p. 177.

[21] Ibid.

[22] 'Advice to Mr Lunardi. By a Lady', *Edinburgh Magazine*, 1785.

[23] 'Confucius the Sage', *Oriental Chronicle*, p. 75.

[24] Holmes, *Age of Wonder*, especially Prologue.

[25] Patrick O'Flighty, *British Magazine*, November 1783.

[26] *Aerostation Displayed*, p. 17.

[27] *Caledonian Mercury*, 26 October 1785.

[28] James Watt to Josiah Wedgwood, 28 January 1784; quoted and discussed by Stewart, 'A Meaning for Machines', p. 263.

[29] S. L. Kotar and J. E. Gessler, *Ballooning: A History, 1782–1900* (2011), pp. 28–9.

[30] *London Magazine*, 27 August 1785.

[31] *St James's Chronicle*, 10 September 1783.

[32] *St James's Chronicle*, 21 January 1784.

[33] *St James's Chronicle*, 10 August 1784.

[34] Keen, 'The "Balloonomania"', p. 510.

[35] Pierre Bourdieu, *Practical Reason: On the Theory of Action* (Cambridge, 1998).

[36] *York Chronicle*, 29 July 1785.

[37] B-P.

[38] *York Courant*, 16 March 1784.

[39] Mary Eleanor Bowes to Thomas Colpitts, 16 July 1786; Strathmore Papers, Glamis Castle (National Register of Scotland 885), vol. C, folio 34. I am very grateful to Wendy Moore for this reference.

[40] *York Courant*, 7 November 1785, from a letter from Paris dated 23 October.

[41] *Annual Register*, 1785.

[42] B-P.

[43] B-P.

Chapter 10: THE SUBLIME

[1] *The Aerial Voyage*, p. viii.

[2] Ibid., p. x.

[3] Ibid., p. 1, lines 1–8; p. 2.

[4] On eighteenth-century thinking about air, see Lewis, *Air's Appearance*.

[5] Edward Young, *The Complaint, or Night Thoughts on Life, Death and Immortality* (1742–45), Night the Seventh, p. 128.

[6] Edmund Burke, *A Philosophical Enquiry into the Origin of Our Ideas of the Sublime and Beautiful* (1757), p. 41.

[7] William Gilpin, *Observations on the River Wye, and Several parts of South Wales, &c. relative chiefly to picturesque beauty; made in the summer of the year 1770* (1782), p. 63. See also Gilpin's *Three Essays: on picturesque beauty; on picturesque travel; and on sketching landscape...* (1792) and Uvedale Price, *An Essay on the Picturesque, As Compared With The Sublime and The Beautiful* (1794).

[8] Cavallo, *History of Aerostation*, p. 80.

[9] Hugh Blair, *Essays on Rhetoric, abridged chiefly from Dr Blair's Lectures on that Science* (Dublin, 1784), pp. 30–1.

[10] Blair, *Essays on Rhetoric*, p. 16.

[11] Lynn, *Sublime Invention*, p. 72.

[12] Andrew Ashfield and Peter de Bolla, *The Sublime: A Reader in British Aesthetic Theory* (Cambridge, 1996), p. 2.

[13] Thomas Baldwin, *Airopaidia: Containing the Narrative of a Balloon Excursion from Chester, the Eighth of September, 1785...* (Chester, 1786), p. 4.

[14] See jokes about Burke at a Whig dinner during a Westminster election, *Morning Chronicle*, 28 July 1788: 'Mr. B----- instantly rose, and with a heart overflowing with extasy, was going to shower down the sublime on Lord G-----'s conversion, but was prevented by a flood of tears.' Grateful thanks to James Naylor for this reference.

[15] Paul Keen, *Literature, Commerce, and the Spectacle of Modernity, 1750–1800* (Cambridge, 2012), p. 49.

[16] Baldwin, *Airopaidia*, p. 29.

[17] 'The Lady's Balloon, or Female Aerial Traveller' (1785); B-P.

[18] *York Chronicle*, 12 March 1784.

19 Blair, *Essays on Rhetoric*, p. 53.

20 *Morning Post*, 16 September 1784.

21 Quoted by Alexander Gerard, *An Essay on Taste* (1759), p. 21, summarising Hume's *Treatise on Human Nature*, Book II, p. 3, s. 8.

22 Baldwin, *Airopaidia*, p. 93.

23 Lunardi, *Five Aerial Voyages*, p. 90.

24 Lunardi, *Ascension and Aerial Voyage from the New Fort, Liverpool*, p. 35.

25 *Aerostation Displayed*, p. 25; the aeronauts were Zambeccari and Vernon.

26 See Dick Pountain and David Robins, *Cool Rules: Anatomy of an Attitude* (2000).

27 Ashfield and de Bolla, *Sublime*, p. 41.

28 Ibid., p. 42.

29 'An Epistle to Sig. Vincenzo Lunardi', in Lunardi, *First Aerial Voyage*, p. 64.

30 Baldwin, *Airopaidia*, pp. 53–8.

31 Price, *Essay on the Picturesque*, p. 81.

32 Lunardi, *First Aerial Voyage*, p. 34; Mrs. [Laetitia] Sage, *A Letter*, p. 15.

33 Lunardi, *First Aerial Voyage*, p. 33.

34 Baldwin, *Airopaidia*, p. 46.

35 Ashfield and de Bolla, *Sublime*, p. 130.

36 William Blake, 'Jerusalem the Emanations of the Giant Albion', *Complete Poems & Prose*, ed. David V. Erdman (New York, 1997), p. 186, lines 19–20.

37 Baldwin, *Airopaidia*, p. 109.

38 Ibid., pp. 37–8.

39 David Hendy, *Noise: A Human History of Sound and Listening* (2013), p. 8.

40 *The Aerial Voyage*, p. vii.

41 Baldwin, *Airopaidia*, p. 91.

42 Ibid., p. 117.

43 [Alcock], *The Air Balloon*, p. 2.

44 Baldwin, *Airopaidia*, p. 39.

45 Ibid., pp. 71–2.

46 Frances Ferguson, *Solitude and the Sublime: Romanticism and the Aesthetics of Individuation* (1992), p. 140.

47 See Richard Hamblyn, *The Invention of Clouds: How an Amateur Meteorologist Forged the Language of the Skies* (2001).

48 Henry Home, Lord Kames, *Elements of Criticism* (Edinburgh, 1762), 3 vols, vol. 1, p. 50.

49 Blair, *Essays on Rhetoric*, p. 54; Burke, *Enquiry*, p. 102.

50 Baldwin, *Airopaidia*, pp. 117–18.

51 Ferguson, *Solitude*, p. 91.

52 B-P.

53 *The Air Balloon, or a Treatise on the Aerostatic Globe, Lately invented by the celebrated Mons. Montgolfier of Paris*, 3rd edn (1783), p. 21.

54 An Aerial Traveller, *The Aerostatic Spy*, vol. 2, p. 75.

55 Baldwin, *Airopaidia*, p. 172.

56 Ibid., p. 38.

57 Alexander Pope, *Windsor-Forest* (1713), lines 13–16.

58 Simon Morley, ed., *The Contemporary Sublime* (Cambridge MA, 2010), p. 1.

59 Paula Amad, 'From God's-eye to Camera-eye: Aerial Photography's Post-humanist and Neo-humanist Visions of the World', *History of Photography*, vol. 36, no. 1 (2012), pp. 66–86, here quoting Donna Haraway, 'The Persistence of Vision', in *The Visual Culture Reader*, ed. Nicholas Mirzoeff (2001), pp. 191–8.

60 Amad, 'From God's-eye', p. 67.

61 *The Aerial Voyager*.

62 Sam Smiles, *Flight and the Artistic Imagination* (Compton Verney, 2012); 'Views from Above' exhibition, Centre Pompidou-Metz, 17 May to 7 October 2013.

63 http://www.youtube.com/watch?v=GJVEtXDVUBk.

64 http://www.centrepompidou-metz.fr/en/views-above#onglet-0.

[65] Smiles, *Flight and the Artistic Imagination* press release.

[66] Alex G. MacLean, referring to 'Views from Above' exhibition: http://www.alexmaclean.com/exhibitions/ArtCetera_tumblr/.

[67] http://www.centrepompidou-metz.fr/en/views-above#onglet-1.

[68] Robert Wohl, *A Passion for Wings: Aviation and the Western Imagination, 1908–1918* (New Haven, 1994); Robert Wohl, *The Spectacle of Flight: Aviation and the Western Imagination 1920–1950* (New Haven, 2005); Smiles, *Flight and the Artistic Imagination*.

[69] Amad, 'From God's-eye', p. 85.

[70] See http://www.yannarthusbertrand.org/ for examples.

[71] Henry James, 'The Figure in the Carpet' (1916), p. 10.

[72] Ibid., p. 16.

Chapter 11: AERONATIONALISM

[1] *Universal Magazine*, 1785, p. 151.

[2] Douglas Bradburn, 'Nation, Nationhood, and Nationalism', *Oxford Bibliographies*, http://www.oxfordbibliographies.com/view/document/obo-9780199730414/obo-9780199730414–0070.xml.

[3] Hart, *The Dream of Flight*, p. 21. The three regions were warm lower; cool middle; hot upper.

[4] Cavallo, *History of Aerostation*, p. 3.

[5] W. H. Boulton, *The Pageant of Transport through the Ages* (n.d.), p. 209.

[6] See the definitive study by Svante Stubelius, *Balloon, Flying-Machine, Helicopter: Further Studies in the History of Terms for Aircraft in English*, Goteborgs Universitets Årsskrift (Goteborg, 1960), vol. 66, pp. 104–40.

[7] The BBC's use of a balloon to animate its customary logo of a global map is discussed in the final chapter.

[8] B-P. See Francis Olivari, *The Balloons of Citizen Campenas, or Aerial Castles Realized* (Dublin, 1798).

[9] David Edgerton, *The Shock of the Old: Technology and Global History since 1900* (2006), p. 103.

[10] 'An Account of the Aerostatical Ball…', *London Magazine*, September 1783, p. 260.

[11] Ibid.

[12] *Benjamin Franklin on Balloons*, ed. W. K. Bixby (St Louis, 1922), n.p.

[13] *Universal Magazine*, March 1784, p. 153.

[14] Ibid.

[15] *London Magazine*, December 1783.

[16] *St James's Chronicle*, 20 January 1784; 20 May 1784.

[17] *St James's Chronicle*, 4 May 1784.

[18] H. E., *London Magazine*, April 1784, pp. 301–2.

[19] *London Magazine*, June 1784, p. 450.

[20] *London Magazine*, December 1783.

[21] *St James's Chronicle*, 23 September 1783.

[22] *St James's Chronicle*, 15 March 1783; 29 April 1783.

[23] *St James's Chronicle*, 15 March 1783.

[24] *St James's Chronicle*, 13 March 1784. The Vauxhall Royal Balloon of 1836 was patriotically red and white too. However, M. Charles and Robert ascended in a red and straw coloured balloon in 1784.

[25] *London Magazine*, October 1784, pp. 312–13.

[26] James A. Williamson, *The English Channel: A History* (1961), p. 290.

[27] *St James's Chronicle*, 20 September 1783, on the precautions to reduce alarm in peasants on the occasion of the hydrogen balloon which landed at Gonesse on 27 August 1783.

[28] *St James's Chronicle*, 11 September 1783; letter from Paris, 4 September 1783.

29 'Extract of a Letter from Dover', *St James's Chronicle*, 2 December 1783.

30 *Caledonian Mercury*, 4 October 1784.

31 Lunardi, *First Aerial Voyage*, p. 48.

32 Advertisement. The drawings were to be designed by Philippe Loutherbourg, a friend of Garrick's. Bell's edition was published, in twenty volumes, from 1785 to 1788.

33 Lunardi, *First Aerial Voyage*, p. 52.

34 Ibid., pp. 2, 9, 18, 19, 23, 37, 41.

35 Lunardi, *Five Aerial Voyages*, pp. 1–2.

36 Freedgood, *Victorian Writing about Risk*.

37 *WLA*, 25 August 1785.

38 *WLA*, 23 September 1784.

39 'Epistle to Mr Lunardi', *Universal Magazine*, October 1784.

40 Pilon, *Aerostation*, p. 31.

41 Ibid., p. 19.

42 Spadafora, *Progress*, p. 60: there were 477 in the 1780s, compared to 294 in the 1770s, and on a diminishing scale back to the 1750s, when only 56 patents were granted.

43 Edward Topham, Epilogue to *Deception* (1784).

44 Gillispie, *Montgolfier Brothers*, p. 36.

45 *Gentleman's Magazine*, 1782, vol. 52, p. 124.

46 Quoted in *The Romance of Ballooning: The Story of the Early Aeronauts* (New York, 1971), p. 23 (both quotations).

47 Gillispie, *Montgolfier Brothers*, p. 87.

48 Attributed to B. A. Dunker in *The Aeronauts*, The Epic of Flight 4, ed. Donald Dale Jackson (Alexandria VA, 1981), p. 27. The whimsical, delicately-coloured drawing is reproduced on p. 26.

49 Willem Bilderdijk, *A Short Account of a Remarkable Aerial Voyage and Discovery of a New Planet* (1813; reprinted Paisley, Scotland, 1987).

Chapter 12: WAR

1 Timothy Garton Ash, 'Why Britain is in Europe', *Twentieth Century British History*, vol. 17, no. 4 (2006), pp. 451–63.

2 N. A. M. Rodger, 'Sea-Power and Empire, 1688–1793', *The Oxford History of the British Empire*, vol. 2, ed. P. J. Marshall (Oxford, 1998), pp. 169–83.

3 Kathleen Wilson, *The Island Race: Englishness, Empire and Gender in the Eighteenth Century* (2003), p. 55.

4 On the long history of *Robinson Crusoe* and its metamorphoses, see Nicholas Rogers, 'Lost in translation? Tracking Robinson Crusoe through the long eighteenth century' (forthcoming).

5 Garton Ash, 'Why Britain is in Europe', p. 451.

6 Winston Churchill, *A History of the English-Speaking Peoples* (1956–58), 4 vols; a shortened version, *The Island Race*, was published in 1964.

7 Jacques Necker, *Memoirs*, serialised in *Universal Magazine*, October 1785, p. 180.

8 John Aikin, *England Delineated* (1788), p. 247; R[ichard] Watson, *Chemical Essays*, 2nd edn (1782), 4 vols, vol. 4, Preface, n.p.

9 On the social complexity of naval power and its patchy relation to patriotism, see Nicholas Rogers, *The Press Gang: Naval Impressment and its opponents in Georgian Britain* (2007), especially ch. 2.

10 *Universal Magazine*, May 1784, p. 225.

11 Ayala, quoted in Peter Bond, *300 Years of British Gibraltar 1704–2004* (n.p., 2003), p. 18.

12 Honoré Gabriel Riqueti, Comte de Mirabeau, *Mirabeau's Letters, During his Residence in England; with Anecdotes, Maxims &c* (1832), 2 vols, vol. 2, pp. 228–9.

13 Bond, *Gibraltar*, p. 29; James Falkner, 'Eliott', DNB.

[14] *WLA*, 23 January 1783.

[15] Captain John Drinkwater, 'A History of the Late Siege of Gibraltar', *Universal Magazine*, December 1785, pp. 346–9.

[16] DNB.

[17] *The Universal Magazine of Knowledge and Pleasure*, vol. 72 [1783], p. 380.

[18] *Universal Magazine*, September 1783, p. 161.

[19] *Harlequin Junior, or The Magic Cestus* [1784]. See also Frederick Pilon's musical farce, *The Siege of Gibraltar* (1780).

[20] *British Magazine*, vol. 2, 1783, p. 64.

[21] Joseph Wright, *View of Gibraltar during the destruction of the Spanish Floating Batteries, 13 September 1782* (1783–85). Oil on canvas, 152.5cm × 259cm. Kingston, Ontario: Agnes Etherington Art Centre. See John Bonehill, 'Laying Siege to the Royal Academy: Wright of Derby's *View of Gibraltar* at Robins's Rooms, Covent Garden, April 1785', *Art History*, vol. 30, no. 4 (2007), pp. 521–44.

[22] William Hayley, *Ode to Mr Wright of Derby* (Chichester, 1783), p. 9.

[23] *Universal Magazine*, June 1783, p. 402.

[24] Gillispie, *Montgolfier Brothers*, p. 16.

[25] Ibid.

[26] M. Dorothy George, *Catalogue of Political and Personal Satires Preserved in the Department of Prints and Drawings in the British Museum* (1938), 6 vols, vol. 6, p. 44; British Museum No. 643.

[27] George, *Catalogue*, vol. 5, p. 771; British Museum No. 6333.

[28] *St James's Chronicle*, 2 September 1784.

[29] *Annual Register ... for 1784 and 1785* (1785), p. 2.

[30] *St James's Chronicle*, 2 October 1784.

[31] *Annual Register ... for 1784 and 1785* (1785), p. 34.

[32] Ibid., pp. 39–40.

[33] *St James's Chronicle*, 2 September 1784; *Universal Magazine*, November 1785, p. 274. Spadafora, *Progress*, p. 62: 'Steam and balloons, power and speed: these were the quintessential symbols of contemporary technological advance.' In the 1780s, lightness accompanied them.

[34] Brian Lavery, *Empire of the Seas: How the Navy Forged the Modern World* (2009), pp. 139–41 on coppering: 'Production in Cornwall expanded quite moderately from around 30,000 tons a year in the 1770s to 50,000 in the '90s, but the great boom was in the Anglesey mines, for which no records were kept.'

[35] Compared to £262 for wood: N. A. M. Rodger, *The Command of the Ocean: A Naval History of Britain 1649–1815* (2006), p. 375.

[36] Ibid.

[37] From Garrick's pantomime, 'Harlequin's Invasion', in *The Muse's Delight: or, the Songster's Jovial Companion* (1760), p. 67.

[38] *Universal Magazine*, 1784, pp. i–ii.

[39] *Five Curious and Interesting Papers* (Glasgow, 1807) – an extract from Robert Hooke's *Philosophical Collections* [originally 1681]; no. 4 of the papers is 'An Account of the Sieur [*sic*] Bernier's method of Flying in Air.' No. 5 is 'A demonstration of how ... to make a ship, which shall be sustained by the Air and may be moved along either by Sails or Oars.' Hooke thought Francesco de Lana's scheme likeliest.

[40] Watson, *Chemical Essays*, vol. 4, Preface, n.p.

[41] *Universal Magazine*, September 1785, p. 114.

[42] *Universal Magazine*, September 1785, pp. 114–17, and October 1785, Necker continued, p. 179.

[43] *Universal Magazine*, February 1783, p. 72, extracting Algarotti, *Letters Military and Political* (1782).

[44] *St James's Chronicle*, 20 September 1784.

[45] *Universal Magazine*, February 1786.

46 Algarotti, extracted in *Universal Magazine*, February 1783, p. 82.

47 Consider also the enduring usages of 'Battle for the Skies' and 'War at Sea'.

48 Jean-Jacques Rousseau, *Emile, or Education* (1762), trans. Barbara Foxley (1911), Book II.

49 The association continues: an American company, Salamander, founded c. 1998, makes equipment for managing emergency situations, including fire.

50 Jonathan Swift, 'The Description of a Salamander', 1705, from Pliny, *Natural History*, Book X, 67; Book XXIX: 'So, when the war has raised a storm,/ I've seen a snake in human form,/ All stain'd with infamy and vice,/ Leap from the dunghill in a trice,/ Burnish and make a gaudy show,/ Become a general, peer, and beau,/ Till peace has made the sky serene,/ Then shrink into its hole again./ "All this we grant—why then, look yonder,/ Sure that must be a Salamander!"'

51 *European Magazine*, April 1804, p. 267; 'Natural History of the Land Salamander' by the Count de la Cepede. A salamander was also an iron tool for grilling. See http://thehistoricfoodie.wordpress.com/2011/07/27/18th-century-kitchen-tools-salamander%C2%A9/.

52 *Monitory Hints to the Minister, or the Present State of the Nation* (1783), p. 15.

53 *St James's Chronicle*, 6 July 1784.

54 *WLA*, 21 October 1784.

55 See Tobias Smollett, *History of England, from the Revolution to the Death of George the Second* (1785), 5 vols, vol. 3, p. 31.

56 *York Chronicle*, 1 April 1785.

57 *London Magazine*, November 1784, p. 378. In 1782 the Comte de Grasse headed to attack Jamaica, richest of Britain's island possessions; he was defeated by Admiral Rodney.

58 *Annual Register ... for 1784 and 1785*, vol. 27, p. 228.

59 MacNally, *Fashionable Levities*. Epilogue written by Mr Norris with some lines added by MacNally. Zambeccari narrowly survived after a midnight balloon flight in Venice ended in the dark freezing Adriatic. *European Magazine*, 1803, p. 347.

60 Michael Paris, *Winged Warfare: The Literature and Theory of Aerial Warfare in Britain 1859–1917* (Manchester, 1992), pp. 17–18.

61 See Lynn, *Sublime Invention*, pp. 33–58 for a review of utility.

62 See my book, *Eighteenth-Century Letters and British Culture*, pp. 267–80.

63 Horace Walpole to H. S. Conway, 15 October 1784, in Hodgson, *Aeronautics*, p. 202.

64 Hodgson, *Aeronautics*, p. 204.

65 Ibid., p. 203.

66 Though my point is that Darwin brings the sea around balloons, he is also evoking diving bells in terms of balloons: 'The diving castles, roof'd with spheric glass,/ Ribb'd with strong oak, and barr'd with bolts of brass,/ Buoy'd with pure air shall endless tracks pursue.' *The Economy of Vegetation*, I.3.VI, lines 195–9, in Erasmus Darwin, *Cosmologia*, ed. Stuart Harris (Sheffield, 2002), p. 53. Darwin's poem is organised into four cantos, each treating an element: Fire, Earth, Water, Air.

67 Paul de Virilio, *War and Cinema: The Logistics of Perception* (1979).

68 Mirabeau, *Letters*, vol. 1, p. 364.

69 'In this period it was the benefits of innovation, not the dangers, to which commentators pointed,' argues Spadafora, *Progress*, p. 60. He cites Erasmus Darwin in 1799 looking forward; *The Botanic Garden*, 4th edn (1799), 2 vols, vol. 1, n. 31: 'As the specific levity of air is too great for the support of great burthens by balloons, there seems no probable method of flying conveniently but by the power of steam, or some other explosive material, which another half-century may probably discover.'

70 Lynn, *Sublime Invention*, p. 34.

[71] *St James's Chronicle*, 28 September 1785.

Chapter 13: BACK TO EARTH

[1] John Lucas, *The Silken Canopy: A History of the Parachute* (Shrewsbury, 1997), p. 19.
[2] *Caledonian Mercury*, 10 November 1784.
[3] Thomas Martyn, *Hints of Important Uses, to be Derived from Aerostatic Globes* (1784), frontispiece.
[4] Lucas, *Silken Canopy*, p. 18.
[5] *Berwick Museum*, vol. 1, p. 333.
[6] B-P.
[7] *The Times*, 16 July 1785.
[8] *York Chronicle*, 10 June 1785.
[9] *Caledonian Mercury*, 18 October 1784.
[10] *The Times*, 4 June 1785.
[11] Ibid.
[12] Lucas, *Silken Canopy*, pp. 19–20.
[13] *The Times*, 7 September 1785.
[14] Gerhard Vieth, *The Pleasing Preceptor, Or Familiar Instructions in Natural History and Physics, Adapted to the Capacities of Youth* (1800–01), 2 vols, vol. 2, p. 98.
[15] *Political Parachute, A Coalition Experiment*, 8 September 1785, made by William Dent, published by J. Nunn.
[16] *The Weekly Entertainer; or Agreeable and Instructive Repository* (Sherborne [1783]-1819), 59 vols, vol. 6, p. 18.
[17] *York Chronicle*, 14 November 1785.
[18] Thomas Holcroft, *The Choleric Fathers* (1785), p. 34.
[19] *Mémoires Secrets pour Servir a L'Histoire de la République des Lettres en France, depuis M.DCC.LXII jusqu'a Nos Jours; ou Journal D'un Observateur* (1788–89), 36 vols, vol. 34, p. 147, p. 308.
[20] Malcolm Macleod, D.D., *The Key of Knowledge, or Universal Conjuror* [1800?], p. 36.
[21] Olivier Blanc, *Last Letters: Prisons and Prisoners of the French Revolution 1793–1794*, trans. Alan Sheridan (New York, 1989), p. 191.
[22] Ibid.
[23] Ibid., p. 173.
[24] Andrew Merry, *The Last Dying Words of the Eighteenth Century, A Pindarick Ode* (1800), pp. 23–4.
[25] François Xavier Pagès, *Secret History of the French Revolution, from the Convocation of the Notables in 1787 to the first of November 1796* (1797), pp. 361–2.
[26] Lucas, *Silken Canopy*, pp. 22–3.
[27] B-P.
[28] Ibid.
[29] Ibid.
[30] Ibid.
[31] B-P for all quotations.
[32] Ibid.
[33] Ibid.
[34] Ibid.
[35] *The Times*, 20 August 1802.
[36] B-P.
[37] *The Times*, 20 July 1802; B-P.
[38] B-P.
[39] Ibid.
[40] Ibid.
[41] Ibid.

⁴² Ibid.

⁴³ The Jester, No. XV, *The Britannic Magazine* (1793–1807), 12 vols, vol. 10, p. 10.

⁴⁴ *Kirby's Wonderful and Eccentric Museum; or Magazine of Remarkable Characters* (1820), vol. 6, p. 382.

⁴⁵ B-P (both quotations).

⁴⁶ Ibid.; letter from Terra-Firma Man, 1802.

⁴⁷ B-P.

⁴⁸ *The Times*, 9 September 1802.

⁴⁹ B-P.

⁵⁰ Ibid.; also Lucas, *Silken Canopy*, p. 26.

⁵¹ B-P.

⁵² *Universal Magazine*, 23 September 1802.

⁵³ B-P; also Lucas, *Silken Canopy*, p. 26.

⁵⁴ *The Times*, 27 September 1802.

⁵⁵ *The Times*, 22 September 1802 and 26 June 1802.

⁵⁶ [Francis Barrett], *The Magus, or Celestial Intelligencer* (1801); additional information from W. H. Brock, 'Barrett', DNB.

⁵⁷ *The Times*, 13 August 1802 (both quotations).

⁵⁸ *The Times*, 14 August 1802.

⁵⁹ B-P for all quotations.

⁶⁰ Ibid.

⁶¹ Ibid.

⁶² Francis Barrett, *Lives of the Adepts in Alchymical Philosophy* (1814), cited in Brock, 'Barrett', DNB.

Chapter 14: ASCENDING AGAIN

¹ 'Airy-fairy' comes from a fusion of rhymes from Tennyson's *Lilian* (1830), a disturbing poem addressed to a fairy who will not reciprocate a declaration of love, and whom the poet then threatens to crush like a rose-leaf. Eric Partridge in his *Dictionary of Slang and Unconventional English* (1984) asserts that 'airy-fairy' (in the sense of shallow and impractical) was current by the 1920s.

² Arnold E. Grummer, *The Great Balloon Game Book and More Balloon Activities* (Appleton WI, 1987), last chapter passim.

³ Further details at http://www.balloonhq.com/faq/history.html.

⁴ *Life*, 15 September 1947, p. 48.

⁵ http://www.cpsc.gov/cpscpub/prerel/prhtml76/76083.html.

⁶ http://www.nasa.gov/audience/foreducators/5–8/features/F_What_Can_I_Wear.html.

⁷ Grummer, *Great Balloon Game Book*.

⁸ Elizabeth Bishop, *The Armadillo* (1965), in which the dangers of fire balloons are visited upon animals.

⁹ http://www.oxford.gov.uk/PageRender/decEH/Balloon_Releases_occw.htm; http://www.nfuonline.com/about-us/our-offices/east-midlands/latest-news/nfu-steps-up-chinese-lanterns-alert/; http://www.bbac.org/lor/conduct. The British Balloon and Airship Club code of conduct is drawn up in association with the National Farmers' Union.

¹⁰ Tilly Balloon packaging, quoted on http://www.balloonhq.com/faq/history.html.

¹¹ *The Daily Mail*, 26 September 2007.

¹² Owen Gleiberman, 'Hope Floats', *Entertainment Weekly*, 30 November 2007.

¹³ Brian Gibson, 'What childhood films are these?', *Vue Weekly*, no. 634, 12 December 2007.

¹⁴ A remake, *Flight of the Red Balloon* by Hou Hsiao Hsien (2008), makes more of puppetry as metaphor than balloons; to the contemporary little boy, a video game is more enchanting than a red balloon.

[15] http://news.bbc.co.uk/local/bristol/hi/people_and_places/arts_and_culture/ newsid_8505000/8505819.stm, accessed March 2010.

[16] Poets make much of children and balloons: among many, see Rachel Hadas's poem *Balloon; Balloon* and the first stanza of *Moon Song* by Robert Service; the penultimate stanza of Sylvia Plath's *The Disquieting Muses*, and the last line of her *Morning Song*.

[17] Jonathan R. Trappe, http://clusterballoon.com/.

[18] See Douglas W. Druick, *Odilon Redon: Prince of Dreams, 1840–1916* (Chicago, 1994).

[19] On panoramas see Denise Blake Oleksijczuk, *The First Panoramas: Visions of British Imperialism* (Minnesota, 2011).

[20] *Le Boulevard*, 25 May 1863.

[21] Wohl, *A Passion for Wings*, ch. 6, 'Painters Take Flight', pp. 157–200.

[22] Leonid Chirtov, 'Perceptographic Code in Visual Culture', *Sign Systems Studies*, no. 1 (2005), pp. 137–58.

[23] See/hear holkham.blogspot.com, a blog documenting a sound project by Simon Keep recording hot air balloons.

[24] A mosaic of coloured parasols at Xohimilco market in Mexico City; dyers' vats at Fez; a patchwork of carpets at Marrakech: all these and more at www. yannarthusbertrand.org.

[25] *Popular Science*, January 1916, p. 63.

[26] http://staging.unep.org/pdf/Ourplanet/2009/may/en/OP-2009-05-en-AWARDS.pdf.

[27] Philippe Pastor, 'Le Ciel Regarde la Terre' exhibition, 19 July to 18 August 2008, Monaco Modern Art Gallery; http://www.philippe-pastor.com/the-sky-is-watching-the-earth/.

[28] Charlotte Smith, Sonnet LXXVII, Elegiac Sonnets (1784–97), *The Poems of Charlotte Smith*, ed. Stuart Curran (Oxford, 1993), pp. 66–7.

[29] Emily Dickinson, *The Single Hound* (1914), p. 30; see http://www.edickinson. org/editions/6/image_sets/64362.

[30] The balloon is now stored in a museum. The launch set of films (1997) is viewable at https://www.youtube.com/watch?v=VQsSIFoAYUo.

[31] For BBC logo history, see http://www.bbc.co.uk/historyofthebbc/resources/ in-depth/bbc_logo.shtml.

[32] David Hastings, 'Back Down to Earth' (2001), at http://www.transdiffusion. org/emc/ident/history/bbc1.php.

[33] 'Steampunk' exhibition curated by Art Donovan at the Museum of Science, Oxford, 13 October to 21 February 2010; *Broad Sheet*, no. 9.

[34] Elaine Scarry, *The Body in Pain: The Making and Unmaking of the World* (Oxford, 1987), p. 292: 'in this one instance we overtly reveal our recognition that the artefact is a materialisation of perception by the widely shared convention of inserting it back inside a drawing of the human head where it stands for the moment when a problem is reconceived in terms of its solution'.

[35] *Monty Python's Flying Circus*, fourth season, episode 40 (screened 31 October 1974); script via http://www.ibras.dk/montypython/episode40.htm.

[36] 'And now for someone completely different...', Anne Shooter, interview with Carol Chapman, *The Daily Mail*, 14 October 1999.

[37] Bachelard, *Air and Dreams*, p. 112.

[38] This blog was hosted by http://www.d2be.org/arc_up.html: 'Your Time to Soar to New Heights'.

[39] Lloyds TSB, 'For the Journey'; ads designed by RKCR/Y&R, 2008–10.

[40] http://www.uktvadverts.com/facts/?list=ch4.

[41] http://www.dailyscript.com/scripts/AmericanBeauty_final.html – script by Alan Ball, directed by Sam Mendes, DreamWorks 1999.

[42] On airships see my article, '*Aeolus*: Futurism's Flights of Fancy',

Interdisciplinary Science Reviews, vol. 34, no. 1, eds Max Saunders, Brian Hurwitz and Neil Vickers (2009), pp. 79–90.

43 http://www.hardcoregaming101.net/kazenonotam/kazenonotam.html; grateful thanks to Rob Gallagher for this reference.

44 Diane Ackerman, 'Traveling Light', *New York Times*, 11 January 1997.

45 As in 'Relax & Escape', a compilation CD box set issued by Classic FM Records (2004), whose soothing classical music is imaged by a white balloon ascending in a blue sky. My thanks to Chris Brant for this item.

Bibliography

Place of publication is London unless otherwise indicated.

PRIMARY SOURCES

Manuscript Sources

Blagden Papers, Royal Society Archives
British Library, MSS 37925
Burke, Edmund, BL Add MSS 37843, folio 9
Hamilton, Mary, 'A Manuscript' (1784)
Innes, George, Papers of George Innes, National Records of Scotland, GD
    113/4/157; 136
Lunardi to Count Bruhl, 21 April 1784, National Archives of Scotland,
    GD 157/3369/1
Montagu, Elizabeth Robinson, Papers, The Huntington Library, San
    Marino, California, MO 3587, MO 6136, MO 3612
Smeathman, Henry, Papers, Royal Society AP/5/12
Strathmore Papers, Glamis Castle (National Register of Scotland 885),
    vol. C, folio 34

Hybrid Sources

Baden-Powell Collection, National Aerospace Library, Farnham, Surrey
Sarah Sophia Banks Collection, British Library

Printed Sources

Aberdeen Journal (1784)
An Account of the Loss of the 'Royal George' at Spithead, August 1782
    (1842)
An Aerial Dialogue between a Male and a Female Traveller above the Clouds
    (n.d.)
An Aerial Traveller, *The Aerostatic Spy: or, Excursions with an Air Balloon*, 2
    vols (1785)
The Aerial Voyage, a Poem. Inscribed to Richard Crosbie, Esq. (Dublin, 1785)
The Aerial Voyager (Dublin, 1785)
Aeronautica, or Voyages in the Air (1823)

Aerostation Displayed (1802)

Aikin, John, *England Delineated; or, a Geographical Description of Every County in England and Wales: With a Concise Account of its Most Important Products, Natural and Artificial* (1788)

The Air Balloon, or a Treatise on the Aerostatic Globe, Lately invented by the celebrated Mons. Montgolfier of Paris, 3rd edn (1783)

Air-Balloon, or Blanchard's Triumphal Entry into the Etherial World; A Poem (1785)

A Journey Lately Performed Through the Air (Litchfield CT, 1784)

[Alcock, Mary], *The Air Balloon; or, Flying Mortal* (1784)

Algarotti, Francesco, *Letters Military and Political* (1782)

The Annual Register

The Answer of Sir R—d W—y to L—y W—y (1782)

Astley, Philip, *Natural Magic or Physical Amusements Revealed* (1785)

An Asylum for Fugitive Pieces, in Prose and Verse, not in any Other Collection: With Several Pieces Never Before Published, 2 vols (1786)

Bailey, William, *Bailey's British Directory; or, Merchant's and Trader's Useful Companion, for the Year 1784, in four volumes*, 4 vols (1784)

Baldwin, Thomas, *Airopaidia: Containing the Narrative of a Balloon Excursion from Chester, the Eighth of September, 1785* (Chester, 1786)

The Ballooniad, 2nd edn (Birmingham, 1785)

The Balloon Jester or, Flights of Wit and Humour (Dublin, 1784)

Banks, Sir Joseph, *Scientific Correspondence of Sir Joseph Banks, 1765–1820*, ed. Neil Chambers, 6 vols (2007)

Barrett, Francis, *Lives of the Adepts in Alchymical Philosophy* (1814)

[Barrett, Francis], *The Magus, or Celestial Intelligencer* (1801)

Belknap, Jeremiah, 'Letter of Rev. Jeremiah Belknap to Rev. Manasseh Cutler, LL.D., 1785', *The Pennsylvania Magazine of History and Biography*, vol. 37, no. 4 (Philadelphia, 1913), pp. 491–8

Berwick Museum, or Monthly Literary Intelligencer, 3 vols (Berwick, 1785–87)

Bilderdijk, Willem, *A Short Account of a Remarkable Aerial Voyage and Discovery of a New Planet* (1813; reprinted Paisley, Scotland, 1987)

Blair, Hugh, *Essays on Rhetoric, abridged chiefly from Dr Blair's Lectures on that Science* (Dublin, 1784)

—— *Lectures on Rhetoric and Belles Lettres* (Dublin, 1783)

Blake, William, *Complete Poems & Prose*, ed. David V. Erdman (New York, 1997)

Blanchard, Jean-Pierre, *Journal and Certificates on the Fourth Voyage of Mr. Blanchard...* (1784)

—— *Journal of my Forty-fifth Ascension, being the first performed in America, on the Ninth of January, 1793* (Philadelphia, 1793)

Blower, Elizabeth, *Maria, A Novel*, 2 vols (Dublin, 1787)

Boswell, James, *Boswell's Life of Johnson, Together with Boswell's Journal of a Tour to the Hebrides and Johnson's Diary of a Journey into North Wales*, ed. George Birkbeck Hill, rev. L. F. Powell, 6 vols (Oxford, 1934–50)

Boyer, Abel, *Anglo-French Dictionary* (1780)

Bristol Courant

The Britannic Magazine, or Entertaining Repository of Heroic Adventures, 12 vols (1793–1807)

British Magazine and Review; or, Universal Miscellany, 3 vols (1782–83)

Burgh, James, *The Art of Speaking* (Dublin, 1784)

Burke, Edmund, *A Philosophical Enquiry into the Origin of Our Ideas of the Sublime and Beautiful* (1757)

Caledonian Mercury (Edinburgh, 1784–86)

Campbell, George, *Poems, on Several Occasions* (Kilmarnock, 1787)

Cavallo, Tiberius, *The History and Practice of Aerostation* (1785)

Cave, Jane, *Poems on Various Subjects, Entertaining, Elegiac and Religious* (Bristol, 1786)

Clark, John, *Observations on Fevers* (1780)

Coleridge, Samuel Taylor, *Sibylline Leaves* (1817)

'Confucius the Sage', *The Oriental Chronicle of the Times: Being the Translation of a Chinese MS...* (1785)

Cowper, William, *The Letters and Prose Writings of William Cowper*, eds James King and Charles Ryskamp, 5 vols (Oxford, 1979–86)

Darwin, Erasmus, *The Botanic Garden, a Poem*, 4th edn, 2 vols (1799)

—— *Cosmologia*, ed. Stuart Harris (Sheffield, 2002)

The Delineator (1784)

Edinburgh Courant

Edinburgh Magazine

An Epistle from L—y W—y to Sir R—d W—y (1782)

The European Magazine, and London Review: Containing the Literature, History, Politics, Arts, Manners and Amusements of the Age. By the Philological Society of London, 40 vols ([1782]-1826)

The European Review and London Magazine (1785)

Felix Farley's Bristol Journal (Bristol, 1785)

Féraud, Jean-François, *Dictionnaire Critique de la Langue Française* (Marseille, 1787–88)

Figaro, *The Novelties of a Year and a Day, in a Series of Picturesque Letters...* [1785?]

Fisher, James, *Poems on Various Subjects*, 2nd edn (Dumfries, 1792)

Five Curious and Interesting Papers (Glasgow, 1807)

The Florence Miscellany (Florence, 1785)

Franklin, Benjamin, *Benjamin Franklin on Balloons*, ed. W. K. Bixby (St Louis, 1922)

Frewen, Thomas, *Physiologia: or, the Doctrine of Nature, Comprehended in the Origin and Progression of Human Life; the Vital and Animal Functions; Diseases of Body and Mind; and Remedies Prophylactic and Therapeutic* (1780)

Gay, John, *Trivia, or the Art of Walking the Streets of London* (1716)

Gazetteer and New Daily Advertiser

The General Evening Post

The Gentleman's Magazine (1781–86)

The Glasgow Herald

Goethe, Johann Wolfgang von, *Aus Meinem Leben, Dichtung und Wahreit*, 4 vols (1811–33)

Gove's General Advertiser

Half Hours in Air and Sky (1899)

An Heroic Epistle (1780)

An History of the Instances of Exclusion from the Royal Society, which were not suffered to be argued in the course of the late debates. By some members in the minority, 2nd edn (1784)

Gerard, Alexander, *An Essay on Taste* (1759)

Gilpin, William, *Observations on the River Wye, and Several parts of South Wales, &c. relative chiefly to picturesque beauty; made in the summer of the year 1770* (1782)

—— *Three Essays: on picturesque beauty; on picturesque travel; and on sketching landscape...* (1792)

Goodwin, William, of Street Farm, Earl Soham, diary, 27 June 1785; transcribed by Mrs J. Rothery of Soham (2001)

Griffiths, William, *A Practical Treatise on Farriery* (1784)

Harlequin Junior, or The Magic Cestus [1784]

['Hawkins, Sir John'], *Probationary Odes for the Laureatship* ([Oxford?] 1785)

Hayley, William, *Ode to Mr Wright of Derby* (Chichester, 1783)

Hibernian Magazine

Holcroft, Thomas, *The Choleric Fathers* (1785)

Hoyle, John, *Dictionaria Musica* (1770)

Inchbald, Elizabeth, *The Mogul Tale, or, The Descent of the Balloon* (1788)

Jackson's Oxford Journal

James, Henry, 'The Figure in the Carpet' (1916)

Jeffries, John, *A Narrative of the Two Aerial Voyages of Doctor Jeffries with Mons. Blanchard; with Meteorological Observations and Remarks* (1786)

Johnson, Samuel, *The Rambler*, 6 vols (1752)

[Johnstone, Charles], *The Adventures of Anthony Varnish; or, a Peep at the Manners of Society* (1786)

Kames, Henry Home, Lord, *Elements of Criticism*, 3 vols (Edinburgh, 1762)

Keane, George, 'Prologue to *Cymbeline*' (1786)

Kearsley, George, *Tax Tables for 1784* (1784)

Kippis, Andrew, *Observations on the Late Contests in the Royal Society* (1784)

Kirby's Wonderful and Eccentric Museum; or, Magazine of Remarkable Characters, 6 vols (1820)

Knipe, Eliza, *Poems on Various Subjects* (Manchester, 1783)

Ladies' Own Memorandum-Book; or, Daily Pocket Journal, for the Year 1786 [1785]

The Lady's Balloon, or Female Aerial Traveller (1785)

The Lady's Magazine, or Entertaining Companion for the Fair Sex (1783)

Lamorisse, Albert, *The Red Balloon* (1957)

Leigh, James Henry, *The New Rosciad, in the Manner of Churchill: Containing a Judicious, Humourous* [sic] *and Critical Description of our Present Dramatic Characters* (1785)

Lennox, Lord William, *Percy Hamilton, or The Adventures of a Westminster Boy*, 3 vols (1851)

Life on the Moon in 1768: Ten Fantasy Engravings of the 18th Century by Filippo Morghen, introd. Brian W. Aldiss (Hythe, 1990)

Linley, Thomas, *The Spanish Rivals: A Musical Farce* (1784)

London Chronicle

London Debating Societies 1776–1799, ed. Donna T. Andrew (1994)

London Magazine

The Lounger, 3rd edn, 3 vols (1787)

Lunardi, Vincent, *An Account of the First Aerial Voyage in England, in a Series of Letters to his Guardian Chevalier Gherardo Compagni. Written under the Impression of the various Events that affected the Undertaking* (1784)

—— *An Account of Five Aerial Voyages in Scotland* (Edinburgh, 1786)

—— *Mr Lunardi's Account of his Ascension and Aerial Voyage from the New Fort, Liverpool, on Wednesday the 20th of July, 1785, in Three Letters, addressed to George Biggin, Esq.* ([London?] 1785)

—— *Mr. Lunardi's Account of his Second Aerial Voyage on Tuesday 9th August 1785* ([London?] 1785)

The Lunardiad, or, The Folly and Madness of the Age (1784)

Mackay, Charles, *Memoirs of Extraordinary Popular Delusions and the Madness of Crowds,* 3 vols (1841)

Macleod, D. D., Malcolm, *The Key of Knowledge, or Universal Conjuror* [1800?]

MacNally, Leonard, *Fashionable Levities, A Comedy in Five Acts* (Dublin, 1786)

MacSweeny, Joseph, *An Essay on Aerial Navigation* (1845)

Man in the Moon, The, *London Unmask'd: Or the New Town Spy* [1784?]

Mandeville, Bernard, *The Fable of the Bees* (1716)

Martyn, Thomas, *Hints of Important Uses, to be Derived from Aerostatic Globes* (1784)

Mason, Francis K., and Martin C. Windrow, *Air Facts and Feats: A Record of Aerospace Achievements* (1970)

Mason, Monck, *Aeronautica; or Sketches Illustrative of the Theory and Practice of Aerostation: Comprising an Enlarged Account of the late Aerial Expedition to Germany* (1838)

Mathias, Thomas, *An Heroic Epistle to the Rev. Richard Watson…* (1780)

Mémoires Secrets pour Servir a L'Histoire de la République des Lettres en France, depuis M.DCC.LXII jusqu'a Nos Jours; ou Journal D'un Observateur, 36 vols (1788–89)

Mercier, Louis-Sébastien, *Memoirs of the Year Two Thousand Five Hundred* [sic] (New York, 1974)

—— *The Nightcap,* 2 vols [1785]

—— *The Waiting City. Paris, 1782–88,* trans. and ed. Helen Simpson (New York, 1933)

Merry, Andrew, *The Last Dying Words of the Eighteenth Century, A Pindarick Ode* (1800)

Mirabeau, Honoré Gabriel Riqueti, Comte de, *Mirabeau's Letters, During his Residence in England; with Anecdotes, Maxims &c.,* 2 vols (1832)

The Modern Atalantis; or, the Devil in an Air Balloon (1784)

Modern Manners: In a Series of Familiar Epistles (1781)

Monitory Hints to the Minister, or the Present State of the Nation (1783)

Morning Chronicle

Morning Herald and Daily Advertiser (1784–85)

Morning Post and Daily Advertiser (1784–85)

The Muse's Delight: or, the Songster's Jovial Companion (1760)

The New Annual Register, or General Repository of History, Politics, and Literature (1782–87)

The Newcastle Magazine: or, Monthly Journal (Newcastle, 1785)

New London Magazine (1785)

O'Keeffe, John, *Fontainbleau, or, Our Way in France* (Dublin, 1785)

Olivari, Francis, *The Balloons of Citizen Campenas, or Aerial Castles Realized* (Dublin, 1798)

Oppian, *Halieuticks, or the Nature of Fishes*, trans. John Jones (Oxford, 1722)

Pagès, François Xavier, *Secret History of the French Revolution, from the Convocation of the Notables in 1787 to the first of November 1796* (1797)

Paltock, Robert, *The Life and Adventures of Peter Wilkins* (1751)

Parker's General Advertiser and Morning Intelligencer (1782–84)

Pilon, Frederick, *Aerostation; or, The Templar's Stratagem. A Farce* (1785)

—— *The Siege of Gibraltar: A Musical Farce, in Two Acts* (1780)

Pinetti, Giuseppe, *Physical Amusements and Diverting Experiments* (1784)

Pope, Alexander, *Windsor-Forest* (1713)

Price, Uvedale, *An Essay on the Picturesque, as Compared with the Sublime and the Beautiful* (1794)

Public Advertiser

Pye, Henry James, *Poems on Various Subjects*, 2 vols (1787)

[Rigby, Edward], *An Account of Mr. James Deeker's Two Aerial Expeditions from the City of Norwich* (Norwich, 1785)

Robinson, Mary Darby, *Memoirs of Mary Robinson*, ed. J. Fitzgerald Molloy (Philadelphia, 1895)

Rousseau, Jean-Jacques, *Emile, or Education* (1762), trans. Barbara Foxley (1911)

Sage, Mrs. [Laetitia], *A Letter Addressed to a Female Friend. By Mrs. Sage, The First English Female Aerial Traveller* (1785)

St James's Chronicle

Scrapbook of Early Aeronautica [assembled by William Upcott], 3 vols (n.d.)

Ségur, Louis Philippe Comte de, *Memoirs of Louis Philippe Comte de Ségur*, ed. Eveline Cruickshanks (1960)

The Selector (1783–84)

Smith, Charlotte, *The Poems of Charlotte Smith*, ed. Stuart Curran (Oxford, 1993)

Smollett, Tobias, *The History of England, from the Revolution to the Death of George the Second*, 5 vols (1785)

Symposia, or Table Talk in the Month of September 1784 (1784)

The Times

Topham, Edward, Epilogue to *Deception* (play of unknown authorship, 1784)

Town and Country Magazine (1784)

Townley, Richard, *A Journal Kept in the Isle of Man, giving an Account of the Wind, Weather and Daily Occurrences*, 2 vols (Whitehaven, 1791)

The Trial with the Whole of the Evidence, between the Right Hon. Sir Richard Worsley, Bart ... and George Maurice Bisset, esq., 7th edn (1782)

The Trifler, No. IV' (1785)

T. T. Hook-Norton, Oxfordshire [*sic*], *A Description of the Fire and Air Balloon: With a Spiritual Use of them Both* (Banbury [1785?])

Universal Magazine

The Universal Magazine of Knowledge and Pleasure, vol. 72 [1783]

Vieth, Gerhard Ulrich Anthony, *The Pleasing Preceptor, Or Familiar Instructions in Natural History and Physics, Adapted to the Capacities of Youth*, 2 vols (1800–01)

[Villiers, George], *Flights of Fancy* (n.d.)

Walpole, Horace, *The Correspondence of Horace Walpole*, ed. W. S. Lewis, 48 vols (New Haven, 1937–83)

Watson, Richard, *Chemical Essays*, 2nd edn, 4 vols (1782)

The Weekly Entertainer; or Agreeable and Instructive Repository, 59 vols (Sherborne [1783]-1819)

White, Gilbert, *The Natural History and Antiquities of Selbourne, in the County of Southampton, with Engravings and an Appendix* (1789)

Whitehall Evening Post

[Whyte, Samuel], *To Richard Crosbie Esq. on his attempting a Second Aerial Excursion, in which he proved unsuccessful* (Dublin, 1785)

Williamson's Liverpool Advertiser

Windham, William, *The Diary of the Right Honourable William Windham, 1784–1810*, ed. Cecilia Anne Baring (1866)

York Chronicle

York Courant

Young, Edward, *The Complaint, or Night Thoughts on Life, Death and Immortality* (1742–45)

SECONDARY SOURCES

Ackerman, Diane, 'Traveling Light', *New York Times* (11 January 1997)

Amad, Paula, 'From God's-eye to Camera-eye: Aerial Photography's Post-humanist and Neo-humanist Visions of the World', *History of Photography*, vol. 36, no. 1 (2012), pp. 66–86

Anderson, Benedict, *Imagined Communities: Reflections on the Origin and Spread of Nationalism* (1983)

Andrew, Donna T., ed., 'London debates: 1784', *London Debating Societies 1776–1799* (1994); http://www.british-history.ac.uk/source.aspx?pubid=238

Ashfield, Andrew, and Peter de Bolla, *The Sublime: A Reader in British Aesthetic Theory* (Cambridge, 1996)

Auckland, R. G., and Keith B. Moore, *Messages from the Sky Over Britain: The Fascinating Story of the Publicity and Propaganda Leaflets*

Disseminated Over Great Britain by Airship, Aeroplane, Balloon and Rocket, in Peacetime and in War (Leeds, 1998)

Bachelard, Gaston, *Air and Dreams: An Essay on the Imagination of Movement* (1943), trans. Edith R. Farrell and C. Frederick Farrell (Dallas, 2002)

Baecque, Antoine de, *The Body Politic: Corporeal Metaphor in Revolutionary France, 1770–1800*, trans. Charlotte Mednell (Stanford, 1997)

Baldick, Robert, *The Duel: A History of Duelling* (1970)

Baron, John, *The Life of Edward Jenner, with Illustrations of His Doctrines...*, 2 vols (1827)

'Barrington, George (1755–1804)', *Australian Dictionary of Biography*, National Centre of Biography, Australian National University, http://adb.anu.edu.au/biography/barrington-george-1746/text1935

Barry, Jonathan, Marianne Hester and Gareth Roberts, eds, *Witchcraft in Early Modern Europe: Studies in Culture and Belief* (Cambridge, 1996)

Barthes, Roland, *Mythologies*, trans. Annette Lavers (New York, 1982)

Benjamin, Marina, *Rocket Dreams: How the Space Age shaped our vision of a World Beyond* (2003)

Bernier, Olivier, *The World in 1800* (New York, 2000)

Bindman, Catherine, 'Odilon Redon: Prince of Dreams, 1840–1916', *Art in Print*, http://artinprint.org/index.php/exhibitions/article/odilon_redon_prince_of_dreams_1840_19161

Blanc, Olivier, *Last Letters: Prisons and Prisoners of the French Revolution 1793–1794*, trans. Alan Sheridan (New York, 1989)

Bloom, Harold, 'The Knight in the Mirror', *The Guardian* (13 December 2003)

Bond, Peter, *300 Years of British Gibraltar 1704–2004* (n.p., 2003)

Bonehill, John, 'Laying Siege to the Royal Academy: Wright of Derby's *View of Gibraltar* at Robins's Rooms, Covent Garden, April 1785', *Art History*, vol. 30, no. 4 (2007), pp. 521–44

Le Boulevard (25 May 1863)

Boulton, W. H., *The Pageant of Transport through the Ages* (n.d.)

Bourdieu, Pierre, *Practical Reason: On the Theory of Action* (Cambridge, 1998)

Bradburn, Douglas, 'Nation, Nationhood, and Nationalism', *Oxford Bibliographies*, http://www.oxfordbibliographies.com/view/document/obo-9780199730414/obo-9780199730414–0070.xml

Brant, Clare, '*Aeolus*: Futurism's Flights of Fancy', *Interdisciplinary Science Reviews*, vol. 34, no. 1, eds Max Saunders, Brian Hurwitz and Neil Vickers (2009), pp. 79–90

—— *Eighteenth-Century Letters and British Culture* (Basingstoke, 2006)

—— '"I will carry you with me on the wings of immagination": Aerial Letters and Eighteenth-Century Ballooning', *Eighteenth-Century Life*, vol. 35, no. 1 (2011), pp. 168–79

—— 'Philosophical Playthings? Balloons and the Play of Ideas', *Sich selbst aufs Spiel setzen. Spiel als Technik und Medium von Subjektivierung*, eds Christian Moser and Regine Strätling (Munich, 2016), pp. 327–46

—— 'The Progress of Knowledge in the Regions of Air? Divisions and Disciplines in early ballooning', *Eighteenth-Century Studies*, vol. 45, no. 1 (2011), pp. 77–86

Brooke, Richard, *Liverpool as it was during the Last Quarter of the Eighteenth Century* (Liverpool, 1853)

Buchwald, Jed Z., 'Egyptian Stars under Paris Skies', *Science and Engineering*, no. 4 (2003), pp. 21–31

Canetti, Elias, *Crowds and Power* (1962)

Carroll, Siobhan, *An Empire of Air and Water: Uncolonizable Space in the British Imagination, 1750–1850* (Philadelphia, 2015)

Chamberlain, Geoffrey, *Airships – Cardington* (Lavenham, 1984)

Chirtov, Leonid, 'Perceptographic Code in Visual Culture', *Sign Systems Studies*, no. 1 (2005), pp. 137–58

Churchill, Winston, *A History of the English-Speaking Peoples*, 4 vols (1956–58)

Claeys, Gregory, ed., *Modern British Utopias, 1700–1850*, 8 vols (1997)

Clarke, I. F., *The Pattern of Expectation 1644–2001* (1979)

Colley, Linda, 'The Apotheosis of George III: Loyalty, Royalty and the British Nation 1760–1820', *Past & Present*, no. 102 (1984), pp. 94–129

Cosgrove, Denis, and William L. Fox, *Photography and Flight* (2010)

Crouch, Tom D., *The Eagle Aloft: Two Centuries of the Balloon in america* (Washington DC, 1983)

Cunnington, C. Willett, and Phyllis Cunnington, *Handbook of English Costume in the Eighteenth Century* (1957; rev. 1972)

Darcy, Jane, *Melancholy and Literary Biography, 1640–1816* (Basingstoke, 2013)

Darnton, Robert, *Mesmerism and the End of Enlightenment in France* (Cambridge MA, 1968)

Davies, Mark, *King of All Balloons: The Adventurous Life of James Sadler, The First English Aeronaut* (Stroud, 2015)

Deane, C.A., Submarine Researches on the Wrecks of His Majesty's Late Ships Royal George, Boyne and OthersDeane, C. A., *Submarine Researches on the Wrecks of His Majesty's Late Ships Royal George, Boyne and Others* (1836; reprinted 2001)

Deploige, Jeroen, and Gita Deneckere, eds, *Mystifying the Monarch* (Amsterdam, 2006)

Dickinson, Emily, *The Single Hound: Poems of a Lifetime* (Boston, 1914)

Donovan, Art, *Broad Sheet*, no. 9, 'Steampunk' exhibition curated by Art Donovan at the Museum of Science, Oxford (13 October to 21 February 2010)

Dorrian, Mark, and Frédéric Pousin, *Seeing From Above: The Aerial View in Visual Culture* (2013)

Druick, Douglas W., *Odilon Redon: Prince of Dreams, 1840–1916* (Chicago, 1994)

Edgerton, David, *The Shock of the Old: Technology and Global History since 1900* (2006)

Evans, R. J. W., and Alexander Marr, eds, *Curiosity and Wonder from the Renaissance to the Enlightenment* (Aldershot, 2006)

Fara, Patricia, *An Entertainment for Angels: Electricity in the Enlightenment* (Cambridge, 2002)

Farquharson, Donald Robert, *Tales and Memories of Cromar and Canada* (Chatham, Ontario [1851?])

Felski, Rita, 'Context Stinks!', *New Literary History*, vol. 42, no. 4 (2011), pp. 573–91

Ferguson, Frances, *Solitude and the Sublime: Romanticism and the Aesthetics of Individuation* (1992)

Ferguson, Priscilla Parkhurst, *Paris as Revolution: Writing the Nineteenth-Century City* (Berkeley CA, 1994)

Fergusson, Sir James of Kilkerran, *Balloon Tytler* (1972)

Foreman, Amanda, *Georgiana, Duchess of Devonshire* (1998)

France, Peter, *The Oxford Guide to Literature in Translation* (Oxford, 2001)

Franck, Walter, 'Tentative de vol: forms définitives d'une économie esthétique de l'aerien', *Exposé*, no. 2 (1995), pp. 45–61

Freedgood, Elaine, *Victorian Writing about Risk: Imagining a Safe England in a Dangerous World* (Cambridge, 2000)

Friends of the United States Air Force Academy Library, *The Genesis of Flight: The Aeronautical History Collection of Colonel Ralph Gimbel* (Los Angeles, 2000)

Fry, Stephen, *The Ode Less Travelled: Unlocking the Poet Within* (2007)

Gamer, Michael, and Terry F. Robinson, 'Mary Robinson and the Art of the Dramatic Comeback', *Studies in Romanticism*, vol. 48, no. 2 (2009), pp. 219–56

Gardiner, Leslie, *Lunardi: The Story of Vincenzo Lunardi* (Shrewsbury, 1984)

Garton Ash, Timothy, 'Why Britain is in Europe', *Twentieth Century British History*, vol. 17, no. 4 (2006), pp. 451–63

Garvey, Nathan, *The Celebrated George Barrington: A Spurious Author; The Book Trade, and Botany Bay* (Sydney, 2008)

Gattrell, Vic, *City of Laughter: Sex and Satire in Eighteenth-Century London* (2006)

George, M. Dorothy, *Catalogue of Political and Personal Satires Preserved in the Department of Prints and Drawings in the British Museum*, 6 vols (1938)

Gibbs-Smith, C. H., *Ballooning* (1948)

Gibson, Brian, 'What childhood films are these?', *Vue Weekly*, no. 634 (12 December 2007)

Gillispie, Charles Coulston, *The Montgolfier Brothers and the Invention of Aviation 1783–1784* (Princeton NJ, 1983)

Gleiberman, Owen, 'Hope Floats', *Entertainment Weekly* (30 November 2007)

Golden, James L., and Edward P. J. Corbett, *The Rhetoric of Blair, Campbell, and Whately: With Updated Bibliographies* (Carbondale and Edwardsville, 1990)

Golinski, Jan, *Making Natural Knowledge: Constructivism and the History of Science* (Chicago, 2005)

—— *Science as Public Culture: Chemistry and Enlightenment in Britain, 1780–1820* (Cambridge, 1992)

Greig, Hannah, *The Beau Monde: Fashionable Society in Georgian London* (Oxford, 2013)

—— 'Leading the fashion: The material culture of London's beau monde', *Gender, Taste, and Material Culture in Britain & North America, 1700–1830*, eds Amanda Vickery and John Styles (New Haven, 2006), pp. 293–310

Grummer, Arnold E., *The Great Balloon Game Book and More Balloon Activities* (Appleton, WI, 1987)

Haffner, Jeanne, *The View from Above: The Science of Social Space* (Cambridge MA, 2013)

Haggerty, Sarah, *Blake's Gifts: Poetry and the Politics of Exchange* (Cambridge, 2010)

Haining, Peter, ed., *The Dream Machines: An Eye-Witness History of Ballooning* (1972)

Hallion, Richard P., *Taking Flight: Inventing the Aerial Age from Antiquity to the First World War* (Oxford, 2003)

Hamblyn, Richard, *The Invention of Clouds: How an Amateur Meteorologist Forged the Language of the Skies* (2001)

Harrison, Mark, *Crowds and History: Mass Phenomena in English Towns, 1790–1835* (Cambridge, 2002)

Hart, Clive, *The Dream of Flight: Aeronautics from Classical Times to the Renaissance* (1972)

—— *The Prehistory of Flight* (Berkeley CA, 1985)

Hawes, Clement, *Mania and Literary Style: The Rhetoric of Enthusiasm from the Ranters to Christopher Smart* (Cambridge, 1996)

Haywood, Ian, and J. Seed, eds, *The Gordon Riots: Politics, Culture and Insurrection in Late Eighteenth-century Britain* (Cambridge, 2012)

Hendy, David, *Noise: A Human History of Sound and Listening* (2013)

Hildenbrandt, A., *Balloons and Airships* (1973)

Hodgson, J. E., *The History of Aeronautics in Great Britain* (Oxford, 1924)

Holmes, Richard, *The Age of Wonder: How the Romantic Generation Discovered the Beauty and Terror of Science* (2008)

—— *Falling Upwards: How We Took to the Air* (2013)

Hornak, Angelo, *Balloon over Britain* (1991)

Jackson, Donald Dale, ed., *The Aeronauts*, The Epic of Flight 4 (Alexandria VA, 1981)

Jay, Mike, *The Atmosphere of Heaven: The Unnatural Experiments of Dr Beddoes and his Sons of Genius* (New Haven, 2009)

Johnson, Steven, *The Invention of Air* (2009)

Jungnickel, Christa, and Russell McCormmach, *Cavendish: The Experimental Life* (1999)

Kaplan, Caren, 'The Balloon Prospect: Aerostatic Observation and the Emergence of Militarised Aeromobility', *From Above: War, Violence, and Verticality*, eds Peter Adey, Mark Whitehead and Alison J. Williams (Oxford, 2013), pp. 19–40

Kareem, Sarah Tindal, *Eighteenth-Century Fiction and the Reinvention of Wonder* (Oxford, 2014)

Keen, Paul, '"The Balloonomania": Science and Spectacle in 1780s England', *Eighteenth-Century Studies*, vol. 39, no. 4 (2006), pp. 507–35

—— *Literature, Commerce, and the Spectacle of Modernity, 1750–1800* (Cambridge, 2012)

—— '"The Good Things Above": The Commercial Modernity of Vincent Lunardi', http://www.18thcenturycommon.org/c18ballooning (posted 20 March 2013)

Kim, Mi Gyung, '"Public" Science: Hydrogen Balloons and Lavoisier's Decomposition of Water', *Annals of Science*, vol. 63, no. 3 (2006), pp. 291–318

Kotar, S. L., and J. E. Gessler, *Ballooning: A History, 1782–1900* (Jefferson NC, 2011)

Lavery, Brian, *Empire of the Seas: How the Navy Forged the Modern World* (2009)

Lewis, Jayne Elizabeth, *Air's Appearance: Literary Atmosphere in British Fiction, 1660–1794* (Chicago, 2012)

Life magazine (1947)

Lucas, John, *The Silken Canopy: A History of the Parachute* (Shrewsbury, 1997)

Lynn, Michael R., *Popular Science and Public Opinion in Eighteenth-Century France* (Manchester, 2006)

—— *The Sublime Invention: Ballooning in Europe, 1783–1820* (2010)

MacMahon, Bryan, *Ascend or Die: Richard Crosbie, Pioneer of Balloon Flight* (Dublin, 2010)

Marvin, Carolyn, *When Old Technologies were New: Thinking about Electric Communication in the Late Nineteenth Century* (Oxford, 1998)

McConnell, Anita, *Jesse Ramsden (1735–1800): London's Leading Scientific Instrument Maker* (Aldershot, 2007)

McPherson, Heather, 'Picturing Tragedy: *Mrs Siddons as the Tragic Muse* Revisited', *Eighteenth-Century Studies*, vol. 33, no. 3 (2000), pp. 401–30

Mee, John, *Dangerous Enthusiasm: William Blake and the Culture of Radicalism in the 1790s* (Oxford, 1994)

Melzer, Sarah, and Kathryn Norberg, eds, *From the Royal to the Republican Body: Incorporating the Political in Seventeenth- and Eighteenth-Century France* (Berkeley CA, 1998)

Midgley, Graham, *University Life in Eighteenth-Century Oxford* (New Haven, 1996)

Mirzoeff, Nicholas, ed., *The Visual Culture Reader* (2001)

Mitchell, L. G., *Charles James Fox* (1991)

Mole, Tom, ed., *Romanticism and Celebrity Culture 1750–1850* (Cambridge, 2009)

Morley, Simon, ed., *The Contemporary Sublime* (Cambridge MA, 2010)

Nicolson, Marjorie Hope, *Voyages to the Moon* (1948)

O'Brian, Patrick, *Joseph Banks: A Life* (1994)

Oleksijczuk, Denise Blake, *The First Panoramas: Visions of British Imperialism* (Minneapolis, 2011)

Oppel, Frank, ed., *Early Flight: From Balloons to Biplanes* (Secaucus NJ, 1987)

Paris, Michael, *Winged Warfare: The Literature and Theory of Aerial Warfare in Britain 1859–1917* (Manchester, 1992)

The Parliamentary History of England, from the Earliest Period to the Year 1803, vol. 25 (1815)

Parrinder, Patrick, *Learning from Other Worlds* (Liverpool, 2000)

Parsons, Mrs Clement, *The Incomparable Siddons* (1909)

Partridge, Eric, *A Dictionary of Slang and Unconventional English* (1984)

Pascoe, Judith, *The Sarah Siddons Audio Files: Romanticism and the Lost Voice* (Ann Arbor, 2011)

Paston, George, *Little Memoirs of the Eighteenth Century* (1901)

Paton-Williams, David, *Katterfelto: Prince of Puff* (Leicester, 2008)

Penny, John, *Up, Up and Away! An account of ballooning in and around Bristol and Bath 1784–1999*, HA Pamphlets, no. 97 (Bristol, n.d.)

Phillips, William, 'History on the Couch', *New York Review* (1 February 1963)

Pitcher, H. J., 'A Scottish View of Catherine's Russia: William Richardson's *Anecdotes of the Russian Empire* (1784)', *Forum Modern Language Studies*, vol. 3, no. 3 (1967), pp. 236–51

Pohl, Nicole, 'Of Balloons and Foreign Worlds: Mary Hamilton and Eighteenth-Century Flights of Fancy', Utopias: The Un-Placed in Language and Politics, *Azimuth: Philosophical Coordinates in Modern and Contemporary Age*, vol. 2, no. 3 (2014), pp. 61–90

Ponting, Betty, 'A History of Mathematics at Aberdeen', *The Aberdeen University Review*, vol. 48 (1979–80); http://www.gap-system. org/~history/Extras/Aberdeen_4.html

Popular Science (January 1916)

Postle, Martin, 'Thomas Gainsborough's "Lost" Portrait of Auguste Vestris', *The British Art Journal*, vol. 4, no. 1 (Spring 2002), pp. 64–8

Pountain, Dick, and David Robins, *Cool Rules: Anatomy of an Attitude* (2000)

Reid, J. S., 'The Castlehill Observatory Aberdeen', *Journal for the History of Astronomy*, vol. 13 (1982), pp. 84–96

Rimbault, E. F., *Soho and its Associations* (1895)

Robbins, John, 'Up in the Air: Balloonomania and Scientific Performance', *Eighteenth-Century Studies*, vol. 48, no. 4 (2015), pp. 521–38

Rodger, N. A. M., *The Command of the Ocean: A Naval History of Britain 1649–1815* (2006)

—— 'Sea-Power and Empire, 1688–1793', *The Oxford History of the British Empire*, vol. 2, ed. P. J. Marshall (Oxford, 1998), pp. 169–83

Rogers, Nicholas, *The Press Gang: Naval Impressment and its Opponents in Georgian Britain* (2007)

Rolt, L. T. C., *The Aeronauts: A History of Ballooning 1783–1903* (1966)

—— *The Balloonists: The History of the First Aeronauts* (Stroud, 2006)

The Romance of Ballooning: The Story of the Early Aeronauts (New York, 1971)

Rose, R. B., 'Utopianism', *Encyclopaedia of the Enlightenment*, ed. Alan Charles Kors, 4 vols, vol. 4 (Oxford, 2003), pp. 215–18

Scarry, Elaine, *The Body in Pain: The Making and Unmaking of the World* (Oxford, 1987)

Shooter, Anne, 'And now for someone completely different...', *The Daily Mail* (14 October 1999)

Smiles, Sam, *Flight and the Artistic Imagination* (Compton Verney, 2012)

Smith, Richard O., *The Man with his Head in the Clouds: James Sadler, the First Englishman to Fly* (Oxford, 2014)

Spadafora, David, *The Idea of Progress in Eighteenth-Century Britain* (New Haven, 1990)

Sprott, Duncan, *1784* (1984)

Stewart, Larry, 'A Meaning for Machines: Modernity, Utility, and the Eighteenth-Century British Public', *The Journal of Modern History*, vol. 70, no. 2 (1998), pp. 259–94

Stewart, Susan, *On Longing: Narratives of the Miniature, the Gigantic, the Souvenir, the Collection* (Baltimore MD, 1984)

Stockdale, Susan Renee, 'An Interdisciplinary Review of the Crowd at Eighteenth Century Hangings in England', MSc thesis, University of Iowa State, *Retrospective Theses and Dissertations*, Paper 15038 (2007)

Stuart, S. E., and W. T. W. Potts, 'Richard Gillow and Vincent Lunardi: Early Balloon Flights', *Contrebis*, vol. 24 (1999), pp. 26–33

Stubelius, Svante, *Balloon, Flying-Machine, Helicopter: Further Studies in the History of Terms for Aircraft in English*, Goteborgs Universitets Årsskrift, vol. 66 (Goteborg, 1960), pp. 104–40

Styles, John, *The Dress of the People: Everyday Fashion in Eighteenth-Century England* (New Haven, 2007)

Sugg, Richard, *Mummies, Cannibals and Vampires: The History of Corpse Medicine from the Renaissance to the Victorians* (2011)

Suriewicki, James, *The Wisdom of Crowds* (New York, 2004)

Survey of London, vols 31 and 32: St James [*sic*] Westminster, Part 2 (1963)

Syson, Lydia, *Doctor of Love: James Graham and his Celestial Bed* (2008)

Taylor, Michael J. H., *The Aerospace Chronology* (1989)

Thébaud-Sorger, Marie, *L'Aérostation au temps des Lumières* (Rennes, 2009)

—— *Une Histoire des Ballons: Invention, culture matèrielle et imaginaire, 1783–1909* (Paris, 2010)

Tilly, Charles, *Popular Contention in Great Britain 1758–1834* (Boulder CO, 2005)

Tomko, Michael, '"All the World have heard of the Devil and the Pope": Elizabeth Inchbald's *The Mogul Tale* and English Catholic Satire', *Tulsa Studies in Women's Literature*, vol. 31, nos 1/2 (2012), pp. 117–36

Turner, Graeme, 'Approaching Celebrity Studies', *Celebrity Studies Journal*, vol. 1, no. 1 (2010), pp. 11–20

Uglow, Jenny, *The Lunar Men: The Friends who Made the Future 1730–1810* (2002)

Valenza, Robin, *Literature, Language, and the Rise of the Intellectual Disciplines in Britain, 1680–1820* (Cambridge, 2009)

Virilio, Paul de, *War and Cinema: The Logistics of Perception* (1979)

Wichner, Jessika, 'Hot Air and Chilly Welcomes: Accidental Arrivals with Balloons and Airships in the Eighteenth century and Beyond', *Citizens of the World: Adapting in the Eighteenth Century*, eds Samara Anne Cahill and Kevin L. Cope (Lanham MD, 2015), pp. 19–42

Williamson, James A., *The English Channel: A History* (1961)

Wilson, Kathleen, *The Island Race: Englishness, Empire and Gender in the Eighteenth Century* (2003)

Wirth, Dick, and Jerry Young, *Ballooning: The Complete Guide to Riding the Winds* (1980)

Wohl, Robert, *A Passion for Wings: Aviation and the Western Imagination, 1908–1918* (New Haven, 1994)

—— *The Spectacle of Flight: Aviation and the Western Imagination 1920–1950* (New Haven, 2005)

Websites

Electronic Enlightenment: www.e-enlightenment.com

The Proceedings of the Old Bailey 1674–1913: http://www.oldbaileyonline.org/

http://www2.tv.ark.org.uk/bbc1national/bbc1national1997.hts

http://www.adam-williams.com/PrintObject.aspx?objectid=125459&dealerid=316>

http://www.balloonhq.com/faq/history.html

http://www.bbac.org/lor/conduct.

http://www.bbc.co.uk/historyofthebbc/resources/in-depth/bbc_logo.shtml

http://botanybaymedallion.com/?page_id=8>

http://www.centrepompidou-metz.fr/en/views-above#onglet-0

http://clusterballoon.com

http://www.cpsc.gov/cpscpub/prerel/prhtml76/76083.html

http://www.d2be.org/arc_up.html

http://www.dailyscript.com/scripts/AmericanBeauty_final.html

http://holkham.blogspot.com

https://www.hybridairvehicles.com/

http://www.ibras.dk/montypython/episode40.htm

http://www.nasa.gov/audience/foreducators/5–8/features/F_What_Can_I_Wear.html

http://news.bbc.co.uk/local/bristol/hi/people_and_places/arts_and_culture/newsid_8505000/8505819.stm

http://www.nfuonline.com/about-us/our-offices/east-midlands/latest-news/nfu-steps-up-chinese-lanterns-alert/

http://www.oxford.gov.uk/PageRender/decEH/Balloon_Releases_occw.htm

http://www.philippe-pastor.com/oeuvres-recentes/ciel-de-la-terre.php

http://www.transdiffusion.org/emc/ident/history/bbc1.php

http://www.uktvadverts.com/facts/?list=ch4

http://www.yannarthusbertrand.org

http://www.youtube.com/watch?v=GJVEtXDVUBk

Podcasts

Brant, Clare, '"Balloon madness": science versus spectacle in early aeronautics', Royal Society (27 March 2007)
White, Jerry, 'Vengeance and the Crowd in Eighteenth-Century London', Birkbeck College, backdoorbroadcasting.net (21 February 2011)

Index